# BIBLE AND TRANSFORMATION

# Society of Biblical Literature

Semeia Studies

Gerald O. West, Editor

*Editorial Board*

Number 81

# BIBLE AND TRANSFORMATION

## THE PROMISE OF
## INTERCULTURAL BIBLE READING

*Edited by*

Hans de Wit and Janet Dyk

SBL Press

Atlanta

Library of Congress Cataloging-in-Publication Data

Bible and transformation : the promise of intercultural Bible reading / edited by Hans de Wit and Janet Dyk.
    p. cm. — (Society of Biblical Literature. Semeia studies ; number 81)
    Includes index.
    Summary: "This book offers the results of research within a new area of discipline—empirical hermeneutics in intercultural perspective. Ordinary readers from more than twenty-five countries in interaction with a distant partner group engage the stories of the rape of biblical accounts. Interpretations from the homeless in Amsterdam, to Indonesia, from African Xhosa readers to Norway, to Madagascar, American youths, Germany, Czech Republic, Colombia, and Haitian refugees in the Dominican Republic offer a (road)map of the sometimes delightful and inspiring, sometimes rough and rocky road to inclusive and transformative Bible reading"— Provided by publisher.
    ISBN 978-1-62837-105-5 (pbk. : alk. paper) — ISBN 978-1-62837-107-9 (ebook) — ISBN 978-1-62837-106-2 (hardcover : alk. paper)
    1. Bible—Hermeneutics. 2. Bible—Reading. I. Wit, Hans de., editor. II. Dyk, J. W., editor.
    BS476.B4928 2015
    220.609—dc23                                           2015021468

Printed on acid-free paper.

# CONTENTS

Part 2. Rape and Outrage: Case Studies on 2 Samuel 13

Part 2.1. In Her Memory: Tamar's Story in Global Perspective

Part 2.2. In Her Memory: Tamar's Story in Local Perspective

# INTRODUCTION

*Hans de Wit and Janet Dyk*

Beginning as a grassroots movement, inspired by Latin American and other contextual hermeneutics, intercultural Bible reading has earned its own place within the field of biblical studies.

In 2001 the first phase of a worldwide initiative called "Through the Eyes of Another" was launched, and, with a focus on John 4, a method for bringing Bible reading groups to interact with one another was developed. The novelty of this project was not that readers from different cultures and contexts were asked to participate, nor that biblical scholars carefully began to listen or "read with" nonprofessional Bible readers. What was innovative was that distance was incorporated as a hermeneutical factor and that encounter and dialogue were organized between readers from different reading traditions and contexts.

The central research question was open and explorative: What happens when Bible readers from sometimes radically different contexts and cultures read the same Bible text and start dialoguing about its significance? Can this way of shared Bible reading become a catalyst for more openness and transformation? More than one hundred fifty groups from over thirty countries participated in the project. Its results were astonishing. Levinas's infinity—texts are inexhaustible—came to the fore. Over three thousand pages of vernacular readings of the story of the Samaritan women were collected. The theological reflection was varied and rich. Several participating scholars developed a qualitative analytical system for coding and decoding the material in order to detect which factors hampered and which promoted successful exchange and growth in intercultural and hermeneutical competence.

During the analysis of the empirical material, the question of the relationship between reading, (new) praxis, and transformation became increasingly intriguing. This relationship is almost always taken to be strong, intimate, and immediate. We noted, however, that the relationship is, to say the least, complex and much less direct than is often claimed. In the three thousand pages of empirical material, we discovered only one example of a group that took immediate action as a result of the reading process. Even in those cases where groups had asked themselves explicitly which directives resulted from reading the text, the reply was almost always that of a *desideratum*: "we will/would now...," "perhaps we should... ," "could we not... ?" The question arose as to what extent a transforming, praxeological effect of intercultural readings could be mapped.

Out of this question, the second phase of the project was born of which this volume bears witness. The research questions are more precise: How, if at all, does transformation occur? Can cross-border encounters become a catalyst for the transformation of the reader, the text, and the perception and acceptance of the other reader? If so, under which conditions? In this second phase, groups mainly focused on 2 Sam 13 (the rape of Tamar) and John 20:1–18 (Mary Magdalene at Jesus's tomb), while a few groups interacted on the story of Cain and Abel, Ruth, the prodigal son, the inopportune guest, or the widow and the unjust judge.

Building on the project "Through the Eyes of Another," this new cycle of reading exchanges marks a step forward, not just more of the same. It culminated in a February 2013 conference in Amsterdam and the essays in this volume. Through a consolidation of insights, the results of the intercultural Bible reading process are brought into a framework in which the theological, sociological, psychological, and personal implications can be analyzed. Results of a cross-border practice of Bible reading are presented that account for the multiplicity of readings.

Central to this volume are the concepts "empirical," "intercultural," and "transformation." "Empirical hermeneutics" refers to an activity of researchers; it is a form of reception or reader-response criticism that analyzes how the interaction between Scripture and contemporary readers takes place. "Empirical" does not refer to a specific type of reading but to the object of analysis, that is, the detailed reports of what readers did in their approach to a specific biblical text. Interpretation practices of contemporary ordinary readers are assessed at the metalevel of theory formation, as well as at the microlevel of qualitative research. An important argument for using the term "empirical" is that the production of empirical data was necessary for a successful application of the method used in the processes analyzed in this book. Participating groups were invited to record how their reading processes and encounters with partner groups took place. Exegetes leave the traces of their labor in books and commentaries, and those traces—empirical data—can be analyzed; however, little evidence is recorded, let alone analyzed, of the way in which the overwhelming majority of current ordinary readers approach biblical texts. The "Bible and Transformation" project concentrates on *their* interpretive practices. That is also one of the reasons why some of the contributors did not want to engage much in more critical, scholarly reflection but preferred rather to offer their readers the opportunity of becoming eyewitnesses to the way in which drug addicts and homeless people in Amsterdam, prisoners in Indonesia, or readers elsewhere read and appropriated the story of Tamar or Mary Magdalene. For several authors, this has been a conscious choice. By offering much of the raw data—almost verbatim descriptions of the reading process—they wanted to create space for the subaltern, enabling them to speak out and letting their voices be heard. The choice was thus not to allow scholarly reflection to overshadow and mute that process, that is, a choice for praxis first and only thereafter for reflection. "Empirical hermeneutics," as here defined, is not interested in the analysis of the genesis and transmission of the text, but explores what has been called "the foreground" of the text, that is, its capacity to shed light on new situations not seen by the original authors and its potential to engender new practices. We wanted to explore the space in which the effect of *reading the text now* becomes manifest, the space where the text becomes embedded in a new context, where, for better or for worse, processes of appropriation take place and readers try to understand the text as a letter directly addressed to themselves and their situation—the space mainly inhabited by ordinary readers.

Over the last decades, the concept "ordinary readers" has been broadly debated. To what extent can biblical scholars, who next to their interpretive interests almost always also have life interests that guide their practice, be considered ordinary readers? Can they ever become nonprofessional readers again? Is a second naïveté really possible? Can "ordinary" be defined according to and in contrast with what knowledge professional readers are supposed to have when they approach biblical texts? Does an Old Testament scholar become an ordinary reader when he or she reads a text of Paul or John? Is the concept class bound?

We propose here an alternative definition of the concept. By "ordinary reader," we prefer to understand both a *space* and *a way of reading*, an *attitude toward the text*. The space is where the *effect* of the process of reading biblical texts is revealed, where Bible reading becomes decisive and ethical. It is the place where the overwhelming majority of Bible readers can be found, where the potential of biblical texts to affect behavior is activated, and where interpretation processes turn into social, political, and religious practices founded on biblical texts. In this space, reading processes become either life-sapping and excluding, or life-giving, liberative, and salvific.

By "attitude," we understand the way readers approach biblical texts. What is the status of the text for the readers, what are their expectations of the outcome of the interpretation process? Which questions would they like to ask the text? What results of the reading process are they looking for, what kind of interaction? Which metaphor would they apply to their encounter with the text—meeting a companion, an ally, a friend, a counselor, an enemy?

In his foundational article "What Is a Text? Explanation and Understanding," Paul Ricoeur (1981) distinguished between two attitudes with which a reader can approach a biblical text: a critical, analytical attitude and an existential one. This distinction is still valid and helps to solve our dilemma. By "ordinary reader," we understand the "existential attitude," an attitude, amply documented in our empirical data, that explores the text in its nearness. The keywords to describe this existential approach to the text are not analysis, history, background, or object, but nearness, expectation, present, and appropriation.

By "empirical" we refer to a specific research method, its direct object (reading reports), and the space from which we collect our empirical data (ordinary readers). To the term "empirical," we add another label: "intercultural." This more normative label refers to how we wanted our empirical data to be gathered and of which processes the data should bear traces. To go further than acknowledging that multiplicity exists and that everywhere—also, and especially, in the margins—the Bible is being read, we invited participants to read "with the other." The "inter" in "intercultural" stands for the normative dimension of the project and the method in which ordinary readers from different contexts were invited to read the same biblical text and dialogue about its significance with other readers, whereas "cultural" stands for the conviction that deep dimensions of culture play an important role in the interpretation process.

In this time of the great paradox of fundamentalisms, on the one hand, and globalization, on the other, we wanted to take up again the fundamental—but too easily forgotten—insight of Gadamer on the importance of distance in interpretation processes. Not only wanting to hear the voices of readers from the margins, we wanted to *organize encounter*, integrating distance as a hermeneutical factor in the interpretation process and inviting readers of the margins to read *together* with readers from the centers: poor readers and more wealthy readers, readers from different ecclesial traditions, political convictions, and cultural settings.

The third component of this book is "transformation." Can Bible reading practices, confronted by exchanges in which distance and differences are made operative, lead to transformation? Can they contribute to open up closed, frozen positions? Can they help people to stop seeing themselves as owners of divine revelation? Empirical evidence is sought that would point to a relationship between Bible-reading processes and transformation.

Empirical data became available from ordinary readers from more than twenty-five countries in interaction with a distant partner group. In its portrayals of transformation and the framework of cross-border Bible reading, this book takes the reader to the contexts of the participating groups—from the homeless and drug addicts in Amsterdam to Indonesia, from African Xhosa readers to Norway, Madagascar, North America, Japan, China, Germany, Colombia, and Haitian refugees in the Dominican Republic. This volume offers a roadmap of the sometimes delightful and inspiring, sometimes rough and rocky road to inclusive and transformative Bible reading.

In a variety of ways participants addressed the three main concepts of the conference. The more theoretically and the more empirically oriented essays complement each other, offering responses to questions such as the place of intercultural Bible reading within hermeneutics, how culture influences reading processes, what is implied in group dynamics, how empirical data can be collected and processed in a responsible way, how Bible reading with others becomes a script for transformation, where and how transformation is to be observed, and which factors facilitate and which factors prevent transformation from taking place.

Several essays contain results not only of intercultural but also of cross-textual reading experiences (Peru, Indonesia, Madagascar). Cross-textual reading, as a specific form of interreligious dialogue, is only one step removed from intercultural reading. Both approaches involve "alterity" and "otherness" in an explicit way in the process of reading sacred texts. Whereas intercultural Bible reading remains within the Jewish-Christian tradition, cross-textual reading practices relate sacred texts from different religious traditions. In this volume a choice has been made for the intercultural method for several reasons, one being hermeneutical: since intercultural Bible reading invites readers from different places who belong to the same religious tradition to read the same text, authority and ownership are problematized, Levinas's "infinity" becomes a prominent theme for reflection, and shared ownership and shared agency can more easily be strived for. The more practical reason for staying within intercultural exchanges is that it would not be easy to organize a cross-textual reading project at the level of grassroots readers with the extensive range of the current project. Furthermore, even if cross-textual reading becomes more important and urgent, the longing for transformation that characterized the current project could have easily been confused with a call to conversion. Analysis and comparison of results of interpretations of the same religious texts and the role culture plays in this are perhaps easier than interpreting two or more texts from different traditions. Finally, the confrontation with the other who also believes to be owner of the text, but nevertheless reads it differently, may take place at a more existential level than would be the case in cross-textual hermeneutics. What intercultural Bible reading strives for is that, within a profoundly divided Christianity, the intercultural encounter becomes a *script* for transformation and leads to *shared* ownership and *shared* agency for justice and liberation.

At the same time, we also take note of where this has not been possible and where the limits of this method become manifest. Like all intercultural encounters, intercultural reading of Scripture is not the easiest way of reflecting on the significance of fundamental texts. The wounded heart cannot easily make the transition from pain to a reflection about how others read the text that one feels to be a mirror of one's own sorrows and grief. It is one thing to recognize yourself as one of the actors in the drama that the text unfolds before you, but it is quite another to read how your role is analyzed or how others do not recognize you in this role.

The essays in this volume could have been arranged in many ways. The difference between more empirically and more theoretically oriented essays makes the text a point of encounter, highlighting the truth of the old talmudic saying that "in dispersion the text is homeland." After the first part treating various aspects of the conceptual framework, essays relating to a particular Bible text are grouped together. The reader will be aware of the multiple thematic cross-connections between the essays.

## Part 1. The Dynamics of Intercultural Bible Reading:
## Conceptual Framework

Within the field of contextual hermeneutics, intercultural Bible reading is a recent offshoot. It distinguishes itself from previous contextually and locally determined Bible-reading processes by defining the concept of communitarian reading in a new way, stressing the need for intercultural encounters and transborder exchanges. The distinctive place of this new field within biblical studies is progressively clearer as the fruits of this type of Bible reading become available.

Fernando F. Segovia addresses the question of the place and role of intercultural biblical hermeneutics within the field of biblical studies, which involves both the conceptualization and formulation of this particular critical approach and its relation to other critical approaches in contemporary biblical criticism. Intercultural reading coincides with the call on the part of political analysts for a return to liberation and embodies such a turn in that it brings a new edge to the hermeneutical mediation of liberation.

In his essay, Hans de Wit scrutinizes the empirical foundations of the universal assumption that reading the Bible does something to the reader, that the dynamics of the encounter has an effect. He attempts to corroborate a workable definition of transformation with an empirically sound understanding of the concept. The question is posed as to what extent cross-border Bible reading should be seen as a quality of the interpretation processes and under which circumstances it can result in transformation of the self, of the social context, of the other reader, and even of the text. This touches the heart of Bible reading and hermeneutic reflection among those who do not want to regard the ancient text solely as an archaeological *deposit* but as a letter addressed to present-day ordinary readers. It is precisely because of the "global presence" of the Bible and the endless procession of people who interact with the Bible that posing the question about the effect of that interaction is so urgent.

Following the methodology of the intercultural reading process, John Mansford Prior examines the integrity of the reader, of the other, and of the text. *The reader*: the greater the openness both in relation to oneself and in the relationships within a group, the greater is the potential transformative power of intercultural readings. *The other*: the other's integrity is respected to the extent readers become bicultural. The more sensitive we become in the conversation with our partner(s), the greater will be the integrity with which we acknowledge their reading. *The text*: no single interpretation is exhaustive. The more we question and probe each other's readings, the greater will be the integrity with which we read the text. Prior's essay closes with an examination of the values behind our reading of the Bible, concluding that intercultural readings clarify not only which God we actually believe in and who our neighbors are to us and we to them, but also the role religion plays in our lives in ideologically framing our reading. We violate a text when we read into it a message that undermines the God of life and love.

From the point of view of practical theology, Daniel S. Schipani explains that four perspectives on intercultural reading are possible: descriptive-empirical, pragmatic, interpretive, and normative. The process of intercultural Bible reading can be seen as a spiritual journey for which five elements are constitutive: a safe space; the moment of incubation through imagination; space for plurality and new insights; the eureka moment that can be full of catharsis or mourning and shared memories; and the moment of acquiring a new identity. On the basis of empirical data, he further defines, analyzes, and evaluates transformation in interdisciplinary terms. He articulates guidelines for further praxis and emphasizes the importance of the factor of spirituality.

Danie van Zyl discerns distinct levels of transformation affected by group dynamics and makes explicit the necessary conditions for a meaningful process to be lasting. Religious communities often develop closed frameworks of understanding within which texts are read, and they become defensive when confronted with those who differ with them. Intergroup exchange of readings is potentially highly challengingly to the groups involved, particularly on the level of integration and (self-)critical reflection. Without some level of self-criticism, the chances of transformation in intercultural exchange are limited. Issues like the choice of texts and the choice of which groups to link together seem to play key roles in the effectiveness of the transformative experience of intercultural Bible reading.

Werner Kahl shows how, from its earliest beginnings, Christianity has been a cross-cultural phenomenon. Cross-cultural processes represent a central feature of the spread of early Christianity, as is seen in Gal 3. Kahl argues that intercultural biblical hermeneutics not only reflects what lies at the heart of early Christianity—a divinely commissioned crossing of boundaries by undermining exclusive claims to salvation—but that it also pushes for further crossing of boundaries. In the situation in which there is little contact between the many African migrant churches and German churches, intercultural Bible study can serve as a space for a propitious encounter of Christians with different cultural and confessional backgrounds within the same neighborhood.

## Part 2. Rape and Outrage: Case Studies on 2 Samuel 13

A large number of groups engaged with the story of the rape of Tamar (2 Sam 13). Some essays reflect the interaction between globally separated groups in which cultural differences often play a role (part 2.1), while others show the exchange within a locally confined environment where the differences still could be so great that the communication was difficult or broke down completely (part 2.2). In one case, essays dealing with the dialogue between two globally separated groups (Indonesia and Germany) is reported from both perspectives, and the transformation of the strategies and ethics of the interaction with the partner group is analyzed.

## Part 2.1. In Her Memory: Tamar's Story in Global Perspective

In the exchange between Indonesia and Germany, Batara Sihombing analyzes the interaction with the German group from the Indonesian point of view. Semantics appears to weigh heavily on the intercultural reading process: the groups use different terms and definitions for the same cases— "rape" (German group) versus "sexual transgression" (Indonesian group). The cultural dimension of collectivism and its influence on the interpretation process are examined. The German group started to see David in his role as father through Indonesian eyes, not as an individual, but as part of a collective—a failed father. This changed the German perception of the plot. The Indonesians, as prisoners, had ample time to gossip and offer new insights into the role of Jonadab. The Indonesian group saw him as a "puppeteer of gossip," and this changed the German groups' perception of Jonadab. In spite of a willingness to learn from the other, both groups also showed a reluctance to change due to their own cultural backgrounds and doctrinal positions, demonstrating that certain attitudes can hamper the promise of transformation in achieving its full potential.

On the other side of this exchange, Rainer Kessler describes how the German middle-class Protestant reading group appears to think they are able to maintain a neutral position in evaluating the partner's interpretation of a biblical passage. While reading the reports and responses of the partner group comprising Indonesian prisoners, an ethical problem arose within the German group. As it was known that some members of the prisoners' group were incarcerated for sexual crimes, German readers were in danger of showing a lack of respect for the partners by replacing a dialogue with them with an attempt to analyze them. Only after discussing the ethical problems was the group able to benefit from the partners' readings. The essay exposes certain colonial mechanisms at work and how these had to be deconstructed before a less biased exchange could take place.

La Rip Marip of Myanmar emphasizes the need for readers to be interested both in connecting the text to one's own context and in understanding the partners' cultural background. Both the Myanmar and the Dutch reading groups recognized injustice and the abuse of power in their intercultural dialogue on 2 Sam 13, but the Myanmar group related their Bible reading to their whole community whereas the partner Dutch group related it to individuals. The more the asymmetry between reading groups comes to the fore in the dialogue, the more transformation can contribute to the well-being of the other. The desire to understand the culture of the other led the groups further toward understanding the biblical text and toward social justice.

Jeff Moore reports on two groups of women, one from the Netherlands and one from a shelter for homeless women in St. Louis, Missouri, who identified and discussed hegemonic language and harmful assumptions across contexts and across time. Their questions and responses opened up a further conversation for a group of ecumenical clergy on the importance of encountering Scripture in context and experiencing transformation therein. Four effects of the intercultural encounter were observed: the groups displayed solidarity with the other, previously unknown group; new interpretive clues were offered; the partner group helped to unmask hegemony; the exchange helped to disentangle ideological codes frequently used in one's own context. This essay reflects on the ways in which hegemony in the text and in front of the text hides the coercive nature of discourse on gender and power, making it seem benignly persuasive, and how readings by ordinary readers expose this hegemony as ideology and lead to a discussion of how working for change and empowerment can be achieved.

Part 2.2. In Her Memory: Tamar's Story in Local Perspective

The exchanges between three pairs of Amsterdam groups who read the Tamar story are presented by Willemien van Berkum: groups from the

Drugs Pastorate, Street Pastorate, a middle-class church, evangelical young people, Dominican migrant women, and women without a direct church affiliation. Van Berkum reflects on how and to what extent the text is freed from its historical setting, is embedded in present life, and is able to empower participants. The aim is to see what conditions may encourage exchanges between multiple sites within the same context to achieve a transformation of attitude toward partner groups.

Godian Ejiogu reports on how the reading with the group of the Amsterdam Drugs Pastorate created a context in which painful personal experiences were shared while reflecting on the Bible story. This group, whose members came from different cultural and national backgrounds and who met only for this occasion, constituted itself as an interpretive community of the Tamar story, and cultural differences were no longer an obstacle to the interpretation process. The hermeneutical process moved from the text to life and back again. Safe space is highlighted as essential for a fruitful reading process. Whereas the Amsterdam middle-class partner group maintained distance to the story and was interested mainly in questions of translation and historical background, the Drugs Pastorate group read the story as though it happened today—which it does. Through the sharing, God's story became one's own story. Using this method to transform culture presents major challenges to the participants since culture represents the deepest levels of human nature, stronger and deeper than love.

Reading with the Amsterdam Street Pastorate group, Luc Tanja explores the limitations of cross-boundary Bible reading and the power of analogy. A reading strategy was developed that did not look for meaning in the text, but focused on reading the story in a direct and personal way, as though one were reading a newspaper. Participants were transformed and felt like actors in a movie about their own lives. Because appropriation was so immediate that there was no place for a more objective reading, a reading report by another more intellectually oriented group, who did not read the text in a personal way, remained empty and meaningless to the Street Pastorate group. The failure to achieve a meaningful exchange with the partner group shows that the manner of engaging with the text can pose limitations to interaction in intercultural Bible reading.

As Charlene van der Walt and Kim Barker make clear, sexual violence is endemic to South African society. Besides being victims of sexual violence, women are often silenced, being perceived by ideologies of male dominance and stripped of hope within a culture of violence. While conducting a qualitative research inquiry exploring the dynamics of the intercultural Bible reading space, especially focusing on the strategies of power and the implications of ideology, the researchers became aware of the inherent possibilities of that space to address issues of sexual violence. Their essay reflects on possible effects that the intercultural Bible reading can have by creating a supportive environment in which women and men may reflect on issues of gender-based violence in the light of biblical stories.

Using Michel Foucault's undeveloped but suggestive notion of "heterotopia," Gerald West explores ways in which the particular reading approach developed in South Africa—Contextual Bible Study—is a heterotopia. The first focus is on how the *reading processes* might be considered as heterotopic. The second focus considers how the processes construct *the biblical text* as a heterotopic site. The essay then explores in detail how the biblical text is an intercultural site, enabling lines of connection to be found and forged between the biblical text and the reception context. The story of the rape of Tamar is used in assessing to what extent this text provides resources for an intercultural dialogue between ancient "biblical" and contemporary "contextual" conceptions of masculinity.

## Part 3. Together at the Tomb: Case Studies on John 20

Again a pair of exchanges is presented, this time involving Bolivia and Indonesia. Reflecting on the Indonesian side of the exchange, Batara Sihombing observes that the Indonesian and Bolivian groups showed a willingness to learn from each other, but also a reluctance to change their own cultural backgrounds and doctrinal positions. The intercultural reading offered an opportunity to learn from the differences and to encourage transformation, but became as well a place to judge others and justify oneself. Factors that obstruct openness and growth are reflected upon. The place of Mary in the story led both groups to reflect on the position of women in their churches. A change of perspective occurred when the Bolivian group became more familiar with the partner group's social position and context.

Esa Autero explores this encounter from the Bolivian side. In striving to map the hermeneutical processes and transformation versus freezing points, he presents an analysis of the exchange and encoding of empirical data. Social and psychological insights and intergroup relations are implemented. He reflects on the extent to which the Bible is merely instrumental or has an added value in these types of exchange processes. References to the ancestral Batak culture of the Indonesian partner group helps the Bolivian group to gain insight in the text and the role of Mary: Mary is the only one who has courage to stay at the tomb, a place of ghosts and darkness.

Eric Nii Bortey Anum offers an analysis of an exchange between eight groups (from Colombia, the Netherlands, and Ghana). What happens if your Easter story is read by your partner group during the Christmas season? By involving the "unfamiliar" (another liturgical time for reading the resurrection story) as a hermeneutical factor in the interpretation process, the "familiar" dominant reading tradition is problematized. New meanings of the text are discovered, and the process of appropriation is reinforced through a new sensitivity to one's own context. Social transformation is aimed at as participants see the importance of developing their lifestyle so as to become a role model in their society like Mary Magdalene was.

Ignacio Antonio Madera Vargas analyzes an exchange between a Roman Catholic group from a slum area in Bogotá and several other groups, in particular a Dutch Reformed middle-class group. Ample reflection is provided on the differences between the groups in reading attitude, approach to the text, and appropriation processes: life and embedding over against reason and distance; reading in a modest home (Colombian group) over against reading in a church building (Dutch group); interest in the foreground of the text instead of in its background; dedication, recognition, and surrender over against reason and logic as interpretive instruments; trust in the resurrection over against questions about the historicity of the resurrection. Where differences were based on prejudice, the Colombian group felt they were being stereotyped. In response, the Colombian group asserted and affirmed their life-loving attitude in spite of adverse circumstances. Thus the differences and even prejudices had a positive transformative effect of making the Colombians more aware of their own identity.

Ricardo González Kindelan describes how, through the input of the Dutch partner group, cultural values existent in the Cuban culture, in particular violence, are problematized. The Dutch partner group offered a biblical-theological perspective that invited the Cuban group to rethink the position and experiences of women in the church and society. The personal testimonies of two women affirm that contextual and cross-border Bible reading can help expose and protect against fundamentalist reading and belief systems. The encounter with these new modes of reading opens new horizons and leads toward a transformation of lifestyle and of position on the hermeneutic playing field, thus inspiring to a new perception and practice of faith and leading to joining a new community of faith. It is demonstrated how the Bible can help Cubans look beyond their fragmented horizon and reflect on their responsibilities to their ecclesial and societal environment.

Marisol Ale Díaz and Manuel Obeso Perez show how the Peruvian ancestral veneration of the dead gives the story of Mary at the tomb a new significance. John 20 appears to be a story of processing trauma and offers the opportunity to convert mourning into a celebration of life. Mary's despair and search for Jesus's body is well understood in the Peruvian culture, where the bodies of so many loved ones have disappeared. A tomb without a body is meaningless. The tomb, as the resting place of the body of the dead, is a place where the community is renewed, memories are reenacted, and reconciliation celebrated. Fidelity to the dead is at stake. The essayists analyze how, through intercultural Bible reading, ordinary readers in the Peruvian context are enabled to reconcile themselves with their original culture.

Hans Snoek explores different visions on how Bible texts are read and appropriated and relates these to different cultural and socioeconomic contexts. Most Dutch groups reject an historical reading of John 20 and prefer a more symbolic approach, thus corresponding to a major trend in Dutch society. According to statistics, a growing segment of the Dutch population views the reader as the key, not the text and its historical trustworthiness. This marks a shift from an orientation focused on God to one focused on the person, implying that the individual and his or her personal opinion become more important than the opinion of another, for example, the text. This difference in attitude can form a major obstacle to transformation in the exchange between groups.

## Part 4. Am I My Sister's Keeper? Case Studies on Other Texts

Knut Holter presents an analysis of an intercultural dialogue on the Cain and Abel narrative in Gen 4 between two Bible study groups in Madagascar and Norway. Though the participants come from similar sociological and ecclesial contexts, different cultural and historical experiences during the colonial period led to divergent readings on key topics, such as the two kinds of sacrifices and the fate of Cain. The analysis focuses on the question of divine and human justice, asking to what extent the encounter with the other reader in the partner group had a potential for increased understanding and personal transformation.

Digna María Adames Nuñez describes how two different cultures that view the other as a threat—Haitians and Dominicans—were brought into contact in an intercultural Bible reading project in the Dominican Republic in 2009, thus bringing about an encounter between two societies that never socialize. As a result of preconceived ideas, inhabitants of both countries have developed a view of the other country based upon prejudice and rejection. Sitting side by side around the holy Scriptures offered the possibility of breaking the imaginary boundary that made them enemies. A new way to look at the world was born, with all its mystery and richness. For this experience, the story of of Ruth (Ruth 1), the migrant worker, was chosen, with immigration and women as main topics. Transformation was observed especially in the way the groups were led to a new perception of the other. Her observations are particularly relevant for the current situation of global migration, not only in Central and Latin America but particularly in the Middle East, Asia, and Europe, where on a daily basis countries have to deal with a massive flood of refugees and migrants.

As described by Louis Jonker, a research project in the Western Cape of South Africa read Luke 11:1–13 and took as its point of departure the hypothesis that a development of hermeneutical skills for reading the Bible together with "the other" could contribute significantly toward the fostering of interculturality in the broader South African society. Additionally, it was hypothesized that studying the process of intercultural Bible reading could provide insights into the dynamics of a shift from multiculturality to interculturality in South African society. It has been established that fear for and a lack of knowledge of "the other" are important factors in the lack of interculturality in society and that the Bible—as liminal meeting place for people from different cultures—can foster a sense of family and hospitality in the South African nation.

Taggert E. Wolverton examines the results of a multiyear study of intercultural Bible reading of Luke 15:11–32 with youth aged thirteen–twenty, involving a total of fourteen groups from North and South America, Western Europe, and Asia (China, Vietnam, Japan). An analysis of the reading reports and transcripts led the author to propose that the youthful participants did indeed show signs of spiritual growth as evidenced by shifts in their understanding and interpretation of the biblical text (acknowledging plurivocity is assessed as growth), changes in their view of themselves, and a modified view of their exchange partners.

José Vicente Vergara Hoyos analyzes an exchange on Luke 18:1–8 between twenty Latin American groups (Peru, Colombia, El Salvador, and Guatemala) whose context is marked by conflict, premature death, and impunity. Through a sincere and supportive interaction between those who share the same reality of pain and suffering due to the reigning impunity, the search for justice can be intensified. Sharing memories and discovering previously unknown places of struggle result in the processing of trauma, and contribute significantly to posttraumatic growth and the overcoming of the trauma. Vergara Hoyos shows how processes of appropriation redirect and activate spiritual and nonviolent resistance.

In the concluding reflections, the editors summarize the main lessons learned from the essays in this volume and the implications for a process in which Bible reading becomes life giving. Conditions for the latter are explicated, and the limitations inherent in the method pointed out.

## References

Ricoeur, Paul. 1981. "What Is a Text? Explanation and Understanding." Pages 145–64 in *Hermeneutics and the Human Sciences: Essays on Language, Action, and Interpretation*. Edited and translated by John B. Thompson. Cambridge: Cambridge University Press.

# PART 1
# THE DYNAMICS OF INTERCULTURAL BIBLE READING:
## CONCEPTUAL FRAMEWORK

# 1

## INTERCULTURAL BIBLE READING
## AS TRANSFORMATION FOR LIBERATION:
## INTERCULTURAL HERMENEUTICS AND BIBLICAL STUDIES

*Fernando F. Segovia*

The present study undertakes a critical analysis of intercultural Bible reading in biblical studies. This critical approach has marked for many years now the global project of scriptural interpretation developed and undertaken under the expert leadership of Hans de Wit and a superb circle of colleagues within the academic scholarly context of the *Stichting* (or foundation) set up in honor and memory of Dom Hélder at the Vrije Universiteit Amsterdam.[1] In 2013 I had the great honor and privilege of serving as the Visiting Professor of the Dom Hélder Câmara Chair and delivering the Dom Hélder Câmara Lecture.[2] That year, the lecture was also designed as the keynote address of a major international conference on "Bible and Transformation: The Promise of Intercultural Bible Reading." Given this context, a specific task was entrusted to me for the lecture: to address the place and role of intercultural Bible reading within the critical trajectory and repertoire of biblical criticism. This study represents, therefore, a

---

1. The foundation comprises a professorial appointment, the Dom Hélder Câmara Chair, and a program of studies. Professor Hans de Wit is the present holder of the professorial appointment, while intercultural Bible reading constitutes the leading project of the program of studies.

2. The foundation further comprises a formal series of lectures, The Dom Hélder Câmara Lectures, and a visiting professorial appointment, the Visiting Professor of the Dom Hélder Câmara Chair, whose main task it is to deliver the lecture. Following the changing nature of the chair over the years—as the professorial appointment changed from a revolving one to a permanent position, with an additional visiting appointment every two years—the lecture was at first given annually and now biennially.

revised and expanded version of that lecture, written for the publication of the conference proceedings as a volume in Semeia Studies.

The task in question, I find, is a daunting one. First, in the spirit of previous lectures, such analysis should address and embody, in some way, the values and ideals espoused by Dom Hélder. It is by no means easy, however, to bear the mantle of Dom Hélder upon one's shoulders and to follow in the footsteps of the distinguished line of speakers who have preceded me in this charge. It is thus a task that I take up with a distinct measure of trepidation; yet it is also one that I assume, duly empowered by that same tradition, with full resolve. In what follows, therefore, I shall strive to capture such ideals and values of the archbishop of Olinda and Recife and to further his memory.

Second, such analysis faces a complex topic, one that involves the question of method and theory as well as the question of methodology and metatheory. It has to do, therefore, not only with the conceptualization and formulation of this critical approach as such, but also with its relation to other critical approaches in contemporary biblical criticism. It is hence a task that I assume with a distinct sense of challenge; at the same time, it is also one that I embark upon with full determination, compelled by the confidence bestowed on me and my desire to make a contribution to the project. In what follows, then, I shall strive as well to capture the critical thrust of the project and its locus within present-day criticism.

For such analysis I have chosen the title of "Intercultural Bible Reading as Transformation for Liberation." I bring together thereby the designation bestowed on the approach and the title chosen for the international conference with its promise for biblical hermeneutics properly identified. Through its proposed approach to the Bible, I argue, the project seeks a transformation for liberation. I thus see the concept of liberation as central to the approach. I also see the concept itself as thoroughly reconceptualized and reformulated in the process, bringing thereby a new edge to the hermeneutics of liberation. I further see this revised concept of liberation as bearing a new meaning for the goal of transformation as well.

To my mind, therefore, the project stands squarely within the legacy of Dom Hélder, for whom the concept of liberation and the goal of transformation were quintessential signifiers. Indeed, I would contend that intercultural Bible reading constitutes a most worthy and praiseworthy embodiment of his values and ideals for our times, as envisioned and promoted by the foundation in his honor and memory. To bring out this connection within the tradition of liberation, it is indeed imperative to set the project against the broader canvas of biblical criticism, both in its historical path and its present configuration. This vision I shall develop in three movements.

I shall begin by tracing the course and shape of biblical criticism through a focus on the problematic of contextualization. In this first section, I argue that intercultural reading constitutes an important advance on the analysis of contextualization at the level of reception, the world of interpreters and interpretive contexts—a new direction for biblical interpretation. I shall continue with a close reading of intercultural reading as such, examining its dynamics and mechanics as a critical project. In this second section, I argue that the new direction on contextualization provides the foundation for a thorough recasting and rearticulation of the hermeneutical mediation of liberation—a new take on the invocation and use of Scripture in the tradition of liberation. I shall close by focusing on the goal of transformation advanced by the project, scrutinizing its position on the question of development. In this third section, I argue that the new take on hermeneutics sets the stage for a similar recasting and rearticulation of the practical mediation of liberation—a new edge on the question of praxis or way of life in the world in the tradition of liberation.

## Contemporary Biblical Criticism: Trajectory and Configuration

The path and shape of biblical criticism can be traced in various ways. For my purposes here, I should like to do so from the point of view of its stance regarding the goal and problematic of contextualization. This is a question that involves both the influence of context and the agency of the reader. It is also a question that has been a long-standing and driving aim as well as a concern of recent vintage and of limited appeal in biblical criticism. Such a statement calls for explication. Its surface contradiction can be readily explained in terms of the constitutive dimensions of interpretation.

Interpretation involves (at least) two realms of activity: the object or focus of analysis and the subject or agent of analysis. In biblical criticism such a twofold framework may be described as follows. On one side, there is the arena of biblical texts and contexts—the object or focus of study. This means the world of antiquity: the world of ancient Israel, as part of the ancient Near East, and the world of early Christianity, as part of the Greco-Roman Mediterranean basin. The boundaries between these two worlds, reflected in the two corpora that make up the Christian Bible, are by no means tight but rather porous. On the other side, there is the arena of biblical interpreters and their contexts—the subject or agent of study. This means, as a field of studies in the academy, the realm of modernity and postmodernity: the world of the West, straddling the area of the North Atlantic, and the world of globalization, comprising all continents. Again, the borders between these worlds are flexible rather than secure.

Within this double framework, the task of contextualization has driven a wedge between the two realms, resulting in a sharp division that only in the last few decades begins to be reconceptualized and reformulated. Thus contextualization has long functioned as a driving concern with regard to the texts and contexts of antiquity. However, only recently has it become a preoccupation with respect to biblical interpreters and their contexts of modernity and postmodernity and then only to a limited extent, embraced in some circles while bypassed in others. In this regard biblical criticism has by no means been an exception in the academy, but has followed the path of criticism in general.

To account for this twofold approach to contextualization, a review of the field's historical trajectory is essential. In so doing, I will draw on my vision of the field as encompassing various grand models of interpretation, which emerge in general (rather than strict) sequential fashion and which end up coexisting as parallel, and oftentimes competing, critical movements.

The foundational grand model of historical criticism, dominant to the point of exclusion for a long time, from the formation of the discipline in the first half of the nineteenth century through the first three quarters of the twentieth century, reveals the wedge at work. Historicism insisted on the importance of context and the task of contextualization with regard to the object of study—the biblical texts and contexts. In order to attain a proper re-creation of textual meaning and reconstruction of historical context, it was necessary to situate and read such texts and contexts within their broader sociocultural frameworks. At the same time, historicism denied any importance to context and contextualization with respect to the subject of study—biblical critics and their contexts. To secure a proper re-creation of meaning and reconstruction of context, there was no need to locate and read interpreters and their contexts within their broader sociocultural frameworks.

The rationale for this wedge lay in the character of objectivity and disengagement attributed to the historical approach as such, as learned and practiced within the scientific environment of the academy and its scholarly tradition of reading. Consequently, what was radically affirmed for one realm of production, the past, was radically rejected for the other, the present. In this regard, biblical criticism followed the path of scientific inquiry laid out by traditional historiography.

It was only in the mid-1970s, when theoretical challenges began to be brought against this initial model, that the wedge of contextualization began to be reviewed and revisioned. This process was by no means universally undertaken or accepted, but was more of a here-and-there affair. Three such sources come readily to mind: one constitutes a discursive development from within the discipline itself; the other two represent developments brought to bear on the discipline by material forces from the outside.

The challenge from the inside comes from the grand model of literary criticism and its emphasis on the analysis of texts as texts. This model gradually turned its attention from texts, with corresponding analysis of formal literary and rhetorical features, to readers: first, by analyzing intratextual readers and yielding a plethora of reader constructs, and, subsequently, by addressing extratextual reader constructs and highlighting the real readers. In this process from narrative criticism to reader response, two issues gained increasing prominence: the context or "social location" of interpretation and the agency or "meaning making" of interpreters.

The challenges from the outside emerge from early moves in two variations of the grand model of ideological criticism, with its emphasis on the dynamics and mechanics of power, both introduced by newcomers to the discipline. In effect, feminist criticism and liberation criticism began to foreground the role of the real readers in interpretation, at first in largely dialectical fashion.

While liberation highlighted the problematic of political economy and the differential formations and relations of power engendered by it, both in the past and in the present, feminism pursued the problematic of gender and the unequal formations and relations of power brought about by it, again in both texts and interpretations. The two approaches argued for a difference in reading, variously articulated, between the dominant and the oppressed: for liberation, this difference was expressed in terms of the rich and the poor; for feminism, in terms of men and women. For both, the consequences for criticism, whether traditional or contemporary, were wide ranging and far reaching. Notable among these was a view of the discipline as shaped by the perspectives and interests of economic and male privilege. To be sure, such considerations did not necessarily lead to a sense of diversity in interpretation, for arguments on behalf of proper reading—proper re-creation and reconstruction—could be advanced as well from the point of view of diverse readers. In all such developments, it should be noted, biblical criticism took up lines of inquiry that were present not only in literary studies but throughout the academy as well.

Under the influence of such developments, the traditional wedge at the heart of the discipline between the object and the subject of criticism began to be overcome. The call for critical analysis to focus as much on contextualizing biblical interpreters and interpretive contexts as on contextualizing biblical texts and contexts would undergo, over time, steady expansion and growing sophistication. This was especially so insofar as the contextualization of antiquity was viewed as a constructive exercise on the part of modernity and postmodernity—an exercise in the representation of antiquity. It was as part of such developments that the full-fledged analysis of contextualizing interpretation would emerge.

Analyzing Context as Project

As point of origin for such analysis, I would identify, as generally recognized today, the project "Reading from This Place," which Mary Ann Tolbert and I undertook in the early 1990s and which saw the light of day in 1995 (Segovia and Tolbert 1995a, 1995b). Its aim, first of all, was to examine the relation between critical production and sociocultural location in a sustained and systematic fashion. Its base, therefore, lay primarily in the academy and the scholarly tradition of reading. This was a project grounded primarily in literary theory, revolving around the topics of multiplicity of meanings and diversity of readings. Its edge, in terms of theory and method, was oppositional and revisionist. The project was undertaken in the face of received critical practices, regarded as objectivist and impartial. This was thus an exercise in methodological and theoretical liberation, a hermeneutical program emerging out of interest in contextualization and perspective. Its scope was ambitious. The project proceeded in expansive fashion, involving scholars from a broad variety of quarters and structured in three major stages.

A first phase addressed the problematic from the perspective of the United States, bringing together scholars from the dominant ethnic-racial formation as well as from minoritized groups. The goal was more or less equal representation from the various groups in question, with parity in gender throughout as a further aim. A second phase pursued the problematic from a global perspective, drawing on scholars from both the

Western and the non-Western world. Again, more or less equal representation from among the various continents was the goal, with parity in gender as an accompanying aim. These two phases involved a conference as well as a publication. A third phase, bearing the title of "Teaching the Bible," expanded the problematic by raising the question of pedagogy in light of the relation between production and location. This phase called on scholars from both the national and the international phases to address the topic of teaching the Bible in terms of its discourses and politics. Once again, care was taken to have balanced representation with respect to race/ethnicity, continent, and gender. This last phase involved only preparing a publication.

As part of this project, I undertook a mapping of the discipline that would outline and explain the present state of affairs in criticism in terms of the past trajectory of the discipline. It was here, in effect, that I first developed the vision of a series of critical paradigms, largely sequential and partly competing. I identified four such models: historical, literary, sociocultural, and ideological.[3] This mapping served as my own rationale for the project. I set out to show thereby how the project could be understood as arising at this particular point in time—in the light of such a trajectory and with such concerns in mind. I carried out the mapping by identifying and tracing a set of constitutive principles through the various paradigms, including the role of the reader presupposed in each case. I pointed out how the discipline had moved from appeal to the reader as universal and informed to deployment of the reader as contextual and perspectival. To my mind, therefore, the project sought to investigate the role of critical context and agenda in biblical interpretation.

Behind such mapping and such a conception of the project lay a variety of movements and discourses: liberation theology, reader-response criticism, and cultural studies.

First, there was the influence of liberation theology. For liberation theology, all theological discourse was tied to context: it emerged from context, and it addressed context. As such, analysis of context constituted a fundamental step in theological production. This it proceeded to do, at first, in terms of the social sciences and a neo-Marxist approach: a concentration on political economy and the class struggle among social

---

3. I used this mapping as an introduction to the first two volumes: the first three models were addressed in the first volume and the fourth in the second volume.

formations as a result of differential relations to the means of production, with the use of analytical models as givens. What applied to theological discourse, I had come to see, applied to critical discourse as well. Analysis of context was of the essence, but it was also necessary to expand beyond political economy and to critique the social-scientific models invoked.

Second, there was also the influence of reader-response criticism in literary studies. In the debate regarding the construction of meaning, which involved the relation between the text and the reader, I had come to a position that favored the reader pole of the spectrum, with a view of the real reader as by no means a passive receptor but rather an active creator in the process of approaching and understanding the text. In effect, I saw the flesh-and-blood reader as proactively involved in the re-creation of meaning and the reconstruction of context, a position that led logically to the acceptance of a multiplicity of meanings and histories. Further, I saw real readers as standing behind all constructions of readers (reader constructs) and all models of reading (reading strategies), indeed as standing behind all constructions of real readers, whether of others or of themselves (reader representations). Consequently, in the light of such an epistemic role, I had come to see the need for close analysis of the relation between real readers and their sociocultural contexts, seeking to know how they stood within and reacted to such contexts (location and agenda).

Third, there was the influence of cultural studies, which I understood along the lines of both ideological critique and cultural critique. With the focus on real readers and their relation to sociocultural contexts, I came to see context itself as complex and conflicted. I saw the need for attention to the multiple constitutive dimensions of human identity and hence for recourse to the multiple discourses dealing with the axes of human formations and relations. With the focus on real readers, I came to realize the need to expand the field of inquiry from the academic-scholarly readers to readers of all sorts as they appeal to and deploy the biblical texts and contexts. Context had thus been blown wide open: horizontally it encompassed new contexts of interpretation, and vertically it took the networks of power across society and culture into account. Context had taken a popular as well as a political turn.

All such influences and preoccupations congealed for me in the project. This was not an easy task: at the time, not many people were working on this problematic. The end result, pathbreaking at it was, can now be analyzed with the benefit of distance.

## Deficiencies in Analysis

The project was certainly not without its weaknesses. Indeed, with the passing of time and the privilege of distance, these have become ever clearer. The following come readily to mind: a disjointed structural layout, a deficient theoretical charter, a deficient geopolitical encasement, and a lack of a religious-theological dimension.

First, the layout of the project separated the national and international critical scenes, although there was some representation from the United States in the global phase. This division was adopted in light of what was perceived as the distinctive nature of the United States scene, given the significant number of racial-ethnic minoritized critics at work in the field. This situation, it was felt, needed close and urgent scrutiny on its own. Such a separation was challenged from the very beginning, especially by participants from outside the United States. Its downside was undeniable. The division prevented the two conversations from interacting with one another, to the detriment of both. On the one hand, the national discussion proceeded without any input from the outside, despite multiple links between the minoritized formations within the United States and the societies and cultures of the non-Western world. On the other hand, the international discussion went on without sufficient input from the United States, even though, as the by then hyperpower in the world, the country cast a long shadow on all continents.

Second, the pursuit of the problematic was granted full freedom in terms of the topic and mode of development. While the problematic was duly conveyed, no theoretical framework or corpus of materials was embraced or suggested by way of orientation and theorization. The reason for such latitude was to make the project as malleable as possible, given the wide range of participants and contexts involved. The downside was evident. The different studies did not connect as much with one another or with a set of common referents. Consequently, while they proved highly informative with regard to the local level, they remained much too divorced at a more global level.

Third, the pursuit of the problematic was not emplaced within any particular political or geopolitical discussion. No such framework was advanced or suggested, even though all of us, regardless of context, were now exercising our craft in a very different world. This was, after all, a world that had witnessed but a few years earlier the breakdown of the post-World War II order: the cessation of the Cold War between East and

West, the breakup of the socialist block of nations, and the collapse of the Soviet Union as a state and a superpower (1989–1991). Such omission was not intentional; it was simply accidental. The downside was obvious. What all of us were doing as biblical critics failed to be connected to the wider international scene or to be seen in terms of an overreaching critical agenda. No discussion of the status and role of the critic in such changed conditions and expectations was even entertained.

Finally, the vision of the project did not incorporate a religious-theological dimension. In effect, neither the status of the Bible as a foundational document for Christianity nor the status of biblical studies as a theological discipline within Christian studies was presented as an item for discussion. The reason for such a course of action was a by-product of framing the project within the parameters of literary theory and its impact on the academic-scholarly tradition of reading. This omission was criticized from the beginning as well, especially by participants for whom, as scholars, the Bible was a religious document of import to the church. The downside was undeniable. A perfect opportunity was missed to discuss, in common, the role of the Bible as a global phenomenon as well as the relation between academic-scholarly reading and religious-theological reading.

A Concluding Word

It is against this background, this historical trajectory and present configuration of the field, revolving around the question of contextualization in interpretation, that the position and role of intercultural reading can be properly discerned and assessed. Its place and impact I find to be quite significant. It represents, to be sure, a descendant of the project *Reading from This Place*, but it also signifies an advance upon it. Indeed, it addresses the weaknesses identified above. It moves beyond a disjointed structural layout, bringing together the local and the global throughout. It corrects a deficient theoretical charter, adopting a common framework, using texts in common, and deploying a common method. It counters a deficient geopolitical encasement, identifying the underlying context. It moves against the absence of the religious-theological dimension, bringing this repressed tradition of reading to the fore. In so doing, I find, intercultural reading is similarly influenced, among others, by the discourses of liberation theology, reader response, and cultural studies. The result, then, is a recasting and rearticulation of the hermeneutical mediation of liberation—a new take on biblical interpretation. To this I now turn.

## Intercultural Bible Reading as Project

The project of intercultural Bible reading had its official debut in 2004 with the publication of *Through the Eyes of Another: Intercultural Reading of the Bible*, although the discussions regarding definition, planning, and execution had started a number of years earlier (De Wit et al. 2004). The project was spearheaded by De Wit and a group of colleagues at the Vrije Universiteit Amsterdam, with the assistance of colleagues both in the Netherlands and from around the world. In time, a coordinating board was formed, the Intercultural Bible Collective, to oversee the process of research, analysis, and publication. The volume reported on the first cycle of research and the climax of three years of intensive work.

This first phase set out to examine the interpretation of a common biblical text, the story of Jesus and the Samaritan woman in John 4, on the part of ordinary readers throughout the world, who were organized in small groups for this purpose. It was conceived as an exercise in empirical hermeneutics, insofar as the actual readers would write a report of their interpretation, as well as an excercise in dialogical hermeneutics, insofar as such reports would be shared with other groups in a different part of the world. Since then, the project has continued apace and now finds itself at the conclusion of another long and intensive cycle of research, this time centered on two stories, one from each testament: the mourning of Mary Magdalene at the tomb of Jesus in John 20 and the rape of Tamar by her brother Amnon in 2 Sam 13. The project is one of several in recent years that have sought to deal with a startling development in religion in general and the Christian religion in particular: the emergence of the Bible as a global phenomenon. One such project was autobiographical criticism (see Anderson and Staley 1997; Kitzberger 1999, 2002). Another was scriptural criticism (see Grenholm and Patte 2000).[4] Such spread, presence, and use of the Bible throughout the world, especially in the non-Western world, has been a result of the growth and expansion of Christianity from the end of the nineteenth century and throughout the course of the twentieth century. The global Bible is thus a consequence of the enormous success of the Christian missionary movements and the underlying

---

4. This approach has given way to a number of projects, such as *The Global Bible Commentary* (Patte 2004), the series Romans through History and Culture published by T&T Clark, and the series Texts and Contexts on individual books of the Bible published by Fortress.

vision of the "Christian century." With such globalization of the Bible as a religious and cultural artifact emerged a distinct problematic, especially in the light of developments in criticism—the ever-increasing emphasis on the influence of context and on the agency of readers in the construction of meaning. With the global Bible, contexts and readers multiply. The problematic may be summarized as follows: interpreting the Bible, the one foundational text—or, better, set of texts—of Christianity, within the religious framework of contemporary global Christianity, in all of its multiplicity and diversity. It is this problematic that various interpretive projects have sought to address, including intercultural criticism. Of these, it is the latter that I find most striking.[5]

It is, first of all, quite innovative as well as quite encompassing. It is highly novel, insofar as it moves beyond the world of the academy and professional critics to include ordinary readers, and it is highly comprehensive, insofar as it involves ordinary readers from throughout the world. It is, in addition, quite sophisticated, invoking a variety of fields as foundation: reader-response criticism—well situated within this discourse; cultural anthropology—well aware of discussions regarding culture; and communication studies—well versed in the dynamics and mechanics of intercultural exchange. It is, lastly, overtly religious-theological. It is grounded in Christian studies and the Christian church and, as such, represents an exercise in the religious-theological interpretation of the Bible.

I shall address its driving vision and force by way of two foundational pieces written by De Wit: the original exposition of the project (De Wit 2004), which functioned as an introduction to *Through the Eyes of Another* (De Wit et al. 2004), and the later, expanded elaboration (De Wit 2012), which appeared as the first volume of the new series Intercultural Biblical Hermeneutics, launched by the Dom Hélder Câmara Foundation. These two pieces are complementary, and I shall look at them jointly, while paying attention to the passage of time. In so doing, I shall follow the structure of the original exposition.

---

5. Works along this line continue to appear (see Keener and Carroll R. 2013). A critical comparative analysis of such approaches is very much in order.

## Overall Design

### Original Exposition

De Wit begins the original exposition by setting forth the essential components of the project: the "core question" behind the venture; the circumstances and reasons that form its background—the "developments and challenges that have come to light in the past decades in the broad field of theology"; and the process that comes to embody it (2004, 4).

(1) *Core Question.* The core question is twofold, the first part setting the stage for the second. The first part summarizes the focus and the problematic of the project, "What happens when Christians from radically different cultures and situations read the same Bible story and start talking about it with each other?" The focus is on Christianity taken as a whole, having in mind the momentous development mentioned above, that is, the phenomenon of global Christianity—the presence of Christians across cultures and situations, sharply different from one another. Such expansion sets up the problematic: communication among Christians regarding the Bible, the common book of Christianity—the reading of the Bible and the sharing of such readings within such a framework of radical differences. The second part reveals the spirit and the vision of the project, "Can intercultural reading of Bible stories result in a new method of reading the Bible and communicating faith that is a catalyst for new, trans-border dialogue and identity formation?" (De Wit 2004, 4). The spirit has to do with undertaking such reading and sharing among Christians. The vision is to establish, through such reading and sharing of the Bible, dialogue and identity as Christians across the boundaries represented by the divergent cultures and situations of global Christianity. In effect, De Wit envisions the intercultural reading of the Bible as a point of convergence for Christians.

(2) *Circumstances and Reasons.* Behind such an undertaking and beyond the globalization of Christianity as such, a variety of circumstances and reasons are identified, four in all. Two of these have to do with the material matrix underlying global Christianity and can be readily brought together. The other two involve the discursive dimension of the project and can be grouped together as well.

The social angle has two dimensions. The first is strictly economic: the negative impact of globalization on the world, above all the growing divide—the "increasing asymmetry"—between the rich and the poor. The second represents a mixture of social and economic factors: the fact of diversity in the world and the need to move beyond such diversity, by way of "new interactions," in order to bring about conscientization and change. For De Wit, therefore, the project constitutes one such "new interaction" to address the worsening condition of inequality in the world: a new approach to reading the Bible among Christians. In this regard, intercultural criticism has a lot in common with liberation criticism, with its stress on poverty and transformation. The cultural angle also has two dimensions. The first reason represents a mixture of the theological and the critical: the riches to be found in the readings of ordinary Christian readers and the absence or omission of such richness in academic criticism. The second is strictly critical: the interest in a new perspective beyond the search for ultimate meaning. For De Wit, the new approach advanced by the project is a fruitful source of wisdom and a necessary method of criticism, not as one more tool, but as an essential modus operandi. Here, too, intercultural criticism reveals itself to have much in common with liberation, with its emphasis on the voice of the community.

(3) *Process.* The process for such intercultural reading was threefold. In the first stage each group read and discussed the text among themselves, and a report of this exercise described both the group and the interpretation. The group was free with regard to its own manner of reading, although various points of reference were suggested to all groups. In the second stage, groups around the world were paired: each read the report of the partner group, seeking to read the text "through the eyes of another," and prepared a response for the other group. In the final stage the partner groups engaged in dialogue: the groups responded to one another's reports, reflected on the process as a whole, and decided on the future of the relation. The entire process was coordinated by a committee at the Vrije Universiteit Amsterdam responsible for the protocol to be followed, the translation of the reports, the pairing of the groups, the running of a website, and the preparation of a volume and a documentary. In this way, De Wit and his colleagues placed Christians from contrasting sides of the world, in all sorts of combinations, in conversation with one another about both a biblical story and their own stories.

## Recent Elaboration

From the beginning of the more recent monograph, De Wit sharply accentuates the economic circumstances and reasons behind the project. The material matrix is again laid out in terms of the prevailing, untoward state of affairs in the world and the corresponding need to move forward in the face of such adverse circumstances. The global situation is portrayed as marked by "exclusion, injustice, and oppression" (De Wit 2012, 5 n. 4), while the path to follow is presented as a quest for "transformation and changed perspectives" on the part of groups coming together from radically different contexts (5). De Wit pointedly asks, "In which ways can an intercultural dialogue on the meaning of fundamental narratives—Holy Scripture—contribute to justice and liberation?" Such dialogue, such reading of sacred texts "through the eyes of another," across cultural and sociopolitical contexts, can lead readers of sacred texts to develop a greater understanding for one another and thus to move toward "reconciliation, peace, and justice" (6).

The years intervening between the two expositions have clearly moved the project toward a greater awareness of global problems and a greater resolve for global action. The primary reason for such a turn is the ever greater impact of the Global South upon De Wit, as the following comments reveal.

In recent years there has been a return toward a contemporary appropriation of texts in interpretation and thus away from a protracted exclusive focus on the historical understanding of texts in the aftermath of the Enlightenment. During the "divorce" that existed between "Brother Text" and "Sister Appropriation," the critic became a *Vormund* or "guardian" of the text, for whom a response to the text was seen "as irrelevant, as a hindrance, and indeed as an assault on the original meaning of the text." De Wit attributes such renewed emphasis on appropriation in biblical studies to the religious-theological circles of the two-thirds world and their "genitive theologies."[6] Scholars in Latin America, Africa, and Asia began to view the relationship between text and response as essential and proceeded to engage in dialogue with "ordinary, socioeconomically poor readers" with the aim of moving toward "a praxis of liberation." Such a development emerged as "fundamental to the hermeneutics of liberation" (De Wit 2012, 11).

Intercultural reading is thereby placed squarely within the trajectory of liberation hermeneutics in general. Its objective is to extend this trajectory

---

6. In the world of the academy in general, such a turn toward response is associated with literary studies, modern hermeneutics, and postmodern philosophy.

along a path not yet taken, the path of empirical hermeneutics: a systematic analysis of the actual responses of ordinary Christian readers, reading together the same texts in and across groups, throughout the world. In so doing, the project seeks to avoid any "romantic" or "essentialist" description of how the poor read and to render instead a sense of how such reading actually takes place. If such reading is good for the poor and serves as a key to liberation as claimed, then, argues De Wit, it is imperative to establish exactly how such reading actually works. Only then can a proper response to the global situation of today proceed as it should.

## Detailed Unfolding

The original exposition of the project follows the succinct presentation of an overall design with an expansive explanation of a number of constitutive components viewed as inherent to the core question. Four such elements are identified: the concept of ordinary readers, the character of stories, the nature of intercultural exchange, and the description of empirical hermeneutics as a new field of research—all are taken up again in the later elaboration. In unfolding these elements, a variety of issues emerge that are key to my task of critical placement: the status of the Bible, the driving objectives of the project, and the mode of Scripture reading.

### Status of the Bible

The status assigned to the Bible within the project is highly significant and needs to be addressed. In the initial exposition, this issue forms part of the second core component—the discussion regarding the power of stories. The subsequent elaboration develops it by placing it in a variety of discursive and material frameworks, with the former as primary—the growing focus on the power of readers. Throughout, the place and role assigned to the Bible are pivotal, but by no means supreme or exclusive. For De Wit, the uniqueness of the Bible lies not so much in its status as the word of God, the deposit of revelation, for and in the world, far above, if not over against, all other sacred texts. It is not its divine origin and content that set the Bible apart, but other traits ranging from the literary and the rhetorical, through the religious and the existential, to the commercial and the spatial. The Bible is thus unique, certainly for Christians, but in neither triumphal nor dogmatic fashion. Its special character and power flow rather from a variety of other sources.

(1) *Original Exposition*. The sense of uniqueness is tied to the power of story, and De Wit points in this regard to a turn to story and narrative in recent times across a number of fields of study. For the Bible, the power of the story is advanced as multidimensional. At a universal level, stories are seen as essential to identity, bringing together the past and the future in and for the present—"awareness, knowledge, culture, experience, community, and personal identity flow together in them." At the circumscribed level of religious stories across religious traditions, stories are described as foregrounding the fundamental questions of life, in which they serve as bearers of authority, memory, and potential: "Religious stories are the central components of tradition." At the particular level of the Christian tradition, stories are viewed as being at the core of its religious worldview and its sacred text: "The Bible, Christianity's basic document, contains all kinds of texts, but the story dominates. The stories make the Bible a Bible" (De Wit 2004, 20).

Thus the power of reading the stories of the Bible together in small groups is described as profound and fruitful. Such reading has multiple repercussions: the reflection on life as it is and as it should be, the acquisition of intimate knowledge regarding the other across differences, the unleashing of the longing for radical transformation and liberation, and the development of a sense of remembering and actualization—making the old new in creative ways by analogy and imagination.

(2) *Later Elaboration*. The sense of uniqueness is explained in a variety of other ways. It is linked, first of all, to the power of appropriating texts in reading, and De Wit points here to a similar turn to the reader and reception in recent times across fields dealing with texts and interpretation. For the Bible, such power is again advanced as multidimensional. At a general level, having to do with texts of all sorts, it is granted that reading does something to readers—"a consequence, a moment of appropriation, an effect." At a restricted level, involving sacred texts, such is all the more true: "all hermeneutical traditions of all religions based on sacred texts argue *a fortiori* that texts do something with their readers." At the concrete level of the Bible as the sacred text of Christianity, the effect of the text on the reader has always been granted (except during the period of "divorce" mentioned earlier), although in different ways: "a response from the readers, is constitutive for the meaning of texts, for the meaning of tradition, for the meaning of revelation itself" (De Wit 2012, 9). Consequently, the power of appropriating the Bible in reading is described as a "condition for survival": "Without readers, without a response the Scripture ceases to

be a source of revelation" (14). The sense of uniqueness is further associated with two other factors: the power at work in the broad dissemination of the Bible—"the most-sold book in the history of humanity"—and the power resulting from its global presence—a volume "read at the same time by so many different people in such radically different contexts and situations" (14–15).

(3) *Concluding Comment.* The Bible emerges thereby as indispensable to Christians for a variety of reasons: it bears the elements of storytelling and leads to appropriation as a text (literary and rhetorical grounds); it is a sacred text and raises the ultimate questions of human life, both present and possible (religious and existential grounds); and it is present everywhere and read throughout (commercial and spatial grounds). Taken together, this set of traits renders the Bible a "unique analytical tool" (2012, 9), insofar as it opens a window to the social, emotional, and active lives of its many and different readers.

Such an approach to the unique or special character of the Bible differs considerably from that of traditional liberation hermeneutics. What is of import here is not the theological message or the divine origin of the Bible as such, nor the structural binomial of wealth and poverty, nor its control by the rich and its loss by the poor. What is of import, rather, is the power of its form as story and its appropriation as text, its character as a sacred text among many and its problematizing of life, its unmatched degree of distribution and its global angles of consumption. The result is a different approach to liberation. It is an approach in tune with recent academic and intellectual currents as well as with social and cultural developments. It is not the discovery of one overarching story and the adoption of the one appropriate response to it, for story and its appropriation proceed in many different ways. Intercultural reading lays out an approach that grants much greater freedom to readers, both in interpretation and appropriation.

On this point De Wit himself is forthcoming. In mentioning the unleashing of the longing for liberation and change among those who engage in group readings of the Bible as one of the consequences of appropriation, he associates such unleashing directly with the sense of freedom, confidence, and "brotherhood" felt by the participants in such discussions and groups. Such freedom De Wit further relates to the power of story over against the restraint of dogma. With reference to Paul Ricoeur's description of narrative theology, he writes, "The assignment of narrative theology is to save the playfulness, stubbornness, incoherence, and ambiguity of the story from the hands of dogmatic argument, absolute certainty, closed formulas" (2004, 22). While liberation also decries the restraints of dogma, insofar as it has occluded the materialist dimension of the Bible, it does not mention such qualities of the Bible, and, indeed, it seems to me, would neither welcome nor praise them.

## Driving Objectives of the Project

The driving objectives behind the project are quite important and call for close consideration as well. In De Wit's initial exposition, this issue arises within the third core component—the discussion on the nature of intercultural exchange. His subsequent elaboration expands upon it by way of a dialogical encounter with the field of missiology, especially the proposal for a postmissionary missiology. At all times, such goals are profoundly religious-theological. This De Wit makes clear from the beginning, as he unfolds the meaning of the term *intercultural*: "The two concepts together also represent the question of what possibilities are offered by the project in the world of ecumenics and mission" (2004, 25). Thus, the driving objectives emerge as ecumenical, or intra-Christian, and missionary, or interreligious.

(1) *Original Exposition.* The point of departure for the formulation of these religious-theological aims is a consideration of intercultural exchange in general, analyzing both the meaning of the base noun, *culture*, and the force of the prefix, *inter-*. On the one hand, the term *culture* is described as one among many factors of social context—alongside such terms as *status, gender, ethnicity, power, education,* and *church*—that impinge on, inform, and guide individuals. Culture is what frames and orients behavior, values and standards, and view of life. It is not static but shifts, always in the process of construction. On the other hand, the modifier *inter-* is said to signify a move toward "exchange, confrontation, interaction" (2004, 28). *Inter-* goes beyond a mere presentation of differences (the province of the multicultural) toward a comparative analysis of difference. It sets the stage for a new understanding of one's own culture and that of the other, away from a hierarchy of difference, toward the legitimacy of difference. In recent times, De Wit observes, there has been much discussion on the question of culture, cultural differences, and cultural identity. In such discussion Christian studies has proved no exception.

The intercultural Bible reading project seeks to bring this turn to culture to bear upon biblical criticism and, more specifically, on the problematic of reading the Bible in a global Christian context. In so doing, intercultural criticism approaches the question of culture as multidimensional and seeks to discern its influence on interpretation across a variety of realms at once: to begin with, the world of the Bible; then, the world of the readers of the Bible; and lastly, the process of reading the Bible.[7] Toward this end, communities of participants from around the globe are given a threefold task: to examine the same biblical text, to do so from their different social and cultural contexts, and to compare the different interpretations of the same text by engaging in a process of exchange with other groups of participants.

In such interaction, De Wit argues, lies the possibility of a "new productive understanding of texts"—a transforming reading—in which "a structure and hierarchy can be detected in the differences in such a way that the weight of the differences is cancelled and can be explained and put into perspective in the light of a common engagement, a common assignment" (2004, 29). Thus global Christianity is brought together in dialogue, in limited and strategic fashion, over the same passage(s), taken from its sacred text. Such exchange is meant to lead to confrontation with differences, given the diversity of interpretations coming forth from the multiple readings and contexts of reading, as a step in moving beyond such radical differences toward a "new sort of catholicity" (30).[8] Only such a transformed sense of catholicity can enable the community not to break apart over differences, but rather to survive as a community in the face and light of difference.

For De Wit, transforming reading of this type signifies major breakthroughs in criticism. To begin with, such reading moves beyond all discourses that address reading and the reader (2004, 30–31): beyond reader

---

7. For the analysis of the influence of culture, De Wit draws on Hofstede 1995. His cultural theory is viewed as most suitable for empirical research insofar as it outlines specific "calibration points." The theory advances a view of culture as "software of the mind," whereby all societies are seen as having to deal with the same fundamental problems. Hofstede identifies five such "dimensions": (1) power and inequality; (2) relationship between the individual and the collective; (3) expected social roles of men and women; (4) fear and uncertainty of existence; and (5) time and tradition. Such dimensions, De Wit argues, can be employed in discerning cultural specifics in the project.

8. For this concept De Wit draws on Schreiter 1997, who presents it as a resolution of opposites—sameness and difference, the local and the global—in faith, toward a universal theology, through the exercise of intercultural communication and with a vision of proper praxis in mind.

response, which remains at a general level, whether with regard to reading strategies, communities of readers, or the text-reader relation; beyond reception theory, insofar as it remains focused on models of identification between readers and characters and the motives behind such patterns; beyond the subjective criticism of David Bleich (1975, 1978) and its call for interaction between professional and ordinary readers, which remains concerned only with a very restricted set of readers in North America; and beyond ideological criticism, insofar as it remains closed to ordinary readers. In contrast, intercultural reading addresses—empirically and expansively—how diversity and confrontation can lead to transformation. In addition, intercultural reading moves against the established and operative, though unacknowledged, ecclesial traditions of reading through the insertion of cultural diversity, forcing thereby a distance from such traditions through confrontation and diversity (De Wit 2004, 32).

It is such catholicity that intercultural reading has in mind through its driving objectives of ecumenical and missionary interaction. The goal of ecumenical intercultural reading is directed at the microcontext of the global Christian community, calling for dialogue among Christians over its sacred text across ecclesial boundaries. Missionary intercultural reading aims at the macrocontext of the global Christian community as one among many religious traditions, calling for dialogue among Christians and non-Christians over sacred texts across religious structures. One could say, therefore, that beyond and underlying the ecumenical and missionary objectives lies the ultimate objective of intra-Christian and inter-religious catholicity.

Thus, from the point of view of the ecumenical imperative, the project sets out to provide "opportunities for enriching relationships of mission and service between Christians, especially at the grassroots level of the churches." The rationale is that Christians find themselves in a situation where they are separated from one another by all kinds of differences, yet confronted by common problems and crises that demand cooperation across such differences. Hence intercultural reading can open a space through dialogue with other Christians on the sacred text for broad ecumenical engagement—"a space where consensus, balance, and identity are sought in a broad ecumenical perspective" (De Wit 2004, 33).

This first objective is deeply grounded in the power of the Bible itself: "unity is not a lost cause as long as the scripture continues to be opened, read, and preached in all Christian churches" (2004, 33). Its effects are far reaching and wide ranging. They have to do with context: getting to know other contexts and critically examining one's own context, acknowledging patterns of prejudice and exclusion as well as recognizing the presence of asymmetry, and searching for the reasons beyond the differences and looking for bonds of union. They also have to do with interpretation: revision of original readings and appreciation for other readings, problematizing the reading process itself, and awareness of the relation to the church, local and global.

Similarly, from the point of view of the missionary imperative, the project sets out to provide an opportunity for Christians and non-Christians to engage "in the discussion on the good world and the merciful God" (2004, 32). Christians find themselves separated from non-Christians by traditions of converting the other and using self-righteous argumentation, while being faced, alongside non-Christians, with the asymmetrical forces of globalization that require a common response. Consequently, through dialogue with non-Christians and the inclusion of sacred texts from non-Christian religions, intercultural reading can clear a space for broad interreligious scriptural engagement—a space to "arrive at solutions to the border-transgressing problems that humanity is confronting" (41).

This objective is deeply grounded in the power of the Bible as well: "The gospel itself is transcultural and trans-border. The scripture is a product of intercultural communication" (2004, 38). Its effects are similarly far-reaching and wide-ranging. For Christians, they include an option for love rather than conversion as well as the adoption of sensitivity and openness instead of self-righteousness in dealing with the religious other. For all religions, they signify: tearing down barriers between nations, eradicating inequality, and combating practices of exclusion and discrimination.

(2) *Later Elaboration.* The question of objectives is further developed through an appeal to the work of Lambert Hoedemaker (2000) on a missiology for a "postmissionary" age. This proposal is taken by De Wit to apply to both the intra-Christian ecumenical and the interreligious missionary objectives outlined for the project. The proposal itself involves a fundamental rethinking and reorientation of traditional missiology in the light of a new era marked by profound inequality, worldwide secularization, religious pluralism, and contextual-cultural diversity. Just as mission has always carried within it an eschatological impulse, similarly these markers reveal an eschatological dimension, a "longing" for something altogether "different" and "new." De Wit describes this longing as follows: "finally a

redeemed and liberated humanity, a deep and complete mutual acknowledgement among people, and a successful communication in which all of humankind is involved—'reconciled variety'" (2012, 81). In this new era, traditional missiology, the preserve of an isolated West, collapses. Difference can no longer be approached at a safe distance, from a normative standpoint, with unity in mind. It must now be approached in context, through dialogue with and respect for the other and with reconciliation in mind. Such is the call of a postmissionary missiology. In this regard, the use of Scripture and tradition stands as foundational.

Within such a transformed concept of missiology, intercultural reading represents an ideal recourse. The project moves beyond a sense of a normative here and a distant other toward the pursuit of dialogue everywhere—beyond formal organizations and structures toward grassroots communities, beyond central validation and proposals toward a multiplicity of conversations and solutions, and beyond recording how the other reads and speaks toward having all read and speak in interactive fashion. Intercultural reading is presented thereby as a "new missionary practice" that stands in critical relation "to institutionalized practices and attempts to do justice to the eschatological dimension of missions," that is, a practice very much in tune with a postmissionary age (2012, 83).

(3) *Concluding Comment*. This formulation of the driving objectives of the project deviates significantly from those of traditional liberation hermeneutics. What is of significance here is the exercise of interchange across intra-Christian and interreligious borders, not the adoption of an overriding (e.g., materialist) angle of vision; allowance for a variety of impinging sociocultural crises, not the focalization of any one problematic; openness to the immense diversity of readings and contexts in the grass roots, not the marshaling of the grass roots toward a common topic or goal; and unrestricted range of exchange between and among countless diverse contexts and readings, rather than the presence of a cohering and overseeing voice of an attendant facilitator. The result is a different approach to liberation, in critical conversation with contemporary events and currents. Instead of an epic oppositional struggle between oppression and liberation, one finds a multilens consideration of common massive global problems. In sum, the ecumenical and missionary goals of the project prove too crisscrossing and the venues too numerous and widespread for any one optic to lord it over the others. Thus, once again, intercultural reading grants a much greater degree of freedom in interpretation and sharing to readers of all sorts.

## Mode of Scripture Reading

The mode of approach to the biblical texts as Scripture, as religious-theo-logical texts, is an equally important issue and demands just as much attention. In the initial exposition, this question is broached within the first core component—the presentation of the concept of ordinary readers. The subsequent elaboration develops it by setting it against a broader theoretical framework: a vision and project of ethical interpretation. Throughout, for De Wit the reading of Scripture as Scripture—not merely as a historical product or a literary classic or a cultural artifact—is tied to the notion of ordinary readers and entails a process of reading together, encountering and dialoguing with one another. It is the type of reading at work in inter-cultural reading.

(1) *Original Exposition.* Ordinary readers represent the foundations, agents, and proprietors of Scripture reading, which is how they approach the Bible. Such a category, however, is a carefully delineated construct, "dynamic" as well as "complex," at once exclusive and inclusive. It is restric-tive, insofar as it is defined vis-à-vis an Other: ordinary readers are consti-tuted as a distinct formation in contraposition to "scholarly readers." It is, at the same time, comprehensive, as it encompasses a multitude of others: ordinary readers from across all social and cultural distinctions—"social status, income, culture, education level, occupation, church background, and religious conviction" (De Wit 2004, 6)—are brought together in the same formation. At first sight, given the numerous and profound differ-ences and tensions at work, such a category would appear to be unstable and unwieldy. What holds it together for De Wit is a combination of two factors: a coalescence of four "melodies" that mark such readers and their mode of reading and the call to read in community.

The four "melodies" are identified as follows. To begin with, Scrip-ture reading possesses a strong spiritual dimension, twofold in nature. It involves motivation: ordinary readers come to the Bible from a situa-tion of fragility and seek in the Bible a word of life—perhaps a measure of assistance or healing, perhaps a sense of direction or transformation. It also involves performance: ordinary readers look for more than intellec-tual understanding and thus accompany such reading with symbols and rituals. In addition, such reading embodies an existential hermeneutical dimension. Ordinary readers respond to and appropriate the Bible in and for the present, bringing new meaning to bear on the texts. Further, such reading carries a decidedly empirical dimension. Ordinary readers are not abstractions but real readers, whose actual readings of the Bible are worthy of analysis and demand extensive research. Lastly, Scripture reading has a resolutely autonomous dimension. The voices of ordinary readers must come to the surface as they are, without a preassigned strategy or model for reading.

These "melodies" readily locate Scripture reading within a variety of interpretive traditions. Its explicitly spiritual dimension situates it within a long tradition of spiritual reading in the church, a trajectory that extends from its early centuries (as in the concept of the spiritual sense or the practice of *lectio divina*) to our own times (as with the practices of Semoya reading in Africa or *lectura orante* in Latin America). Its spontaneous hermeneutical dimension sets it within recent theoretical developments in literary criticism, a view of the reader as contextual and engaged and of meaning as construction. Its pronounced empirical and autonomous dimensions place it within the tradition of biblical scholarship in the Global South (Africa, Asia, Latin America) arising in the 1970s, an angle of vision that foregrounds the reading of the Bible by the poor and oppressed.

Underlying all four traits lies the imperative of reading in community, a practice designed to bring about interaction and confrontation among ordinary readers. Its effects may be outlined as follows. With regard to the search for a word of life in Scripture, through the use of symbols and rituals, communal reading brings about an ambience of celebration and commemoration. In terms of the existential response to Scripture, it acts as a check on any closure of meaning by individuals or groups of ordinary readers. In terms of the emphasis on real readers, it serves as a guard against any flattening representation of ordinary readers. With regard to the focus on actual voices and corresponding modes of expression, communal reading prevents any possible metaphorization of ordinary readers as privileged and exclusive.

Such traits and such reading in community touch directly on the problematic of ethics in interpretation, which lies for De Wit at the heart of Scripture reading in general and intercultural reading in particular. This problematic is well captured by the concepts of plurivocity and plenitude. Plurivocity refers to the seemingly unending diversity of meaning: ordinary readers produce ever new interpretations of the same text. Thus De Wit declares, "Texts are multidimensional and are simultaneously read at different levels by communities with different interests." Plenitude addresses the issue of validation in the face of plurivocity: meaning involves the range of readings advanced, including those of ordinary readers. Thus, "The interpretation that includes the maximum number of facts offered by the text, including possible connotations, is the most probable" (2004, 14). Consequently, Scripture reading demands an ethics of interpretation that allows for plurivocity in plenitude, as ordinary readers, in approaching the Bible, produce ever new readings from their respective sociocultural contexts and religious-theological communities.

(2) *Later Elaboration*. The call for an ethics of interpretation is amplified in the subsequent elaboration by drawing on cultural and philosophical studies, grounded in the work of Hendrik Procee and Emmanuel Levinas. Procee, a professor at the University of Twente, addresses the situation of heightened ethnic-cultural diversity in the Netherlands brought about by the influx of migrants and refugees. He proposes to move beyond the usual analytical approaches to diversity, universalism, and relativism, by advancing a third approach—pluralism (Procee 1991). A leading French intellectual in the decades that followed World War II profoundly imbued with the ethical-religious tradition of Judaism, Levinas pursued the question of alterity and the corresponding question of subjectivity raised by the other. Moving beyond the traditional aims of metaphysics (analysis of being) and epistemology (analysis of knowing), he argued for the primacy of personal ethical responsibility in the face of others (Levinas 1961).

Along the lines of Procee, De Wit envisions Scripture reading as an effort to move beyond the divide between the traditional universalism of Western hermeneutics and the recent relativism of contextual hermeneutics. Toward this end, Scripture reading is said to embody the basic concepts of pluralism: interactive diversity and eccentricity. The former foregrounds cultural diversity in human interaction, while the latter grounds such strategy in a fundamental structural relation of the individual to the cultural as both producer and product. This relation is described as follows: it yields a "multiformity of human individuals" and "a great diversity of cultural patterns"; it posits interaction as "essential for human beings"; and it involves two principles of praxis, that is, nonexclusion and promotion of diversity. Scripture reading implements interactive diversity through confrontation in organized communal readings of the Bible; it further appropriates eccentricity by calling for knowledge of other interpretations, without exception and without cease, for it considers all interpretation as "incomplete and vulnerable" (De Wit 2012, 22).

Along the lines of Levinas, De Wit looks upon Scripture reading as an attempt to move away from the totality and mastery by the self and toward the welcoming of the unfamiliar. As such, it is said to integrate essential aspects of ethical responsibility: orientation to the other, infinity, and engagement. Orientation to the other means looking beyond one's horizon for new possibilities, a stance that captures the eschatological disposition of Tanak, which looks beyond the present and toward the future. Infinity involves a determination to cross boundaries—especially, as specified by Tanak, those of the marginalized (widows, orphans, strangers)—in search of plenitude and transcendence. Engagement signifies a commitment to peace and justice, yielding transformation and passion, activating thereby the tradition of the Hebrew Bible. Spiritual reading displays all such features: welcoming the other, through its view of texts as "polysemic, polyphonic, and diverse" (De Wit 2012, 23); espousing infinity by adhering to the position that there are as "many readings as there are readers" and that "each reader is irreplaceable" (24); and opting for engagement, by having respect for and interaction with all others, "prevent[ing] the interpreter from standing on the sidelines unwilling to dirty his hands"—especially so in "historical situations of suffering and exclusion" (25).

(3) *Concluding Comment.* This conception of Scripture reading departs considerably from that of traditional liberation hermeneutics. Indeed, on this issue De Wit himself is forthcoming, both when unfolding the notion of ordinary readers and when laying out the vision of ethical responsibility.

First, when addressing the existential dimension of ordinary readers and the importance of appropriation, De Wit mentions how the context of antiquity is applied to the context of today, especially in terms of the relation oppressor-oppressed. Such a move, he warns, may turn "egocentric" or "narcissistic": appropriation may become "annexation," so that readers "only hear the echo of their own voices, and always take the side of the good and just" (2004, 10). Second, in emphasizing the empirical dimension of ordinary readers, De Wit observes how little analysis of popular readings has actually been done, even by those in the South, who have stressed the transformative nature of such readings. Such absence makes one wonder "how those social changes come about, what role reading the Bible plays in this process, what factors are decisive, and which impede it" (16). Third, in highlighting the autonomous character of ordinary readers, he points to how such voices can easily become a metaphor—say, "the poor." Such abstraction may result in a privileged and exclusivistic category: the poor as the best interpreters of the text, with reference to a specific category of people, while "other poor people are left off the boat" (17). Finally, when discussing ethical responsibility and expounding the option for pluralism between universalism and relativism, De Wit situates contextual hermeneutics, regardless of the genitive in question, squarely within the latter pole, given the emphasis on the local situation and values. Such a stance may easily turn into a "strong reductionism," whereby readers "merge with their context" (2012, 21).

What is of importance here is the multitude and cacophony of ordinary readers in conversation with one another. It is the ever-expanding diversity of appropriation by readers yielding an ever-expanding reservoir of meaning of the text, not an absolute, unquestioned identification on the part of any one formation of readers with the text. It is the detailed analysis of transformation, its dynamics and mechanics, in all readers, not a general, unexamined attribution of transformation to such reading. It is the individual voices of real readers across social and cultural divisions and the way in which such voices express themselves, not a circumscribed, undifferentiated designation of any particular formation. It is the full array of situations of need from which readers emerge and seek comfort in the Bible, not the focus on any one such situation. The result, I would submit yet again, is a different approach to liberation—one that is in contact with recent developments in interpretation and philosophical reflections on alterity. The mode of Scripture reading that emerges is unremittingly open and unremittingly communal. In sum, intercultural reading grants much greater freedom to readers as ordinary readers who engage in interactive religious-theological reading of the Bible as Scripture.

## Intercultural Bible Reading and Praxis: A New Direction

A further direction in the recasting and rearticulation of liberation must be noted, especially because it has to do with the mediation of praxis, the critical way of life in the world. This takes place in De Wit's later elaboration of the project, at the very end and by way of a hint (2012, 85–86). It involves the contribution envisioned for intercultural reading with regard to development theory—the strategy that has informed relations between the developed world and the undeveloped and underdeveloped world, within the geopolitical project of modernization, since the mid-twentieth century. It is a framework—a way of thinking and a way of acting—that De Wit finds severely wanting.

To begin with, development organizations are depicted as suffering from a common "demonic dilemma" of concentrating on the economic dimension of life—the poverty of the other and its attending manifestations. As a result, the other is approached from the secularized perspective of the West and is instrumentalized in the process. In addition, Christian development organizations, drawing for their rationale and policies on the ethical-religious traditions of Christianity, are portrayed as misguided in their service: failing to engage the other in the process—the exclusion of the other from the discussion. They approach the other from the outside, as having nothing to offer regarding their own situation, even in terms of the ethical-religious traditions to which they adhere. Intercultural reading, De Wit proposed, can make an important dent in this regard.

Such a reading respects the "'other' in the Two-Thirds World" as a twofold "epiphanic space," signifying simultaneously a condition, in life as in death, beyond the imagination of the developed world, and a profound bond to religious tradition, which allows them to survive in such a situation. Intercultural reading allows the other to voice their concerns and perspectives at all levels of life, not just on economics. Because intercultural Bible reading allows the other to express themselves on the basis of their religious tradition, such a reading should be adopted as a "development strategy" in the work of developmental organizations. This strategy would allow such organizations to enter into dialogue with the other directly, learning about their situation from the inside, sharing their problems and hopes. Even in the secularized West, religion is still much "a part of that world." Such a strategy would allow Christian organizations to pursue such dialogue with the other through the Bible. The Bible represents "the most important compass" of this "religious universe" (2012, 85). Thus development organizations, Christian or not, "should look carefully at such stories—not simply at the misery but also at the dreams, power, and hope that people derive from the biblical story in situations of obvious suffering" (86).

Such a course of action brings a decided shift in the traditional optic of liberation. Development is not to be approached solely through the eyes of dependency theory and defined as underdevelopment, but from the grass roots. It goes directly to the people and asks what they think and what they dream. Thus intercultural reading "can contribute in a modest but yet fundamental way to the process of identity formation" (De Wit 2012, 86) by serving as a place from which dominant development models can be critically analyzed and where alternative models can be allowed to surface. This is indeed a move on De Wit's part that shifts intercultural reading into a very different and suggestive sociocultural role—the critical analysis of praxis.

## Conclusion

I began by stating that intercultural Bible reading represents a signal attempt to address the problematic of liberation in and for our times and that, as such, the approach has been most faithful to the legacy of Dom Hélder Câmara, as intended and advanced by the foundation in his honor and memory. This I set out to show in three steps.

In the first section, I argued that intercultural reading brings a new direction to the problematic of contextualization in biblical criticism at the level of reception, a development at work in the field, in principle since the 1970s but pursued in earnest only in the 1990s. Intercultural reading, I pointed out, brought greater theorization to this line of investigation on a variety of issues regarding the reading of the Bible: the relation between local and global dimensions of reading, the articulation of a process of reading, the exposition of the sociocultural global framework underlying such reading, and the integration of the religious-theological tradition of reading. Such advance sets the stage for a new angle on the appeal to and deployment of Scripture in the tradition of liberation.

In the second section, I argued that such recasting and rearticulation of liberation takes place at all levels of the intercultural Bible reading project. This revisioning is very much in evidence in the explanation of its overall design: the core question, its attending circumstances and reasons, and the process of reading. It is also much in evidence in the exposition of the constitutive elements undergirding the core question, given the critical positions taken along the way on fundamental issues of biblical interpretation: the status accorded to the Bible, the objectives identified as driving the project, and the mode of reading deployed for approaching the texts as Scripture. The result represents a marked expansion in the hermeneutics of liberation. This expansion reveals a threefold nature. First, from the point of view of overall design and the core question in particular, the project views the phenomenon of global Christianity as a problematic, with its many and radical differences in context and culture, and seeks to bring it together through the Bible, given its status as both global phenomenon and common book. Such a sense of identity and dialogue the project sets out to achieve through a set process of reading together, in community, on the part of ordinary readers throughout the world—a way of reading that extends the tradition of liberation in a novel, empirical direction. Second, in terms of the attending reasons for the overall design, the project emphasizes the ever growing divide between the haves and have-nots in the wake of globalization and hence the urgent need for global Christianity to address this fundamental disparity present in its own midst. The project seeks to take on this sense of inequality and exclusion by pressing ordinary readers across the globe, haves and have-nots alike, to work together for transformation, with justice and liberation in mind, through their reading of the Bible in dialogue—a focus of reading that extends the tradition of liberation onto a new, global plane. Third, from the perspective of the critical positions assumed regarding biblical interpretation, the project grants ordinary readers a tremendous degree of freedom in such a reading of the Bible together. This sense of openness the project promotes by moving well beyond previous parameters regarding all such issues—a mode of reading that sets the tradition of liberation on a novel, multidirectional footing.

In the third section, I argued that such expansion in the hermeneutics of liberation led, although only by way of a glimpse at this point, to a further recasting and rearticulation of its vision of praxis or way of life toward transformation in the world. This revisioning, I noted, leads to a radical shift in the understanding of the long-standing project of development regarding the relation between the haves and the have-nots. It moves away from its old grounding in economic theory, reflecting the perspective of outside, expert observers, and toward a new grounding in the grass roots, expressing the dreams and visions of ordinary readers themselves. The goal here is not at all the abandonment of theory, but rather a synthesis between theory and people, one in which theory emerges from the perspective of and for the sake of the have-nots. The result, I observed, constitutes a decided expansion of the praxis of liberation as well.

In closing, I can only reiterate what I expressed at the beginning: I find the project of intercultural Bible reading to be a most faithful witness to and tradent of the values and ideals of Dom Hélder. At the same time, I should like to offer a respectful and hopeful challenge. Can the project move on to a sustained, detailed analysis of society and culture today in the world—a reconceptualization and rearticulation of the contextual dimension of liberation? I hope, and urge, that it does. Not only is such a step, properly informed, much needed, given the critical times before us, but also the project as it stands, given its trajectory and achievements, is well poised for such a move and would have much to contribute. Such a step I see as a further, and decidedly significant, step in its goal of transformation for liberation.

## References

Anderson, Janice Capel, and Jeffrey L. Staley, eds. 1997. *Taking It Personally. Semeia* 72. Atlanta: Society of Biblical Literature.

Bleich, David. 1975. *Readings and Feelings: An Introduction to Subjective Criticism.* Urbana, IL: National Council of Teachers.

———. 1978. *Subjective Criticism.* Baltimore: John Hopkins University Press.

Grenholm, Cristina, and Daniel Patte. 2000. *Reading Israel in Romans: Legitimacy and Plausibility of Divergent Interpretations.* Romans through History and Culture 1. Bloomsbury: T&T Clark.

Hoedemaker, Lambert. 2000. *Met anderen tot Christus: Zending in een postmissionair tijdpark.* Zoetermeer: Boekencentrum.

Hofstede, Geert. 1995. *Allemaal Andersdekenden: Omgann met cultuursverschillen.* Amsterdam: Uitgeverij Contact.

Hofstede, Geert, Gert Jan Hofstede, and Michael Minkov. 2010. *Cultures and Organizations: Software of the Mind.* 3rd ed. New York: McGraw-Hill.

Keener, Craig, and M. Daniel Carroll R., eds. 2013. *Global Voices: Reading the Bible in the Majority World.* Peabody, MA: Hendrickson.

Kitzberger, Ingrid Rosa. 1999. *The Personal Voice in Biblical Interpretation.* London: Routledge.

———, ed. 2002. *Autobiographical Biblical Criticism: Between Text and Self.* Blandford Forum. Dorset, UK: Deo.

Levinas, Emmanuel. 1961. *Totalité et infini: Essai sur l'exteriorité.* The Hague: Nijhoff.

Patte, Daniel M., ed. 2004. *The Global Bible Commentary.* Nashville: Abingdon.

Procee, Hendrik. 1991. *Over de Grenzen van Culturen: Voorbij Universalisme en relativisme.* Amsterdam: Contact Uitgeverij.

Schreiter, Robert J. 1997. *The New Catholicity: Theology between the Global and the Local.* Maryknoll, NY: Orbis.

Segovia, Fernando, and Mary Ann Tolbert, eds. 1995a. *Social Location and Biblical Interpretation in the United States.* Vol. 1 of *Reading from This Place.* Minneapolis: Fortress.

———, eds. 1995b. *Social Location and Biblical Interpretation in Global Perspective.* Vol. 2 of *Reading from This Place.* Minneapolis: Fortress.

Wit, Hans de. 2004. "Through the Eyes of Another: Objectives and Backgrounds." Pages 3–53 in De Wit et al. 2004.

————. 2012. *Empirical Hermeneutics, Interculturality, and Holy Scripture.* Intercultural Biblical Hermeneutics 1. Elkhart, IN: Institute of Mennonite Studies.

Wit, Hans de, Louis Jonker, Marleen Kool, and Daniel Schipani, eds. 2004. *Through the Eyes of Another: Intercultural Reading of the Bible.* Elkhart, IN: Institute of Mennonite Studies.

## 2

# BIBLE AND TRANSFORMATION:
# THE MANY FACES OF TRANSFORMATION

*Hans de Wit*

> To approach the Other in conversation is to welcome his expression.... It
> is therefore to receive from the Other beyond the capacity of the I, which
> means exactly: to have the idea of infinity.
> —Emmanuel Levinas (1969, 51)

Much has been published on intercultural Bible reading over the past few
years; the method has been applied in the most divergent variants, in the
most diverse contexts involving forty countries—with varying results. A
large quantity of often impressive empirical material has been produced.

The conference in Amsterdam in February 2013, with its central theme:
"Bible and Transformation: The Promise of Intercultural Bible Reading,"
was a moment of intensification in which we could make ourselves vulnerable and dare to change a nearly universal assumption into a critical
question: To what extent and under what circumstances can cross-border
Bible reading, involving sometimes a radically different reader, result in
transformation of the self, of the social context, of the other reader, and,
yes, even of the text? Can cross-border reading of Scripture result in reading for justice, in a life-giving, instead of a life-taking, process?

The question touches the core of forms of Bible reading and hermeneutic reflection of those who do not want to regard the ancient text
solely as an archaeological *depositum*, but also and foremost as a letter
addressed to present-day ordinary readers, understanding by the concept "ordinary reader" not so much a flesh-and-blood "naïve" reader, but
rather an (existential) *attitude* toward Scripture. The question concerning the relation between Bible reading and transformation touches on

the practice of millions of people around the world who read, interpret, apply, use, and otherwise engage with the Bible on a daily basis. It is precisely because of this global presence of the Bible and the endless procession of people who interact with it, each in her or his own way, that posing the question about the effect of that interaction is so urgent. It is curious that there is so little empirical reflection on it.

In this essay I explore the space implied in the title of this volume—an exploration that is given more body via the other essays which, as their titles and themes demonstrate, make this volume so special, so exciting, and, I hope, so relevant.

## Outline

What does the relationship between Bible reading and transformation in an intercultural perspective entail? The terrain clearly has many subthemes, a number of which are discussed in the essays in this volume. To prevent us from sinking into a morass, I split the theme of transformation into two parts, first looking at the relationship between the Bible and transformation, discussing examples that suggest an unbroken, direct relation between the two terms. In a second step I will analyze how, at a more abstract and reflective level of theory formation, transformation is seen and defined. Is transformation a concept that can be hermeneutically applied and that can offer enough clarity to act as a criterion for good Bible reading? Or do the definitions of the concept lead us into a labyrinth, so that transformation appears to be just "a hoped-for" effect of Bible reading? To approach this, I will consider how the stories about Bible and transformation are structured. Was enough attention given to what James Bielo (2009b) called the relationship between "textual ideology" (the set of presuppositions held about the Bible) and "textual practices" (the various interpretive procedures of the readers of the Bible) and to the relationship between "textual practices" and the ecclesiastic and "social environment" of Bible readers? Has the outcome been empirically tested?

This theme is further dealt with by reflecting on "the promise of intercultural Bible reading," with all the pretensions of the absence of the question mark. With Vincent Wimbush (2010), I would like to ask, "If we want to read the Bible interculturally, then what is 'the work we want to make Scripture do for us'?"

### "Because Immediately, at the End of This Sentence, a Flow of Certainty Entered My Heart"

Everyday millions of people throughout the world approach the Bible, and do so with confidence, awe, bemusement, and suspicion. They find meaning, comfort, inspiration, council [sic], strength, and conviction. They are surprised and encouraged, puzzled and troubled. All this begs an important question. How? How do people—as conflicted and complex individuals, as inheritors of institutional and cultural resources, as practitioners of distinct expressions of Christianity—interact with the Bible? (Bielo 2009a, 1)

Many diverse metaphors for the experience of reading the Bible have been used in the course of church history: the Bible is a mirror, fundament, "God's lisping," "God's speaking like a nurse" (Calvin quoted by Labberton 1990, 16–17), a guide, a guideline. The metaphors have in common that reading Bible texts is of a performative nature: something happens when you read the Bible. The effect of Bible reading is expressed in a nearly endless series of concepts: conversion, liberation, remorse, reconciliation, seeing the light, insight, introspection, change, healing, salvation, deliverance, hope, inspiration, persistence, and love.

For the most part, the path of that interaction is not pursued: there is no report on how it ended, how long the change lasted or for what reason, or what the person was liberated from. If one were to design a typology of testimonies about that interaction, the stories about an immediate effect, in particular an immediate transformation, would figure prominently. They represent an ideal description of how people imagine the encounter between the Bible text and the reader. We are all acquainted with these stories, they are precious to us and of special interest. They vitalize our profession and raise it above the criticism that we are merely performing an autopsy on dead objects (Ricoeur 1998, xii).

Some of these descriptions from the past and the present provide the aspects that we wish to question. Our random selection of examples begins with Saint Augustine. This should suffice as far as the past is concerned, for it is a model of what could also said about Wesley, Luther, Barth, and many other leading figures in church history.

Past: Saint Augustine

In his *Confessions,* Augustine tells about his lying under the fig tree in his garden in Milan when he was thirty-two. He was in a crisis, weeping bitterly, and did not know how to escape from his past and God's wrath (Augustine 1886, 29). Suddenly he heard a child singing, *Tolle, lege! Tolle lege!* ("Pick up and read"). Is this a children's game or a command from God to pick up the Bible? He walked toward the book, opened it to a random page, and found the text of Rom 13:13–14 about stopping with binges and drinking sprees. The text hit him like a bolt of lightning. Augustine tells about the transformation as follows: "No further would I read, nor did I need; for instantly, as the sentence ended—by a light, as it were, of security infused into my heart,—all the gloom of doubt vanished away" (127–28). With his friend Alypius, Augustine went to his mother and told her about this immediate and irreversible transformation, after which she burst forth joyously.

At possibly the most crucial moment of his life, the learned church father did not apply exegesis but used the method that has been used frequently in circles of pietistic, evangelical, and Pentecostal communities to this day—the thumb-verse method: one asks a question, struggles with a problem, has to preach; one places one's thumb on an arbitrary place in the Bible and, voilà, there is the answer. Experts say it always works!

Present

*"Treasures out of Darkness"*

Jumping to the present, a similar example comes from the North American church Victory Outreach International, which runs a relief center for drug addicts in Amsterdam (Osman 2011). The drug addicts are called "treasures out of darkness," taken from a text of Deutero-Isaiah (45:2–3) in which Cyrus, the anointed, is told: "I will give you the treasures of darkness and hidden riches of secret places."

This text is a tool in the Amsterdam Victory Outreach International Home for drug addicts. It is the text that the founder of the church, Pastor Sonny, a former drug addict himself, "received" as an instrument for his work with drug addicts. "Now after forty-one years this Scripture still speaks to the hearts of people of Victory Outreach and the lives of many are being transformed," one staff member observes. When one of the former drug addicts was asked about the meaning of this Bible text in his life, he said,

> It is a promise given to one person. It started to live in me too. *I was born out of this promise. I run with this Scripture and I have made it my own and I now live it* [italics mine].

Other similar testimonies:

> I have always thought that I would die as a junkie. That isn't true. God has changed my mind and made me a new person. It gives me hope to know that I was not born to live and die as a drug addict, but I am a "treasure" in this the world.

> I found a life of dignity in that I now believe that I was not born to live a life of drug addiction, but I am a treasure in the eyes of God.

> My application and understanding of these scriptures has made me become involved in reaching out to those who were like me.

The effect of the Bible text is described as immediate, radical, and final. The Bible text acts as a speech act (Searle 1969): it causes the hearer to take a particular action. Just as in the case of Augustine, transformation is fundamental—a turning point, a taking leave, a restoration of life, a regaining of dignity.

*Pentecostals*

Ample analogous examples can be found in circles of Pentecostal and evangelical churches, such as the healing gatherings where people are delivered from their illness or problem by means of a Bible text and the so-called *toque mágico* ("the magic touch") or such as the relation between Bible use and transformation focused on prosperity in circles of neo-Pentecostal churches.[1] In one of the major Pentecostal churches in

---

1. Ocaña F. (2002, 40–41) gives an example of a minister of the *Iglesia Pentecostal Dios es Amor*, Lima, Peru: "Hoy usted está sembrando lo que después va a cosechar y no pasará siete días para la respuesta del Señor. Dios, creador del cielo y de la tierra, confirma esta revelación de prosperidad; haz que el hermano conozca sólo prosperidad; llega a tu casa hermano, marca tu calendario; primero de setiembre empieza tu

Ghana, active participation in political life has long been taboo, but after reading Nehemiah, Daniel, Rom 12, and Deut 28:13, Reverend Odoom was convinced that he had to enter politics. This radically changed his life (Quayesi-Amakye 2013, 218).

*Social Transformation*

For those interested in the social effect of Bible reading, it is a feast to have a look at what has been said on this in Latin America since the 1970s and 1980s. In a case study, Dutch sociologist Geert Banck describes the great commitment of the local churches in Brazil to the transformation of the local context and how much Bible reading contributes to it. Banck affirms the intimate link between the celebration of the Word and reality, which implies "the problem of the relationship between a Christian life-style [*vivência cristã*] and transforming political action" (1997, 296).[2]

Where the so-called *lectura popular* is practiced, the relationship to the biblical text is one of recognition and familiarity: "We are Abraham" (De Wit 1991, 69); "We are the widow in Luke 18 who keeps going to that judge" (De Wit and López 2013, 329–38). The landless farmers who occupied a government building in one of Brazil's states *are* the frogs in the story of the plagues in Egypt. They kept the officials from doing their work for over a week: "All of them hungry negroes, all of them inside the gates and making trouble" (De Wit 1991, 57–58).

Since the 1980s the direct connection between reading, transformation, and praxis has been expressed in many testimonies. The statement in one of the closing documents of the CEBs (Basic Christian Communities, Comunidades Eclesiales de Base) meetings serves as a model:

> We saw the power the Word of God provides us on our journey and in our battle for the transformation of society. The Word of God, read from the reality of the people and celebrated in community, is the food that

---

prosperidad." ("Today you are sowing what you are going to reap afterward, and in less than seven days the response from the Lord will come. God, the creator of heaven and earth, confirms this revelation of prosperity; cause this brother to know only prosperity; it will arrive at your house, brother, put a mark on your calendar; on the first of September your prosperity will begin.")

2. For multiple examples of how in the Latin American Bible movement Bible reading and (new) social praxis are connected, see De Wit 1991, 42–54.

keeps us going for the service of love and for our faithful involvement in
the journey of the people. (De Wit 1991, 45)

The relationship between the Bible, transformation, and the subsequent
action or praxis is intimate here. It often involves protests and strikes to
change the social situations, but it can also involve more personal matters
like coping with trauma, reintegration into society, changing one's self-
image. Looking back on twenty years of Bible movement in Latin America,
Carlos Mesters compiles an exhaustive list of connections between Bible
and praxis (1988, 2–3; see De Wit 1991, 9–10). Numerous examples of the
desired and assumed relationship between reading the Bible and (social)
transformation can be found in Africa, Asia, and elsewhere as well.

*Transformation in Hermeneutics*

This longing for there to be a close bond between Bible reading and transformation is evident not only in the examples provided, but also in the
ultimate goal and expected results of Bible reading found in modern
hermeneutics and in certain handbooks for Bible reading methods. Transformation is regarded as the culmination of the process of understanding.[3]
The emphasis on the importance of transformation and action can also be
found in the method "see, judge, act" (*ver, juzgar, actuar*), so popular in
Latin America. A similar emphasis on transformation as an effect of Bible
reading is encountered in the handbook for contextual Bible reading by
the Contextual Bible Study Development Group, published by the Scottish
Bible Society. There we read: "Our approach encourages TRANSFORMA-
TION of the individuals and group in their particular social and religious
contexts.… [The] belief that, as the community of believers, all Christians
are called to express their faith in action that seeks to transform the world"
(Contextual Bible Study Group 2004, 12). At the same time transformation is problematized in the handbook under the header "Moving For-
wards and the Struggle for Transformation":

> There is no doubt that the experience of this project has changed the
> faith-in-action of a number of the trainees. At a different level however,

---

3. On appropriation and naiveté, see Ricoeur 1976, 89–95; LaCocque and Ricoeur
1998, xi–xiii; on the praxis that results in knowledge, see José Severino Croatto 1994,
52–56, 80–84, 109–11, 123–25; De Wit 1991, 175–80.

the CBS Development Group has become more conscious of how much a struggle it is to enable transformation within individuals and communities through this approach. While most people who take part clearly enjoy Conversations-CBS sessions, it would be hard to say where exactly what we have done has had any clear or measurable effect on a church or community. (Contextual Bible Study Group 2004, 43)

The method of the CEBI (Centro de Estudos Bíblicos, Brazil) is called "the Bible transforms life," and the biblical model for this is the Emmaus story (Luke 24) with a strong emphasis on "the encounter (also with the Scripture) that opens the eyes" (Mesters and Orofino n.d., 7).

## Conclusion

The selected examples bring two things to light. First, these stories of the impact of Bible reading on people cannot be ignored, for something indeed often happens when people read the Bible! Second, the trajectory of this assumed or hoped for transformation is rarely, if ever, followed; what it consists of is never clarified; and how this transformation is brought about is not explained. In other words, we rarely receive a clear answer as to what elements in the interaction between Bible texts and readers changes this interaction into a script for transformative action (see Salomon and Niño-Murcia 2011, 153).

## Transformed for What?

## Definitions

Going a step beyond what the stories have to offer, we now look at definitions of transformation on a more abstract and reflective level. As in the case of other disciplines, such as mathematics, genetics, literary theory, sociology, and dramaturgy, transformation is defined in theology as a profound, durable process of change. Transformation is something fundamental, but since people are complex, the same variety in definition appears as in the stories. In religious psychology, it concerns acquiring new coping styles that enable one to overcome situations that could be threatening to one's self image and value system. Transformation implies that:

A person comes up with a strategy in order to cope with situations that can be threatening to his self-image and value-system. According to Pargament, psychological objectives of coping are, "Self-esteem, a sense of power and control in life, a sense of meaning in life, personal growth, a sense of hope in life, feelings of intimacy and belonging with other people, a release of feelings, a sense of personal identity, restraints on undesirable impulses and feelings, and feelings of comfort in life." (Alma 1998, 201)

In emancipation hermeneutics transformation often concerns social structures. Andrew Rogers (2009, 29) writes, "The goal for Christians and their communities, especially when encountering Scripture, is to be transformed into the likeness of Christ." In neo-Pentecostal circles where the prosperity gospel is proclaimed, transformation is defined as raising the social and financial status of the faithful. Churches where faith healing is practiced consider healing to be the most important effect of Bible reading, while in hermeneutics, transformation has to do with a new understanding of texts. Not to be forgotten is the fact that there is also such a thing as fundamentalist transformation, which is transformation resulting in hatred of differences.

## Conclusions

We are still far removed from a sound ethnography of the relationship between textual ideology, textual practices, and transformation. Transformation refers to a multitude of changes and effects that are not always complementary. Transformation as an effect of Bible reading in the sense of "literacy enablement" is something other than the transformation of the "treasures out of darkness":

> This concept relates to those activities, qualities and devices which, in a particular socio-religious field, are seen as necessary for attempting to bridge between the divine-scriptural sphere and the worldly realm. These literacy procedures, qualities and devices are mostly understood as being secondary to the actual beholding or interpretation of the Bible. Yet, as I suggest, each "enablement" is essential and highly influential for scriptural readings and processes of religious authorization. The concept of "literacy enablement" is therefore useful in comparing the literacy practices of different religious communities. (Kirsch 2011, 145)

Social transformation can happen at the expense of attention to new coping styles.

In short, transformation turns out to be a container concept, defined according to the religious orientation, the hermeneutic model, and the expectations of the effect of what is considered to be good Bible reading. The definition of transformation follows the reading process.

## Lessons

### No Empirical Research on Transformation

Along with Brian Malley (2009, 195), I conclude "that many claims about scripture are not really empirical claims at all, despite appeals to historical evidence." Rogers (2009, 17) sighed, "Given the huge literature on academic hermeneutics, and in the light of the ... postmodern turn towards context and the local, it is surprising how little empirical research has been done, as yet, on the hermeneutics of ordinary Christians." Elsewhere I have called that the "empirical fallacy" (De Wit 2008, 21–22; 2010, 145–46): "This alludes to the fact that transformative or transforming reading is often more speculation, more of a *hoped for* effect than based on an empirical foundation." I hope that the empirical setting of this volume can contribute to filling in this void.

### As If the World Were Not on Fire

Empirical research done on the relationship between (ordinary) readers and the Bible (see Rogers 2009, 17–37) chiefly looks at existing reading practices: one analyzes attitudes toward the Bible, looks at what hermeneutic and church traditions play a role in what type of Bible reading, and analyzes the coherence between character typologies and reading processes (see Village 2007). This analysis is primarily comparative and descriptive, rarely normative, though Rogers does map the transformative potential of religious communities. This potential can be found, according to Rogers, where a "hermeneutical plasticity that encouraged encounter with difference," is involved (2009, 264, section C). One analyzes as if the world were not on fire, as if asymmetry were nonexistent. Little attention is focused on how the damage caused by Bible reading can be contained: the Bible is, after all, also a dangerous book! In my opinion the emancipation hermeneutics and the contribution from cultural studies, feministic hermeneutics, and postcolonial criticism are true exceptions here.

The Message from Other Disciplines

Empirical research of Bible reading practices also takes place outside theology and biblical science. In the *Anthropology of Christianity*, for example,
a new research area is involved indicated by the term *biblicism* (see Village 2007). Biblicism is an analytical framework to facilitate comparative
research on how Christians interact with their sacred texts. Biblicism is
intended to investigate the dynamic relationship between how Christians
conceptualize their Scriptures and what they do with them through various forms of individual and corporate practice (Bielo 2009a, 2). Anthro-
pologists and sociologists analyze biblical ideologies, interpretive styles in
biblical hermeneutics, biblical rhetoric, and the role and effect of the Bible
as an artifact. Biblical ideologies refer to "the presuppositions that Christians nurture about the nature, organization, content and purpose of the
Bible as a text." *Interpretive styles* refer to the types of approach to the text
advanced in which hermeneutic model, why, and with what result; *biblical rhetorics* refers to the analysis of the process of appropriation and use
(Bielo 2009a, 5–7).

    Biblical scholars and exegetes can learn a great deal from such
research. If one takes note of the results, one can only agree with Malley
(2009, 195) that "theological accounts enormously underdetermine the
ways in which people actually use and experience the Bible; so an anthropological account is needed, regardless of one's theological commitments."
Biblicism research points out how extraordinarily intimate and universal the relation is between textual ideology and textual practices, between
prevalent reading and church traditions, and between social factors and
reading practices and how complicated it is to bring about any radical
change, as Bielo (2009b, 174) demonstrates among, for example, American evangelicals. Such research puts pressure on the optimism theologians
have concerning the space for transformative reading. It shows that the
majority of Bible readers read for success, for power, for affirmation—not
for transformation.

    Biblicism research results in recognizing the necessity of building
bridges also between disciplines. Anthropology has a tendency to underes-
timate the textual aspect of the interpretation process (the encounter with
the text) and reduces the interaction between text and reader to the effect
of social factors ("the social life of Scripture"). It pays little attention to the
power of the Spirit—and, based on its epistemological statute, it cannot do
otherwise. "Thus, *contra Malley*, transformation of congregational horizons

was actual and potential through hermeneutical traditions that aided scriptural encounter" (Rogers 2009, 268; italics mine).

On the other hand, exegetes have all too little attention for the power of extratextual factors such as reading tradition, inequality, might, and empire. Exegetes like to assume that *el papelito manda* ("the little paper commands"), as they say in Peru, but that is, at the very least, naïve (cf. Salomon and Niño-Murcia 2001, 153–57).

The analysis of empirical data will have to reflect the advantage of this interdisciplinary character. Evidence of Bible reading as a seizure of power and confirmation of the existing order, and therefore a source of sorrow and trauma for others, will have to be exposed. Evidence of cultural definitions that can thereby frustrate reading processes and interaction must be pointed out, but also the evidence of the power of the text and the Spirit leading to coping with trauma and to healing. In practice, this will mean a combination of discourse analysis ("a method for disclosing the relation between making meaning and power") and a more narrative approach that also does justice to what are sometimes called prenarrative stories of traumatic experiences (for a combination of these methods, see Grung 2010, 112–16).

If the purpose of Bible reading is to renew a religious ethical tradition aiming for reconciled plurality, for rights, justice, and peace, Bible reading should certainly also be able to contribute to an increasing sensitivity to the unending obligations and responsibilities of persons to and for one another. The ethical assignment for the analysis of our empirical material is then to clarify where the obstacles to a shared agency for justice lie.

People Read in Solitude

Many types of Bible reading apparently focus on totality. While Scripture itself in content and origin suggests an attitude focused on welcoming the other, and thus is oriented toward what Levinas called infinity, in practice it turns out that Bible reading is primarily a totalitarian activity, a seizure of power, a reading in solitude and isolation inside a rigid interpretive system and within a closed dominant reading and church tradition. With Levinas one could say:

> Orientation to the other in interpretation processes implies welcoming what every exegete in fact experiences—namely, that texts are polysemic, polyphonic, and diverse. Totality's opposition to infinity represents

> exclusion, or not welcoming the other. The other is the enemy. Totality is not only destructive and leads to war—there are only enemies on the battlefield.... Totality is not prepared to take texts' reserve of meaning into consideration; rather, it dehumanizes by erasing the particulars and reducing them to its own objective and ultimate meaning, regardless of the reality of the variety of possible meanings. The varied nature of the meaning of texts is continually sacrificed, always through an appeal to the objective meaning. (De Wit 2012, 23; cf. Levinas 1961, 8)

However, the content of Scripture itself demands an attitude open to encounter and confrontation. "Infinity [the possibility to go beyond oneself and beyond one's own limited interpretation—my definition] is produced in the relationship of the same *with the other*.... Infinity does not pre-exist" (Levinas 1969, 26; emphasis added). The truth of the text in all its dimensions is only discovered when no single voice is omitted.

> What a text can say depends on the multiplicity of readers and readings. No reader can be missed. The truth of the text, the revelation of its mystery, lies therefore precisely in the contributions of a multiplicity of people: the uniqueness of each act of listening carries the secret of the text; the voice of Revelation, in precisely the inflection lent by each person's ear, is necessary for the truth of the Whole.... The multiplicity of people, each one of them indispensable, is necessary to produce all the dimensions of meaning; the multiplicity of meanings is due to the multiplicity of people. (Levinas 1989, 159)

Precisely because in the era of globalization this encounter with the other is more possible than ever, it is so bewildering to see how little this encounter with the totally different reader is organized, and, yes, how much that confrontation is avoided. The secret of the text actually remains hidden when the Bible of the Other is missing.

No Hermeneutic Impotence, but Tremendous Challenges

It is my intention not to bog us down by emphasizing our hermeneutic impotence, but to prepare ourselves for disappointments and to restrain exuberant optimism. I problematize the concept of transformation in order to arm us against speaking too naively about the connection between Bible reading and change and to make us sensitive to instances of small-scale transformation—the simple gestures of love, of compassion, and of vulnerability. Since people are complex and Bible texts are polyphonic, transformation must have many faces. We need to accept not only that transformation is a complicated concept, but also that transformation cannot be programmed. In her dissertation on the method of the *lectura popular* of CEBI in Brazil, which is so focused on (social) transformation, Isabel Aparecida Felix comes to the conclusion:

> Despite being defined as an approach to a liberating biblical interpretation [the CEBI method] shows some gaps in relation to this goal.... We perceive ... the absence of analytical tools which could facilitate the transformation of the concrete socio-religious realities, the analysis of the experiences of the subjects of interpretation, and the reflection on criteria to define the place of revelation and authority. (2010, 4)

The wish to achieve a certain type of transformation as an effect of Bible reading implies imposing restraints on the interpretation process and on the many dimensions of the text, causing the latter to become utilitarian. In learning processes where the other is involved as an authentic dialogue partner and the outcome is uncertain, we advocate that such restraints are impermissible.

The assignment is thus profoundly ethical and extraordinarily difficult. On one hand, we strive for openness to and inclusion of that which is "strange" (not one voice can be omitted!). On the other, we do not want to ignore "the strange" but propose and practice a method that makes that which is strange interact with other interpretive styles. This method is intended as a catalyst for a new hermeneutic ethos, for a way of reading by which "readers are formed and transformed ... so as to be open to new experiences, new relationships and new forms of cultural existence" (see Stone 1998, 150, paraphrasing Foucault).

Over the past few decades much has been written on the importance of otherness in interpretation processes, as well as much on ethics and interpretation. Years ago Daniel Patte wrote:

> Concerns for oppressive (anti-Semitic, patriarchal and sexist, racist, classist, as well as economically and socially unjust) pragmatic/scriptural readings, as well as wishes for pragmatic/scriptural readings which would instead promote justice and other expressions of goodness by contributing to the transformation of problematic situations have always been at least the implicit starting point for any critical biblical study.... Why not make it systematically the explicit starting point? (1998, 280)

We have taken up these challenges: to honor otherness and design a method that will enable pragmatic/scriptural readings, "promote justice and other expressions of goodness by contributing to the transformation of problematic situations," and adhere to what Patte, entirely in keeping with Gadamer, Ricoeur, and Levinas, wrote:

> Finally, the sacredness, holiness of the Bible as Scriptures is most definitely affirmed *by those readings which reflect an experience of the Bible which totally transcend our conventional views*, because the Bible is for readers "a participatory dreamwork" in which a vision of new relationships is possible and a new self is formed. (Patte 1998, 280, emphasis added)

The most innovative aspect of this project is the combination of the pragmatic and the scriptural. We want to cultivate our reflections where more than 95 percent of the Bible readers are, where the direct and unrelenting effect of Bible reading is manifested more than in any commentary whatsoever—among ordinary readers who read from a proud and hardened, or simply a wounded, heart.

Involvement in this project over the past few years often reminded me of what Rabbi Ashi once said, "Those who love studying the *Thora* amongst many people shall reap the harvest" (Levinas 1994, 67). Our experience thus far affords a perspective of a tremendous responsibility and challenge, rather than of hermeneutic impotence. This brings me to the second part of my essay: a cross-border Bible reading in which one does not omit the other is an ethical imperative and assignment, but is it a promise as well?

### The Work We Want to Make Scriptures Do for Us

Vincent Wimbush's question (2010)—"What is the work we want to make Scriptures do for us?"—can be given the following answer from our intercultural Bible reading project: we want to promote the intercultural encounter with Scripture in such a manner that it becomes a script for life-giving and life-transforming reading.

### The Stubborn Method

The road chosen is not an easy one. Like all intercultural encounters, the process is complicated and lengthy. A great deal of patience, sensitivity, and vulnerability is demanded. Readers mainly interested in a pleasant experience soon turn away. Since change involves a process of loss and mourning, not everyone is up to it. To some wounded and despairing groups, not communicating with others about what words of consolation they found in the Bible is a survival strategy.

Analysis of the empirical material involves questions concerning the method of encoding the material, the interpretive style to be applied to these texts about Bible texts, and the envisioned result (see De Wit 2004, 395–436). It is clear that on this point we are at the beginning of a new road. I expect to learn a great deal from those who examine their empirical material for evidence of transformation.

Ordinary Readers

When entering those places where the effect of Bible texts manifests itself, one needs to pay attention to current ordinary readers. That means that the Bible of the *Fracasados* in the slums of Buenos Aires has a place in the encounter process. "Bible drinkers," they call themselves: they put shreds of Ps 23 in their tea to protect them from the omnipresent powers of the dead (Althaus-Reid 2003). Similarly, there will be a place for the Bible of the Haitian refugees, the "treasures out of darkness," the raped Dalit women in India, and the HIV victims around the world.

Intercultural

The label *intercultural* is only one among other possibilities. It also could have been called diatopic (Pannikar), intercontextual, or transcontextual. The core of the *inter* is that we explicitly want to make alterity fruitful in the understanding process and to heed the call of "reading with" twice. Not only do professional readers have to read much more with ordinary readers, but ordinary readers need to do so among themselves as well. Real dialogue is equipped to welcome otherness: "Dialogue … exists only where there is a real respect for the otherness of the other. Such respect, born of awareness, is intrinsic to an historical understanding of human existence" (Gadamer 1989, 306). It is the only way that the Bible of the *Fracasados* or the Dalit women will be heard by entirely different Bible readers, Bible readers who will only in that way be able to leave the comfort zone of their established reading traditions. "It is not the insufficiency of the I that prevents totalization, but the Infinity of the Other" (Levinas 1969, 80).

We use the concept of culture, because it represents context and the awareness that what people do with their Scriptures is deeply and directly informed by their circumstances and cultures and also that what they do with their Scriptures exerts a formative impact on those circumstances. We want to listen to what happens when the poor and the rich, the healthy and the ill, the victims and the perpetrator, and the colonizer and the colonized read together. We want to see whether the Bible texts that very frequently become places of conflict can also become places of encounter and reconciliation. In practice this means that "two different epistemological languages, two different modes of affirmative reading," each with a number of its own "kernelistic impulses," are brought together in discussion with one another (see Rogers 2009, 116; see also 134).

## Normative

In all of this, we do not want to limit ourselves to descriptive work, standing along the sidelines, keeping our hands clean. We want to test the effect of a method that is normative, because it is based on ideas about what good Bible reading is. In our opinion, good Bible reading finds its point of orientation in ethics. "The great miracle of the Bible," writes Levinas, "[lies] in the confluence of different literatures toward the same essential content ... the ethical" (Levinas, cited in Cohen 2001, 263). We want to arrive at shared knowledge, shared ownership, and shared agency by means of dialogue, confrontation, and encounter. We want to arrive at a diapraxis, in which the Bible text becomes intertext and has more than one owner (Grung 2010, 26, citing Rasmussen 1997, 110). In the essays in this volume, I expect to find out whether, and under what conditions, this was successful, or whether a healthy dose of pessimism would be appropriate after all.

## Paradigm Shift?

Elisabeth Schüssler Fiorenza has defined a new paradigm for biblical scholarship with which I feel comfortable:

> Thus, this third hermeneutical-postmodern paradigm of biblical studies also cannot address the increasing insecurities of globalized inequality nor accept the constraints that the ethical imperative of emancipatory movements places on the relativizing proliferation of meaning. There-

fore, a fourth rhetorical-political paradigm needs to be acknowledged, one that inaugurates not just a hermeneutic-scientific but an ethical-political turn. (Schüssler Fiorenza 2010, 391)

It is a paradigm capable of meeting the challenges of globalization, and implies not only a hermeneutic-scientific change, but above all an ethical-political one:

Such a critical rhetorical understanding of interpretation investigates and reconstructs the discursive arguments of a text, its socio-religious location, and its diverse interpretations in order to underscore the text's possible oppressive as well as liberative performative actions, values, and possibilities in ever-changing historical-cultural situations. This approach understands the Bible and biblical interpretation as *a site of struggle over authority, values, and meaning.* (Schüssler Fiorenza 2010, 392)

Varying on this paradigm description by Schüssler Fiorenza, I can summarize the task of intercultural hermeneutics as follows: "To examine the conditions for the possibility of constructing, analyzing, and using (intercultural) methods of Bible reading that do *not* reinforce the structural violence of the status quo in society, church and academy."

The assignment that Schüssler Fiorenza gives to biblical scholars strongly resembles Gramsci's Organic Intellectual concept, and is not a minor one. The biblical scholar shall regard himself as "a public, transformative, connected, or integrated intellectual who is able to communicate with a variegated public with the goal of personal, social, and religious transformation for justice and well-being for all" (Schüssler Fiorenza 2010, 392–93).

Pretension or Promise?

These are inspiring words on the theoretical level, but how does that work at the empirical level? Is intercultural Bible reading a pretension or a promise? Because of the material gathered and researched, the impressive examples of the effect of otherness, the inclusion of the discipline of intercultural hermeneutics in many curricula, I am convinced it is a promise and not a pretense. That much remains to be done to transform the Bible texts into places of encounter, that we have to be modest, and that the method is difficult are all too clear. But what is also clear is that we are acquiring new and unexpected knowledge about Bible texts and that revelation and transformation have new opportunities via the intercultural encounter. We cannot disregard what a victim of the rampant impunity from one of the conflict zones in Colombia said after reading with a partner group about the widow who kept going to the judge who would not give her justice (Luke 18):

> I hope that this experience is repeated, that it is distributed. It was a divine experience; I cannot find the words to express what it meant in my life. (De Wit and López 2013, 436)[4]

Or what the woman from El Salvador, who participated in the same project, told her Colombian partners:

> The way you read that text is a tremendous lesson in life to me, a lesson in persistence, faith, power, solidarity. I admire you! (De Wit and López 2013, 417)[5]

Such experiences should be heard and examined with awe and deep respect, and that is precisely the project we have committed ourselves to.

## References

Alma, H. A. 1998. *Identiteit door verbondenheid: Een godsdienstpsychologisch onderzoek naar identificatie en christelijk geloof.* Kampen: Kok.

Althaus-Reid, Marcella. 2003. "The Bible of the Frascasados." Pages 109–26 in *One Gospel—Many Cultures: Case Studies and Reflections on Cross-Cultural Theology.* Edited by Mercy Amba Oduyoye and Hendrik M. Vroom. Amsterdam: World Alliance of Reformed Churches.

Augustine, Aurelius. 1886. *The Confessions of St. Augustine, Bishop of Hippo.* Translated by J. G. Pilkington. In vol. 1 of *A Select Library of the Nicene and Post-Nicene Fathers of the Christian Church, Series 1.* Edited by Philip Schaff. Buffalo: Christian Literature.

Banck, Geert. 1997. "Brazilian Christian Base Communities: Organizing Rituals for Democracy." Pages 291–301 in *The Diversity of Devel-*

---

4. *¡Ojalá que se repita la experiencia, que se divulgue. Fue una experiencia divina. No hallo palabra para decir lo que ha significado en mi vida!*

5. *Para mí es una gran lección de vida, de tenacidad, fe, fortaleza, solidaridad, ¡¡¡son admirables!!!*

*opment: Essays in Honour of Jan Kleinpenning*. Edited by Ton van Naerssen, Marcel Rutten, and Annelies Zoomers. Assen: Van Gorcum.

Bielo, James S. 2009a. "Introduction: Encountering Biblicism." Pages 1–9 in *The Social Life of Scriptures: Cross-Cultural Perspectives on Biblicism*. Edited by James S. Bielo. New Brunswick, NJ: Rutgers University Press.

———. 2009b. "Textual Ideology, Textual Practice: Evangelical Bible Reading in Group Study." Pages 157–75 in *The Social Life of Scriptures: Cross-Cultural Perspectives on Biblicism*. Edited by James S. Bielo. New Brunswick, NJ: Rutgers University Press.

Cohen, Richard A. 2001. *Ethics, Exegesis and Philosophy: Interpretation after Levinas*. Cambridge: Cambridge University Press.

Contextual Bible Study Group. 2004. *Conversations*. Edinburgh: Scottish Bible Society.

Croatto, José Severino. 1994. *Hermenéutica Bíblica: Para una teoria de la lectura como producción de sentido*. Buenos Aires: Lumen.

Felix, Isabel Aparecida. 2010. "Anseio por danzar diferente: Leitura popular da bíblia na ótica da hermenéutica feminista crítica de libertacao." São Bernardo do Campo. PhD diss., Universidade Metodista de São Paulo.

Gadamer, Hans-Georg. 1989. *Warheit und Methode*. Tübingen: Mohr Siebeck.

Grung, Anne Hege. 2010. "Gender Justice in Muslim-Christian Readings." PhD diss., University of Oslo.

Kirsch, Thomas G. 2011. *Spirits and Letters: Reading, Writing and Charisma in African Christianity*. New York: Berghahn.

Labberton, Mark. 1990. "Ordinary Bible Reading: The Reformed Tradition and Reader-Oriented Criticism." PhD diss., University of Cambridge.

LaCocque, André, and Paul Ricoeur. 1998. "Preface." Pages ix–xix in *Thinking Biblically: Exegetical and Hermeneutical Studies*. Chicago: University of Chicago Press.

Levinas, Emmanuel. 1961. *Totalité et infini: Essai sur l'extériorité*. The Hague: Nijhoff.

———. 1969. *Totality and Infinity: An Essay on Exteriority*. Translated by Alphonso Lingis. Pittsburgh: Duquesne University Press.

———. 1989. "Revelation in the Jewish Tradition." Pages 190–210 in *The Levinas Reader*. Edited by Sean Hand. Oxford: Blackwell.

———. 1994. *Beyond the Verse: Talmudic Readings and Lectures*. Bloomington: Indiana University Press.

Malley, Brian. 2009. "Understanding the Bible's Influence." Pages 194–204 in *The Social Life of Scriptures: Cross-Cultural Perspectives on Biblicism.* Edited by James S. Bielo. New Brunswick, NJ: Rutgers University Press.

Mesters, Carlos. 1988. "Balanço de 20 Anos." Pages 2–10 in *Suplemento do Boletím 'Por Trás Da Palavra'* 7. Belo Horizonte: Centro de Estudos Bíblicos.

Mesters, Carlos, and Francisco Orofino. n.d. De Bijbel verandert het leven. Dutch translation of Portugese original. Belo Horizonte, Brazil: Centro de Estudos Bíblicos.

Ocaña F., Martín. 2002. *Los Banqueros de Dios: Una aproximación evangélica a la Teología de la Prosperidad.* Lima: Puma.

Osman, Raffic. 2011. "Treasures out of Darkness." MA thesis, Vrije Universiteit Amsterdam.

Patte, Daniel. 1998. "When Ethical Questions Transform Critical Biblical Studies." *Semeia* 77:271–83.

Quayesi-Amakye, Joseph. 2013. *Christology and Evil in Ghana: Towards a Pentecostal Public Theology.* Amsterdam: Rodopi.

Rasmussen, Lissi. 1997. *Diapraksis og dialog mellem kristne og muslimer: I lyset af den afrikanske erfaring.* Aarhus: Aarhus Universitetsforlag.

Ricoeur, Paul. 1976. *Interpretation Theory: Discourse and the Surplus of Meaning.* Fort Worth: Texas Christian University Press.

Rogers, Andrew. 2009. "Ordinary Biblical Hermeneutics and the Transformation of Congregational Horizons within English Evangelicalism: A Theological-Ethnographic Study." PhD diss., King's College, London.

Salomon, Frank, and Mercedes Niño-Murcia. 2011. *The Lettered Mountain: A Peruvian Village's Way with Writing.* Durham, NC: Duke University Press.

Schüssler Fiorenza, Elisabeth. 2010. "Rethinking the Educational Practices of Biblical Doctoral Studies." Pages 373–93 in Schüssler Fiorenza and Richards 2010.

Schüssler Fiorenza, Elisabeth, and Kent Harold Richards, eds. 2010. *Transforming Graduate Biblical Education: Ethos and Discipline.* Atlanta: Society of Biblical Literature.

Searle, John. 1969. *Speech Acts: An Essay in the Philosophy of Language.* New York: Cambridge University Press.

Stone, Ken. 1998. "Biblical Interpretation as a Technology of the Self: Gay Men and the Ethics of Reading." Pages 139–55 in *Bible and Ethics of*

*Reading*. Edited by Dana Nolan Fewell and Gary A. Philips. Semeia 77. Atlanta: Society of Biblical Literature.

Village, Andrew. 2007. *The Bible and Lay People: An Empirical Approach to Ordinary Hermeneutics*. Burlington, VT: Ashgate.

Wimbush, Vincent L. 2010. "The Work We Make Scriptures Do for Us: An Argument for Signifying (on) Scriptures as Intellectual Project." Pages 355–66 in Schüssler Fiorenza and Richards 2010.

Wit, Hans de. 1991. *Leerlingen van de Armen*. Amsterdam: Vrije Universiteit.

———. 2004. "Codes and Coding." Pages 395–436 in *Through The Eyes of Another: Intercultural Reading of the Bible*. Edited by Hans de Wit, Louis Jonker, Marleen Kool, and Daniel Schipani. Elkhart, IN: Institute of Mennonite Studies.

———. 2008. "Exegesis and Contextuality: Happy Marriage, Divorce or Living (Apart) Together." Pages 3–30 in *African and European Readers of the Bible in Dialogue*. Edited by Hans de Wit and Gerald West. Leiden: Brill.

———. 2009. "'It Should Be Burnt and Forgotten!' Latin American Liberation Hermeneutics through the Eyes of Another." Pages 39–60 in *The Bible and the Hermeneutics of Liberation*. Edited by Alejandro Botta and Pablo Andiñach. SemeiaSt 59. Atlanta: Society of Biblical Literature.

———. 2010. *Por un solo gesto de Amor: Lectura de la Biblia desde una práctica intercultural*. Buenos Aires: Instituto Universitario ISEDET.

———. 2012. *Empirical Hermeneutics, Interculturality, and Holy Scripture*. Intercultural Biblical Hermeneutics 1. Elkhart, IN: Institute of Mennonite Studies.

Wit, Hans de, Louis Jonker, Marleen Kool, and Daniel Schipani, eds. 2004. *Through The Eyes of Another: Intercultural Reading of the Bible*. Elkhart, IN: Institute of Mennonite Studies.

Wit, Hans de, and Gerald West, eds. 2008. *African and European Readers of the Bible in Dialogue*. Leiden: Brill.

Wit, Hans de, and Edgar López, eds. 2013. *Lectura intercultural de la Biblia en contextos de impunidad en América Latina*. Bogotá: Universidad Javeriana.

## 3
## THE ETHICS OF TRANSFORMATIVE READING:
## THE TEXT, THE OTHER, AND ONESELF

*John Mansford Prior*

### Location in a Cyber World

In a cyber world rapidly globalizing economically and therefore also radically shifting socially, culturally, and politically, one clear reaction has been for some to recast themselves in a mythical past set in stone. Whether withdrawing into isolated enclaves or confronting the outside world violently, signs of cultural and religious fundamentalism can be seen everywhere. For as Paul Tournier (1968) pointed out long ago, however disrupting social change, everybody needs a sense of place, an awareness of belonging to a location, a culture, a community.

Another reaction is simply to go with the flow, to allow oneself to be swept along by the tsunami of change, exerting as little effort as possible and claiming little or no personal responsibility. Consumer society, run by the captains of casino capitalism, is busy trying to format societies such as these.

Then there are Christians who reject such shallow market-driven values, who consciously reroot themselves in the biblical values of the freedom of the children of the God of compassionate justice, communities that are willing, and with God's grace able, to give prophetic witness to the gospel. Gospel communities remain rooted locally in numerous ways despite the rapid uprooting of local cultures, and yet in a market-driven globalizing world they cannot remain isolated and purely local and so are aware of the need to connect and act in global networks. Thus they engage in global countercultural movements from below. Intercultural

Bible reading for transformation is one vital node in these interlocking local-global (glocal) connections effecting prophetic change.[1]

How ethical are such readings of the Bible? This essay follows the three phases of the intercultural process, highlighting the issue of integrity at each stage. Personal and group integrity is crucial in our first reading, the integrity of the text and of the other comes to the fore as we exchange and comment upon our reports with our partner group, and honesty about our core beliefs and the transformative potential of the process becomes clearer as the conversation continues.

Phase One: The Naïve First Reading—The Integrity of Oneself

What are the minimal requirements for the first, naïve reading to be potentially transformative?

Trust

The first condition is for the group to create an atmosphere of trust among its members, where each one is utterly honest, true to whom they are, where they are in their faith struggle, and where each is able to be as open as they feel they can be.

Openness is, by and large, decided by the level of trust. To be open is to be vulnerable: most of us guard against any perceived possibility of being wounded by the insensitivity of others. Some cultures nurture greater openness than others. In some cultures reticence is a major way of preserving privacy and of avoiding feeling threatened. Reticence is present in status societies where the "voiceless" tend to remain quiet in the company of persons of higher status. Also, a community of battered women living in a temporary safe house, a group of long-term prisoners in jail, or a support group of HIV carriers needs time to develop trust among themselves as a Bible group. It surely demands a greater effort to place trust in a partner reading group in another corner of the world.

The greater the openness and honesty to one's own reality, the greater the potential transformative power of intercultural readings of the Bible. True and important as that is, we need also to respect the degree of open-

---

1. The term *glocal*, first coined in World Council of Churches circles, is becoming increasingly serviceable in mission studies. See, for instance, Engelsviken et al. 2010.

ness or reticence of any group member, particularly those in defenseless situations at the margins of society.

## Method

Some groups have members who are long acquainted with the Bible, while others possibly remember only those narratives once heard in school or maybe still heard on occasion from the Sunday pulpit. When convinced that Bible reading is not the monopoly of religious teachers, preachers, or the ordained, "new readers" give a fresh take on the text, reading it spontaneously from where they are—transparently naïve yet frequently disarmingly astute. Quite a few groups are intuitive, some imaginatively identifying with (or failing to identify with) one or more characters present in, or indeed absent from, the text, perhaps tracing their autobiography along the narrative plot. The more theologically academic members of some groups consult Bible dictionaries and biblical commentaries and make their initial reading with assistance from one or more of the classic historical-critical, literary-narrative, social-science, feminist-rhetorical, or reader-response methods, or indeed from a combination of such approaches.

In this first naïve reading, the key ethical principle is personal and group authenticity, rather than reading strategy or theoretical model. There should be no limits placed on the method a particular group or individual members choose to employ, no boundary set upon anyone's imagination, as long as they are being true to themselves. Whether the readings are more literal or allegorical, more moral or eschatological, the interpretations should be sincere, coherent, and authentic for the readers themselves.

For this first naïve reading, honesty and openness are crucial, not the selection of any particular method, let alone the privileging of one over another, nor the questioning of any latent "preunderstanding."

## Presuppositions

Thus there should be no demand for particular readings, such as a liberationist reading or a gender-sensitive take, if that is not yet where readers are. The key "preunderstanding" demanded by transformative intercultural readings of the Bible is the acknowledgment that others have differing takes and others read with different presuppositions, and precisely because their perceptions are different we can, and indeed need to, learn from them. Such readings are "highly rewarding," for "by making explicit the specific context and the concerns from which they read the Bible, scholars show the significance of aspects of the biblical text that readers in other contexts have often taken for granted or overlooked" (Patte 2004, xxi), as indeed scholars also learn from the imaginative readings of "ordinary readers."

I acknowledge that my take is one possibility among many; this is where I am—and the group is—at this moment. I do not possess absolute certainty. I am committed to searching for a greater truth beyond the truth elicited by myself, my group, and my ecclesial tradition. Just as I listen to myself carefully and listen attentively to other members of my group, so I am prepared to listen deeply to the readings of another group or groups.

Following from that, I acknowledge that it is important that I am also ready to allow "the other" to question my (our) reading(s), for I am engaged in a quest for greater clarity, ready to explain and question and learn from people I respect, but with whom I may initially disagree.

Thus I freely acknowledge that no one cultural interpretation is final, that I can and need to learn from people embedded in other cultural contexts, that classical methods, even if they are my way of entering the language of a text, are not the one infallible way to understanding.

While group members living in marginal rural or urban cultures need to put aside any feelings of cultural inferiority and place themselves alongside a partner group who may be at the "metropolitan center," the educational and social elite will need to bracket any arrogant feelings of cultural superiority and be willing to learn from voices not usually heard in the academy let alone in the corridors of power.

While one reading may be more helpful, or indeed be considered more truthful than another, willingness to listen and learn from others who start from a different position demands that we, at least initially, place "the other's" reading alongside ours, acknowledging a vital complementarity between a critical reading of scholars and an intuitive reading of "ordinary" believers. This demands humility and patience from those more academically qualified.

Bible

Clearly, no Christian fundamentalist or literalist will see any point of joining in intercultural reading of the Bible; anybody who accepts the Bible as a collection of primary documents summoning people to faith "from every nation, race, tribe, and language" (Rev 7:9) may well do so. Nonetheless, the greater the character of "sacredness" I place on the text, the narrower and more exclusive the potential range of my interpretation. Likewise, the greater the authority I give to church hierarchs or to overarching, biblically based creedal statements, the less sensitive I find myself when confronted with very different approaches.

We can be open to others when we regard the word of the Bible as our primary witness to the living word of God made flesh in Jesus the Nazarene, in whom is life, life that shines in darkness, a light that darkness could not overpower (see John 1:5). The Bible gives witness to what God has done and is doing through the Word and the Spirit.

Nevertheless, faith commitments and practices vary, not just between partner groups but within groups themselves. For some, their particular ecclesial allegiance, consciously or unconsciously, guides how they treat and read the Bible, while others are more independent of any ecclesial commitment. Whatever the level of faith or denominational engagement, all who take part in intercultural reading surely see a point in reading the Bible as an indispensable witness to the truth of God as revealed in Jesus, the Word, a living word capable of forging history, then and now.

In-Group Conversation

Some groups are embedded in a more or less homogeneous culture, resulting in a common understanding, although even here gender questions and the different social status of members do lead to alternative readings within the group.

Other groups are embedded in more individualistic cultures where the initial reading gives rise to much discussion, even opposing appraisals. The important point here is to record faithfully each and every voice, every nuanced exchange, whether harmonious or dissonant. However, we need also to acknowledge that the very fact that the conversation will be sent to a partner group influences what is said and how the report will be framed.

As the reading is to be exchanged with, and discussed by, another group from a quite different background, it would be surprising if, even at this initial stage, the social and cultural background of the text is not mined one way or another, such as noting obvious contrasts with attitudes and practices between the world of the text and the world of the reading group. Academics use their linguistic and exegetical skills, while "ordinary readers" often fuse complementary cultural horizons while questioning the sharper cultural contrasts between their world and that of the Bible.

To sum up: an ethical first reading is a reading that is honest both to each individual's reading of the text and to any possible conversation between individual members' takes on the reading. The more open the groups are internally, the greater the possibility of transformation even at this first naïve stage. The key is the integrity of oneself as reader.

### Phase Two: Mutual Listening and Questioning— The Integrity of the Text and of the Other

In the second and critical stage of the process, we send our report to our partner group and receive theirs, remembering that "a critical analysis of real readers and their readings becomes as important and necessary as a critical analysis of the ancient texts themselves" (Segovia 2000, 119).[2]

Often the first transformation to take place in academic groups results from the insight that the imaginative readings of "ordinary" readers are as sharp and gifted as their own scientific exegesis, while for "ordinary" participants transformation often begins when they realize that they are being acknowledged, respected, and listened to by more academically qualified others. Furthermore, the partner's report can be treated as a "text" holding a certain hermeneutical autonomy of its own, although we can interrogate, and indeed shall be interrogating, its authors, just as the interrogation of the biblical text is always an exercise in intercultural communication between the group's culture and the culture embedded in the text.

Each group uses a set of responses to a text provided by its experience within its own particular culture. However, we can understand the responses of another group only to the extent that we are able to break away from any ethnocentrism that might still bind us to our home culture. We need to alter the cultural lens we usually look through and tune the frequency with which we listen to others.

Willingness to engage in cross-cultural exchange, however sincere, will not on its own trigger greater sensitivity to the partner. Our ethno-

---

2. While some partner groups use a common tongue, many reports are translated into another language, sometimes into a third, and each translation is an act of interpretation. For the crucial role of the facilitator/translator, see the subsection "Facilitator as Cultural Broker."

centric readings are not challenged as long as we remain rooted in our home culture, but they can be questioned when faced with the alternative reading provided by our partner who holds to another system of meanings, another culture. The transformative power of such contrasting readings takes place to the extent that we are able to break away from the ethnocentrism that binds us to our first culture. In a word, we need to become bicultural.

## Integrity of the Other

To read our partner's report, we need to become conversant in their group's culture. We are concerned not just with intercultural readings, but crucially with *intercultural relationships*. At least some members need to develop the ability to "recognise, define, analyse and select an approach to problems that involve cultural values, beliefs and assumptions from contexts other than one's own" (Stallter 2009, 544).

The fact that I, a marginal European, born in the Atlantic-swept British Isles, have been living in Southeast Asia for the past forty years does not automatically mean that I am bicultural. To listen to the partner group's reading, I must learn to leave my own cultural mindset, leave its cherished ideas and values, its familiar perspectives, its seemingly "superior" philosophy, theology, and exegesis.

### Bennett's Principles

Janet Bennett (2011) has found that an intentional and developmentally sequenced program design can lead to competence in intercultural communication. Bennett has outlined no less than nine principles for enhancing cultural curiosity for any person wishing to be "at home" in more than their home culture. Both Janet and Milton Bennett developed their theory and practice in working with North American business people intending to work abroad. Many of their insights are applicable to anybody wishing to enter into the thinking of members of another's cultural domain. Let me outline them briefly and apply them to our program.

First, we need to learn to *suspend our assumptions and value judgments*. For an intercultural reading of the Bible, that means we need to read our partner's report as they themselves intended it to be read, putting aside our initial, spontaneous questioning of anything that seems "odd," if not downright wrong.

Second, this entails that we *practice cultural humility*, treating the partner with respect on equal terms, presuming that their reading is valuable, life-giving, and important both to themselves as well as to us.

Third, we need to *enhance our perception skills* and look for cultural patterns and values that shape the other's reading however different it may be from our own. This may well involve seeking clarification and background on key differences.

Fourth, we need to *develop multiple perspectives*, acknowledging that each Bible passage is polyvalent and open to any number of interpretations, none of which is absolutely correct, for the one absolute is God.

Fifth, this means that we need to *increase our tolerance of ambiguity* and not read the Bible as a set of clear-cut faith propositions; we need to be open to "meaningful inconsistencies." Truth is beyond a single understanding, beyond any one language or culture; truth cannot be confined to one age, nation, or people.

We do ask questions on points that we either do not yet understand or find ourselves in disagreement with. So, sixth, we correspond with our partner, and in doing so *learn to ask culturally appropriate questions*. Here the role of the translator is crucial: learning how to translate the questions of one cultural group for the members of another. Initial questions seek to clarify our understanding of the other, to see and appreciate the reading as they intend.

Seventh, ideally the translator/reporter/go-between has been a *"participant observer"* in the other culture, has engaged in a regular, enduring relationship with the other's context, so as to be able to draw upon the ideas, feelings, and values of the other in order to "translate" the other's reading in terms of their own values, symbols, frame of thinking, and acting. This is crucial both in maintaining the integrity of the other and of oneself.

Eighth, bicultural sensitivity is essential and ought to increase as the conversation continues; it should not, however, result in "ecumenical over-politeness," but rather should teach us to *become analytically inquisitive* as we probe away at seemingly dissonant voices, while allowing such voices to probe and question our own. We learn to be non-threatening yet incisive, to respect difference while noting both convergence and discrepancy.

Ninth, we need to *assess the credibility of our intercultural sources*, that is, the credibility of sources used by our own group as well as those of our partners.

Exchanging reports encourages groups to reread the text in the light of the other's report, to take up aspects of the text we have not highlighted, to place ourselves in the other's position, and then reread our own report anew. We freely question and probe preconceptions of ourselves and the other, their methods and ours, their selective reading and ours, but always with respect in order to enhance understanding. Our exchanges are only of value where differences are honored.

## Intercultural Sensitivity Model

It may be useful to filter and appraise our reports and exchanges through the intercultural sensitivity developmental model utilized by Milton Bennett (1993). Bennett's model sketches out how to navigate difference with increasing sophistication. His model begins with three ethnocentric stages in which our own culture (our initial reading of the biblical text) is experienced as central in some particular way. Beyond them the last three stages are ethnorelative, in which our own cultural reading is viewed in the context of our partner's.

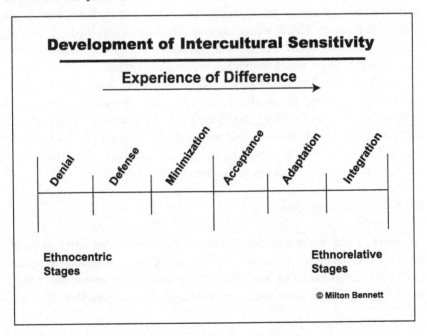

"Development of Intercultural Sensitivity" (Milton 1993, 42). Reproduced by permission of Milton Bennett.

Reading the group reports, I suggest that all of us passed beyond
Milton's first stage of "denial of difference" before we entered the program:
we began our intercultural reading of the Bible already acknowledging the
dignity of difference. However, first reactions to the report of our partner
may well have elicited a few defensive responses, at least in some of us.
This is normal, but we need to go beyond any sense of feeling threatened,
to accept quite opposing readings as viable in certain situations and quite
possibly in our own too. Conversely, we might have been tempted, at least
initially, to overplay the "being polite" card and tended to minimize differences that, indeed, may well have been present, while overemphasizing
common patterns in our readings.

Fortunately, responses to partners' reports also show that we are capable of getting past these ethnocentric mindsets. We accept that different
readings are not just possible but necessary, and not just for the partner
but also for ourselves. This comes about through a struggle, first within the
group itself and then in the ongoing conversation with our partner. So we
learn to adapt, to relativize, to go beyond previous boundaries and adjust
our long-held parameters. Ideally, we can move from our reading to our
partner's and back again, understanding each one as it is understood by its
respective authors. This is a process that can come about through sudden
insights, but more often incrementally as our exchange continues: we find
ourselves crossing a street we have never crossed before.

While Milton Bennett places "integration" as the final stage in cross-
cultural conversion,[3] for us the final stage is transformation: we do not
emulate our partner's reading nor integrate the two, but allow our partner's
reading to transform our own, finding sense and so finding our way to our
own beliefs. The insights gained by each group are distinctive, more than
the sum or synthesis of an integrated amalgam of both.

*Cross-Cultural Conversion*

As we read our partner's comprehension of the text, we learn through
practice the necessary theological and anthropological vision, attitudes,
and skills that allow us to "exit" from our own cultural home and "enter"
into the other's. On their own, knowledge and understanding, however

---

3. The term *intercultural conversion* comes from Jon Kirby; see Kirby and Lange
2000.

deep, do not trigger cross-cultural conversion. In dialogue with the other, we learn to leave our own cherished ideas and values, familiar perspectives, enhanced academia, seemingly "superior" exegesis, and, ironic as it might seem, our familiar religious forms. That is, we must constantly guard against evaluating the partner's reading through an "un-evaluated insider's mythical understanding of [our]selves" (Redfield, cited in Kirby and Lange 2000, 6). While sensitivity and cross-cultural skills are not automatic, many groups do seem to have been able to "grope" their way past the hazards of an ethnocentric straightjacket.

Authenticity, that is, truly ethical readings, demand such bicultural skills, skills developed through communicating cross-culturally. The more successful conversations will balance challenge with support as both reading partners cultivate their curiosity and their cognitive flexibility.

Obviously we are not dealing with abstract hermeneutics distanced from life. The intercultural communities we are creating between partners, however ephemeral, are sites that "increase our attention, our presence and our appreciation for what is around us." Intercultural reading of the Bible "requires time and stretching and self-examination, and trust building, and vulnerability." The love and the friendship that develop between partner communities are rooted in "a wholly uncomforting, wholly contingent, wholly creative, wholly open-ended, wholly vulnerable and risky act of human imagination" as the words of Scripture are recast in a quite new and unique ways, "opening something up in a way which can only be described as 'with jagged edges'" (Alison 2003, passim). Transformation through intercultural reading

> is the strange combination of the contingent, the creative, the brave, the unimagined, the revealing, the not yet clear or tied up which is quite outside all the normal forms of comforting and regular [readings]. It is this jagged edge of creative imagination in the midst of contingency which seems to be one of the indispensable qualities of [intercultural readings of the Bible], and one of the most difficult to learn and to perform. (Alison 2003, 10)

Integrity of the Text

No single reading will give "appropriate" attention to each aspect of the text: all readings are selective. Any attempt to "lock up *the* meaning of a text is futile and unreal ... [for each] text is open to various patterns.... The plurality of readings ... is not due to the ambiguity of a text but to its capacity to say many things at once" (Croatto 1987, 21). For interpretation "is a chain process, not repetitive but ascending. The text contains a reservoir of meaning, ever exploited never exhausted" (29). The transforming "word" is in the reading event itself, the text appropriated through the lens of faith. Our focus, then, is on context, perspective, location, and agenda (Segovia 2000, 119).

## Scholarly Readings

Historical-critical methods help us give shape to the text, while intercultural readings draw out its capacity to give meaning to our life as readers. For while classical historical exegesis gives us insights into the possible history of a text, it does not give us the meaning of the text.

The literary form—the legal, historical, prophetical, sapiential, evangelical, epistolary, or apocalyptic genre of a text—does place parameters on our reading. While Paul Ricoeur (1981, 16) rejects the assumption that to understand a text is to understand the intention of the author or to grasp the text's meaning as it was grasped by the first hearers or readers who shared the author's cultural situation, nevertheless, without privileging classic exegesis, it still plays a vital role in our reading a text with integrity. Genre guides our reading, but it need not unduly limit our interpretation. Linguistics and narrative semiotics help us construct the world behind the text; while this is an important referent, it is a point of departure, not the end of our reading (Croatto 1987, 9).

Nonetheless, the language and genre of individual texts do need to be taken seriously. Through literary criticism, we read a coherent narrative with plot and setting, characterization, speech patterns, irony, symbolism, an implicit author/redactor, and implicit readers. Through social-science criticism we read the text in its relation to cultural and social contexts understood through social-science models, theories, and assumptions. Through liberationist readings, we focus on issues of power and dependency, injustice, and vulnerability. Through postcolonial criticism we ask whether the text supports or subverts imperial intentions (see Sugirtharajah 2012, 43–46).

## Fragments and Collections

Shorter texts need to be placed in their broader textual context, within the frame of the complete biblical book in question, for instance, and within the biblical collection as a whole, and read "with the reverence they derive from and address, yet with the intelligence God gave us to help us find him" (Wills 2008, 209).

In reading each text as part of a greater whole, we discover patterns that play themselves out again and again. Isolating certain texts out of their narrative and/or cultural contexts usually leads to misunderstanding and confusion.[4] For instance, the "warrior God" of Joshua can be used to justify going to war, while accounts of the conquest of the land of Canaan can be quoted to justify the contemporary Jewish state's annexation of Palestinian land.

*Reading Violent Texts*

To avoid violating violent texts, the group might place itself as "the other" in the text and imagine how they believe and behave the way "the other" does, for instance, as the losers in a battle (e.g., the Philistines) or as the dispossessed in a land grab (e.g., the Canaanites). "The Bible does not present a single, unified perspective. Rather it gathers together witnesses to a passionate, historical argument over what it means to be 'God's people'" (Howard-Brook 2010, 4). Reading the Bible interculturally requires wrestling with these issues from at least two divergent cultural settings. Listening deeply to our partner, we learn to listen to "absent" voices in the text, and so to read texts with the eyes of anyone marginalized or maligned in the text.

We gradually learn to discern when, and in what way, specific biblical statements were composed to reread, and thus replace, readings of earlier texts. For instance, Deuteronomy rereads Exodus, the prophets reread Samuel and Kings, and the entire apostolic writings of the New Testament are a commentary on the Hebrew Bible in the light of faith in Jesus as the Christ (Wills 2008, 8–9).

---

4. I personally greatly appreciate contemplative *lectio divina*—the silent breathing in of a biblical word or a phrase, a living mantra. The meaning extended to a single word or phrase in contemplative prayer is (unconsciously) understood by the one who prays within a more general presupposed hermeneutical framework. The danger is the obverse: building up a hermeneutical frame from a single verse.

*Surfacing Cultural Givens*

Our partner makes us aware of the choices we make in our interpretation, and which particular aspects of the text have triggered our reading. Further, we can become more aware of the cultural, religious, and ideological presuppositions behind our take on the text. We are transformed when our instinctive, perhaps even obstinate or unintellectualized, convictions are brought to the surface and enter into conversation with those of our partner. Such disclosures are truly revelatory to both groups.

We ask how our partner's reading of a text transforms our view of our life context. Also, how does approaching the text with the concerns and insights arising from our partner's particular context transform our group's understanding of the Scriptures (see Patte 2004, xxiv)? In exchanging readings across cultures, "we begin to adopt a totally different attitude towards our own interpretations. As we learn to respect their interpretations, we find that the differences reflect divergent but plausible interpretative choices of three kinds: textual, contextual and theological" (xxx). When Gospel narratives have become too familiar to move us, too big and bald and flat to penetrate our souls, in the face of our partner's reading they "become once again a surprising, disturbing, challenging, prodding, demanding or wooing address that we cannot ignore" (xxiv).

Thus we must keep the way wide open for further thought, for ongoing discussion, for additional investigation, and for quiet reflection. What most blocks transformative reading is allowing oneself to be permanently categorized, embedded in a single, tight cultural matrix. Those who tie their biblical faith onto a single culture within a particular political structure end up serving the structure and losing faith to ideology. We have to keep thinking and asking questions with meticulous curiosity, forever listening with inspiring patience.

*Surfacing Faith Commitments*

Exegetical methods are guides, but the faith commitment of the group members is decisive. The word is revealed as we read in common, as we "fuse" the text and our life commitments. In reading our partner's report, we learn of their commitment and thus how and why they prioritize one experience over others. In order to enter into the understanding of our partner, we need to enter into their life, if only vicariously. Thus intercultural readings become transformative when our partner helps us place the text in their cultural and political contexts, both that of the text itself constructed through exegetical criticism as well as that of ourselves, the readers.

To sum up, the more biculturally sensitive we become in our conversation with our partner, the greater the integrity with which we will acknowledge their reading. The more we question and probe each other's reading, the greater integrity with which we will read the text. The less the pretense, the greater the search for truth.

## Facilitator as Cultural Broker

Here I must say a word about the key role played by the facilitators who negotiate between partner groups as a bridge to the other and a source of new ideas. In fact, neither group knows fully what is going on. The facilitator must deal internally with the tensions of two cultural worlds, internalizing both cultural worlds, despite, on occasion, not being able to resolve fundamental differences between them. As such the facilitator finds herself at home in each group, yet an outsider to both, particularly where certain cultural assumptions do not fit into any of the other's cultural categories. Relationships of integrity depend upon understanding the fundamental assumptions of the other. Adopting the role of listener and learner enables the facilitator to enter the cultural world of the partner and study its ways.

Facilitators need to identify as closely as possible with the mindset of both groups, remembering that "at the deepest level identification begins with attitudes: with a sense of love and oneness with the people and an appreciation for their culture and history" (Hiebert 1985, 237). Clearly, group members have some basic idea of how to act and respond, and this makes it easier to initiate and sustain relationships. What is important is not how we see ourselves but how the other group sees us; surely this determines the effectiveness and outcome of our intercultural exchange.

When groups interact over long periods of time, they can develop stable patterns of relating to one another. Further, intercultural exchange becomes truly creative and innovative where cultural patterns are not rigidly adhered to. With patience and understanding, the two groups enter into an interdependent relationship and learn to work as equals, without withdrawing to "superior-inferior" roles when misapprehensions arise. The facilitator must avoid prescribing answers, but be ready to suggest alternative courses to help both groups to think through the consequences of each one's understanding of the text.

Phase Three: Extending Horizons—Committed to Transformation

If at all possible, the exchange continues as each group probes deeper into the world of the other and so into the world of the text. Apparently not many partners continue their exchange for any length of time; it seems we react to our partner's responses twice at most. Clearly we are prepared to listen, but transformation of self (conversion) and of our theology may necessitate a longer, more challenging conversation.

One example is the rather heated conversations that took place in the Ecumenical Association of Third World Theologians (EATWOT) in the 1980s. Asian liberationist readings (e.g., Aloysius Pieris) were taking the culture and religion of the marginalized as seriously as the economic and political context that was being mined by their Latin American colleagues. This heated yet nonthreatening discussion triggered an expansion of the horizon of first-generation Latin American liberation theologians (e.g., Leonardo Boff) who moved into popular religiosity and ecological issues, just as the economic and political (social class) readings of that pioneering Latin American generation had provoked widespread liberationist readings in Asia. Within a nonthreatening context, EATWOT undertook intercultural readings where the fundamental liberationist thrust united very different ecclesial and societal contexts and thus allowed for cultural challenge and transformation. That creative discussion was between academics only, although many of them were engaged in grassroots communities locally. Crucially our "through the eyes of another" program has drawn "ordinary" readers into the conversation as equal partners, and we are not tied to any particular liberationist model. This gives rise to a different dynamic.

These intercultural readings have much in common with postcolonial criticism (Sugirtharajah 1998, 2012; Segovia 2000). Readers acknowledge theirs is not the only take; readers try to avoid any cultural hegemonic imperialism; and academics and ordinary readers listen to each other with respect as equals, neither attempting to dominant the other. We have left behind any attempt at "objective," "neutral," "impartial," "universally applicable," and "exhaustive" readings. Our readings, richly diverse, are not mutually exclusive, but on core issues do converge. Our readings are always exploratory, engaged readings birthed from within the context of our eschatological hopes and day-to-day struggles. We listen in order to learn, so as to be transformed.

Historical, literary, and social-science criticism in which academics feel at home keeps all of us attuned to the integrity of the text, preventing any too easy outside ideological takeover, while our conscious engagement with societal issues of love and reconciliation, compassionate justice and human rights in local and global contexts, prevents us locking ourselves into any spurious academic "objectivity." The Bible does not present a single, unified perspective, and so it is our core engagement with society that frames coherence with the scriptural witness. Our core values give coherence to the Bible and inform us as to which God we believe in.

Intercultural readings should, then, bring to the surface in each group the core themes and values that are central to each group's life and reading of the Bible.

## Classic Themes

Many scholars, for instance, frame their reading in terms of covenant (Eichrodt 1961–1967); righteousness (von Rad 1962–1965); promise (Childs 1979; Clines 1978); hope (Moltmann 1967, 1974); freedom (Gottwald 1979; Pixley 1987; Croatto 1987); justice (Limburg 1977); and joy, thanksgiving, and fidelity (Brueggemann 1997). Linking the more recent theological themes are *fidelity* and *solidarity*, an active solidarity that overrides social, class, and cultural divisions within and between Christian communities. Each of these key themes, or a certain combination of them, is framed somewhat differently in each cultural context. Some groups read the entire Scriptures within a broad liberation frame, others more modestly as a journey, a pilgrimage moving toward ever deeper understanding.

## Opposing Magnetic Poles

In his fascinating book *"Come Out, My People!"* Wes Howard-Brook (2010) reads the entire Bible through the prism of opposing magnetic poles, poles he labels "creation" and "empire." The collections of documents gathered into the Hebrew-Christian Bible, where one author/redactor reinterprets earlier authors, where contemporary events are read in the light of earlier pivotal events, the Scriptures "gather together witnesses to a passionate, historical argument over what it means to be 'God's people'" (Howard-Brook 2010, 4). Thus what unites different readings, however contradictory they may initially appear to be, are fundamental human and religious values and commitments. Each text challenges us: which God are we talking about? Whose side are we on?

A Central Kerygma

For Croatto, these core values are expressed in a "linguistically coded central kerygma" that gave rise to the apostolic writings in which Jesus's disciples reread the entire Hebrew Bible (1987, 57). Thus for Croatto, it is not the level of exegetical expertise that is essential but our grasp of the central kerygma: God's creative and saving presence in creation and history. "The authority of scripture must ultimately be articulated in confessional terms by communities that assert that they have discerned the truth of power and the power of truth precisely in this text" (Bruggemann, as quoted by Thatcher 2008, 147). Core values are expressed differently in a variety of cultural and ecclesial communities.

Just as the experience of the risen Christ by the first disciples led to a kerygmatic rereading of the Hebrew Scriptures, so many accept Christ as *the* "hermeneutical key" for discovering God in the Bible, our lives, and contemporary society. Others take up the "great commandment" as the axis to read the entire Scriptures (Matt 22:40): loving the God of love and life and loving others as ourselves. This overarching God experience opens us to a sharing in God's own life (John 15:10). Intercultural reading of the Bible clarifies who this Christ is in whom we believe.

So, in reading the Scriptures, which God are we talking about? Whose side are we one? Have we created a "god" to justify our cultural/political/gender hegemony, or does our reading express an experience of the *Abba* of Jesus the Nazarene who invites us into a covenant with God in the Spirit in order that we be a blessing for the entire community of creation? Reading the Bible interculturally allows us to recognize God in "the other." Our readings are ethical when we listen to voices that have long been silenced.

Intercultural readings clarify not only which God we believe in, but also the role religion is playing in our life. Religion can be a source for restraint and restriction, but also for freedom and creativity. Whichever role religion plays in our life will tend to frame our reading ideologically. Intercultural readings bring our ideologies to the surface.

Identity, History, Purpose

This central kerygma—with its concomitant core values expressed in diverse cultural contexts, when maintained in honest and open intercultural conversation, listening carefully to the whole symphony of voices, suppressing none—allows us to discover a shared identity, history, and purpose within and beyond our cultural plurality.

Intercultural readings are ethical (authentic) when they question not just the biblical reports of the partner group, but also allow themselves to be questioned by the social location of such readings. How is each partner perceiving our globalizing world with its imperialistic economy, its deepening divide between the superrich and the expendable poor as we hurtle toward ecological disaster? What role is biblical faith playing in each one's engagement with poverty and injustice, communal violence, and political power struggles? Where are our cultural values, social location, and reading of the Scriptures placing our partner as marginalized groups throughout the world struggle for acknowledgment with a modicum of dignity?

Our contemporary struggle for hope and freedom, justice and love, fidelity and solidarity, frame our reading of the attitudes, beliefs, and practices that bind together the Hebrews of old and the disciples of apostolic times as a people, namely, family, ethnicity, language, nationality, neighborhood, common interests, membership in an organization, and social or political concerns. Then we compare and contrast the scriptural witness with our own. The kaleidoscope surely alters in accordance with the cultural perceptions of the readers, yet the underlying values remain the same and so does our core experience of God as a God of inclusion and love.

Faith Framework

Our experience and praxis of faith set the parameters of our first naïve reading, which was then questioned by both the reading and feedback of our partner. These readings inform us which God we actually believe in (our God experience) and who our neighbors are to us. We violate a text when we read into it a message that undermines the God of life and love.

To Conclude: Boundary Crossing

In intercultural readings, we learn to practice "boundary crossing." We are not tied to a specific theory as such, but are open to the use of a variety of exegetical methods in order to construct the cultural world behind the text, but without prioritizing or absolutizing any one critical method. We cross boundaries between these critical approaches by academics and the more spontaneous approaches by ordinary readers who in conversation consciously unearth each other's cultural and political assumptions in the particular reading strategies pursued. We cross cultural boundaries by attempting to understand the other, acknowledging an underlying convergence in conviction and values while the world around us becomes increasingly divided. As state and religious institutions become increasingly sidelined and casino capitalism deterritorialized, we form intercultural networks to galvanize movements for change. Seeing through the eyes of another is crucial in a multicultural world for those of us who reject any manner of imperialistic cultural hegemony, who give equal respect to each and every human being and culture, and who are committed, under God, to building up a community of equals.

Intercultural readings by academics and "ordinary readers," emerging from both local and global contexts, bring out inconvenient truths that recognize the complex nature of studying the Bible for transformation. We are engaged in decentring the universal and transhistorical values of post-Enlightenment categories of knowledge while articulating readings from the margins together with those of the mainstream. Yet, no matter how committed we may be to a view of biblical studies that does not privilege Western conceptual frameworks, we cannot actually be rid of them. We are working through what it means to be local and universal in the face of competing hegemonies of method and conclusion. It does not hurt to acknowledge that we are not only among the doctors but also among the patients with the disabilities of each one's individual cultural particularities. At the heart of the intercultural approach is the willingness and ability to listen carefully to each and every voice—to listen deeply from the cave of the heart where buried intuitions are laid bare, intuitions that have been running deeply and quietly and unnoticed beneath everything else—and the willingness and ability to be open to the Spirit in others who start from a quite different location (see Prior 2012, 177–78).

We are transformed when we acknowledge that we need each other, the academic and the "ordinary" reader, when we experience how intercultural conversations shock and liberate, disturb and challenge, prod and sensitize, refute and confirm, question and transform, interfere and create anew. The more we enter and find ourselves at home in both cultures—our own and that of our partner—the more our understanding and commitment are open to transformation. Intercultural readings force us to be conscious of our location, perspective, and agenda.

The deeper the analysis of the text and context, the greater the responsibility of the analyst/facilitator in engaging in a conversation with partners who are more intuitive either because of their cultural background or due to their level of schooling. To remain ethical we need the ability to translate our abstract analyses into concrete, imaginative narratives accessible to the other,[5] and, yes, translate them into social commitment. "The more believers read the Bible as a Word-to-live-by in all aspects of their life context, the more aware are they of the moral and religious gap that separates them from the biblical text. Thus, our ethical and scriptural sensibility is sharpened" (Patte 2004, xxiv). Only then does the Word get through the door, into the heart, and ignite.

## References

Alison, James. 2003. "Worship in a Violent World. Dublin." James Alison: Theology. http://www.jamesalison.co.uk/texts/eng13.html.

Bennett, Janet. 2011. "Developing Intercultural Competence." AIEA Conference, 22 February. www.jbennett@intercultural.org.

Bennett, Milton. 1993. "A Developmental Model of Intercultural Sensitivity." Pages 1–51 in *Education for the Intercultural Experience*. Edited by R. Michael Paige. Yarmouth, ME: Intercultural Press.

Brueggemann, Walter. 1997. *Theology of the Old Testament: Testimony, Dispute, Advocacy*. Minneapolis: Fortress.

Childs, Brevard S. 1979. *Introduction to the Old Testament as Scripture*. London: SCM.

Clines, J. A. David. 1978. *The Theme of the Pentateuch*. Sheffield: JSOT Press.

Croatto, J. Severino. 1987. *Biblical Hermeneutics: Toward a Theory of Reading as the Production of Meaning*. Maryknoll, NY: Orbis.

Eichrodt, Walther. 1961–1967. *Theology of the Old Testament*. Translated by J. A. Baker. 2 vols. Philadelphia: Westminster.

---

5. Sugirtharajah (1998, 124) outlines five categories of readers as described by C. D. Narasimhaiah. The *Achariya* is the discriminating reader, one who puts into practice what is read. The *Panditha* is the academic reader, one who has considerable knowledge but is not necessarily a committed reader. The *Bhakta* is the devoted reader, the reader with a cause and a commitment. The *Rasika* is the aesthetic reader who reads for satisfaction and whose interest ceases the moment expectations are satisfied. Narasimhaiah's fifth category is the *Alpabuddhijana*, whom he describes as the ignorant reader with an inferior taste. Most readers might identify with more than one category; perhaps monocultural readings in multicultural societies are primarily reduced to the last category.

Engelsviken, Tormod, Erling Lundeby, and Dagfinn Solheim, eds. 2011. *The Church Going Glocal: Mission and Globalisation*. Oxford: Regnum.

Gottwald, Norman K. 1979. *The Tribes of Yahweh: A Sociology of the Religion of Liberated Israel, 1250–1050 B.C.E.* London: SCM.

———, ed. 1983. *The Bible and Liberation: Political and Social Hermeneutics*. Maryknoll, NY: Orbis.

Hiebert, Paul G. 1985. *Anthropological Insights for Missionaries*. Grand Rapids: Baker Academic.

Howard-Brook, Wes. 2010. *"Come Out, My People!" God's Call out of Empire in the Bible and Beyond*. Maryknoll, NY: Orbis.

Kirby, Jon P., and Kofi Ron Lange. 2000. "The Crisis in Missionary Formation." *Tamale Institute of Cross-Cultural Studies Newsletter* 25 (January): 5–9. www.sedosmission.org/old/eng/kirby_1.htm.

Limburg, James. 1977. *Prophets and the Powerless*. Atlanta: John Knox.

Moltmann, Jürgen. 1967. *Theology of Hope: On the Ground and the Implications of a Christian Eschatology*. Translated by J. W. Leitch. London: SCM.

———. 1974. *The Crucified God: The Cross of Christ as the Foundation and Criticism of Christian Theology*. Translated by R. A. Wilson and John Bowden. London: SCM.

Patte, Daniel M. 2004. "Introduction." Pages xxi–xxxiv in *Global Bible Commentary*. Edited by Daniel M. Patte, J. Severino Croatto, Nicole Wilkinson Duran, Teresa Okure, and Archie Chi Chung Lee. Nashville: Abingdon.

Pixley, Georg V. 1987. *On Exodus: A Liberation Perspective*. Maryknoll, NY: Orbis.

Prior, John Mansford. 2012. "Biblical Studies and Mission Study Group: The First Thirty-Five Years." Pages 157–78 in *Witness to World Christianity: The International Association for Mission Studies, 1972–2012*. Edited by Gerald H. Anderson, John Roxborough, John M. Prior, and Christoffer H. Grundmann. New Haven: OMSC.

Rad, Gerhard von. 1962–1965. *Old Testament Theology*. Translated by D. M. G. Stalker. 2 vols. London: SCM.

Redfield, Robert. 1960. *The Little Community and Peasant Society and Culture*. Chicago: University of Chicago Press.

Ricoeur, Paul. 1981. *Essays on Biblical Interpretation*. London: SPCK.

Segovia, Fernando F. 2000. *Decolonizing Biblical Studies: A View from the Margins*. Maryknoll, NY: Orbis.

Stallter, Tom. 2009. "Cultural Intelligence: A Model for Cross-Cultural Problem Solving." *Missiology* 37:543–54.

Sugirtharajah, R. S. 1998. *Asian Biblical Hermeneutics and Post-Colonialism: Contesting the Interpretations*. Maryknoll, NY: Orbis.

———. 2012. *Exploring Postcolonial Biblical Criticism: History, Method, Practice*. Oxford: Wiley-Blackwell.

Thatcher, Adrian. 2008. *The Savage Text: The Use and Abuse of the Bible*. Oxford: Wiley-Blackwell.

Tournier, Paul. 1968. *A Place for You*. New York: Simon & Schuster.

Wills, Garry. 2008. *What the Gospels Meant*. New York: Viking.

# 4

## TRANSFORMATION IN INTERCULTURAL BIBLE READING: A VIEW FROM PRACTICAL THEOLOGY

*Daniel S. Schipani*

The connection between reading a sacred text and experiencing human transformation is an assumption inherent in the very value assigned by religious communities to certain texts deemed sacred. That is the reason for those communities to engage in reading, interpreting, and appropriating their message. This applies as well to the Bible, even though, strictly speaking, Christianity should not be considered a "religion of the Book" in ways that Judaism and Islam might. The expression "people of the Book" appears in the Qur'an (29:46) in reference to Jews and Christians. Recently it has become commonplace to characterize the so-called Abrahamic traditions as "peoples of the Book." However, as a corrective view on this issue, Hall (2013) persuasively argues against bibliocentrism, biblical literalism, and fundamentalism as modern phenomena and makes the case that Christianity is not accurately described as a religion "of the Book." Hall includes the chapter "Not a Religion 'of the Book'" in his sixfold "apophatic" theological presentation from a Protestant perspective (2013, 42–58).

During the last decades of the twentieth century, Walter Wink became one of the better-known North American scholars concerned with transformative reading of the Bible. Wink's views are documented in his manifesto (2010—an earlier version was published in 1973), in which he starts by denouncing what he calls the "bankruptcy of the biblical critical paradigm" and then presents a dialectical hermeneutic involving "fusion," "distance," and "communion." Wink (1980) presents an approach of intensive group study and dialogue of a biblical passage, involving new presuppositions, new methods, and a new view of knowledge (see also Wink

1984, 1986, 1992, 2003). Wink explicitly states that the goal of Bible study is "the conscious transformation of persons ... centered on commitment to the will of God.... Our interest is ... in finding that subtle intersection between the text and our own life where ... we encounter the living God addressing us at the point of our and the world's need" (2010, 82, 126–27).

Roughly at the same time, a number of liberationist, feminist, and postcolonial contributions began to demonstrate the potentially trans-forming power of reading Scripture contextually in deliberate and sys-tematic ways. Even though one does not find in those endeavors many references to "transformation" as an explicit goal, they clearly represent what has been characterized as the "liberation model" of transformation (social-relational transformation).

Yung Suk Kim (2013, 6–7) discusses four models of transformation depending on their emphasis on different forms of human existence: autonomy (a mode of rule by self), relationality (a mode of rule by com-munity), and heteronomy (a mode of rule by Other). He asserts that these modes reflect scholars' views of an ideal transformation in terms of indi-vidual life (autonomy), communal life (relationality), and religious experi-ence (heteronomy). The four models discussed are: usual Western model (*individual-autonomous* transformation), liberation model (*social-rela-tional* transformation), religious community model (*traditional-commu-nal* transformation), and religious individual model (*mystic, charismatic* transformation). Kim proceeds to present his *holistic* model of transfor-mation, seeking to integrate the aim of transformation in personal and public life by connecting those three modes of human existence, three moments of human life ("I am no-one, I am some-one, I am for-others"), and the three subjects of human transformation (self, neighbor, and God).

For its part, the much newer field of empirical intercultural herme-neutics also offers the hope of fostering holistic human transformation in settings where the Bible can be read not only contextually but also *inter-contextually*. In the words of Hans de Wit (2012, 5) about the new space provided for relevant and topical research, "This space ... of empirical hermeneutic in intercultural perspective ... has to do with the question of whether reading Bible stories jointly by groups from often radically differ-ent cultural and sociopolitical contexts can contribute to transformation and changed perspectives."

I approach the question of transformation in intercultural Bible read-ing as a practical theologian. Practical theology contributes a unique per-spective and approach that includes four methodological dimensions (see

Osmer 2008). The *descriptive-empirical* dimension focuses on the real-life situation and specific practices of Bible reading groups in a variety of sociocultural situations; it gathers information that helps us discern patterns and dynamics in intercultural reading of Scripture. The *interpretive* dimension is concerned with analysis in order to situate the empirical research within a more comprehensive explanatory framework; such a hermeneutical task draws on theories of the arts and sciences to better understand and explain why those patterns and dynamics occur. The *normative* dimension consists in the use of theological tools to contextually interpret ("judge") particular events, episodes, and situations, to construct ethical norms to guide our responses, and to learn from good practices of intercultural Bible reading. Finally, the *pragmatic* dimension of practical theology determines strategies of action that will influence situations of intercultural reading in desirable ways.

In the following section I consider briefly a multiple case study of reading the Bible in the context of impunity in Latin America. Such documented experience serves to illustrate my understanding of transformation and of the creative process that potentially yields transformative outcomes for the people who participate in intercultural Bible reading. Finally, I present a theological perspective on the deeply spiritual nature of the transformation process.

Reading the Bible in Contexts of Impunity in Latin America

For this reflection on transformation in the intercultural reading of the Bible, I chose to focus on an empirical study that involved "ordinary readers" who live in contexts of impunity in Latin America.[1] In this section I summarize the recorded empirical evidence of the study that supplies material for the analysis and evaluation necessary to identify criteria and principle, that is, dependable guides to the practice of transformative Bible reading.

Eighteen groups from Colombia, Peru, El Salvador, and Guatemala participated in an intercultural reading process focused on the text of Luke 18:1–8 (De Wit and López 2013). The groups did not know each other beforehand, nor did they know that they shared experiences of violence,

---

1. In addition to the intrinsic value of the unprecedented study edited by Hans de Wit and Edgar Antonio López (2013), my choice was also motivated by my own experience as an Argentine minister and scholar who also lived in a context of terror and impunity.

corruption, lack of protection, crime, and impunity. Each group studied the text in their usual manner. The groups could also consider guiding questions such as: What is the central message of this story? Which character(s) do you identify yourself with? What personal experiences does the widow's story elicit for you? (see De Wit et al. 2004). During the first phase of the project, each group created a written report on the material generated in the study. Reports included personal introductions, descriptions of the sociocultural context, and descriptions of their reading experiences. All reports were sent to the project's central coordinating office.

In the second phase, each group connected with a partner group from another country. Partner groups received each other's report and the text was read for a second time, now with the input provided by the partner group. That was the beginning of the mutual encounter or confrontation with the possibility of reading the story "through the eyes of another." Each group could thus reflect on the reading, the context, and the experiences of the other group, discovering commonalities as well as differences. Most importantly, the readers could realize that the text "offers" a multiplicity of possible interpretations and applications beyond those locally discovered in the communal, contextual reading and that those different views and insights are potentially transformative. Second reports based on the reading and discussion of the partner group's first report were then exchanged. These told how the partner group's first report was received and included explanations of what was found meaningful or problematic.

The third phase in particular tested the sensitivity of each group and their willingness to sustain a real encounter with the partner group. By then the groups had had considerable interaction and could seek further mutual understanding and even collaboration. They had realized the richness of communal intercontextual reading of the Bible and with it the possibility of overcoming isolation and of empowering those involved with courage, resolve, and a renewed sense of solidarity and hope.

For the researchers and project directors, the most important question was to what extent the shared reading of Luke 18:1–8 had been a catalyst for overcoming isolation and suffering:

> Our interest went beyond registering how ordinary readers deal with a biblical text in different cultural settings. We wanted to know to what extent the interaction … had been a means to heal their wounds, to recover hidden memories and talk about them, and to move forward towards overcoming their traumas. (De Wit and López 2013, 99)

Having just described succinctly that unprecedented Latin American study, we must now address the question: Why might transformation happen in intercultural reading of the Bible? I have divided the response to that question in two parts. In the following section, I will highlight a few interpretive observations focusing primarily on the very nature of the Bible as sacred Scripture and the unique potential and dispositions of so-called ordinary readers. In the second part I propose that one way of understanding transformation in intercultural Bible reading is by framing it in terms of the theory of creativity and the creative process in particular.

## Holy Scripture and "Ordinary Readers"

In this context, a succinct definition of transformation could be as follows: a process of significant change that unfolds to the extent that people reading the Bible together find new insights, perspectives, and deepened understanding, while strengthening their experience of community and solidarity in ways that encourage commitment to and involvement in praxis for reconciliation, justice, peace, and healing. Transformation can take many different forms. Even if one is suspicious of grandiose claims regarding (macro)political transformation as the possible effect of intercultural Bible reading, there is evidence that micro- and mid-level transformations are possible, as in the case of the healing of trauma documented in the Latin American study. The next paragraphs suggest several reasons why transformation might happen due to the particular connection between holy Scripture and "ordinary readers."

First of all, transformation might happen because of the very nature of the Bible as sacred text. "The text comes first and is the main Other.... It is more than the reader" (De Wit 2012, 47). The sacred text of the Bible has great disclosive potential and inexhaustible meaning. Throughout the centuries, readers have assumed, implicitly and explicitly, that the Bible has an enduring potential to offer manifold meaning that can actually guide, instruct, teach, challenge, convict, sustain, inspire, and empower the faithful.

It is further assumed that such power is potentially operative and relevant across cultures and throughout the ages. The reason for such assumptions is that sacred texts address fundamental human needs, existential longings, and potentials. "Readers experience the texts as fundamental for their own lives, and their lives meet on a level of depth in the light of the text.... The intercultural discussion on Bible texts leads to dialogue on the in-depth dimensions of existence" (De Wit 2012, 48–49). In other words, biblical texts can engage people's *spirits* and *spirituality*, both at a personal level and at group and communal levels.

Those who make the sacred text their own do experience a strong sense of normativeness and directiveness as they interact with those texts. At the very least, they are open to experiencing significant personal and social change as a result of certain forms of intercultural Bible reading. Ordinary readers can approach the text with an existential attitude that creates "a space in which the effect of Holy Scripture is evident … a dynamic playing field in which Bible texts are not soiled but called into new life" (De Wit 2012, 79).

Significant correlations can thus be established between the readers' disposition—their interest, attitude, needs, aspirations, and expectations—in a setting characterized by a safe place of trust, respect, and their collaborative and creative participation. The text is somehow effectively expected to become a source of inspiration, orientation, learning, growth, and healing. That is precisely when and why the Bible becomes *Scripture*:

> Being scripture is not a quality inherent in a given text, or type of text, so much as an interaction, a relationship between that text and a community of persons.… "Scripture" is a bilateral term.… It inherently implies, in fact, names, a relationship.… People—a given community—make a text into scripture, or keep it scripture: by treating it a certain way. I suggest *scripture is a human activity*. (Smith 1993, ix, 17–18)

This also implies that there might be "asymmetry" concerning the nature and degree of motivation when comparing reading groups as well as when comparing within each group. Further, another possible dimension of asymmetry has to do with the function of the *imagination*. An important question is raised as to whether imagination is the key to a hermeneutical and epistemological "privilege" often enjoyed by ordinary readers who happen to be marginalized or otherwise oppressed, when compared to either "experts" or other readers who enjoy a socioeconomically comfortable life situation. The work of Bob Ekblad (2006; United States), Carlos Mesters (1984; Brazil), and Gerald West (1999; South Africa), among others, offer additional testimony in favor of a positive answer to that question. The North American theologian Robert McAfee Brown (1984) demonstrates that confrontation with a radically different point of view offers the opportunity for "perspective transformation" and liberation from ideological captivity.

Last but not least, the very nature and dynamics of intercontextual reading of the Bible offers a unique opportunity to encounter "others" who bring different perspectives and alternative views. The "others" can become places of revelation with transforming potential as they critically challenge our own perspectives and views and invite further work of the imagination to visualize the shape of a better future.

Intercultural Reading of the Bible as Creative and Spiritual Process

When we consider the rich plurality of reading group experiences, it is possible to identify a fundamental pattern that appears in multiple cultural settings. Indeed, the intercultural reading of the Bible can be viewed as a special way of generating a *creative process* with five identifiable "steps." Contextual reading in the face of critical situations such as violence and impunity can thus lead to transformation as described above. It can happen whenever, or to the extent to which, the actual intercontextual reading is analogous to the creative process in areas such as scientific discoveries, art, music, and literature. My research on intercultural Bible reading over the last several years has uncovered such patterns in the structure and dynamics briefly discussed and illustrated in the following paragraphs.

First, there is always a community context where trust and mutual respect are key, together with an attitude of trust in the text, coupled with receptive expectation. Such groups of readers usually include celebration practices that generate the kind of emotional and spiritual "climate" that can foster transformation. Groups of ordinary readers who live in contexts of impunity approached Luke 18:1–8 in this manner. The groups sought to create a spirit of trust and safe intimacy. As expressed by a Colombian group, in order for good reading to take place it is necessary to be in a space free from domination and fear:

> We need to build spaces and environments of trust, spaces where we can speak and listen, pray, recover courage, and cast away fear.... Speaking and listening are a first step even if it makes us cry or be silent. We break the strategy of fear when we are able to gather together in order to engage in conversation and to recover memory and trust. (De Wit and López 2013, 320)

Second, the search for meaning and direction always consists in what can be called "incubation period(s)." Hermeneutical explorations thus take place as an interplay between text, participants, and partner group.

Imagination plays a crucial role. The groups must have competent, "demo-cratic" leaders and optimal structures that encourage spontaneity, include openness to take risks, and engage in dialogue. Bible reading and interpre-tive dialogue occur as a search for understanding, consolation, reorienta-tion, and resolution. As readers explore plausible meanings of the text, many possibilities emerge, most of which were not even imagined by the "experts" or the academic, scientific readers:

> Our extensive empirical material from the participating groups showed first of all the multiplicity of readings and the almost unending amount of interpretations. We discovered the hermeneutical and theological import of multiplicity ... [and] the multiplicity of readings also demon-strated for us that contextuality is another dimension of the process. (De Wit and López 2013, 429)

Third, sooner or later those "ordinary readers" experience and artic-ulate new insights, intuitions, and meanings elicited from the text and the hermeneutical collaboration that is taking place. Typically, a plural-ity of opinions are considered that, for instance, in the case of the impu-nity study, connect with "visceral memories" that are reremembered and, potentially, integrated and transformed. Diverse new knowledge and understanding or new perceptions emerge, both within the group and in the exchanges with the partner group. During this phase there is a rich harvest of interpretations:

> Life and text illumine each other. It is an important moment in the pro-cess of understanding.... The readers filled the narrative gaps in the text.... They began to be coauthors and participating actors of the event narrated by the text.... They began to articulate their local theologies, to reflect on the presence of God in the text and in their own lives.... [They imagined the "world of the text" and then, in a second movement, they brought the text to the present as an appropriation process].... The reading reflected the process of *fusion of horizons*. (De Wit and López 2013, 430)

Fourth, energy is released, a kind of "eureka effect," as in the case of the disciples who, after welcoming new insights at the table with Jesus, decided to return immediately to Jerusalem (Luke 24:13–35). Depend-ing on the circumstances, there can be catharsis and lamentation as well as celebration and motivation for new action. There tends to be a sense of empowerment. The release of energy can be expressed in the joy of participation, in wanting to know more about the other group, or to participate further in a worshipful activity. Two windows into this phase of intercultural reading as creative process in the case of those Latin American groups follow:

> The connection between reading and celebrating, remembering and sharing, freely expressing emotions and healing, is very meaningful. It is a process that reflects something of that space in which the spirit of the text can unfold, its transcendent nature can be manifested, and its reserve of meaning can be explored.... It was very impressive to perceive how this simple text with just a few verses [Luke 18:1–8] could mobilize deep [*visceral*] memories and how, in the intimacy of the small group, the readers began to open their hearts and to share about what was moving them at the deepest level of their life and faith. (De Wit and López 2013, 317, 431)

Fifth, the transformation process is not complete until validation and confirmation take place in two ways: both retrospectively, that is, how the new insights or changed views effectively connect with the critical or conflicting situation that participants face, as well as prospectively and praxeologically, which can also generate further praxis. The "hermeneutical loop" is thus completed by way of a dual process of analysis and verification. The groups further confront social reality and look for possible reorientation and new praxis. The review of the empirical material suggests that the intercultural Bible reading process was analogous to the three phases identified in the psychology of trauma processing: first, the creation of a safe and empathic space; second, remembering the losses and owning one's grief and mourning by way of retelling stories with connected anxieties, fears, and impulses of revenge; and third, movement toward a new "normal" enriched state by sharing traumatic experiences and giving and receiving support and solidarity in the face of isolation and loneliness (De Wit and López 2013, 431). Further assessment of the lingering effects of the process in the case of at least some of the participant groups suggests that the experience of intercultural Bible reading has been transformative (De Wit and López 2013, 437–40).

Finally, it must be noted that the transformation process is not only psychosocial and cultural, but also spiritual; in fact, participants themselves can experience their (inter)contextual reading of the Bible as a spiritual process that, together with the encounter with Scripture, includes practices such as prayers for illumination, support, and intercession; music and singing; personal testimonies; and communal meals. In short, the process is profoundly spiritual, precisely because it engages people's spirituality and their very human spirit, as discussed in the following section.

### A Constructive Proposal for Understanding Transformation

As already indicated, "transformation" is the main aspiration and goal of intercultural reading of the Bible. Transformation can be viewed as a process of systemic change detectable on three different *levels* and within three *dimensions* in the lives of those who participate in intercultural Bible reading.

First, strictly speaking, transformation must be viewed as *systemic change,* that is, second-order change. Whereas a change within a given system is a "first-order change," the change of the system itself can be called "transformation," including personal conversion experiences such as that of Saul of Tarsus (Acts 9:1–9; 26:12–18).

Second, transformation can be identified and appraised on three interrelated levels: interpersonal, intrapersonal, and community. Intercultural Bible reading has been shown to foster transformation on the interpersonal and small group levels, as already indicated above. Even though it should not be expected that it will directly effect "macro-" social-structural changes, intercultural Bible reading can affect ecclesial communities structurally. In turn, the proliferation of "radical" ecclesial communities can affect institutions and, to a certain degree, the larger social order: one can argue that grassroots ecclesial communities in Brazil played a significant role in the democratization process of that country in the 1980s.

Third, genuine transformation takes place within three dimensions. Transformations happen when, or to the extent that, the following inter-related outcomes are met: (1) contextual appropriation of biblical material results in new, revelatory *meaning* (e.g., paradigm shift/perspective change, as in the case of Peter and others, according to Acts 10:35); (2) *experience* of community, solidarity, and integrity is enriched (e.g., sense of fraternal communion); and (3) empowerment and reorientation with movement toward creative, liberating, or healing community *action* (e.g., civil disobedience, service in solidarity, reconstruction strategies, and reconciliation). We might say that the kind of transformation hoped for can be experienced and witnessed as a revolution in three dimensions: ortho-doxy (belief, convictions), orthokardia (heart, passions), and orthopraxis (action, enactments).

## Transformation at the Existential or Spiritual Level

I approach the question of the shape and content of transformation by claiming that there is a significant analogy between what clinical research shows in the case of intercultural and interfaith spiritual care and the process and dynamics of intercultural Bible reading (see Schipani 2013). In that light I propose that transformation can be viewed as a process that reshapes the self at the level of *spirit* as follows: (1) from deception, falsehood, illusion, and meaninglessness to a new vision and understanding; truth is revealed afresh—*faith* (new orthodoxy); (2) from isolation, alienation, division, and enmity to connectedness and communion; community and solidarity are strengthened—*love* (new orthopathy or orthokardia); and (3) from inertia, resignation, disorientation, and hopelessness to reorientation and empowerment for justice and peace—*hope* (new orthopraxis). These three dimensions must be considered as dynamically interrelated, as suggested in the following diagram.

HOPE
Reorientation and Purpose
   (against resignation, inertia,
   deception, disorientation, despair, ...)

FAITH
Knowledge and Truth
   (against falsehood, illusion,
   meaninglessness, ...)

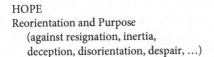
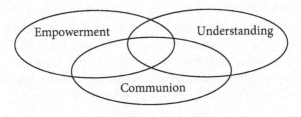

LOVE
Community and Solidarity
   (against loneliness, isolation, division, enmity, ...)

A Model of the Spiritual Self within Family, Social, Global, and Cosmic Contexts

## Additional Notes from Practical Theology

One of the main contributions of the movement concerned with "ordinary readers" of the Bible consists in its bringing into focus both the lived faith of the latter as well as their capacity to function as contextual grassroots theologians doing "popular theology." Such a twofold focus is usually eclipsed in scientific and academic approaches in biblical studies. Here I follow the classification of three levels of theologizing—"professional," "pastoral," and "popular" (Boff and Boff 1987, 11–21). The intercultural Bible reading project thus provides a unique opportunity to explore certain fundamental issues of faith and theology, particularly in regard to the understanding of the connection between reading the Bible and transformation. The directors of the Latin American study included a helpful theological reflection that I summarize in terms of two observations (De Wit and López 2013, 347–59).

The first observation is that the group of common readers became a kind of *communio sanctorum* within which reading the Bible went hand in hand with rereading people's life stories. The group also became the place where new, local, inductive, and contextual theologies began to be fashioned. This process amounted to doing theology in places of violence, injustice, and impunity; the process could lead both to new interpretations and to spiritual renewal. Indeed, together with new formulations of theodicy ("if God is just, why is this happening to us?"), participants were able to transform anger, frustration, and the desire for revenge into a posttraumatic spirituality nurtured by faith, prayer, Scripture, and worship (De Wit and López 2013, 349–54).

The second observation has to do with articulating a theology of memory that starts with the recovery of visceral and dangerous memories of suffering and perseverance (De Wit and López 2013, 388–417). The empirical study supplied rich material pointing to the possibility of developing a theology with the potential to support and guide a liberating and evangelical faith in contexts of impunity. Normatively expressed:

> Theology and hermeneutics must invest in the transformation of alienation and victimization, from lament to … a just struggle … this is the fundamental message of the biblical witness: mourning, suffering, and injustice will not have the final word; rather, healing, restoration, and life renewal are possible as well. (De Wit and López 2013, 304)

The theological reflection toward the end of the study then proceeded with a discussion of grieving, justice, forgiveness, and the healing process as illumined by the human sciences and, especially, Christology.

In addition to these reflections, I propose that our understanding of transformation in intercultural reading of the Bible must include at least three further considerations usually beyond the scope of traditional academic biblical studies—an explicit four-dimensional view of reality and knowing, a normative ethical-eschatological vision, and a practical pneumatology.

A Four-Dimensional View of Reality and Knowing

Traditionally, academic and scientific studies operate within a bidimensional ontological and epistemological frame of reference that focuses on people in social contexts; fundamental existential and spiritual realities tend to be collapsed within such a frame of reference. The disciplined exploration that takes place in empirical contextual hermeneutics, however, makes it imperative to work and reflect systematically according to a four-dimensional view as in the following diagram (adapted from Schipani 2013, 165):

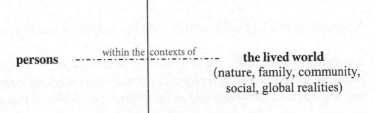

The Holy—*offer of new being in community*
"abundant life"(liberation, healing and wholeness, communion, meaning,
hopefulness, purpose, destiny...)

persons — — — within the contexts of — — —  the lived world
(nature, family, community,
social, global realities)

The Void—*threat of nonbeing, annihilation*
"languishing life" (oppression, trauma and emptiness, alienation,
meaninglessness, despair, aimlessness, fate ...)

A Four-Dimensional Frame of Reference

The empirical material validates the conclusion that readers experience the texts as fundamental to their lives, that in the light of the text their lives meet on a deep level, and that the intercultural discussion on Bible texts leads to dialogue on the deeper dimensions of existence (De Wit 2012, 48–49). The report on the Latin American study supplies abundant material supporting this observation and my related claim regarding the need for a four-dimensional view. That is why I argue that it is impossible to fully appreciate the wealth of knowledge and the implications resulting from the study unless we work with such a perspective and frame of reference.

The following reflection from the directors of the Latin American study supports the point that the realities of evil and grace (the "vertical" dimensions) must be acknowledged and addressed in connection with the realities of people suffering in specific sociocultural contexts (the "horizontal" dimensions):

> Theology and hermeneutics must have an investment in the transformation of alienation and the victimization of lament toward the response of a just struggle. This is an enormous and urgent investment because we can never be fully prepared to confront evil, injustice, and impunity.... Narrative memories invite the victims to be set free from the alienation of evil, that is, to move from a position of silent defenselessness to coming to voice, to denounce and protest and, if possible, to self-renewal.... This is a fundamental message of biblical witness: mourning, sorrow, suffering, and injustice will not have the last word; there also exists the possibility of healing, recovery, and renewal of life. (De Wit and López 2013, 402–3)

## A Normative and Critical Vision Always Reinterpreted and Reappropriated

Intercultural Bible reading is not ethically neutral, and much less so when practiced in contexts of injustice and impunity—readers are engaged with one another and with the Bible as Scripture. Specifically in this case, they interacted with a gospel narrative (Luke 18:1–8) that presents Jesus as proclaimer of the good news of divine grace in the face of delayed justice and faithful perseverance. Readers realize that the good news of the nearness of the "kingdom of God" is the central symbol of Jesus's teaching, healing, and forgiving ministry. The ethical-eschatological and prophetic-utopian vision encapsulated in the biblical symbol "kingdom of God" can function as a critical principle with prophetic import for naming and denouncing injustice and oppression. It can also serve to envision an alternative reality and future with well-being, justice, and peace for all. Such vision is always both "revealed" and at the same time needing to be unveiled and reimagined: it must be (re)envisioned and (re)appropriated contextually, interculturally, and intercontextually again and again, through an open-ended hermeneutical and discerning process:

> Where cultural studies speak of a third-culture perspective, we will use this term in a hermeneutical-religious sense and then analyze whether the learning process has enriched the group or broadened its horizon. Has the faith of the group become deeper? Are people freer with respect to their own faith tradition? Is there a richer, more liberating way of reading and reflecting on one's own faith? Has a new perspective developed, nourished by the interaction with the partner group and the longing for a new "third" look at the text and the praxes manifested in the text?... The Third Perspective immediately becomes ethically charged: it becomes a Third Faith Perspective nourished by the longing for the kingdom of God. It is a perspective that is also eschatologically loaded and within which power differential (asymmetry, inequality), premature death, and oppression are determinative. Concepts such as justice, guilt, love, liberation, one's neighbor, and redemption carry the discussion on the differences. (De Wit 2012, 29–30)

## Pneumatology: A View of the Spirit's Participation in the Hermeneutical Process

From the early days of the church, Christians have assumed and somehow experienced the participation or partnership of the Divine (Spirit of God or Holy Spirit) in the process of interpreting the Bible contextually. This observation is nicely documented in the account of the Jerusalem council in Acts 15:1–35, which itself can be viewed as a case study in intercultural hermeneutics.

Acts 15:1–35 provides a richly textured, prototypical illustration of the early church doing practical theology. The initial success of the gentile mission generated new questions pertaining to requisites for belonging to the church, and thus for salvation itself. Conflict, debate, and dissent occurred; a genuine threat to the life of the church was felt and a meeting was called in which Paul, Barnabas, and others had the opportunity to tell their story, while others insisted that converted male gentiles be circumcised and keep the law of Moses (v. 5). We are told that this was the concern of the whole church (vv. 4, 12, 22), even though the leaders had a special role to play: Peter and James spoke persuasively, and the apostles and the elders made significant choices with the consent of the whole church (vv. 6, 22). In this, a reinterpretation of Scripture provided key foundational input and orientation; indeed, a connection was explicitly made between the perceived work of the Holy Spirit, personal testimony, and the message received in the words from three prophets (vv. 15–18). The discernment process was experienced as Spirit led and culminated in a unanimous decision (v. 25) to send Judas and Silas as special representatives "to the believers of Gentile origin in Antioch and Syria and Cilicia" (v. 23) with a letter of accord. The letter clarified the scope of key expectations concerning gentiles in keeping with Mosaic law (vv. 20, 29) and reaffirmed the work of Paul and Barnabas. Luke's narrative also tells us that the Antioch believers rejoiced at the exhortation and were encouraged and strengthened by Judas and Silas (vv. 31–32). The very presence of converted gentiles became a gift to the early church as an opportunity to challenge and enrich its practical theological imagination.

In somewhat similar manner, the empirical material from the Latin American study includes numerous references to the readers' sense of communion with God as they long for healing and justice. Witness some of the testimonies from the study (De Wit and López 2013):

Maruja: "Truly, life is sometimes hard and one has to endure times of need and pain; and all of that can be overcome only with God's help, by recalling scripture in which God encourages, supports, and gives us hope." (418)

Susana: "The message we received from our brothers and sisters from North San Salvador is so wonderful because it helps us experience the presence of Father God in all the groups and Christian communities no matter how far apart we find ourselves." (418)

Jaime: "the Word of God is hope; how capable [they are] to read the Gospel of Luke!; in spite of their poverty they can take time to reflect, to be together, and to honor our Lord." (419)

Lidy Rocío: "I'm amazed at the Word of our Lord that comes to us and to the whole world, and everybody according to their experiences and relationship with God can continue to interpret it." (419)

Many readers do not necessarily refer to the Holy Spirit or the Spirit of God as such, but speak of experiencing the very presence of God in their lives, especially as they practice communal and intercultural reading of the Bible with a partner group. They offer testimonies of a deeply felt, immanent reality that illustrates the Pauline understanding that the presence of the Spirit is the reality of God's personal presence in the midst of the people. For Paul, the Spirit is always understood in personal terms, as God's own personal presence in people's lives, individually and corporately, not some impersonal force or influence (see Fee 1994, ch. 13).

## Conclusion

The empirical study of intercultural Bible reading in Latin American contexts of impunity provides documented evidence of the potentially transformative power of thus engaging Scripture contextually as well as intercontextually as two inseparable dimensions of the same process. In addition to the contributions from biblical, philosophical, and social-science perspectives and analyses, practical theology offers a unique point of view and considerable resources to deal with several key questions raised by the intercultural Bible reading project's stated aim of fostering transformation. This essay seeks to demonstrate that a practical-theological approach is necessary, although by no means sufficient, in regard to the following areas: the unique psychosocial and spiritual dynamics of faith communities engaged in Bible reading; the special relationship that is engendered between "ordinary readers" and the sacred text; the dynamics of intercultural and intercontextual communication mediated by the sacred text; the very understanding of transformation as a processes of systemic change; and the anthropological, epistemological, and theological issues that any comprehensive study must address. In the last analysis, however, those "ordinary readers" can joyfully receive the fruits of their endeavors as a blessing of wisdom and grace. We, the biblical scholars, scientists, and practical theologians, have the opportunity and the privilege in turn to be blessed by them.

## References

Boff, Leonardo, and Clodovis Boff. 1987. *Introducing Liberation Theology.* Maryknoll, NY: Orbis.

Brown, Robert McAfee. 1984. *Unexpected News: Reading the Bible with Third World Eyes.* Philadelphia: Westminster.

Ekblad, Bob. 2006. *Reading the Bible with the Damned.* Louisville: Westminster John Knox.

Fee, Gordon D. 1994. *God's Empowering Presence.* Peabody, MA: Hendrickson.

Hall, Douglas John. 2013. *What Christianity Is Not: An Exercise in "Negative Theology."* Eugene, OR: Cascade.

Kim, Yung Suk. 2013. *A Transformative Reading of the Bible: Explorations of Holistic Human Transformation.* Eugene, OR: Cascade.

Mesters, Carlos. 1984. *Flor sin defensa: Una explicación de la biblia a la luz del pueblo.* Bogotá: Clar.

Osmer, Richard R. 2008. *Practical Theology: An Introduction.* Grand Rapids: Eerdmans.

Schipani, Daniel S. 2013. "The Heart of the Matter: Engaging the *Spirit* in Spiritual Care." Pages 149–66 in *Multifaith Views in Spiritual Care.* Edited by Daniel S. Schipani. Kitchener: Pandora.

Smith, Wilfred Cantwell. 1993. *What Is Scripture?* Minneapolis: Fortress.

West, Gerald. 1999. *The Academy of the Poor: Toward a Dialogical Reading of the Bible.* Sheffield: Sheffield Academic.

Wink, Walter. 1980. *Transforming Bible Study.* Nashville: Abingdon.

———. 1984. *Naming the Powers.* Philadelphia: Fortress.

———. 1986. *Unmasking the Powers.* Philadelphia: Fortress.

———. 1992. *Engaging the Powers.* Philadelphia: Fortress.

———. 2003. *Jesus and Nonviolence: A Third Way.* Philadelphia: Fortress.

———. 2010. *The Bible in Human Transformation: Toward a New Paradigm for Biblical Study.* Philadelphia: Fortress.

Wit, Hans de. 2012. *Empirical Hermeneutics, Interculturality, and Holy Scripture.* Intercultural Biblical Hermeneutics Series 1. Elkhart, IN: Institute of Mennonite Studies.

Wit, Hans de, Louis Jonker, Marleen Kool, and Daniel Schipani, eds. 2004. *Through the Eyes of Another: Intercultural Reading of the Bible.* Elkhart, IN: Institute of Mennonite Studies.

Wit, Hans de, and Edgar López, eds. 2013. *Lectura intercultural de la Biblia en contextos de impunidad en América Latina.* Bogotá: Pontificia Universidad Javeriana.

# 5

## TOWARD TRANSFORMATION:
## FACTORS IN TRANSFORMATIVE READING

*Danie C. van Zyl*

### About Transformation

Since its inception, the intercultural Bible reading project had a dual aim: to serve the academic community with insight in the way ordinary readers read the Bible and to achieve a practical result in such communities through their participation (see De Wit 2004). Behind this lies the acknowledgment that grassroots communities in particular read the Bible "for life" and that their readings have (transformative) consequences. The project seeks to open up the community of readers by linking groups that would otherwise have no knowledge of one another, in the hope that this interaction would serve transformation through reading the Bible in a more comprehensive manner.

At the 2013 conference "Bible and Transformation: The Promise of Intercultural Reading of the Bible," questions were asked as to what level and under what conditions traces of transformation resulting in *shared ownership* (of the texts) and *shared agency for justice and peace* can be detected (De Wit 2013, 5). Hans de Wit continues:

> Transformation is (used as) a container concept that refers to a nearly universal but rarely empirically researched claim or presumption, namely that the encounter with Scripture results in transformation. It is a container concept because it is used undefined for all sorts of effects of Bible reading. In a typology of that interaction, stories about an immediate transformation in particular would take a prominent place. They represent as it were a typically ideal description of how many imagine the encounter between the Bible text and the reader to be. Only rarely,

however, does one follow the route of that interaction and rarely does one get an answer to the question of which components led to the fact that the Bible text became a *script for transformation* in the encounter.

To be able to discuss factors that influence transformative reading, it is necessary to be clearer on what is meant by transformation and what the project expects to happen:

> Transformation is defined according to the religious orientation one has, the hermeneutic model one uses and the expectation one has of the *effect one considers to be good* Bible reading. The more massively the concept of transformation is defined, the more unrealistic the expectation and the greater the pressure exerted on the interpretation. (De Wit 2013, 5; emphasis added)

De Wit suggests that one define transformation "more modestly and not, as is often the case in liberation theologies, as a (comprehensive and radical) social transformation" (2013, 5–6). He gives a description of how "the effects of the interaction" can be scientifically analyzed and measured (2012, 27–32), and provides a number of concrete examples from reading reports (2013, 6).

Important as it may be, the question remains whether simply asking whether "there (has) been *development and growth* or stagnation and freezing" (De Wit 2012, 27; my italics) is sufficient to justify the claim that "transformation" has taken place. Writing within a socialist, anticapitalist context, Erik Wright distinguishes three approaches or "transformative strategies" (2008, 211–14): (1) "Ruptural transformation," which brings a total *break* with the existing understanding of reality and seeks to bring about a totally new (in his case, social) structure. What he calls the metamorphosis approach is divided into "interstitial metamorphosis and symbiotic metamorphosis." (2) "Interstitial metamorphosis" seeks to grow clusters of *alternative* thinking and acting alongside what is existing. (3) "Symbiotic metamorphosis" seeks to influence existing structures, renewing and *changing* them from within.

Paulette Gabriel, making use of the theoretical framework of Jack Mezirow, describes transformation as "a reconstruction of one's perspective and worldview based on a set of altered and more inclusive basic assumptions" and argues "that deep level transformative change results in broader, more differentiated perspective, increased personal autonomy and personal efficacy, and better decision making" (Gabriel 2008, vi).

When this "fundamental change" occurs, one looks at the world differently and one's belief system is changed; this is called "perspective change" in learning theory (37). Following Mezirow, Gabriel continues:

> Most profound transformative learning occurs when individuals change their meaning perspective or schemata by using cognitive skills to examine, challenge, and potentially reformulate the assumptions and beliefs influencing their experiences of the world, emancipating them from the libidinal, linguistic, epistemic, institutional and environmental forces that limit our options and control our lives. (38)

Marcia Daszko and Sheila Sheinberg (2005, 1–5) discuss transformation on the level of beliefs, assumptions, patterns, habits, and paradigms. The *Oxford English Dictionary* describes transformation as "a marked change in form, nature, or appearance." The term is used in physics, mathematics, logic, linguistics, biology, and various social sciences. Essentially "transformation" entails a process through which something new comes into being. At a first level, this transpires in the persons involved, in terms of a totally new understanding and approach to the way in which matters are *perceived*; this may be restricted to certain aspects of an issue or reality or to a person's total understanding of life, thus involving a new worldview. The second level, which is included in most definitions of transformation, says that that personal change will result in more or less new, original *actions*. On a third level, the second level of transformation should ideally result in transformation in the society, that is, some *social change*. In terms of the intercultural reading project, De Wit formulates the latter as a "pursuit of reconciliation and justice." Whether his formulation of transformation as "*acquiring new knowledge and experience so that someone is enabled to act differently in the future*" (De Wit 2013, 6; emphasis added) meets the definition should be challenged. Transformation is more fundamental than that. David Bosch (1991, 182–85) appropriates Thomas Kuhn's theory of paradigm shifts according to which transformation occurs when individuals perceive reality *qualitatively* different from their predecessors or from their own up to that point, which brings *breaks* with previous ways of thinking, of seeing things, and thus of acting.

Social theorists point out a number of issues in the social environment that inhibit transformation (Wright 2008, 202–5, 207–9). In what follows, we look at different aspects of the intercultural Bible reading process to highlight positive and possible negative factors regarding the transformative potential of the project.

## Regarding Members of Reading Groups

Within the context of the intercultural reading project, transformation starts with the individual within the context of the reading group (Daszko and Sheinberg 2005, 1). Every group is uniquely composed of ever so many unique individuals. The unique features of individuals impact on their level of participation in the group, on the way they read and appropriate the Bible, and on their social involvement. Obvious aspects of individuality are personality type and features, level and nature of education, age and gender, and economic and social status. The sociocultural environment and family contexts and one's life experiences shape the perceptions and assumptions that color the lens through which one sees reality. A person's "meaning perspective functions as a structure of assumptions with which each of us uniquely sees the world and which creates the context in which we actively or mindlessly assimilate and integrate experience" (Gabriel 2008, 37). One spontaneously perceives and interprets new information from the perspective of one's acquired frame of reference and integrates it within the existing network of beliefs. Usually new information is rationalized to fit and confirm existing assumptions (Zimbardo and Leippe 1991, 204–15). These assumptions are more than attitudes, simple likes, and dislikes. They form the basic value system held by a person that sometimes consciously, but more often unconsciously, inform one's perspectives, the way one sees and handles matters (Wright 2008, 192–99). It is only when these integrated meaning perspectives, or "schemata," are shaken and start to change that one can speak of transformation (Gabriel 2008, 37). In psychology many volumes have been published on attitudes and attitude change. Although the way the concept is handled often comes close to the more fundamental level of values and worldview (Bohner and Wänke 2002, 3–9, 50–61), it is seldom explicitly dealt with (Zimbardo and Leippe 1991, 215–17).

Due to different influences, some individuals are "intrinsically" skeptical of the status quo, or at least susceptible to change, while others are more conservative and even fundamentalist. Within the context of the intercultural Bible reading project, this observation should be taken seriously. The type of communication into which most Bible readers are socialized is what Paulo Freire (2000, 72–73) calls "banking," that is, simply receiving information from outside. In church they are authoritatively told what the truth (of God!) is. This unquestioned acceptance of external authority inhibits critical awareness, which could make transformation difficult. Many grassroots Bible reading groups have sprung up in exactly such ecclesial contexts, with the result that this way of dealing with biblical texts is subconsciously continued in reading groups. In such contexts, the text is mostly held in high esteem. Readers in other contexts, who may be their partner group, have a totally different appreciation of the authority of the text. While one would expect that these attitudes toward the text would be mirrored in attitudes to social issues, the opposite is often the case.

Transformation starts to take place when the acquired frame of understanding with which a person operates begins to change. Wardekker (2002, 208–10) identifies three phases in such transformative learning: acquiring (new) knowledge, reflection on and integration thereof into one's own understanding, and critical reflection on one's position, which affects one's practices. When one is confronted with gaps or inconsistencies in one's frame of understanding, when aspects thereof are questioned, or through "consciencization" (Gabriel 2008, 37), one becomes aware of matters that previously escaped notice or caused no concern. It may happen when confronted with one's own prejudices or narrow perspectives. While this process could be triggered in many ways, a discussion group like a Bible reading group could be an ideal setting, provided it is inclusive, differentiated, and open. This process could take place over a period of time and may have less or more drastic implications for one's understanding of and approach to life (Gabriel 2008, 37; Daszko and Sheinberg 2005, 5–7). This self-critical attitude is a skill that has to be acquired and that will ideally become part of a person's habitual way of dealing with matters. This is a complex process, as is shown by Gabriel (2008, 38–39) in his discussion of Mezirow's ten phases of transformative learning, which could serve as triggers for transformation.

Although the process of transformation may develop subconsciously, especially initially, in the next phase the person seeks to integrate new perspectives, assumptions, and values into his or her existing frame of reference. In a sense, a new identity is formed over time and will motivate future actions. While this reflection and integration should happen in each individual, the context of a sympathetic discussion group clearly promotes this process (Dashtipour 2012, 1–13, 53–63).

If this integration is effectively achieved, it will result in a change of conduct—in attitudes and in the way one deals with people and with life situations. It should result in some social action in whatever relevant regard, and here again the group can play a significant role in reflecting and acting together.

## Regarding the Functioning of Reading Groups

It is clear that the group plays a pivotal role in the process of transformation. Literature on groups, the relations between individuals and the group, and the functioning and influence of groups on members abound (see Forsyth 1999, 5–20). In this regard several factors are to be highlighted. Each group is composed of unique individuals, as discussed above. Groups differ widely in terms of geographical location, culture, traditions, level of education, and things that the members of individual groups share to some extent. A particular reading group may not always consist of the same persons. Interpretation of a particular text by even the same group may differ from time to time due to a variety of factors. Recent experiences by members or in the context where the readers live, for example, may dramatically influence a reading and appropriation of the text at a particular time. Furthermore, the homogeneity or diversity within a group has a significant influence on its functioning and on approaches that may be followed. The length of time that the group is in existence has considerable influence on its functioning. Groups that are established particularly for the purpose of this project seem to be less effective in their functioning and interaction with partners than is the case with established groups (Lanser-van der Velde 2004, 288, 292).

The level of interaction within the group is a key factor to its effectiveness. Aspects mentioned in literature in this regard deal with mutual trust, solidarity, friendship, fellowship, love, and care for one another. To the extent to which a safe environment is created, members will feel free to be honest and put themselves on the line. Those who easily feel threatened or who cannot handle being challenged or criticized will withdraw at the expense of the whole exercise (Freire 2000, 83–89; Gabriel 2008, 38). Relationships of trust and openness between all members of the group can develop only over time. Power plays, domination, and egocentric behavior disrupt the free flow of ideas and perspectives and impair transformation. Depending on the spirituality of the group, prayers and songs help create an atmosphere conducive to trust and sharing.

Maximum participation and personal involvement by members of the group are essential to the growth of the individuals and of the group as such (Forsyth 1999, 69–75). Members should be considerate and beware of talking too much or unduly forcing their views on others. While frankness is important, members who may be shy or not very affirmative by nature must be encouraged to partake. Even those expressing dissident opinions should be handled in a way that they do not feel threatened or sidelined.

In order to facilitate transformation of individuals and the group, it is important to foster critical thinking. Instead of just repeating and accepting what is known and confirming the status quo, one needs a probing attitude. A questioning approach toward the biblical text, toward the opinions expressed, including one's own, and toward practices in the religious community and social context is conducive to growth. Groups that are too homogeneous will probably be quite likeminded. Diversity of gender, age, social background, and denominational background brings a variety of opinions and perspectives into the discussion that will stimulate meaningful dialogue. While some cultures are more geared to cognitive learning than others, learning for life more readily happens through experience, in interaction and participation.

Freire, an educationist who worked in a liberation struggle context in Latin America and who contributed significantly to principles of adult education, contrasts "banking learning" to "problem-posing learning" (2000, 72–87). The former approach sees life as static; it makes people passively and uncritically accept the status quo. A problem-posing approach sees life as open-ended, as something that can and should change. It involves everybody in the development of life-related practical knowledge and makes them take responsibility for life. It is empowering and fosters a critical and creative spirit that leads to transformation. Learning through probing and discovery is meaningful and life-changing; it has the potential to affect one's belief and value systems. A group in which dialogue between equal partners thrives is the ideal situation for this to happen.

## Regarding the Facilitator of Reading Groups

Alma Lanser-van der Velde, who analyzed reading reports from the first cycle of the Bible reading project from the perspective of the hermeneutical significance of group interaction, has pointed out the considerable influence that the group leader or facilitator has on the way the group interacts. She described the difference in functioning and the effect in groups of "task-oriented" as compared to "relationship-oriented" leadership styles. The first followed the guidelines of the project more or less closely and guided the group more directly (2004, 292, 295–300). The latter is closer to what Gerald West (2004, 213) suggests in terms of a facilitator "who creates conditions for the group to function as a group."

Literature on leadership styles and theories abounds. In terms of the conventional distinction between autocratic, democratic, and laissez-faire leadership models, aspects characteristic of a democratic style are most applicable to the aims of the intercultural Bible reading project. This corresponds to what Freire calls a "problem-posing" approach to learning, as contrasted to a "banking" approach (2000, 79–80). Gabriel describes this as "transformative leadership" (2008, 38–39, 200–210), which has become standard in adult education.

For effective functioning, the relationship between the leader and the members of the group is of key importance. Leadership suggests power, but for effective transformation of the members of the group, power must be shared as far as possible. The ideal is that the facilitator should have more knowledge than the members of the project—knowledge of the Bible and of interpretation, of how a group functions, and of how transformation happens. Ideally the leader should be of the same cultural background and social level as the rest of the group. Thus she or he must act as an equal among equals and, as far as possible, be regarded as such by members of the group (Lanser-van der Velde 2004, 297).

The leader/facilitator should aid free and open dialogue within the group. In a spontaneous and friendly style, she or he should take care that some members do not dominate the conversation and make sure others are not sidelined. In a subtle manner, the leader must act as a catalyst while guiding the discussion to explore new perspectives and possibilities. Instead of introducing other possibilities, it is more effective to make hypothetical suggestions or pose probing questions. Alternative readings should not be introduced too soon and must be done in such a way that stimulates further exploration and development. The leader should invite reflection by challenging members to elaborate on the meaning and consequences of their contributions. Growth and transformation can be facilitated by encouraging responses to opinions with a potential of opening new perspectives. A skilled facilitator will be able to detect gaps or inconsistencies in the reading of texts and in the arguments and conclusions reached during discussion, and carefully bring these into the discussion (West 2004, 215–24). Use of the counseling principle of reflection—"is this what we are saying?"—gives the group the opportunity to reflect on the way they have come. Through offering summarizing statements from time to time, the facilitator can help the group to reflect on what is happening and to move forward. By asking a few members at the end of sessions to give their perspectives on what has happened in the group and to point out meaningful aspects and the direction the discussion took or the conclusions reached, the facilitator can further the process of transformation.

## Regarding Intergroup Exchange

What should happen in intergroup exchange of readings is in a sense simply a continuation and extension of what happens within local reading groups. Despite the distance, the best possible level of dialogue between partner groups must be sought. Everything said above about relations within the reading group, like trust, openness, and frankness, should be fostered between groups. Partners must accept the other as equals; any feelings of superiority or inferiority, for whatever reasons, are destructive. The personal and group profiles that the partner groups exchange must therefore be as informative and relevant as possible. Wherever possible, partner groups should meet in order to come to know one another as well as possible on a social and functional level.

True dialogue must be strived for. The communication between groups must be of such a nature that the groups will be able to get as close as possible to what the other said and understand why they said it. Careful listening through close reading of the partner's report is essential. A tourist's attitude of looking to find something "interesting" or "exotic," idealizing the other group and their context, or prejudice all lead to a dead end. It is essential that groups read the reports of the other not only to understand the partner better but particularly to understand themselves better. That means that they must ask themselves what the other group brought out that they had missed, either in the text or its consequences or in probable resulting actions. The reading must help them to see gaps, alternatives, and potentials that will help them advance and grow. Not only should the text and life be seen "through the eyes of the other," but the other must act as a mirror in order to see oneself better. This way of reading promotes self-critical reflection that will lead to deeper integration and transformation. The partner can also be challenged and questioned on their reading, and the group itself should be open to be challenged in the interest of growth and transformation.

The question as to which groups are linked to one another is important. The essential principle here should be that of optimal potential for transformative interaction. Groups that are too far apart—and this does not refer per se to geographical distance—may find it difficult to really understand the other and experience transformation. On the other hand, being too similar could prove equally ineffective. A group should ask itself why it is partaking in this project in the first place—what is the motivation? The policy of allowing groups to choose a partner seems wise, though groups must be aware of their motivation for choosing a particular partner.

The choice of texts to serve as a catalyst between groups should be carefully made with the main purpose of interaction in mind. According to Wim Wardekker (2002, 204–5), for learning/transformation to be effective, participants should be able to see the relevance of the process for their lives.

A final issue in this regard is the duration of the exchange between partner groups. If too much time elapses between the different sessions of reading and receiving responses from partners, much of the dynamic of the process tends to get lost. In order to establish a relationship of mutual appreciation between groups, exchange should be not only regular but also continued over an extended period of time. It is advisable that groups repeat the reading process using other texts jointly chosen. In follow-up readings, the transformative influences of the process will become clear. It is often only by working together in this way over a fairly long period of time that positive transformation can be detected.

## Regarding Reporting and Evaluation

Perhaps the Achilles heel of the intercultural reading project lies in the manner of communication between groups. Verbatim reports of sessions give the partner direct information on what the others said. The problem is that nonverbal elements of interaction within a group cannot easily be communicated in this way. Video recordings can be helpful in this regard, though culture-specific gestures may be missed or misinterpreted by the partner group. A major factor affecting communication is the translation of the report, sometimes twice, from the local vernacular into English and again into the language of the partner group. The usual problems of translation apply. The semantic and the emotional value of words, which often conveys the deeper sense of what is being said, can hardly be captured and transferred in writing.

Other means of interpretation and communication include symbolic objects, visual arts, drama, and songs. These may succeed in communicating aspects that in a purely verbal presentation are difficult to bring

across. When these interpretations are communicated visually to the partner, be it through photos, Internet, or Skype, there are limitations. Often
these forms of interpretation and reporting are very culture specific, which
makes them prone to serious misinterpretation. Also, they tend to highlight a particular aspect of the text. While the focus may be on an aspect
that the partner group missed, the partner would not know what the original group did not see. Inevitably these have to be accompanied by some
verbal explanation.

Another issue meriting consideration is the person and function of
the reporters, those responsible for the communication between groups.
Whether the person is a member of the group could have a bearing on the
report. A member may be subjectively involved and objectivity could be
compromised; nonetheless, because of being involved closely in the process, a member might be in a better position to pick up salient motives and
nuances than would an uninvolved observer (Forsyth 1999, 29–35).

## In Conclusion

Social theories point out a number of issues in the social environment that
inhibit transformation (Wright 2008, 202–5, 207–9). The project will have
to ascertain whether it is enough to leave it to the spontaneous interaction
within groups and between groups to (by chance) address the factors that
influence transformation or whether the project needs to find means of
dealing with these more explicitly. If the aim is hermeneutical research,
then it is wise to leave groups to read as they spontaneously do and analyze the data. If the point is intercultural exchange, the focus shifts to the
interaction process and its results. In that case factors impacting interaction and communication between groups need attention. Alternatively, if
transformation is the main aim, aspects of inner-group dynamics and the
role of the facilitator are of key importance. Careful consideration has to
be given to guidelines provided in order to achieve an optimal functioning
of the intercultural reading project. Above all it is those who interpret the
reading reports who have to be mindful of those factors that influence the
process at the different levels.

## References

Bohner, Gerd, and Michaela Wänke. 2002. *Attitudes and Attitude Change.*
East Sussex: Psychology Press.

Bosch, David J. 1991. *Transforming Mission: Paradigm Shifts in Theology of Missions*. Maryknoll, NY: Orbis.

Dashtipour, Parisa. 2012. *Social Identity in Question: Construction, Subjectivity and Critique*. London: Routledge.

Daszko, Marcia, and Sheila Sheinberg. 2005. "Survival Is Optional: Only Leaders with New Knowledge Can Lead the Transformation." http://www.mdaszko.com/theoryoftransformation_final_to_short_article_apr05.pdf.

Forsyth, Donelson R. 1999. *Group Dynamics*. 3rd ed. Belmont, CA: Wadsworth.

Freire, Paulo. 2000. *Pedagogy of the Oppressed*. Translated by Myra Bergman Ramos. 30th anniversary ed. New York: Continuum.

Gabriel, Paulette. 2008. "Personal Transformation: The Relationship of Transformative Learning Experiences and Transformational Leadership." PhD diss., George Washington University. http://www.keyleadership.com/Downloads/dissertation_full_7_08.pdf.

Lanser-van der Velde, Alma. 2004. "Making Things in Common: The Group Dynamics Dimension of the Hermeneutic Process." Pages 288–303 in *Through the Eyes of Another: Intercultural Reading of the Bible*. Edited by Hans de Wit, Louis Jonker, Marleen Kool, and Daniel Schipani. Elkhart, IN: Institute of Mennonite Studies.

Wardekker, Wim. 2002. "Religieuze vorming via participatie: deelname en reflectie." Pages 197–212 in *Participerend Leren in Debat*. Edited by Chris A. M. Hermans. Amsterdam: Damon Bundel.

West, Gerald. 2004. "Artful Facilitation and Creating a Safe Interpretive Site." Pages 288–303 in *Through the Eyes of Another: Intercultural Reading of the Bible*. Edited by Hans de Wit, Louis Jonker, Marleen Kool, and Daniel Schipani. Elkhart, IN: Institute of Mennonite Studies.

Wit, Hans de. 2004. "Through the Eyes of Another: Objectives and Background." Pages 3–53 in *Through the Eyes of Another: Intercultural Reading of the Bible*. Edited by *Hans de Wit*, Louis Jonker, Marleen Kool, and Daniel Schipani. Elkhart, IN: Institute of Mennonite Studies.

———. 2012. *Empirical Hermeneutics, Interculturality and Holy Scripture*. Intercultural Biblical Hermeneutics 1. Elkhart, IN: Institute of Mennonite Studies.

———. 2013. "Bible and Transformation. The Promise of Intercultural Reading of the Bible." Conference report. Amsterdam, 17–20 February 2013.

Wright, Erik O. 2008. *Envisioning Real Utopias.* http://www.ssc.wisc. edu/~wright/ERU_files/ERU-full-manuscript.pdf.

Zimbardo, Philip G., and Micheal R. Leippe. 1991. *The Psychology of Attitude Change and Social Influence.* New York: McGraw-Hill.

# 6

## GROWING TOGETHER:
## THE BENEFITS OF INTERCULTURAL BIBLE STUDIES
## AT THE LOCAL LEVEL

*Werner Kahl*

### The Gospel and Cross-Cultural Transgressions

About one hundred years ago, in 1906, at Azusa Street Mission in Los Angeles, Christians at the margins of power shared the overpowering experience of celebrating the presence of God together as one people, in spite of the ideology of racial segregation so prominent in the United States at that time. This became one of the birthplaces of modern Pentecostalism. One chronicler of the movement, Frank Bartleman, captured that experience in the following words: "The colour line was washed away in the blood (of Jesus)" (1925, 54). The believers saw the Spirit of God at work. The phenomenon of "speaking in tongues" under the influence of the presence of the Spirit of God was initially interpreted as xenolalia, that is, speaking in foreign languages as in Acts 2, not as glossolalia, as in 1 Cor 12–14. It seemed obvious: the Spirit of God enables cross-cultural communication and an appropriate understanding of the meaning of the gospel. White opponents of the Azusa experience, however, were appalled that blacks and whites, rich and poor, women and men celebrated services together in expressive and emotional manners.

Interestingly, when the movement took root in Germany as early as 1907 during a tent evangelization meeting in the city of Kassel, the police intervened and dissolved the gathering due to spectacular emotional outbursts among those celebrating the service. The general critique of the gathering within evangelical circles was that the spirit at work was not from "above" but from "below," as indicated, for instance, by the following observation: "Die Übermittler sind meist Frauen. Das hat an verschiedenen Punkten der Bewegung dahin geführt, daß gegen die klaren Weisungen der Schrift Frauen, ja sogar junge Mädchen, leitend im Mittelpunkt der Arbeit stehen."[1]

Both Azusa and Kassel represent attempts at undermining societal power structures, be it with respect to "race"/ethnicity, class, or gender. Those who felt empowered by the Spirit of God to act, speak, and become agents of the divine mission were those who were expected to keep quiet in society and in the church. These early Pentecostal experiences can be described as actualizations of essential and widespread early Christian interpretations of the meaning of the gospel and of corresponding attempts at organizing faith communities across ethnic, cultural, and status boundaries (see, e.g., 1 Cor 1:18–31; 9:19–23; Gal 2:1–14; Philemon; Eph 2:11–22; Acts 2:42–47; 4:32–5:12; 10–15; John 4:21–24).

Galatians 3:28 poignantly expresses Paul's fundamental insight into the meaning of the gospel as the message of Christ that puts into effect the crossing of societal boundaries that divide people of different status and origin. The usual translation of the verse, however, is misleading and clouds the intended meaning: "There is neither Jew nor Greek, there is neither slave nor free, there is neither male nor female; for you are all one in Christ Jesus" (RSV). In the context of the discussion in Galatians, this rendering does not make good sense. For in Antioch (Gal 2:11–21), as in the Galatian communities, there were Jews and Greeks, slaves and free persons, men and women. Their distinctness is not transcended. The question at stake in these communities was how their members as Jews and Greeks, slaves and free persons, men and women could constitute a faith community that makes transparent the *dikaiosynē theou*, that is, the justice of a God who is not partial, but who, in Christ, has included all of humanity in the covenant with his people. I render verse 28 in the narrow context of verses 25–29 as follows:

(25) Since the faith has come, however, we are no longer under a custodian. (26) For you all are sons (and daughters) of God by means of the faith (that you have) in Christ Jesus. (27) For as much as you have

---

1. Giese 1987: "The mediators [of the spirit] are mostly women. This has led, at certain points of the movement, to the phenomenon that women and even young girls have featured in leading positions at center stage, against the clear instructions of Scripture" (my translation).

been baptized into Christ, you have put on Christ—(28) *be it as* Jew or Gentile, as slave or free person, as male or female. For *you* all are (joined together as) one in Christ Jesus. (29) But since *you* belong to Christ, it follows that you are progeny of Abraham, that is, heirs according to the promise.

Paul denies here, as elsewhere, any exclusivist claim to salvation or justice (see Boers 1994). This understanding of the function of the motif *dikaiosynē theou* in Paul has been emphasised by Boers and other proponents of the New Perspective on Paul.[2] According to his understanding of the gospel, the justice of God and his salvation have been extended universally. This does not require a change of identity on the part of the believers. A Greek gentile does not have to become a Jew in order to be counted as a child of God and as full member of the Christ believing community. Here each and every one is supposed to be regarded and appreciated as a child of God with his or her particular divinely bestowed gifts and abilities for the formation of the community (see Boyarin 1994). Boyarin correctly attributes the imperialist attitude of much of Christianity up to present times to an interpretation of Gal 3:28 that denies the right of others to exist as others. I would, however, contest that this is what Paul intended.

Cross-cultural processes represent a central feature of the spread of early Christianity; as such, they were the outcome of a widespread understanding of the meaning of the gospel in the first century as essentially implying the crossing of boundaries (see M. Barth 1968). My concept of an intercultural biblical hermeneutics takes into account cross-cultural processes with respect to both early Christianity and present interpretations of biblical writings. Drawing on insights of the new perspective on Paul, one can show that cross-cultural transformations lie at the very heart of much of the interpretation of the gospel or the meaning of Christ, as expressed in New Testament writings. What is at stake with respect to this understanding of the gospel is a divinely commissioned crossing of boundaries by undermining any exclusivist claims to salvation in the biblical sense, that is, to life in abundance. Interestingly, the quest for "life in abundance" in the here and now, as influenced by a reading of John 10:10b, among others, has been shared by quite different Christian movements and from quite different theological perspectives, such as classical African theology of the first generation, Pentecostalism, liberation the-

---

2. For a discussion of the social dimension of *dikaiosynē theou*, see Kahl 2013.

ology in Latin America, and World Council of Churches theology. This common interest and theological insight could serve as a basis on which to merge to a certain extent such opposing views, and it could help in identifying and overcoming problematic tendencies in interpreting the world and the gospel. Intercultural biblical hermeneutics not only reflects on this crossing of boundaries, it actually pushes for breaking through boundaries. This can be quite irritating to a traditional understanding of critical exegesis, but it constitutes the theological and ethical dimension of the academic interpretation of the Bible situated in theological faculties and seminaries. The frictions caused by the correlation of contextual interpretations from the Global South and the Global North, from both the academic and the popular levels, could, however, be productive. These frictions could lead to a more appropriate understanding of biblical writings, in conjunction with a sharpened awareness of the fact that each and every interpretation of the Bible—including Western exegesis—is context bound (see Kahl 2007).

The church, however, is not just a cross-cultural reading community. It is also, and more importantly so, supposed to be a *cross-cultural living community*. To create such communities of Christ believers with different backgrounds and dispositions in culture and status was the great challenge within the early Christian movement once it spread in the Greco-Roman world. The letters of Paul give ample witness to this challenge, which is also clearly reflected in the narrative of Luke's Acts of the Apostles (see Acts 10–15). While Paul was concerned predominantly with establishing equality between Jewish and non-Jewish believers in Christ without denying each groups' cultural particularities (see Gal 1–3), he was hesitant in demanding the abolition of slavery (see Philemon; 1 Cor 7:17–24) and negligent with respect to gender equality (1 Cor 11:2–16; 14:33b–36). His theological insight into the meaning of the gospel did not translate fully into appropriate organizational structures of Christ-believing communities. What exactly compromised his theological insight in his practical ministry remains an issue of debate. It was probably cultural and societal conventions of his time. The large narrative of Luke-Acts—of all writings of the New Testament—comes closest to describing Christ-believing communities in which cultural (Acts 11:19–30; 13:1–3) and socioeconomic differences among members were balanced (see Acts 2:42–47; 4:32–37; 5:1–11)—as an expression of the meaning of *gospel* (see also God's and Jesus's predilection toward the poor and toward women throughout the Gospel of Luke).

As in the Mediterranean world of antiquity, in Europe and in North America today we find a population marked by recent processes of global migration. The old indigenous churches in these regions have largely remained monoethnic while new churches with a predominantly or exclusively Asian, African, or Latin American membership have sprung up. The challenge today, as in early Christian times, is to create spaces for processes of mutual integration of believers of different confessions, backgrounds and walks of life, within the one church—by resisting the temptation of superimposing any one opinion or tradition on the others. An openness for such a process within the church requires a prepared-ness (1) to appreciate the other *as other*, (2) to *share* power and resources, and (3) to *change*. Cross-cultural encounters are encouraged by the very meaning of *gospel*, and the New Testament gives witness to early Christian attempts at tackling the challenge. These encounters at the local church level will eventually not leave anyone involved unchanged. The conditions for the emergence of transcultural church communities in which *equality in all respects is realized* as a reflection of the fundamental meaning of the gospel are today certainly better than they were two thousand years ago.

## Intercultural Bible Studies at the Local Level

Protestant church life in Germany within the Evangelical Church of Germany (EKD), with its roughly twenty-three million members, has been up till recently a rather monoethnic phenomenon. Within the past generation, however, the society in general has become vastly diversified with respect to ethnicity and fragmented with respect to religion and confession, due to processes of global migration. Before 1990 in Germany, there were hardly any faith communities with an Asian or African membership. With respect to the latter alone, today there are roughly one thousand such congregations with African membership and leadership, representing predominantly neo-Pentecostal, but also classical Pentecostal and so-called mainline churches, many of which have undergone processes of charismatization. The majority of members of these congregations have migrated from West African countries, especially from Ghana and Nigeria. Many of these churches celebrate their Sunday services on premises of EKD churches; however, contacts between the two congregations at the local level are still the exception. The new situation of a multiethnic population in Germany reminds us not only of the experiences and challenges of the early Christians in forming characteristic Christian faith communities marked by the ideals of equality, justice, and the appreciation of distinctness, but also of the very meaning of the gospel. In this regard, see Acts 11:26, according to which the believers in Christ from various religious and ethnic backgrounds were called "Christians" for the very first time; and Acts 13:1–3, where Paul and Barnabas are being blessed and sent out on their journeys by three persons, two of whom were Jewish migrants from Africa: Symeon, who was called Niger (Latin for "black man"), and Loukios of Cyrene. This could encourage us to find ways that allow us as Christians with different origins and traditions to grow together. Brought about by the recent processes of global migration, this is a great opportunity for the church to live up to its call.

Inspired by the work of Gerald West from South Africa, I devised a model of joint Bible studies for German and African Christians at the beginning of the new century (see West 1993; West and Dube 1996; Kahl 2002). My own focus on encounters with Christians from Africa is accidental and due to my personal history. Intercultural Bible study (IBS) can serve as a space for a qualified encounter of Christians with different cultural and confessional backgrounds who reside in the same neighborhood. It responds to the phenomenon of global migration in a responsible and distinctly Christian manner. Christians from the Global South generally represent versions of Christianity that have become mainline in their places of origin but that are not as widespread in Europe (i.e., Pentecostalism). IBS is one project that could facilitate ecumenical encounters in local settings. It seems to be an appropriate and promising way to bring Christians with various cultural and confessional backgrounds together, since the Bible, which is of fundamental importance to Christians the world over, can serve as the foundation and main reference point. Combined with the method of Bible sharing, IBS ensures that everybody can contribute his or her observations, insights, or questions, allowing for the meaning of the gospel to become actualized in the process of a Bible study where everybody, whether young or old, male or female, working person or professor, of European or African descent, is important due to his or her very presence.

A Bible sharing session could be organized according to the following steps:

(1) Liturgical entry: song and/or prayer
(2) Reading the passage around the circle of participants

(3) Listening to the passage read in one piece in different languages

(4) Meditating on the passage (with music playing in the background)

(5) Sharing of words or verses without comments

(6) Discussing the passage

(7) Summary/conclusion by the moderator

(8) Liturgical conclusion: song, prayer, blessing

A moderator guides the group through the process, making sure that no one—not even the moderator himself or herself or pastors present—dominates the conversation. If the study group consists of members of two distinct churches (e.g., German Lutheran and Ghanaian Pentecostal), the biblical passages should be chosen by the two groups equally. The method expresses the underlying conviction that each participant has a dignity to be appreciated and an opinion to be respected. The method helps to balance extreme and maybe problematic readings. IBS is first and foremost an attempt at understanding, on various levels. When conducted continuously over a period of time, this approach will not leave the participants unchanged.

IBS fulfills a variety of functions. (1) IBS could help in shaping our Christian identity as members of the worldwide church as an ecumenical body. As such, it expresses and actualizes a fundamental dimension of what the gospel means according to a good number of New Testament witnesses: God has come close so that all may be one body, that is, no one is superior to the other, and no one inferior. Everybody counts as a beloved child of God with his or her distinct perspective.

(2) IBS helps us learn about the other: his or her cultural background, tradition, social location, and spirituality. People get to know one another and respect one another in their distinctiveness. This is a challenge to everyone involved since we perceive reality and organize life in different ways. Widespread in the Global South, and especially in West Africa, is the following worldview, which clashes with that of secular Europe. Most West Africans and migrants from Africa of the first generation living in Europe see the visible world as embedded in a wider spiritual world. Therefore, problems in the visible sphere can be attributed to spiritual forces, and acts in the visible world can have spiritual repercussions. It goes without saying that among West Africans there is a wide range as to the intensity with which they reckon with the activity of spiritual forces.

Many Europeans tend to restrict reality to what can be seen and measured, often in combination with a claim of superiority in the understanding of the world. IBS could help them to consider the possibility that reality in its totality might be different from the European construction of it. Karl Barth described this problem and even the chances of ecumenical encounters in this respect about fifty years ago, long before global migration to central Europe had set in:

> Magisches Weltbild? Ob uns wohl unsere Mitchristen aus den jungen Kirchen von Asien und Afrika, die ja in dieser Sache noch von frischerer Anschauung herkommen, hier eines Tages zu Hilfe kommen könnten? Hoffen wir nur, dass sie sich unterdessen von unserem Weltbild nicht allzusehr imponieren und dann ihrerseits von der Augenkrankheit, an der wir in dieser Hinsicht leiden, anstecken lassen! (K. Barth 1976, 373)

> Magical worldview? I wonder if our fellow Christians of the young churches from Asia and Africa, whose firsthand experience in this respect is fresher, might come to our aid one day. But let us only hope that in the meantime they allow themselves not to become all too impressed by our worldview and then become infected by the ailment of sight by which we have been suffering in this respect. (my translation)

> Wir dürften es in dieser Sache mit einem der nicht seltenen Fälle zu tun haben, in denen man sagen muß, dass nicht alle, aber bestimmte unter den Menschen, denen man heute ein sogenanntes "magisches Welt-bild" zuschreibt,—allerlei zufälligen Hokuspokus abgerechnet—faktisch mehr und deutlicher gesehen haben, der Wirklichkeit in ihrem Denken und in ihrer Sprache näher waren als wir, die glücklichen Besitzer eines rational-wissenschaftlichen Weltbildes, denen die aus diesem abzule-sende klare (aber vielleicht doch nicht so ganz klare) Unterscheidung von Wahrheit und Illusion schon fast unbewusst zum Maß alles Mögli-chen und Wirklichen geworden ist.

> It seems that we are dealing here with one of the not too few cases where we have to admit that some, though not all, among those people to whom is ascribed a so-called magical worldview—once we have sub-tracted various forms of occasional hocus-pocus—have actually seen more and clearer and are closer to reality in their thinking and in their language than we, the happy owners of a rational-scientific worldview, for whom the unambiguous (or possibly not so unambiguous) distinc-tion of truth and illusion, as derived from our worldview, has become almost subconsciously the criterion of anything possible and real. (my translation)

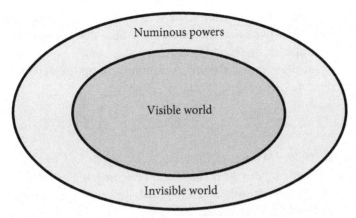

Spiritual Knowledge Systems in Sub-Saharan Africa

(3) IBS could help to balance problematic interpretations of the Bible. If in one interpretation a particular verse is being overemphasized and portrayed as representing absolute truth, it is helpful that others point to the literary context of that verse or to other biblical verses or passages that express different or even contradictory views.

(4) The whole canon of the New Testament, consisting of twenty-seven writings expressing a wide range of understandings of the meaning of Christ, illustrates both the necessity and the possibility of a contextual interpretation of what Christ or gospel may mean in ever-changing situations.

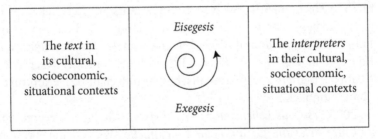

Contextual Interpretation of Scripture

(5) IBS helps to understand the necessity of the ecumenical variability of the church worldwide. It provides a space for the development of an ecumenical reading community in a local setting, which could help pave the way for an ecumenical living community. The migrants have come to stay, and many have already become naturalized inhabitants of European

countries. There is no viable alternative to a mutual and "fluid" integration. This process will be accelerated and will take shape in unforeseeable ways with the upcoming second generation.

(6) As a local, ecumenical living community, the church could serve as model of peaceful integration for the wider society.

## References

Barth, Karl. 1976. *Das christliche Leben.* Vol. 4.4 of *Die Kirchliche Dogmatik: Fragmente aus dem Nachlass, Vorlesungen 1959–1961.* Edited by Hans-Anton Drewes and Eberhard Jüngel. Gesamtausgabe 2/7. Zurich: Theologischer Verlag.

Barth, Markus. 1968. "Jews and Gentiles: The Social Character of Justification in Paul." *JES* 5:241–67.

Bartleman, Frank. 1980. *Azusa Street: The Roots of Modern-day Pentecost.* 1925. Repr., Gainesville, FL: Bridge-Logos.

Boers, Hendrikus. 1994. *The Justification of the Gentiles: Paul's Letters to the Galatians and Romans.* Peabody, MA: Hendrickson.

Boyarin, Daniel. 1994. *A Radical Jew: Paul and the Politics of Identity.* Berkeley: University of California Press.

Giese, Ernst. 1987. "Berliner Erklärung." In *Und flicken die Netze: Dokumente zur Erweckungsgeschichte des 20. Jahrhunderts.* 1909. Repr. Metzingen: Ernst Franz.

Kahl, Werner. 2002. "Dialogisches Verstehen: Chancen einer interkulturellen Hermeneutik des Neuen Testaments am Beispiel eines religionspädagogischen Projekts zu populären Bibellektüren." Pages 111–35 in *Interkulturelle Hermeneutik und lectura popular: Neuere Konzepte in Theorie und Praxis.* Edited by S. Joneleit-Oesch and M. Neubert. Beiheft zur Ökumenischen Rundschau 72. Frankfurt am Main: Lembeck.

———. 2007. *Jesus als Lebensretter: Westafrikanische Bibelinterpretationen und ihre Relevanz für die neutestamentliche Wissenschaft.* Frankfurt: Lang.

———. 2013. "Gottesgerechtigkeit und politische Kritik: Neutestamentliche Exegese angesichts der gesellschaftlichen Relevanz des Evangeliums." *ZNT* 16:2–10.

West, Gerald O. 1993. *Contextual Bible Study.* Pietermaritzburg: Cluster.

West, Gerald O., and Musa W. Dube, eds. 1996. *"Reading With": An Exploration of the Interfaith between Critical and Ordinary Readings of the Bible; African Overtures. Semeia* 73. Atlanta: Society of Biblical Literature.

PART 2

RAPE AND OUTRAGE:

CASE STUDIES ON 2 SAMUEL 13

SECTION 2.1

IN HER MEMORY:

TAMAR'S STORY IN GLOBAL PERSPECTIVE

# 7
# THE EFFECT OF CULTURAL SETTING:
## SEMANTICS, THE ROLE OF THE FATHER, AND GOSSIP
## (A DIALOGUE BETWEEN INDONESIA AND GERMANY)

*Batara Sihombing*

In this essay I focus on the effect of the combination of cultural setting, context, and personal experiences, using an intercultural exchange between two quite different reading communities. The Indonesian Metanoia group from Maumere, Flores, consisting of prisoners, read the story of the rape of Tamar together with the German partner group BibelWeltWeit (Bible World Wide). I analyze the extent to which this encounter transformed readers of both groups, looking at whether the exchange enabled the participants to become more aware of the importance of semantic conventions when dealing with issues of sexual abuse and whether this would aid in bringing about change.

## Terminology as an Expression of Cultural Differences

The Metanoia group, many of whose members are in prison for sexual crimes, decided that the theme of 2 Sam 13:1–20 is "sexual transgression between a brother and sister." This decision made the German group uncomfortable, feeling that the members of Metanoia group had softened the impact of the rape case due to their having similar backgrounds. For the German group, the story is clearly about Amnon's rape of his half-sister, Tamar, while the Metanoia members called it "sexual transgression."

In response to the German group, the Metanoia group divided into two camps. The first agreed that Amnon raped his half-sister. Quite possibly, the problem is one of terminology. While the group in Maumere expressed the case in more veiled terminology, following the Indonesian custom, the German group did so in more blunt terms, consistent with the European way. This conclusion is supported by the second Indonesian group report, which states that they did not intend to soften the rape case, but that this is the story of their own life and that was how they ended up in prison.

The problem seems to lie in the words used to designate the case—*rape* and *sexual transgression*. Are these two the same? The German group denied the similarity, while the Metanoia group maintained it. Both groups seemed to share the same judgment of the case, but expressed it in different terms. The intercultural dialogue provided the opportunity to bring a more mutual understanding of the different terms used to name the case.

## The Role of the Father in Different Cultural Settings

A theme that attracted much attention was that of David as a failed father. One member of the Metanoia group pointed out that David had no success in raising his children, but just kept the scandal out of the law courts and settled it within the family. This statement precipitated a long discussion among the German members on the difficult relation between parents and children. The German members willingly listened to the perspective of the Metanoia group. According to the German group, the education and the structure of family among the Metanoia members play a more important role than among the Germans. This might reflect the social situation in Germany, where the role of the family has become increasingly less important. One member of the German group admitted that before this sharing he viewed David as a wise man and a father who easily forgave, but due to the intercultural exchange he realized that David just let things happen. Thus the intercultural reading provided a new perspective on understanding the position of David in the story.

The Metanoia group viewed David's role from the perspective of Asian culture, where men hold important positions in most spheres and are dominant in decision making. Apparently, David made his decisions without knowing the character of his own son Amnon. David was too busy with his work as king and neglected his family. One member of the Metanoia group identified himself with David, because he had seen a problem that needed solving but did nothing. In response to this, the German group confessed that none of them had come up with such a clear and sharp self-reflection. The German group realized that their guilt lay in doing nothing, which in turn led them to feel guilty and to do the wrong things.

## Identification with the Biblical Characters

In their report, the Metanoia group focused on the question of to which God the biblical characters prayed. In this way, the religious roles and attitudes of Amnon, Absalom, Yonadab (Jonadab), David, and Tamar were brought to the surface. The German group found these answers to be highly speculative, because the story tells nothing about the religious feelings of the actors: they found that the Metanoia group was merely projecting their own ideas onto the figures in the story. In response to this, the Metanoia group was divided into two camps. The first said that they did not simply read the story, but also tried to identify with the characters and see themselves in the characters' place. Involving themselves emotionally with each of the characters made this personal rather than speculative. The story is close to their own experience—it is their story that was being narrated in the Bible. The second camp confessed to a similar sentiment in relation to the descriptions of the characters' religious attitudes, which were rooted in their own experiences. The story of the biblical characters and their own personal stories "read each other." They learned not only how to read the Bible but also how to read themselves.

What was speculative for the German group was personal for the Metanoia group. The Metanoia group was able to enter into the story, because it was their own story. They were able to express the religious feelings of the biblical characters, because this was simply expressing their own religious feelings. This identification with the characters in the story seemed to help the German members to understand that what the Metanoia group said was not mere speculation.

## The God of Yonadab

The Metanoia group held a long and heated discussion on Yonadab and his God, particularly about whether Yonadab was representative of those who view God as personally concerned with human beings. On the one hand, Yonadab believed in God and used a tactic to help Amnon that finally proved to be wrong. On the other hand, Yonadab is understood as a typically two-faced person in that his actions indicated that he did not always follow God. According to the German group, the long arguments in the discussion of the Metanoia group showed that they understood God as a God who intervenes, who organizes things concerning our lives. In contrast, the German group were of the opinion that human beings themselves organize their lives. This difference could be, it seems to me, due to living in a settled situation in a wealthy country.

The Metanoia group maintained that they feel God's presence in every difficulty they face, in the bitterness of life. This is different from the experience of the partners in Germany, whose life flows on calmly. The Metanoia group said that in Genesis God gave freedom to human beings, but the authority for any particular decision remains in the hands of God. They questioned why the German partners were unable to see God's presence in their daily lives. Indonesia is a prime nation for natural disasters—earthquakes, floods, and tsunamis. People see God in all these tragedies either in the compassion shown to survivors or in the natural disaster itself.

The differences between the contexts of the German and Indonesian groups prompted a different understanding of God's intervention and presence in their lives. It was the hope of the Metanoia group that from this discussion the German group would understand why the Metanoia group felt the presence of God in every difficulty they faced. Conversely, the German group hoped that the Metanoia group understood why the German group had a different point of view due to their situation of living in a wealthy country quite different from Indonesia.

## The Role of Gossip

The Metanoia group discussed the role of gossip in the story. Where did "that gossip about all the king's sons being killed" (2 Sam 13:30) come from? How was it possible for the story to reach the king's ears when the eyewitnesses were still on their way to report to him? It may have been spread by Yonadab, but in any case it is important in the story. The German group found the Metanoia group's interpretation of Yonadab as a talebearer to be convincing, though the topic of gossip had not arisen in their discussion. This led the German group to wonder whether gossip might play a crucial role in prison.

The Metanoia group admitted that they gossip a great deal, as they have little to do, but that they do not take it too seriously. When gossip is taken seriously, it all too often triggers problems in prison life, as there is no proof or disproof of the gossip. Since prison life is limited and enclosed, the inmates spend their time gossiping, though not every prisoner is equally intrigued by gossip: it often depends much on one's education. While gossip is not important, it fills up the time. John Prior, the facilitator of the Metanoia group says, "Gossip is a vital part of village life. Despite all problems it causes, it is very addictive!" According to his ministudy of gossip, it is an indirect way of articulating tensions in relationships. Gossip is a kind of "nature spirit" that symbolizes what we cannot control in life.

The idea that they might be addicted to gossip was an eye-opener to the Metanoia group. It is understandable that they easily caught on to the role of gossip in the story of 2 Sam 13. This innovative insight into the role of gossip in the story of 2 Sam 13 opened new dimensions to the German group to understand the role of Yonadab as a talebearer.

## Conclusion

The intercultural reading brought to light that the reader's cultural context frequently influences the way a text is understood. This provides the opportunity of being challenged by the insights from those of a different cultural context. The reading brought about new insights and influenced attitudes toward friends within the same group as well as toward friends in the partner group. Sticking to the culture and context in which they live, a group may resist accepting new ideas brought forward by other readers or be challenged to open up new perspectives on the topics that arose in the exchange.

## 8

## Reading the Text—Reading the Others—
## Reading Ourselves
## (A Dialogue between Germany and Indonesia)

*Rainer Kessler*

During the process of reading 2 Sam 13:1–22 with German and Indonesian partner groups, it became clear that the German group did more than just read the text and the response of the partner group: they indeed *read the others*, and only by discussing this point did they begin to *read themselves*.

Due to her commitment to ecumenical contacts, I asked the minister of the small village of Oberrosphe to form a German group for the reading cycle of 2011–2012. The group comprised about ten persons, all from the rural area north of Marburg, a traditional university town in central Germany; the group called themselves BibelWeltWeit (Bible World Wide). The age of the participants was between forty and eighty, all Protestants and active members of their communities. Four members of the group, including the leading persons, had theological training; the others came from diverse backgrounds. The discussions were in German, which I translated for the partner group and vice versa.

Via the Internet linking process of the intercultural reading program, we found our partner group—the Metanoia group:

The Metanoia group has sixteen members, prisoners in the local jail of Maumere town, Flores Island, eastern Indonesia. All but two are men! A majority are Catholic, a small minority Protestant (Reformed). Many are jailed for sexual offenses (rape, molestation, adultery, etc.), others for murder (problems of land or women), a few for corruption or robbery, one for male prostitution and trafficking. We have been gathering more or less weekly for the past five years—the group changing as some members are released and others incarcerated. The members come from the islands of East Nusa Tenggara.... All have small-scale farming backgrounds, though their professions, apart from farming, range from teaching and the civil service to NGOs and small-time traders. Formal education: lower high school.... We work in the national language of Bahasa Indonesia; our facilitator, English-born priest and seminary lecturer John Prior, translates our sharing into English. (see original at http://www.bible4all.org/Content/view_group.aspx?groep_id=281)

## Reading the Text

Of the two texts proposed for the reading process—the story of Tamar and the one of Jesus and Mary Magdalene—the BibelWeltWeit group chose the story of Tamar's violation in 2 Sam 13:1–22 due to its relevance today: though the story is situated in ancient times, the issue of violation is very much a present-day problem, especially within the church. The story is taken from real life, and the roles both of women and of families are important.

The German group started a close reading of the selected text. The discussion brought a number of issues to the fore. To begin with, none of the persons acting in the story is really transparent; all are ambivalent. This becomes clear by the many questions raised about the characters of the story. Did Yonadab (Jonadab), Amnon's friend and adviser, really not suspect Amnon's bad intentions? Or did he know what Amnon actually wanted? Did he perhaps even consciously want to harm Amnon by bringing him into this situation? With regard to Amnon, did he initially really love Tamar, or does what the text calls "love" only refer to his sexual desire? David, too, plays a dubious role. Why does he send Tamar to Amnon? The group totally denounced his reaction after the rape: when David as the king becomes "very angry," he has to act; doing nothing is no solution. Absalom also acts in an ambivalent manner. He shelters his sister and even later avenges her, but he also downplays the affair. His later revenge is ambivalent as well. It is not clear whether Absalom acts for the benefit of his sister or whether he only wants to remove the successor to the throne so that he himself becomes the next crown prince.

The person discussed the most was Tamar. Is she really the only unequivocally "good" person in the story? Is she "good" because she is the victim? If we look at Tamar as a "good" person, do we not lock her up in the role of the victim? Could Tamar have acted differently at the beginning? The text states that Tamar was a virgin. Did she not perhaps expect an erotic adventure? Could she have contradicted the orders of David to go into the house of her (half-)brother? Was this a realistic option for a woman in a patriarchal society?

The group appreciated the fact that Tamar made a reasonable proposal to solve the conflict before it came to violation. All agreed that after the rape she made things public by running outside crying. After the rape she was paralyzed and had no means of resisting the ensuing developments. Tamar was traumatized, perhaps even unable to feel anger and no longer able to resist. The members of the group suffered together with Tamar.

The group then asked how the story made them feel. Words like *depressive* or *nightmarish* were used. These feelings arose from the fact that the story at every point could have developed in a different way; there could have been an alternative. Nothing in the story was mere fate. Everything depended on the decisions taken by the actors.

At the next meeting the group tried to get closer to the actors by interviewing them. Three members of the group became Yonadab, Amnon, and Absalom. The interviews confirmed the ambivalence in the characters of each of these figures.

After the interviews, the group discussed why this story is in the Bible. They concluded that it is a sort of memorial to Tamar. Especially the interview with Amnon demonstrated that: though she is the victim, Tamar is the only strong person in the story. Criticizing Amnon, she assumes the role of the prophet Nathan in the story of David's adultery with Bathsheba and his killing of her husband Uriah. In the story of 2 Sam 13 males are the active persons, and Tamar comes from the outside. Coming in from the outside is exactly the role of the prophet in 2 Sam 11–12.

The last meeting before linking up with the Metanoia group was dedicated to the one question that remained open from the first meeting: Where is God in the story? God is not mentioned. What does this mean? Where in the story could God find a place? In the preceding chapter, God announced judgment on the house of David because of his adultery and murder: "Now therefore the sword shall never depart from your house" (2 Sam 12:10). This becomes reality. God does not intervene directly. The story belongs to the traditions in the Hebrew Bible that are critical of the monarchy (1 Sam 8).

God does not act directly in this story, nor do the actors seek contact with God. No one prays. They all only look out for themselves. No one admits making a mistake; no one pleads guilty. Though all the actors had alternatives, but they did not take them. That is their guilt.

At the end, the group was looking forward to reading the comments of the far-away partners from Indonesia.

## Reading the Others

The German group met three times to discuss the reports of the Metanoia group from Indonesia. In the following paragraphs, I articulate my personal impressions based on the group's utterances while reading the reading report from Indonesia.

The group's attitude toward the report from Indonesia manifested a mixture of curiosity and gratefulness, as well as reflected upon the idea of being a neutral observer or analyst of the partner group's reading. The group was curious about the situation of the members of the Metanoia group. How do they live in prison? How long have they been there, and how long will they be incarcerated? Why are there two women in the group? The German group was also thankful for the partner's reading. It opened their eyes to new aspects of the text that they had not thought of. Eventually, the reading of the partner group provoked new discussions about their own situation in the light of the partner's reading, for example, the impact of traditional (family) structures.

The third aspect (the idea of being a neutral observer of the other's reading), however, was the most difficult. Sometimes it was as though the group found itself in the role of having to analyze the partner's reading from a neutral point of view. The (virtual) dialogue with the group was in danger of being replaced by an analysis of the partner's reading as objective observers. It was necessary at times for the facilitator to intervene in the process. True dialogue is characterized by questions like: What do they read? What can we learn from their reading? Where do we disagree with their reading? The attitude of analysis is characterized by the questions like: Why do they read the way they read? Are we able to find out the deeper reasons for their utterances? This attitude can reflect a lack of respect for the partners, though it could also indicate a sincere wish to understand the partners better. However, in this case it indeed appeared to be more like a feeling of superiority.

Nonetheless, the danger of replacing the dialogue by analysis did not have the upper hand in the meetings. The dominant feelings were curiosity and thankfulness, though sometimes intermingled with the third aspect. The latter was strengthened by the German group knowing from the Internet presentation of the Indonesian partner group that some of the prisoners were jailed for sexual offenses, even rape, as in the story of Tamar. How would a rapist read a story about the violation of a girl? Would he defend himself? Would he try to avoid the question? It seems evident that questions like these are inevitable. At the same time, however, they are ethically problematic. The members of the partner group were then no longer treated as real partners with their personal points of view, but became objects of curiosity.

An example can serve as illustration. The German group was irritated by reading in the report from the Indonesian group: "The group, many of whom are in prison for sexual crimes, decided that the theme of the passage was 'sexual transgression between a brother and sister.'" The German readers rebutted: "Is the story not about rape, a violation committed by a brother against his half-sister, and not only about 'sexual transgression between a brother and sister'?" To the German group, this description sounded like an attempt to soften the impact of the story. They suspected that this was motivated by the fact that many of them "are in prison for sexual crimes." However, the question remains: what gave the German readers the right to draw such conclusions?

Only after having discussed these ethical problems was the group able to progress to benefiting from the partners' readings. By starting to read the text through the eyes of the other, they could learn about themselves. Only then could the reading process come to a good conclusion.

## Reading Ourselves

When the group began to read the text through the eyes of the partners, they began to question why they themselves read the text the way they did. There are three points in which the German group learned much about themselves.

The first point is the role of family structures. When the German group read the Indonesian reports, they noticed that they themselves had not discussed David's role as a father, while the partners' report stressed David's role as a father who had failed in raising his children. One member remarked: "Before the discussion of the reports from Indonesia, I saw David as a wise man who is ready to forgive. But now I have learned that he simply is a man who lets things be." Generally, the German group noticed that family constellations played a much more important role for the Indonesian partners than they did for Germans. This might reflect the social situation in Germany, where the role of family is increasingly less important due to various factors such as the emancipation of women and older children, the necessity of mobility for jobs, and a high income that allows for independent housing. These factors may not exist in Indonesia.

A second point that the German group learned from the partners was the emphasis on the dark sides within themselves. Generally, the German group appreciated that the partners discussed not only the dark sides of the characters in the story, but also the dark sides within themselves. The German group noticed that they themselves had avoided this question. Some of the partners, for example, detected the "Yonadab within themselves": "I also recognize elements of Yonadab within me, when I prefer to provoke and incite another for my own benefit, when I use a friend to smooth the way for my own purpose." Another said about David: "David is myself when I see a situation that needs putting right and yet I do nothing." No one in the German group had ever made such a clearly self-critical statement, and the group was thankful to the partners for opening their eyes.

The last point concerned God's role within the story. The members of the Indonesian group were asked by their facilitator to answer the question: "What God do the biblical characters pray to?" The answers were enlightening:

> In Tamar's eyes God is her father, her helper; this is the God she believes in and worships by doing good and by not sinning.... Tamar is sure that God is her advocate and so, when face to face with insuperable problems she does not give up or lose hope.... Tamar's whole life is in God's hands. Whatever she experiences or suffers, she is convinced, is part of God's plan. Whatever the predicament, she is in God's hands.

The German group found readings like these to be mainly speculative, because the story tells nothing about the religious feelings of the actors. Though they did not deny the positive possibilities seen by their Indonesian partners, the German group was more ambivalent. They could imagine that perhaps the situation was quite different with Tamar: she could just as easily been seen as having fallen into depression and despair. The end of the story is open to both possibilities.

The greater role of family in the thinking of the Indonesian group has already been explained by the different social situations in the two cultures. Maybe this is also true for the differing views on Tamar's future after her violation. It is generally agreed that for solving conflicts traditional societies often have mechanisms that have been lost in more industrialized societies. Perhaps it is true that in a Western type of society, characterized by individualism and a lack of social networks, a victim of violence runs a greater risk of isolation and consequent depression and despair. Perhaps a more traditional society has the means to help such a person, but this idea may also be a Western romanticizing of traditional societies. The reading of two groups in the frame of the intercultural Bible reading project cannot answer the question. It is, however, important to have raised the issue.

In spite of some critical remarks of the German group on various readings of the Indonesian partners, they admitted learning much about themselves from the Indonesian partners' reading. The Indonesians said they had had a "heated discussion on Yonadab and his God." The Germans wondered how much the Indonesians had found out about this person who plays only a marginal role in the biblical story.

The differences between the readings were conspicuous and caused the Germans to take a fresh look at their own situation and beliefs. For the Indonesian readers, God is much more an intervening God who organizes things concerning their lives. According to the German reading, it is mainly we ourselves who organize things. This understanding may be due to the more settled context of the German group in a wealthy country, where one is able to cope with the problems of daily life. This situation has perhaps made them blind to the things that they in fact cannot manage, and perhaps blind to God's possibilities.

After having overcome the ethical problems of analyzing instead of dialoguing, the German group learned to read through the eyes of the others and thus had their own eyes opened.

# 9

## PERSONAL APPLICATION, SOCIAL JUSTICE, AND SOCIAL TRANSFORMATION (A DIALOGUE BETWEEN MYANMAR AND THE NETHERLANDS)

*La Rip Marip*

A reading group from Myanmar consisting of participants from several different tribes was linked with a Dutch group from a rather homogeneous village near Amsterdam, the Netherlands. Together they read the story of 2 Sam 13. This essay shows how enormous the differences between both contexts and both groups are. It also shows how determinative the sociopolitical context, and awareness thereof, can be for Bible reading. Is the exchange process able to point to more than differences? Can common ground be found going beyond those differences? Can the connection between two separate local groups lead to more global awareness? Is shared agency for social justice possible if differences are so deep?

Myanmar theological students and Protestant Christians from Ouderkerk aan de Amstel, the Netherlands, were engaged in an intercultural dialogue on 2 Sam 13 at the same time that the former military leaders of Myanmar were transforming their military ruling system into the democratic parliamentary system. In this transitional period, many problems, old and new, created instability and disharmony in the country, including poverty, low level of education, joblessness, opium poppy cultivation, drugs and human trafficking, exploitation, injustice, ethnic conflicts, fighting, wars, refugees and internally displaced persons, rape, torture, murder, killings, foreign investments that cause land confiscation and abuse of natural resources, and environmental problems. The problem of ethnic conflicts is the oldest and most heated issue among these, having begun when the Union of Burma (now Union of Myanmar) gained its independence from the United Kingdom in 1948. The process of peace and reconciliation is still ongoing. People are demanding justice that would guarantee a long-lasting peace in Myanmar.

The Union of Myanmar is a beautiful country both in nature and in culture. It produces jade, gold, hydropower, timber, ruby, petroleum, coal, natural gas, pearl, copper, lead, and many other natural resources. Culturally, there are 135 official ethnic groups in Myanmar. They are grouped into eight major national ethnic races: Kachin, Kayah, Kayin, Chin, Bamar, Mon, Rakhine, and Shan. Fortunately, the group of Myanmar theological students was formed with eight people from Kachin, Kayin, Chin, Bamar, Shan, Lisu, Wa, and Akha ethnic groups, each with its own language, history, and culture. The reading group can thus be said to represent the ethnic peoples of the Union of Myanmar.

In contrast, the Dutch group, comprising ten members, did not mention ethnic information in their reading report, probably because all members are Dutch, though the Netherlands, like Myanmar, also has ethnic and religious diversity. That the Dutch partner group did not mention ethnic conflicts in their group portrait suggests that there are no social conflicts among the ethnic groups in the Netherlands and that the country is secure, peaceful, and harmonious.

In terms of religious diversity, the Netherlands has Christians, Muslims, Buddhists, Hindus, and other religious groups, as well as nonreligious groups. While 50 percent of the population practice Christianity in the Netherlands, 89 percent of the Myanmar population practice Buddhism. Myanmar has Buddhism, Christianity, Islam, Hinduism, Spiritualism, Judaism, and other religions.

Both the Myanmar and the Dutch groups live in a multicultural world; however, the Myanmar theological students live in the poor, unstable, unjust, and corrupt developing country, whereas the Dutch group live in a secure and stable, rich country. In the Dutch group, there is no hint of social injustice or poverty, while such social problems are common issues in the Myanmar group. These two groups read 2 Sam 13 together from their respective different worlds, and both drew out of it a message of social justice for social transformation.

In the following, I will discuss how the three components of text, reader, and the other reader interact in the process of communal, intercultural reading that strives for personal and social transformation.

## Personal Application and Social Justice

In order to achieve the goal of social justice, liberation, and personal transformation, the readers should have a desire to personally apply the passage from the biblical text. The Dutch group found the text strange. None of them had ever heard about the story of 2 Sam 13. One reader said, "We don't know this passage either from our youth or from a sermon." A woman searched for the text in a children's Bible and could not find it. How could the Dutch group interact with the text? How could their reading bring about social justice?

The members of the Dutch group approached the text from three perspectives: from the perspective of someone in the biblical period, from the author's perspective, and from a modern perspective. This produced three different meanings of the text.

Viewing the text from the perspective of someone from biblical times, a man found the story of Amnon and Tamar to be an affair between a brother and a sister: "Abide by the laws of Israel, the laws of Moses. Then you can have sex with your half-sister if you ask her." According to a woman, "from the perspective of that time it is not an incestuous story: marriage between brother and sister was permitted. However, it is a story about rape. It was of little importance what women thought of it."

Viewing the text from the perspective of the author, some members highlighted the words *love* and *hatred*. A woman noticed that *hatred* occurred much more frequently than *love*. The group then applied psychology to their reading and observed Amnon's lust and hatred for Tamar and Absalom's hatred for Amnon. They clarified the notions of love and lust so that they did not see any "love" in this story, concluding that the story was not about rape, but about "Absalom's revenge on Amnon's lust." A woman said that "in the end Amnon will pay the price for this behavior: Absalom will have his revenge."

Finally, the group approached the text from a modern perspective. This final approach to the text involved a personal application of the leading question about what we learn from the Bible. Their desire to find a personal application recurs several times in their reading report. All agreed that what had happened in the story could still happen in modern life, but that there were differences between the biblical story and modern life. In the story, Tamar publicly put ashes on her head when she was deflowered; she tore her virgin dress, put her hand on her head, and cried aloud as she went away. In contrast, people in a modern context would keep silent about rape. Though the Dutch group did not use the word *justice* directly in their report, they concluded that the perpetrator would not go unpunished, as Amnon did at first, and the victim of rape was to be revenged, as Absalom did later. They identified with Absalom, as they assumed that his action brought justice in the end. The Dutch group concluded that the theme of justice was the contribution the text could make to real life: "Most of us think it is possible to make a sermon about this subject, but we realize that it will not be possible to do so in every church in the Netherlands yet." Their concern had to do with the presence of children in the congregation—they did not want to scare the children. They themselves had never before heard a sermon on this kind of passage. Nevertheless, it would be possible to make a sermon for any congregation as long as it focuses on social justice.

## Culture and Social Justice

Without understanding the other readers' cultural background, one will not achieve social justice, liberation, and personal transformation during the reading process. The necessity of understanding the partner group's cultural background becomes evident from the Myanmar group's interpretation of 2 Sam 13.

The Myanmar group approached the Scripture liturgically. They sang a song and prayed before they read the text. They found 2 Sam 13 to be about the rape of Tamar, because Amnon forced Tamar, although Tamar appealed to him repeatedly. The group sympathized with Tamar, because she was helpless. Even her father kept silent about her case. Her brother also silenced her. She publicly showed signs of sorrow, but her suffering was suppressed by the three powerful males around her: the crown prince Amnon, King David, and the handsome prince Absalom. The three males did not take any immediate proper action on Tamar's behalf. The Myanmar group saw the suppression of Tamar's suffering as the inattentive behavior of the powerful: "At this point, we feel that authoritative people give very little attention to those who are suffering." The Myanmar group identified with Tamar as the victim of rape. Tamar's life became their life. This identification created the opportunity for reading and personal transformation to go side by side.

In their interaction with the story, the Myanmar group thought of three possible psychological reasons for rape. First, it was a bad consequence of David's polygamy: David had taken many women as wives so that Amnon himself lacked a feeling of family spirit; this allowed him the room to sexually abuse his sister. Second, David himself committed adultery, and Amnon followed in his father's footsteps and raped Tamar. The group quoted a saying, "As mother crab cannot walk straight, the children crabs cannot either." Third, Amnon raped Tamar, because in his isolated palace Amnon might not have seen other beautiful women besides Tamar.

It is interesting to pursue why the Myanmar group interacted with the text in this way, for their response to the text appears to reflect their culture. For instance, the successive military rulers in Myanmar fenced off their military compounds and mostly lived separated from ordinary people. This helps one understand why the Myanmar group imagined the social world of King David's family in a similar fashion and why the Myanmar group identified with Tamar.

The cultural background of the Myanmar theological students, coming from different geographical locations and from different ethnic groups, will help in understanding their reading of the text.

One reader is a Lisu woman who lives in Mogok of Mandalay Division, where ruby, jade, gold, and lumber are produced. In spite of these riches, most of her native people are poor and with little education. She said that the businesses were monopolized by the military government and tycoons who enjoy a close relationship with the government. She saw herself as one of the powerless among her people, which led her to identify with the victim in the story.

Another reader, who belongs to the Shan ethnic group and lives in Namsang, said that his native village produced teak for export to Thailand by foreign logging companies, though the native people gained no benefit from the business. Exploitation and poverty are not uncommon in his area. In addition, his region is situated near the well-known Golden Triangle so that opium growing, drug trafficking, and the low level of education force many youths to leave their native regions. Another woman, who belongs to the Wa ethnic group, and another man, who belongs to the Akha ethnic group, also share the same experiences, as their people live around the Golden Triangle.

A woman belonging to the Karen ethnic group said, "Because of gas pipeline projects conducted by some companies, the native people [of Karen State] are forced to leave their homes and lands." During the civil war between the military government and the armed Karen ethnic group, hundreds of Karen women were raped by the government troops. In fact, many ethnic women had been raped by the military personnel in civil wars in ethnic areas. Karen, Shan, and Kachin women's organizations, for instance, have documented hundreds of rape cases perpetrated by the military. Many ordinary people sympathized with the victims of rape during the civil wars.

A reader belonging to the Kachin ethnic group said that "this year is a year of sorrow for the Kachin people as they are struggling for survival under the fearful war." Thousands of Kachin people had to flee their homes, because the government troops burned them down, arrested many Kachin people, and raped dozens of Kachin women, even inside church buildings. He also said that although the Kachin state produced jade, gold, and other natural resources, the native people benefited little. The Kachins suffer from war, rape, destruction, exploitation, internal displacement, drug abuse, HIV, low level of education, and environmental crisis.

A man of the Chin ethnic group, coming from Chin State, said that Chin regions did not produce any natural resources or good crops. Due to the poverty and the exploitation by the Myanmar military personnel, who often forced Chin people to carry food and weapons up to India border, many Chin had gone abroad for a better future.

A woman of the Bamar ethnic group, the culturally and politically dominant ethnic group in Myanmar, said, "I am very sad when many ethnic people assume all Bamars are members of the military government and Buddhists. Actually, not all Bamar people belong to the military; most of the Bamar people are also suffering from many kinds of exploitation as well."

The Myanmar group identification with Tamar is clear. Like Tamar, they were suffering from various forms of exploitation. As Tamar's voice was ignored, so the voices of the Myanmar ethnic people are largely ignored by their government and, until relatively recently, by the international community. Tamar was expelled by Amnon after he had satisfied his own lust. Likewise, the ethnic people are systematically forced to leave their regions. The natural resources from the ethnic areas are taken by the powerful—their land is raped. Physically, many women were raped during civil wars. Metaphorically, all the people and their ethnic rights are abused. Amnon abused Tamar and took no responsibility. Likewise, the military government abused the ethnic groups and took no responsibility, as stated in the reading report:

> Similarly, citizens of Myanmar are abused and exploited. Metaphorically, all males in this story represent the powerful people in Myanmar today. The victim, Tamar, represents the powerless. According to the Bible, Tamar was a virgin and a very beautiful lady. It is her virginity and beauty

that made her a victim of rape. Similarly, ethnic groups in Myanmar are being exploited in many ways for their invaluable natural resources.

The group said their life was very painful, similar to what Tamar had suffered. The story of Tamar became their life story. No matter whether they were male or female, they felt like Tamar. This brought about a kind of personal transformation.

Their partner group also noticed these points. In the second reading report of the Dutch group, a man said, "There is a clear division in society in Myanmar, and besides they are abused as laborers." A woman also shared her experience when visiting Myanmar where she saw how the people lived in fear: people could not speak freely.

What did interaction between the text, the readers, culture, and the other readers bring about? A woman of the Dutch group said, "The solidarity with the people is apparent in the report from Myanmar. We know that, too, don't we? We could emphasize it more."

At the end of this project, the Dutch group collected €500 and sent it to the Myanmar partner group as the token of their solidarity. When the Dutch partner group sent the money, another ethnic conflict was taking place, starting after a Buddhist woman was gang-raped by three Muslims in Rakhaing State. Nearly a hundred people were killed. Hundreds of houses were burned. Ten thousand people fled from their homes. The Myanmar Institute of Theology and other seminaries in Yangon held a peace prayer service in Yangon. The service collected a donation for Internally Displaced Persons (IDP) in Rakhaing State and Kachin State. The facilitator of the Myanmar group wrote a letter to the Dutch partner group saying, "We divided your gift into three portions. Two portions have been donated to Internal Displaced Persons in Kachin State and Rakhaing State. We spent the third portion. We bought some books that are the most valuable for our future ministry." The Dutch action was noted as an action for social justice, liberation, and social transformation, however modest in extent. When the other readers understand the partner group's cultural background, social justice, liberation, and personal transformation can be achieved.

## Conclusion

In this intercultural Bible reading of 2 Sam 13, both groups discovered injustice and abuse of power in their intercultural dialogue, although their approaches and applications were different. The Myanmar group related their Bible reading and application to their whole community, whereas the Dutch group related their Bible study to individuals. Nevertheless, both groups exchanged their perspectives on social justice. The exchange of cultural information took place in the final phase of this intercultural Bible reading process. The groups' desire to apply the text and to understand the other's culture led them to achieve something concrete toward the goal of understanding biblical truth and achieving social justice, even though the methodology of the groups differed in the process of intercultural Bible reading.

## 10

# "Baby, It's Cold Outside": Coercive and Persuasive Discourse and Hegemony (A Dialogue between the United States and the Netherlands)

*Jeff Moore*

> When an individual tells a lie, it's an individual lie. When an institution
> tells a lie, it becomes a conspiracy that changes the course of a community.
> —Dan Jackson (2014)

"What happens when Christians from radically different cultures and situations read the same Bible story and start talking about it with each other?" (De Wit 2004, 4). This question has many possible answers, most of which must be answered from within the contexts of particular groups engaged in particular readings. I propose here to provide some responses to the more specific question, "What happened when Christians from radically different cultures and situations read the story of the rape of Tamar in 2 Sam 13?"

Four primary issues arose in the course of this study. The first was that of *solidarity*. The women of the group with which I read felt and voiced the power of reading a challenging text with one another and with a group of women they had never met. The second was the importance of *translation*. Through reading with and reporting to a group whose primary language was different from our own, we were given interpretive clues that we might not have seen otherwise. The third issue was *hegemony*. In the course of the study the women began to name their intuitions in ways that began to unmask themes in the text and in their own context. The fourth and final issue was that of *transformation*. The insights of this contextual Bible study, when shared with a group of ecumenical clergy and seminary professors, transformed conversations and understandings about the ideology-laden codes and practices in the United States.

## The Groups

In 2011, at the invitation of one of my students who was serving as a chaplain at Shalom House in St. Louis, Missouri, I began facilitating contextual Bible studies with a group of women who were clients and staff members of Shalom House.[1] These studies went on for many months, and I learned to value greatly the women's questions, challenges, insights, and contributions to ongoing interpretations of biblical texts and social contexts. After a few months of weekly sessions, I asked the Shalom House chaplain whether she thought the women might be willing to participate in an intercultural contextual Bible study exchange. After being told of the structure and parameters of the intercultural project, the women thought, prayed, and discussed the possibility for a week and then informed me that they would like to participate and that they would like to read 2 Sam 13 on the rape of Tamar.

The first partner group considered by the women was a group of men in Indonesia, many of whom were incarcerated for assault against women. The Shalom House group, consisting of nine women—two staff members and seven clients—discussed animatedly the possibilities and difficulties of engaging in a study of the story of Tamar with this group of men. Many of the women claimed that perhaps this would provide an opportunity to speak the truth to these men within the relative safety of an intercultural, long-distance Bible study. Some, however, expressed strong concerns about being able to share safely and openly in the context of an exchange with the men in the Indonesian group. Many of the women at Shalom House—as is, regrettably, the case with women around the world—have experienced violence at the hands of men.

Our search for a partner group resumed, and we came across a group of four women from Driebergen-Rijsenburg, the Netherlands, who were also looking for a partner group with which to read 2 Sam 13. The Shalom House group members settled on this choice of a partner group and were excited about the possibilities inherent in learning from and with women from a context different from their own.

---

1. Shalom House is an "organization specializing in working with homeless women with mental illness and chemical dependency to help them stabilize and rebuild their lives.... Shalom House residents are single, homeless women ages 18 and older, many of whom are chronically homeless and suffering with persistent mental illness and chemical dependence" (Shalom House, n.d.).

The women of Shalom House met each Monday evening for several weeks to study the text of 2 Sam 13:1–22 and to prepare their reports for the partner group. Study sessions began and ended with prayer, including a prayer for the partner group in the Netherlands. Transcripts of the digitally recorded sessions were submitted to the group members for review and approval prior to submission to the website and the partner group in the Netherlands.

## Solidarity

The women of the Shalom House group were gratified to realize that there was a group of women on another continent who were thinking about them and who were interested in what they might have to say about this biblical text. One of their reports to the Driebergen-Rijsenburg group included the following:

> We know we won't all be here at the Shalom House when we receive word from you again, so we want to say: "Thank you!" It was really helpful to read this passage knowing others were doing the same, and we were glad to learn from your report, and also felt happy that you would take our report seriously. Sometimes we feel like people don't hear us—like they think what we say doesn't matter. We know it does matter. Many of your insights helped us to ask new questions or think in new ways. We're glad that even though we are across the globe from you, we are connected.

Reading "together" through the exchange of reading reports and responses provided the women of Shalom House with a strong sense of solidarity with the group in the Netherlands. Even though the inquiries and responses of the groups differed in significant ways, the women in St. Louis articulated satisfaction and joy in the fact that they were struggling with this difficult text and both contributing to and receiving from the reading process of another group of women. Additionally, the Shalom House group exhibited growth in their own willingness to listen carefully and caringly to one another's stories and to see themselves as a true group. Themes, issues, and concerns were remembered and valued from one meeting to the next. Women felt free to question and challenge one another as they offered interpretive possibilities. They also took great care to voice only their own perspectives and to respect the perspectives of others. Before one of the study sessions, a member remarked to me that the experience of sharing reports with the Netherlands group made her more aware of differences *and* similarities between her and other group members. This sense of diversity, even in the midst of the unity of a shared Bible study, helped the group develop a sense of solidarity as they questioned, taught, and learned together.

## Translation

One important, and perhaps unexpected, insight arose from the fact that the Shalom House group and the Driebergen-Rijsenburg group were reading from different translations of the Bible and in different languages. The Shalom House group, made up of English speakers, made use of four versions of the Bible: King James Version (KJV), New Revised Standard Version (NRSV), Good News Bible (GNB), and Common English Bible (CEB). Though we never specifically inquired, we presumed that our partner group was made up of Dutch speakers and that they would be reading from a Dutch Bible. It was around what at first seemed to be a simple issue of translation that our Shalom House group began to think more deeply about the story of Tamar.

Second Samuel 13:3 introduces Jonadab, the son of David's brother Shimeah. The NRSV says that Jonadab was "a very crafty man"; the GNB has "a very shrewd man"; the CEB renders it "a very clever man"; the KJV translates it "a very subtil man." These words ("crafty," "shrewd," "clever," "subtil") seemed to the Shalom House group to implicate Jonadab in instigating a manipulation both of Tamar and of the rules of propriety in David's court. This led the study group members to focus on Jonadab's personal character and motives. When I asked the group their evaluation of Jonadab, some of the responses were:

Woman 1: That he's no good. Deceitful.
Woman 2: Bad advice.
Woman 1: No. That he was the cause of this. Really. He was the cause.
Woman 3: Well, they say he was a shrewd man anyway, so that was part of his nature to be deceitful.

This final comment about the nature of a shrewd person being deceitful fits the overall understanding that these English translations seem to impart. It makes sense in the story to read it this way: Jonadab seems to be operating in a sly way to aid his friend, the prince. In fact, one of our group members labeled Jonadab as a "wingman," referring to the street slang for a male who works in concert with another male to create situations in which at least one of them might have sexual relations with a specific woman. All group members agreed emphatically that Jonadab was an identifiably culpable wingman for Amnon.

Our group even noticed that in two of our translations the word describing Jonadab was the same word used to describe the serpent in Gen 3:1:

> Now the serpent was more subtil than any beast of the field which the Lord God had made. (KJV)

> Now the serpent was more crafty than any other wild animal that the Lord God had made. (NRSV)

The serpent even seems to fare better than Jonadab in the CEB. The CEB translation describes Jonadab as "clever" and the serpent as "intelligent." To our English-speaking group in the United States, "intelligent" conveyed a more innate sense of knowledge. "Clever" seemed to indicate context-bound skills of manipulation. Our group had identified the wingman and had agreed upon his guilt: "He was the cause."

Then we received the first report from the women of Driebergen-Rijsenburg. The women of Shalom House were excited to read what their partner group had written. They expected to see similarities with their own thoughts and also discussed the possibility of being surprised by insights from the Netherlands group. Both things happened. The Driebergen-Rijsenburg report contained questions and thoughts about the situation, about Tamar, and about David's family, just as the Shalom House discussions had. The Driebergen-Rijsenburg report also contained a few concerns that the Shalom House group had not discussed. One simple but important question, however, in the Driebergen-Rijsenburg report surprised the Shalom House group and helped them to pursue their discussion more deeply and with more focus. The Driebergen-Rijsenburg report began with a brief outline of the text, retelling, verse by verse, the story of Tamar. The report presented 2 Sam 13:3:

> Amnon had a friend: Jonadab, a very wise man. This friend was at the same time his cousin.

In a later section the Driebergen-Rijsenburg report asks:

> Jonadab was a wise man. Why did he gave [sic] this advice? Did he knew [sic] what Amnon was going to do? Did he do this on purpuose [sic]? Didn't he want Amnon to be king?

The Shalom House women and I were surprised to see the word *wise* in the Driebergen-Rijsenburg report. No English translation we were using denoted or even seemed to connote "wise" in connection with Jonadab. I had not given the description of Jonadab much thought and had not looked up the Hebrew behind our English translations. "Crafty," "subtil," and "shrewd" seemed to fit the character very well. Perhaps, we mused, our Dutch interlocutors had misunderstood the semantic range of "wise" in American English. After all, given their verb usage, as in their reported questions above, it seemed likely that English was their second or possibly third language.

We consulted the Hebrew, expecting to find that Jonadab was "crafty" and "subtil," just like the serpent in the garden of Eden. Imagine our surprise when we discovered that the Hebrew word used to describe Jonadab was not the word *ʿārûm*[2]—used to describe the serpent, the "craftiest" character we could imagine, but rather the Hebrew word *ḥākām*—used in 1 Kgs 3:12 to describe Solomon, the wisest person we could remember from Sunday school lessons. How could this be? Why had all of their translations used words other than "wise"? A quick search of many other English translations revealed that *ḥākām* is almost never translated "wise" in 2 Sam 13:3. A search of many Dutch translations revealed that the same is sometimes true in Dutch, where *ḥākām* is repeatedly translated *wijs* in 1 Kgs 3:12 and translated, in at least a couple of cases, as *schrander* or *vernuftig* in 2 Sam 13:3. In the beginning the women of Shalom House agreed with what the women of Driebergen-Rijsenburg seemed to indicate: Jonadab certainly did not seem very wise to them. This is how the Shalom House reading report presented this to the Driebergen-Rijsenburg group:

> At first, we wondered if the passage was trying to tell us he was wise. We noticed that in some of our English translations, the word used was "crafty." That reminded some of us of the way Genesis 3 talks about the serpent. We wondered if we were supposed to see Jonadab as less wise like Solomon, and more shrewd like the serpent in the garden of Eden. We looked it up in a Hebrew lexicon after we read your report, and were glad we did, because we found out that the Hebrew word for Jonadab was the same word for Solomon's wisdom, and not the same word used for

---

2. For ease of reading, I have used only transliterations of the Hebrew words in my presentation of the Shalom House discussions. These are similar to the transliterations the women found in the lexicon and discussed together.

the serpent's "craftiness," even though it looked the same in our English translations. We would not have seen that on our own. We wondered if perhaps the way Dutch translations for those passages were done helped you to see this differently. We were glad you helped us to see this, but then puzzled, because we really thought Jonadab acted more like the serpent and less like Solomon in his "wisdom"!

Then the women of Shalom House began to revisit their own conversation.

## Hegemony

The women of Shalom House had discussed many issues surrounding the story of Tamar, including the culture of David's family, the political implications of actions, and the wisdom of Tamar in the face of structures that seemed to be working against her.

> Woman 2: This story is about David's children, and I think all of this, the rudiments came from David having stolen Bathsheba and had her husband killed. And the prophet told him that the sword will never leave your house.

Later another woman commented on the structures around Tamar:

> It's just like these unspoken rules, that whatever action the man takes, it's always the female reason why he's upset, because you did this or you did that. You know those structures are all in place.

As the conversation continued, one woman remarked: "some people don't see where they're doing anything wrong. But they see that as a norm."

What the women had begun to discuss as they thought about power and structures and norms was *hegemony*. Through their reflections on this biblical text, they were beginning to unwrap systematically the layers of hegemonic expectation in their own context and in the context of the Davidic court as presented in 2 Samuel.

Jean and John Comaroff offer a helpful definition of hegemony:

> we take hegemony to refer to that order of signs and practices, relations and distinctions, images and epistemologies—drawn from a historically situated cultural field—that come to be taken-for-granted as the natural and received shape of the world and everything that inhabits it. It consists, to paraphrase Bourdieu (1977:167), of things that go without

saying because, being axiomatic, they come without saying; things that, being presumptively shared, are not normally the subject of explication or argument (Bourdieu 1977:94). This is why power has so often been seen to lie in what it silences, what it prevents people from thinking and saying, what it puts beyond the limits of the rational and the credible. In a quite literal sense, hegemony is habit forming. (Comaroff and Comaroff 1991, 23)

The women of Shalom House had discussed emphatically the structures, settings, power, and norms presented by the Comaroffs in this description of hegemony. As much as they lamented these elements of hegemony, though they did not name them as such, in their deliberations they returned to Jonadab as a primary culprit.

Here the distinction the Comaroffs draw between hegemony and ideology is instructive:

Here, then, is the basic difference between hegemony and ideology. Whereas the first consists of constructs and conventions that have come to be shared and naturalized throughout a political community, the second is the expression and ultimately the possession of a particular social group, although it may be widely peddled beyond. The first is nonnegotiable and therefore beyond direct argument; the second is more susceptible to being perceived as a matter of inimical opinion and interest and therefore is open to contestation. Hegemony homogenizes, ideology articulates. Hegemony, at its most effective, is mute; by contrast, says de Certeau (1984:46), "all the while, ideology babbles on." (Comaroff and Comaroff 1991, 24)

The Shalom House group seemed to be saying that everything would have been all right if only Jonadab had not been so shrewd, so deceitful. His particular ideological understandings—his "craftiness"—brought foolishness to an otherwise relatively (pun intended) stable setting. Then they read the report from Driebergen-Rijsenburg and got "wise."

The women of Driebergen-Rijsenburg used a few English-language constructions that were unfamiliar to the women of Shalom House, some of them quite remarkable. For example, when in 2 Sam 13:19 the NRSV reads that Tamar "tore the long robe that she was wearing," the Driebergen-Rijsenburg report renders this as the "cracking of Tamar's clothes." While "cracking the clothes" is a light example of the vagaries of translation, the presentation in the Driebergen-Rijsenburg report of Jonadab as "wise" helped the Shalom House women in "cracking the code" of hegemony in the text of 2 Samuel.

One of the most helpful readings of 2 Sam 13 is that of Phyllis Trible (1984, 46), in which she identifies the voice of Tamar as a voice of wisdom in the text:

> Though Jonadab advised Amnon to seek David's help, how different was that counsel. Over against Jonadab stands Tamar. Wisdom opposes craftiness. In light of her words, not only Amnon but also Jonadab is a fool. Yet in this story victory belongs to the fools.

Compare this with the statement from the Shalom House group: "Tamar didn't have a lot of power, but she used a lot of wisdom in her few words." Both Trible and the members of the study groups were attentive to the presence of wisdom in the character and actions of Tamar. What Trible can only discuss in terms of Jonadab's craftiness, the Shalom House women, aided by their reading partners in the Netherlands, unmask as hegemony. The key is the translation of *ḥākām*. Trible (57) clearly sees the structural issues present in the Davidic court and in our own cultural interactions:

> Moreover, compassion for Tamar requires a new vision. If sister wisdom can protect a young man from the loose woman, who will protect sister wisdom from the loose man, symbolized not by a foreigner but by her very own brother? Who will preserve sister wisdom from the adventurer, the rapist with his smooth words, lecherous eyes, and grasping hands? In answering the question, Israel is found wanting—*and so are we.*

In translating the description of Jonadab in 2 Sam 13:3 as "crafty," Trible, and nearly every English translation of the passage, seems to miss the final, deep connection between the "adventurer, the rapist" and Israel and us. Just before the passage quoted above, Trible (56) writes, referring to a passage in Prov 7:4–5:

> Obedient to the first line of the proverb, Amnon did say to Tamar the wise woman, "My sister are you." His embrace, however, produced a royal rape of wisdom. In light of his action, the parallel line heightens the contrast: "Call insight an intimate friend (or kinsman)." This advice Amnon skewed. For his intimate friend he chose the crafty Jonadab, who offered the plan that would gratify the lustful sight of the prince. Thus, iniquity, not insight, came from this kinsman.

Here Trible, along with the Shalom House women before they read the
report from Driebergen-Rijsenburg, focuses on the "crafty" nature of
Jonadab, implying that perhaps another kinsman might have provided
insight. Trible's introduction of Jonadab near the beginning of her essay
establishes her translational choice: "Jonadab is 'very crafty (ḥākām).'  His
entrance gives Amnon the friend he needs to surmount the impossible"
(39). Trible's note on the translation of ḥākām refers the reader to R. N.
Whybray (1968, 58), who writes:

> The fact that Jonadab, David's nephew, who counselled his friend
> Amnon how to seduce Tamar (II Sam. 13:3–5), is described as "very
> wise" (ḥākām me'ōd) shows that "wisdom" is a purely intellectual and
> morally neutral quality.

That is what hegemony has taught us to assume. Clearly, the narrator cannot
mean to tell us that Jonadab is "wise" in any kind of morally positive sense,
considering the terrible crime his advice precipitates. Translating ḥākām
mĕōd as "very crafty" leads us to focus on Jonadab and Amnon and to miss
the deeper, hegemonic truth. Jonadab's plan *was what passed as wisdom*
in David's court! If the narrator gives us "very wise" as a description for
Jonadab, then the narrative begins to instruct us on systemic problems—
it unmasks hegemony. If we change the descriptor to "crafty," "subtil," or
"shrewd," we overlook the hegemonic, and one person becomes a distrac-
tion or even a decoy. What the Shalom House group began to understand
as they considered the narrator's assertion that Jonadab was "very wise"
was that, through story and character, the narrator was revealing the hegemonic nature of understandings about power and relationships in Israel
during the rule of David's family.

Considered as a part of a prolonged narrative beginning with 1 Samuel,
the story we find in 2 Sam 13 seems to be one of many instances in which
the reader is given clues that the Davidic monarchy was a failed experiment with regard to God's wisdom and care for the people of Israel. These
instances expose in various ways, from the narrator's point of view, the
flawed ideological precepts upon which the monarchy had been founded,
and through which the monarchy had functioned. Seen as an isolated
instance of miserable behavior and horrific abuse, the rape of Tamar
becomes one disappointing story about what happens when the wrong
"crafty" adviser gets too close to a good and honorable future monarch
or his brother, and the story becomes an abhorrent aberration. Seen as

an expression of the behaviors and consequences of the "wisdom" of the Davidic court, the story exposes ideological assumptions upon which the monarchy rests. It reveals the hegemonic construct within which Jonadab's advice could be seen as "very wise." Reading the succession narrative, of which 2 Sam 13 is a part, along with the story of the beginnings of monarchy in Israel in 1 Samuel reveals important keys to understanding the story of Tamar as a story less about the "craftiness" of Jonadab, or anyone else for that matter, and more about the taken-for-granted nature of the "wisdom" employed by members of the royal family and the calamity for people and nation that this sort of wisdom brings.

Aided by the translational clue from the women of Driebergen-Rijsenburg, the Shalom House women were able to articulate the ways in which the structures of the monarchy had created a system within which the advice of Jonadab and the actions of Amnon had become the norm. The reader is given a primer on the dangers of monarchic ideology and its opposition to God's intentions for Israel in 1 Sam 8. Verse 9 sets the stage:

> Now then, listen to their voice; only—you shall solemnly warn them, and show them the ways of the king who shall reign over them (NRSV).

What follows in verses 10–18 is a list describing, in social and economic terms, all the ways kings will establish themselves in Israel. What is more, this list is presented in profoundly theological terms. The very stage upon which all of this has been set is the exchange between Samuel and God in 1 Sam 8:6–8:

> But the thing displeased Samuel when they said, "Give us a king to govern us." Samuel prayed to the LORD, and the LORD said to Samuel, "Listen to the voice of the people in all that they say to you; for they have not rejected you, but they have rejected me from being king over them. Just as they have done to me, from the day I brought them up out of Egypt to this day, forsaking me and serving other gods, so also they are doing to you." (NRSV)

Though this exchange occurs just prior to the rise of Saul as ruler of Israel, it provides the theological groundwork for the entire question of the monarchy. The Davidic monarchy is the centerpiece of this discussion. Even in the midst of language about anointing and covenant promises, the presentation of the Davidic monarchy throughout Samuel is thematically prefaced as a departure from God's intention for Israel. The story of Tamar is a clear indication that what has been called "wise" within the society over which David and his household have ruled is actually quite foolish. Frankly, as the Shalom House group recognized, even the "wisdom" ascribed to Solomon was not enough to keep him from folly. Thanks to a combination of their own experiences of structural misogyny and the possibility of translating *ḥākām* as "wise," the Shalom House group discovered that the story of the rape of Tamar could be read as a revelatory critique of the unspoken hegemonic presumptions about "wisdom" prevalent in the Israelite monarchic household portrayed in 2 Samuel. This presumed "wisdom" created situations in which what might appear as persuasion was actually coercion. The wisdom of Jonadab suggested that Amnon do exactly what David had done in 2 Sam 11—make use of his power and position to effect a rape and cover-up. Jonadab "wisely" suggested a situation seemingly ambiguous enough to appear as one with the possibility for persuasion. From the standpoint of the hegemonic understandings within the court, this collaboration for coercion was the order of the day. The narrator seems to tell us plainly: "Look at this terrible truth. The cruel coercion and violent rape of Tamar is a representative instance of the hegemonic presumptions of the Israelite monarchy." We cannot merely blame Jonadab, though he is certainly culpable. We cannot only single out Amnon, though his guilt is clear. We must also see what the narration has been presenting to us all along: a system has been promulgated in which violent coercion is disguised as ambiguous persuasion.

## Transformation

One important, and often difficult to answer, question about any engagement with a biblical text is whether and how that engagement can be seen to have led to anything substantive in the way of transformation. Subsequent questions would seem to be: What, exactly, counts as "transformation"? How might we recognize or measure it? Leaving aside the inherent epistemological and hermeneutical issues, I propose that the Shalom House group experienced and facilitated transformation in three critical ways.

First, and importantly, the women in the Shalom House reading group experienced a sense of the possibility for learning and growth inherent in any project of group engagement. Through their gathering and sharing, reading and discussing, reporting and exchanging, they learned new information, gained new insights, and fostered new connections. In hearing and considering different perspectives, they participated in transforming their own horizons of understanding. As they read and engaged with the reading reports from another group, their perceptions about the possibilities of learning and sharing with others from another culture were stretched and changed.

Second, the Shalom House group members experienced a transformative widening of their expectations for the overall enterprise of biblical study. They also became more aware of the potential for personal, interpersonal, and intercultural learning, growth, and challenge. As they discussed the hegemonic structures that still exist today and that still call those behaviors and assumptions that oppress and endanger the most vulnerable among us "wisdom," they began to see that there is value in identifying, naming, and resisting such structures in the company of others who share their concerns. As Hans de Wit (2010, 288) has written:

> Resulta que leer la Biblia con otros es más que tomarse una taza de té con otros. No, es aprender a reconocer que hay otros lugares de lucha que no conocíamos antes. Es comenzar a romper la soledad y comprender que no somos los únicos que estamos inmersos en esa resistencia. Es comenzar a resistir *juntos*.

> The result is that reading the Bible with others is more than drinking a cup of tea together. Indeed, it is learning to recognize that there are other sites of struggle that we did not know about before. It means beginning to break through the solitude and understand that we are not the only ones that are engaged in this resistance. It is about beginning to resist *together* (editors' translation).

Realizing that there are others engaged in the struggle and resistance is transformative in itself. The possibilities for unmasking and opposing harmful actions and beliefs are multiplied as, in De Wit's words, people begin "to resist *together*."

One final and quite unexpected way in which the Shalom House group enacted transformation occurred in another setting among other people. A few months after the completion of the intercultural contextual Bible study at Shalom House, I was sharing the story of the women's engagement with the Driebergen-Rijsenburg group with an ecumenical group of pastors and seminary professors in St. Louis. I explained that one of the key things learned involved a heightened awareness of the presence of hegemonies that are exposed only when people challenge the harmful and seemingly natural assumptions upon which they are based. We discussed the difference it made to the Shalom House group to consider the story of Tamar as an exposure of the widely systemic misogynistic assumptions of the Davidic court, rather than merely as a story about the poor behavior of one adviser and his cousin, the prince.

The discussion that ensued led these pastors and professors to ask about ways that attitudes and behaviors that disempower, devalue, and harm women remain hidden in our present-day experience. Our discussion took place on a December morning, and one of my colleagues remarked that she and her son had discussed something quite similar that very morning as they rode together in the car. On the radio, a familiar tune began to play. As she was humming and tapping her fingers, enjoying the familiar tune, her son—a high school senior—said, "Mom, you know this song is about rape." The song, "Baby, It's Cold Outside," written by Frank Loesser, is often played on radio and television during the winter in the United States. It is a duet in which usually a man and a woman sing alternating lines describing the woman's desire and intention to go home for the night, and the man's insistence that she stay.

Though this song has been performed with a man singing the initial lines and a woman responding and by same-sex couples, it is most often performed with a woman singing the first lines of each stanza and a man singing the responses. The timing of the tune is such that the woman's line is not completely finished before the man's reply begins. This song has been perceived again and again as a charming and witty presentation of the sort of persuasive banter that might occur between two people. It has often been performed with a wink and a smile, indicating that the complaints of the woman are veiled expressions of desire and that the insistence of the man is always most welcome and appropriate. The setting is intimate, cozy, and nonthreatening—just like serving your brother cakes when he is ill. No problem at all. Until the text is truly examined and the hegemonic assumptions are interrogated.

The initiating lines of each stanza of this song (labeled "The Mouse" in the musical score) introduce concerns about family, the wider culture, and accountability. The responding lines (labeled "The Wolf" in the musical score) discount these concerns. This song plays out, in disconcerting ways, the kind of situation we find in 2 Sam 13. What at first seems to present the possibilities of persuasion turns out to be the calamity of coercion. Certainly the setting described in the song fits the kinds of situations described by the women of Shalom House as they discussed their experiences of men expressing desire, either directly or through innuendo, and women being expected to demur but in the end not to resist.

The difficulty in claiming that a song such as this is anything other than a completely innocent conversation between two equally responsible and free individuals who may very well share a mutual attraction is the same difficulty we have with identifying hegemony in any situation. Because we assume that men should initiate desire and women should show initial delay but eventually give in, the song seems to relate a silly, somewhat sexy and fun exchange. It could only go wrong if the man were something of a cad—if he were, perhaps, "crafty." Surely a wise man would not use his amorous persuasive efforts coercively, would he?

Hegemony hides. Ideology "babbles." Hidden within the lines of this often enjoyed song one can find assumptions about male and female behavior that presume a certain "wisdom" about gendered relatedness. When searching the Internet for "Baby It's Cold Outside Rape," I found the following type of response:

> The only thing delusional here is you! Rape? Seriously? People like you have taken political correctness to the extremely absurd. You're the first person I have EVER heard say that about this cute, clever, romantic and fun little song. It's obvious the woman wants to stay. Almost everytime he references something (like "Baby you'll freeze out there") in an attempt to get her to stay, she responds with a comment about the different forms of guilt (not her own, but from others such as her parents) or gossip she'll have to deal with if she stays. It's about being flirtatious in a fun way. That's the whole reason it's a back-and-forth, call-and-response song. You're saying a person can't even playfully try to persuade the person they have feelings for to spend the night due to the weather? If she really feels like he's forcing himself on her, why does she even engage in the flirty conversation about whether or not to stay? Remember the line about maybe just a cigarette more? She wants to stay. She's flirting too. It's that guilt and gossip she wants to avoid, and even that is used in a play hard to get sort of way. She's taken with him. Remember her line about wishing she could break this spell? They both want each other. Every woman who has ever sung it (from Esther Williams to Zooey Deschanel) does so without even the slightest hint of "NO MEANS NO! HELP, RAPE!" ("Baby It's Cold Outside Lyrics," n.d.)

Where does hegemony hide? In plain sight. That, after all, is its nature. If one were to accept the premise that men and women enjoy equal access to relational and societal power and resources, all of the comments in the quotation above would seem logical and helpful. When two people can express their agency equally, persuasion is possible, but when encounters are embedded within a system where there are clear (though often seemingly subtle) imbalances, the context is coercive.

Perhaps when those who have experienced the deleterious effects of sexual violence read texts about "crafty" advisers who create intimate situations and "coy" hosts who press their guests to stay a bit longer, they will see simple persuasion. Perhaps they will see possible danger. Maybe they will only blame individuals for any harm that ensues. Or perhaps, if enough people read and listen together, the hidden and silent reality of the hegemonic norms around gendered violence will be unmasked, be named as an ideology of misogyny, and be systematically resisted.

The pastors and professors who considered what the women of Shalom House and Driebergen-Rijsenburg had discussed and learned were challenged and encouraged to look closely at and to question the assumptions we make about gendered interactions and systemic norms. When more people engage with biblical texts and with one another, more interpretive and transformational possibilities arise.

When women from radically different cultures and situations read the story of the rape of Tamar in 2 Sam 13, they shared experiences and entered into a process through which they could learn from one another and express solidarity. Lies were exposed and truths were considered, assumptions challenged and hope engendered. Seemingly individual persuasion was unmasked as systemic coercion. A text, its readers, and the cultures surrounding each were transformed. In the words of the Shalom House final reading report:

> This study connected us, but the story of violence against the powerless also connects us. That means we can work and pray together to "have each other's backs"—to watch out for, speak up for, and stand up with women like Tamar everywhere. May God Bless you!

## References

"Baby It's Cold Outside Lyrics." http://www.metrolyrics.com/baby-its-cold-outside-lyrics-louis-armstrong.html#comment-1161404390.

Bourdieu, Pierre. 1977. Outline of a Theory of Practice. Translated by Richard Nice. Cambridge: Cambridge University Press.

Certeau, Michel de. 1984. *The Practice of Everyday Life.* Translated by Steven Rendall. Berkeley: University of California Press.

Comaroff, Jean, and John L. Comaroff. 1991. *Of Revelation and Revolution: Christianity, Colonialism, and Consciousness in South Africa.* Chicago: University of Chicago Press.

Jackson, Dan. 2014. *Remarks to Webster Groves Clergy Alliance for Inter-Racial Dignity.* North Webster Coalition, Webster Groves, MO.

Shalom House. n.d. www.shaloamhousestl.org.

Trible, Phyllis. 1984. *Texts of Terror: Literary-Feminist Readings of Biblical Narratives.* Overtures to Biblical Theology. Philadelphia: Fortress.

Whybray, R. N. 1968. *The Succession Narrative: A Study of II Samuel 9–20 and I Kings 1 and 2.* Studies in Biblical Theology 2/9. Naperville, IL: Allenson.

Wit, Hans de. 2004. "Through the Eyes of Another: Objectives and Backgrounds." Pages 3–53 in *Through the Eyes of Another: Intercultural Reading of the Bible.* Edited by Hans de Wit, Louis Jonker, Marleen Kool, and Daniel Schipani. Elkhart, IN: Institute of Mennonite Studies.

———. 2010. *Por un solo gesto de amor: Lectura de la Biblia desde una práctica intercultural.* Buenos Aires: Instituto Universitario Isedet.

# Section 2.2
## In Her Memory:
## Tamar's Story in Local Perspective

11

# How to Share Stories of Trauma:
# Reading Tamar in Amsterdam

*Willemien van Berkum*

This essay reflects on the exchanges between three pairs of groups in Amsterdam who read the Tamar story. Beforehand we anticipated having good exchanges, with mutual understanding. We hoped links would develop between separated worlds and that prejudices would be broken down. This hope proved vain. The exchanges between groups were difficult and brought little change in the thinking of the groups. It did not go as anticipated—it proved a failure.

In this essay I reflect on the course of the exchanges and the factors that contributed to the absence of a deepened understanding of oneself, of one another, and of the text. The exchange in intercultural Bible reading occurs in two phases. In the first phase, a group reads the Bible story independently. The groups discuss the story in a way with which the members feel comfortable. A change in the way of thinking of the group members can occur by reading the Bible story together. During the second phase of exchange of reading experiences between two groups, the groups read a report from the other group and respond to it. This phase can give new insights in the biblical text. It can be an opportunity to level prejudices by learning more about those in other circumstances. I will introduce the reading partners and provide an outline of both phases of the reading process. I conclude with some recommendations and conclusions.

## The Groups

The first group consists of about twelve women who call themselves Bakkie Troost, a Dutch expression meaning "cup of consolation," which refers to a cup of coffee. These women have gone through much in their lives. Usually the women meet to discuss some theme; for the intercultural Bible reading project, they read and discussed the story of Tamar and Amnon. This group entered an exchange with immigrant women connected to Casa Migrante, a center for Spanish-speaking people in Amsterdam. The women in this group emigrated from Latin American countries to the Netherlands for a variety of reasons.

The second set of reading partners was formed by people connected to the Drugs Pastorate in Amsterdam and a group from the Keizersgrachtkerk ("church on the emperor's canal"). The Drugs Pastorate organizes activities for people with drug-related problems and their families and friends. The reading group consisted of about ten people. The group from the Keizersgrachtkerk is connected to a mainstream Protestant church. They describe themselves as liberal, emphasizing the social value of the Bible and attaching little importance to dogmas. This group is of mixed gender and consists mainly of those over fifty years of age.

The fifth group consisted of people associated with the Street Pastorate. The Street Pastorate is an initiative of the Protestant Diaconate Amsterdam and offers pastoral care to (former) homeless people and their relatives and friends. Activities for this target group include a philosophy group, which discusses different aspects of life. The philosophy group joined the reading project and was linked to a group related to the Christian community Stroom ("stream"). The latter group consisted of about eight highly educated young people between the ages of twenty and thirty-five who regularly share meals and discuss a theme. Many of the members of Stroom were raised in a traditional Christian environment where there was no room for questions, doubts, or criticisms. Stroom is in search of new ways to live out Christian freedom. For the members of the group it is important to have room to doubt.

Phase 1: Tamar and Amnon Confront Us with Our Own Stories

When one reads the reports of the various Amsterdam groups, it is striking that two of the groups, those of the Keizersgrachtkerk and Stroom, read the story from a distance. These groups seem to look for an underlying meaning in the text; they want to know the intention of the author. In these groups there is little identification with the characters in the story. This seems to be a typical Western way of reading: instead of identifying themselves with the story, readers tend to keep their distance. The story is objectified, and questions of historicity, authorship, and reader tradition play an important part in the conversation. The other four groups use the story of Amnon and Tamar as a mirror for their own experiences. Text-critical issues of authorship and reading tradition are of no interest to them. The story and the characters within it call for identification. As a result, personal stories of abuse, male-female relationships, and family relationships are shared in response to the biblical story. The discussion consists mainly of sharing stories from the participants' own life and sharing the emotions the Bible story evoked.

Looking closer at the discussions in the individual groups, we see that the group of the Drugs Pastorate recognized strong parallels between the biblical story and the lives of the participants of the group. Indeed, contrary to all expectations of the group members, the story became relevant in a natural way. In this way the group underwent a change, a small transformation in the way they viewed the Bible. Instead of it being a book far removed from real life, the Bible became relevant to the everyday life of the readers.

The Drugs Pastorate is not the only group that experienced that the Bible can have a strong connection to one's own personal life. The women's groups, Casa Migrante and Bakkie Troost, and the group of the Street Pastorate shared this experience. All those groups had personal sharing in response to the biblical story. A few members of Bakkie Troost had experienced situations of abuse or exclusion, making the story evoke many emotions. The same was true for the Casa Migrante group, though for different reasons, for instance, by recognizing that relationships between parents and children can be poor. One of the women felt that sometimes it is hard to give your children the restrictions they need. A woman who had to leave her child behind still experienced a lot of grief because of it: "This is a big story because I didn't say no to one of my children in time and I never told him I am his mother (and deserve respect)."

It is clear that the sharing itself is special and touched members emotionally. Unprocessed pain surfaced. There are few spaces where people can share stories like this. Through these vulnerable stories room was created for processing the feelings involved. This can be a small step in the process of recovery, one part of a gradual process of transformation.

Besides creating space for personal stories, the story of Tamar and Amnon called for a reaction. When people identified with a person in the story, the story evoked many emotions, not always linked directly to their own personal experiences. One of the women of Casa Migrante was angry and irritated with King David: "and the king is mourning, and mourning and mourning, out of love for his sons. What kind of attitude is that?" Some could identify with the anger of Absalom: "What if it was your little sister, what would you do?"

There were also other responses to the story. Several groups asked themselves why this story was in the Bible and what role God played in the story. The Stroom group was raised with the idea that biblical stories relate life lessons. In vain they searched for a lesson in this story. The tension that arose was solved by concluding that not all biblical stories provide a lesson. Some—like this one—just reflect the reality of life. Readers are not called upon to act like the people in this story, but they are shown how wrong decisions can have terrible consequences.

A member of the Street Pastorate group resolved the tension of the story by bringing up the story of the good Samaritan. Tamar needed a good Samaritan to take care of her. A similar line of thought arose in the women's group Bakkie Troost. When asked with whom they could identify, one of the women responded that she would like to be Tamar's sister. This woman saw that Tamar needed someone to help her, someone to whom she could talk and with whom she could cry. If she had had a sister, Tamar would have been less lonely. This appealed to the other women at once: "try to be like a brother or sister for the people around you, because they need you." In the end the women of Bakkie Troost concluded that the circle of violence can be broken only by love. One of the women spoke from experience: "Love can be unsafe and egocentric. I was blamed. I was the dirty male fucker. But by meeting you the good in me was stimulated. Now I'm changed."

During the first phase, the groups each read in their own way. From the reading reports, it becomes clear that the two groups who read the text more objectively showed little evidence of change as a result of the reading project. However, if one reads the biblical story in a personal way, in search of parallels to one's own life, there is a greater chance that the biblical story will have a real impact on the personal life of individuals. People need to be able to identify with the persons in the story. Reading in such a way leads to sharing personal stories and creates the possibility that the Bible sheds new light on their own lives. By sharing personal stories, one has the possibility of healing; sharing gives the other group members the possibility of caring for one another. This gives a good foundation for change, which is the essence of transformation.

## Phase 2: How a Lack of Reflective Capacity
## and a Lack of Information Leads to Stagnation

In phase two the groups send each other their reading reports and discuss the report of their partner group.

As Godian Ejiogu wrote in his essay in this volume, the Drugs Pastorate group looked forward to the exchange with the group from the Keizersgrachtkerk. It was exciting: what would ordinary church members think about the way they—as addicts—read the text? Unfortunately, the group from the Keizersgrachtkerk sent their report to the Street Pastorate instead of to the Drugs Pastorate, so that the Drugs Pastorate group was left with no exchange at all. This was all the more a pity, because those of the Drugs Pastorate clearly struggle with feelings of inferiority and rejection. The exchange with another group could possibly have given them a feeling of acceptance. Due to the miscommunication, the Keizersgrachtkerk also received no response to their report. However, the members of this group did not regret this. After two independent sessions on the biblical story, they felt they were done with the story and that it was time for something new. An exchange with another group possibly would have made this group aware of the dynamics of the text. It could have given them the possibility of exploring other angles in approaching the story that they had not discovered on their own. With an exchange of reading reports, the group could have been able to discover the possibility this text offers of meeting other Amsterdam people. Unfortunately, this never happened.

The groups Casa Migrante and Bakkie Troost did have an exchange. It proved hard for the women of Bakkie Troost to discuss the report of the partner group. The subjects of rape and rejection that emerged in the biblical story proved to be so intense that it was necessary in their response to avoid going too deep. The story touched the pain of the women, and they did not know how to cope with it. Only a short response was given to the partner group; the report was not discussed extensively. The result was that there was only a superficial exchange.

On the other hand, the report of Bakkie Troost provided many points of recognition for the women of Casa Migrante. At the same time new topics were provided by the report, especially that of breaking through the circle of violence by love and the call to be there for the other, like a sister. The women of Casa Migrante could identify with the stories of the women of Bakkie Troost. They expressed the wish to be like a sister to these women who had been hurt so much: "They need to know they can cry on our shoulders."

For Bakkie Troost the reading process ended with the reaction that they sent to Casa Migrante. Although all the women received the encouraging and loving words of the women of Casa Migrante by email, it is doubtful whether they read the report, so that this message did not get through to the women of Bakkie Troost. This leaves phase two only halfway completed. The whole process involves reading and realizing how one's own report is received by the other and reading their response to it. In this way prejudices can be overcome and questions answered. If that does not happen, there is a good chance that no changes will take place in one's view of the other group or in one's manner of thinking. Among other things, this has to do with the avoidance of material that would confront one's own beliefs. In the end, for Bakkie Troost phase two was purely a prolongation of phase one: the discussion of the biblical text within their own group was continued on the basis of the partner's reading report. An extension of phase two, which would enable both groups to respond to each other several times, would have required a greater investment of time from both groups. For the exchange to be successful, this would have been desirable. Bakkie Troost was accustomed to discussing a different theme every month. The discussion of the story of Tamar was an exception to this rule. To discuss the story longer was a step too far.

The last two groups we need to comment on are Stroom and the Street Pastorate. The reading group Stroom consisted of socially accepted and highly educated people with positions in the heart of society. It would be expected of such a group that they would be able to reflect on the reading report from the partner group. Stroom, however, observed how the partner group made the story more personal, but saw no reason to take another look at their own reading. In this second reading phase, just like in the first phase, there was no appropriation. The reading of the other's report did not bring them to take another look at their own convictions. On the other hand, the discussion of the reading report of the partner group and the reflection on their own reading proved a step too far for the Street Pastorate group, the partner group of Stroom. All attention was drawn to the story of Tamar. The story of the partner group received no independent consideration but was merely an inducement to discuss the biblical story again. A more thorough analysis of this process can be read in the essay of Luc Tanja in this volume.

The inability to analyze and reflect that came to the fore in groups like the Street Pastorate and Bakkie Troost is striking. Reading the report of the partner group in these cases resulted in a renewed discussion of the text. The report immediately evoked personal stories and brought the discussion back to the story of Amnon and Tamar. It proved nearly impossible to distance themselves from the biblical story and their own life and to focus on the partner group. This hindered a successful completion of the second phase. In order to make the second phase a success, the group must empathize with the partner group by asking questions like: Who are these people? What are our prejudices about them? What is important to these people? In other words, the group has to look for the people behind the report. This proved to be a step too far for the members of the Street Pastorate and Bakkie Troost.

## Conclusions and Recommendations

The intercultural Bible reading project seeks to break down prejudices and build bridges between groups from different and sometimes opposed contexts. With the Amsterdam groups some things went well; others provided us with learning opportunities for the future. In light of the above, I would like to make the following recommendations.

- A reading of the text in which people's personal lives are mirrored in the biblical story or which makes the readers try to identify with the characters in the story generates a greater impact than reading with objective distance. In the current approach, groups are encouraged to read the text in a way they are used to. For some groups this might mean they read the text objectively. In light of the reading process in Amsterdam, I would suggest to encourage groups to read biblical texts in a contextual and personal way, which, of course, can be embedded in a known structure. If a group is used to eating, singing, or praying together, these are customs to be continued; but at all times the discussion should focus on a personal and contextual reading of the story.
- In order to generate a meaningful exchange between two or more groups, it is not enough just to discuss one report of a partner group. The response to one's own report should be read as well. Only by reading the responses of the partnering group can prejudices come to the fore and be overcome.

- Hardly any of the Amsterdam groups created a conscious picture of the partner group. Most of the people treated the report of the other group as a text without context. To the readers it did not matter who said what. In order to overcome prejudices, it is necessary to know the other readers. The exchange between the groups could become more powerful if groups would consciously pay attention to images or even prejudices about the other group. To make this work it is necessary that groups send each other a good description of their own group. Part of a meeting could be spent discussing the image one has of the partner group. Taking the Street Pastorate as an example, one could ask the following questions: (1) Do you know the other group? (2) What springs to your mind if you hear about the Street Pastorate? (3) Do you know any people who live on the streets? (4) What are your experiences with these people? (5) Are there differences or maybe similarities with yourself? By consciously taking time to become aware of the images and prejudices people have about one another, they can create an opportunity to overcome these prejudices.

The above-mentioned recommendations cause the process of exchange to be long and intense, but at the same time give it a chance of being more fruitful. In recruiting groups, it is important to make this time investment clear. Not every group will be available for such a long process. It might be better to have fewer groups and be sure they will take enough time for the whole process. Sometimes it might be better to create a new group instead of working with an already existing group. In this way one can make expectations clear to all participants, and one can make sure that all those involved are willing to spend the time needed for the project. On the other hand, an established group also has advantages, but one has to be very clear about the mutual expectations.

In addition to changes in the way the groups work out the exchange, the exchange between the Street Pastorate and Stroom and their partners leads to the question whether intercultural Bible reading is appropriate for everyone. Maybe some groups lack the ability to analyze and reflect on their own and one another's behavior. What are the criteria for a group to be able to participate in the project? This is a question worth asking. Personally, I think there are many possibilities, given the right group coordinator, especially if special time is reserved to discuss how the group members think about the other group. But even with the right coaching it might be that intercultural Bible reading is not suitable to every group. There are groups that benefit greatly from phase one, that is, from the appropriation of the biblical text to their own context and lives. It might well be that these same groups lack the reflective capacity to read the story from someone else's point of view.

In sum, the exchange in Amsterdam showed many things can go wrong during the process of intercultural Bible reading. A part of the process involves problems that need to be overcome. These problems do not mean that intercultural reading is without value. Although the exchange between the Amsterdam groups did not go as hoped, still many valuable things came out. Very personal stories were shared, both beautiful and unpleasant. People were challenged to take a closer look at themselves. If we look at the Amsterdam groups, we realize that transformation does not happen overnight. Transformation might well be a lifelong process. Reading the text together and being engaged in a mutual exchange may well have contributed to a process of transformation.

## 12

# "We Are All Tamar":
# Transforming Culture through the Bible
# (A Dialogue within Amsterdam)

*Godian Ejiogu*

The title of this essay might seem strange for a Bible story that happened hundreds of years ago in the Middle East, with no connection to India at the time. I chose the title because of the contemporaneity of this story in worldwide news. At the time we were reading this story (2012), a twenty-three-year-old lady in India was raped and died. It could be that raping a lady without any consequences for the offender was normal at the time of Tamar. In present-day India, the justice system takes little or no action, just like King David in the case of Tamar. Tamar and the lady in India shared the same fate of suffering rape without compensatory justice from the authorities. In India, the lot of rape victims lay in the hands of those who sympathized with them and organized protests in order to achieve justice.

I find this title fascinating, because the group members were in touch with one another many weeks after reading the story. When the news of the rape in India broke, groups members exchanged text messages like: "See Tamar in India, the Bible is really not a dead book"; "This is the reality of the situation." Our group recognized this experience in their personal lives as well and in the lives of family, friends, and others around them. The story of the rape in India showed that the Bible deals with problems present in our world today.

## Meeting and Report

When we met together to read this story, we made an effort to create an open and safe atmosphere in which people felt free to talk about their personal feelings and experiences. We explained that nothing said was right or wrong, but it was the way one views it. Therefore, all expressions should be respected and should remain within the group. Participants were encouraged to share personal experiences and feelings and not to generalize and judge opinions of others.

A verbatim report of the meeting was made so that participants could recognize themselves in the report. Some of them found the report to be too confrontational and pleaded not to have their names made public. One of the participants was sick with fear of what the family would do should this report come out. It would mean exposing the families' shameful episode, which they wanted to keep secret. Some knew some members of the partner group and feared that their personal story would be recognized. The feelings of vulnerability among these participants made clear that the report had to be treated with utmost care. In accordance with the protocol of the intercultural reading project, the verbatim report sent to the partner group was made anonymous.

Any communication on the content of such meetings demands extreme caution. I present this essay in such a way that it does justice to the meetings and our report while protecting the names of the participants and the content they shared. This report of the process the group went through during this reading project reveals aspects of the dynamics within a group and between groups.

Drugs Pastorate Group

The Drugs Pastorate is a religious organization that provides pastoral care especially to drug and alcohol users. The twelve people contacted were interested in coming together to share in the story of Tamar. The number seemed felicitous, as it accorded with the biblical number of twelve tribes and twelve apostles, representing both the first and second Testaments that make up the Bible. The number of actual attendants turned out to be less than this congenial number due to health problems, which kept some away.

The group was made up of people who never came together for any other reason. Some had never met before. This was not a conscious choice of the drugs pastor, but came about because those interested happened to come from different contacts that the drugs pastor had all over Amsterdam. The group comprised men and women between the ages of forty and fifty. Those receiving pastoral guidance from the Drugs Pastorate are known to have had experiences that have made them highly sensitive to injustice.

Some of the group responded enthusiastically when they heard that they were coupled with a reading group from a particular church in Amsterdam. They saw the members of that church as middle and high class and were interested in sharing a Bible story with them to see how they viewed the story. Three participants doubted whether the church group would want to meet and share with them, because they thought that people with such a status would not see the Drugs Pastorate group as worthy of being God's children, that they could never imagine that those of the Drugs Pastorate could be involved with matters having to do with God. Two participants thought that the members of the church might be afraid to meet them: they might fear the bluntness of the members of our group. These were reactions before the group came together to read the story.

When the group came together, they prepared dinner and one person read the Bible story out loud. Immediately after the reading, the group began sharing impressions and experiences. This lasted almost two hours before they closed the session and shared dinner.

## The Partner Group

The partner group Keizersgrachtkerk is from a church community where people know one another through church services. The reading group was used to coming together for various activities. For a long period of time they have come together every Tuesday morning for Bible reading or other activities. The pastor of the church community is the leader of the group. The church itself is in the center of Amsterdam and is well known. Some members are active as volunteers in the Drugs Pastorate. At the organizational level, the church and the Amsterdam Diaconate, which sponsors the Drugs Pastorate, cooperate together. The groups from Drugs Pastorate have their own image of the members of the Keizersgrachtkerk.

The pastor confused the Drugs Pastorate group with the Street Pastorate group. All three work together at an organizational level and therefore know one another. He sent the reading report to the Street Pastorate group instead of to the Drugs Pastorate group. He later realized his mistake, but by then it was too late. Due to this mistake, the reading of one another's report did not take place. The pastor regretted his mistake, but the Keizersgrachtkerk group was not interested in reading the report of the Drugs Pastorate group after having worked through the report of the Street Pastorate group. They wanted to get on with other activities instead.

## Sharing Excerpts from the Group Reading

### The Bible: A Dead Book from the Past?

Several within our reading group doubted the relevance of the Bible to us today:

> It is an old book written for people in the past, a revelation to and a message for the people living at the time it was written.
> The story has nothing to do with us.
> What we need is our own story relating to our own times.
> The messianic work of Jesus Christ ended with Jesus's death.

Due to these preconceived notions, reading and understanding the Bible presented a serious challenge to the group.

Reading the story of Tamar radically changed the tone of the discussion. From their own life experiences, all the participants identified with some aspect of the story. The Bible story became so close that it could be compared with one's personal experience. The title of this essay arose out of the reality of the Bible in our world today. Our group related directly to the Bible story, recognizing themselves and the world around them in it. Once the reading and sharing had begun, the issue of the Bible being outdated did not come up again.

The interaction within the group turned into a dialogue between the members' own real experiences and the experience of Tamar. There were continuous interactions between the Bible story and what the group members saw and experienced around them. They shifted from the biblical story to personal stories and then back to the biblical story. The discussion was characterized by touching not only on personal life but also reflecting on the world around and the reality of the same type of injustice going on in the world today. The group truly met one another in the Bible story they read: they saw one another in the Bible.

Not only the rape case in India but also the sexual abuse within the Roman Catholic Church was mentioned more than once by a participant who was sexually abused as a child after his mother left him to be taken care of in a monastery. He was never listened to, neither by the parents nor by the church. He lost his trust in people and suffered lifelong damage. The church kept silent. Just as with Tamar, the victims were not heard.

Tamar's situation of being violently raped and thrown out is sadly similar to that of the many girls and women who are raped weekly in

Amsterdam, India, and around the world. Some of them are lured into situations where they cannot resist their attacker. Some are subjected to violent rape. Though not mentioned during the group reading, it is known that such women accept the abuse as a way of life, because no authority ever believes them. The participants continued sharing these kinds of observations weeks after reading the Tamar story together. The reading gave a means of looking into society through the window of the Bible story.

The group concluded that the Bible is just as alive today as it was of old, because the story of Tamar then is like our story today—we are all Tamar. The Bible is God's story, but it is also the story of our lives.

Human Race: The Same?

The first reaction from a participant after reading this story was quite emotional: "This story is horrible, everything about it is deception. A young girl was invited in a clever way, violently raped and thrown to the street." The story shows the deeply human side of the word of God. It shows how things worked then and how things still work.

In that respect, the human race has always been the same. The role of King David, as the authority that exercised justice, was to protect the weak in society. He, however, sent his daughter to his son, who raped her. After that King David only became angry, but did nothing to safeguard Tamar or to give her justice.

One participant shared a case of a girl who was raped by her brother. Nobody believed her, because it was a taboo in the family. She is now a drug addict and lives on the street. Tamar was also on the street until her brother Absalom took her in.

Incest occurs in some families. Because it is a taboo, it is not talked about, and the offender and the victim suffer from guilt feelings. These feelings of guilt can be healed through God's forgiveness, but the conclusion of the group was that by breaking the taboo and talking about it the parents can set free the brother and sister who committed incest. The role of David was recognized in the behavior of some fathers whose children had comparable experiences. That the parents have the power and authority to set their children free from guilt feelings was repeated several times by a participant.

Another participant brought up the fact that research has shown that one third of the drug addicts have had inappropriate sex within the family.

Feelings of guilt are chronic. The lack of listening to the victims of a fate such as Tamar's causes even more damage. There will always be abuse of power, but much damage could be repaired if the victims were listened to. "Drug addicts suffer from lack of being heard," was his conclusion.

## Jonadab's Role

The group shared experiences concerning people like Jonadab who lie and make devious plans to harm innocent people. A mediator who schemed and brought the family of a participant into difficulties was compared to Jonadab. Jonadab was also compared to a voodoo man who made a charm for a client in order to procure the love of a girl he wanted to marry but who had rejected him. Through the charm the client was able to marry the girl. After having some children with her, he wanted to kill her, but neighbors intervened and rescued her from him. The voodoo man confessed his role and was very angry with the man he had helped. The girl in the story was the sister of one of the participants.

The role of Jonadab provoked serious discussion. Some were favorable to him, because he trusted his friend, Amnon, and made plans to alleviate his pain. Jonadab tried to help his friend, but did not ask or expect Amnon to treat Tamar as he did. Some argued that Jonadab should have known better and should not have lied twice. Two participants condemned Jonadab as being guilty alongside Amnon. It is remarkable that the group particularly condemned Jonadab in this story for coming up with the plan that made David cooperate and submit his daughter to a compromising situation. In the biblical story his role is not given further attention, while the role of the other actors and the consequences thereof are more in focus.

On the other hand, other participants found that what Jonadab did was all right, because it involved a love affair. They saw nothing wrong in bringing a brother and sister together. In love and war, someone brings the two together. What both parties do with each other is not the responsibility of the mediator.

## God Present in the Story/Our Story

The role of God in the story evoked a lively discussion. One participant painfully missed the presence of God in this short story: "I miss the word *God*. A short history of abuse of power by authority. How can God play a role in this story? The story did not teach anything about God. A sorrowful story about a poor girl. That is why we need God. But God did not appear in this story." Another participant reamrked: "God did not do anything to save or protect Tamar. He just let it happen." Another one argued that God was just showing that this was wrong: "You cannot do these things, then evil will happen. Then death will be the consequence. This story shows clearly a God who punishes. They did not act with the spirit of love, and then they received punishment." One participant remarked: "Because of the absence of God, that is why there is an absence of justice. There was no place for God, and there was no place for justice." Another participant reacted: "In the church people were sexually abused. If you do that then you cause damage to God. The victims were sentenced for life and the offenders were silent and walked around happily. If God were present, he could have given strict justice."

As the sharing continued, a participant told a story of a sexual act within a family. Though the issue was discussed in the family decades later, the participant thinks that only God can forgive such an act. A chain of evil happens in a family, and the question remains, how can God save and heal us?

It is noteworthy that the name of God came up often in the sharing on the story of Tamar. The participants read God into this story, looking for a divine solution. At first it seemed that this was because the story came from the word of God and that the participants therefore expected God to appear in the story. Later it became apparent that this was not the reason, but that it stemmed from their own personal need for God. They recognized their own pain and suffering in Tamar's story. No authoritative figure was able to set them free from their pain. Reading God into the story revealed how they sought God to set them free from situations comparable to Tamar's experience. Tamar was victimized and locked up in her painful experience; the powers that should have provided justice were silent. Tamar suffered in silence and loneliness.

Some participants shared their experiences of seeking deliverance from being locked in pain. All hope in an authority that could deliver them was lost. God was the only way out. Therefore, they reasoned, God must be present in this story in order to carry out the healing. This is what is theologically being expressed in this story. A solution in the form of a contrasting experience is God's presence in the story. God was the missing link. The absence of God means the presence of evil. The message of this story as the group understood it is connected directly to God.

## Comparison with the Partner Group

The approach of the partner group was quite different from that of the Drugs Pastorate group. The partner group shared insights into the story in the form of more theological and psychological analyses. They read two different Bible translations to compare the different wordings of the story, and they looked up the meaning of the names. They still had questions about the story and guessed at what might really have happened. There was little connection to their personal lives and to the reality in contemporary society. They also criticized Tamar's role. In contrast, the group from Drugs Pastorate was continually in dialogue with the Bible story and their own life's story.

## Intercultural Reading and Culture

What is remarkable in this method of Bible reading is that people within the same group tend to influence one another in their way of thinking and acting. The culture developed and maintained within a group is deeply and powerfully rooted. Social behavior and communication are significantly influenced by it. The language used and the level of openness are decisive for cultural acceptance. The cultural norms for social interaction are so deep that any social behavior outside that culture is not readily accepted.

The Drugs Pastorate group read the story of Tamar within their own cultural realm. Personal feelings relating to the story were expressed. The group looked at, read, and shared the story in a subjective manner. They sought a connection to the story, identifying and explaining it from the reality of their contemporary situation. They did not search for the aim of what the writer wanted to portray with this story. They saw the evil and the pain caused to the victim by the offenders, and they identified with the victim.

This direct identification breaks down cultural barriers and reveals another realm of language and communication. People are no longer locked into reading the Bible story from the perspective of their own cultural heritage, but another cultural heritage can be shared through the same story. The members of the group came from different countries and continents, men and women from different social and academic backgrounds. They were conscious of their differences before the reading started. They were all victims of drug addiction and shared the same culture of addiction. The Bible story of victimized Tamar brought them together. They forgot their differences in the reading. The Bible is a universal book with the potential of being shared across cultures.

When one compares the reports of the two groups, it is clear that the Drugs Pastorate group expressed a different culture in its language, openness, and communication. The participants themselves were also close to one another in social life and experience and could identify with feeling victimized in life without receiving justice. In contrast, the social context of the church group was far removed from that of the Drugs Pastorate. They could not easily enter the worldview of the partner group because of differences in language and cultural context. They remained objective in their reading of the story.

One of the problems intercultural reading poses is that of the difference in the approach to the text. Not everybody has the capacity to read and think theologically, like asking what is really written in the text and what the aim of the writer was. To do that one needs academic training in hermeneutics. The church group was able to read in that way, but the Drugs Pastorate group could not. On the other hand, reading and sharing at the level of experience and social and cultural context is an approach available often to those less hindered by an academic training. The difference in approach to the text may result in not being able to meet one another in the Bible.

What is necessary to bridge the gap between objective and subjective readings and reflections on the same story? Perhaps groups should be paired according to their social and cultural context or maybe according to their worldview or tradition. In other words, people with a comparable understanding should be coupled, rather than higher class and lower class. The disadvantage of this suggestion is that the bridge between the poor and the rich, lower and higher class, will not be effectuated, and the deeper challenges of intercultural Bible reading are avoided.

## Reflection

The reading and sharing in the group of the Drugs Pastorate created a realm of telling personally painful life experiences through reflecting on the story of Tamar. God's story became one's own personal story. This happened through the sharing and not through the reading of the story. This is the power of the method of intercultural Bible reading. When personal experience is shared, one feels invited to reflect on one's own experiences in the light of the story. It awakens and creates new possibilities for looking at issues present in the life of the participant.

The realm created by this brings the Bible to life and makes it a practical instrument in working together on life issues. This domain emerged within the sphere of the group culture of the Drugs Pastorate. Our group did not meet together with the partner group but only received their report. Their report did not spark enough interest to pursue further interaction with them.

## Conclusion

The report of the Drugs Pastorate ended with positive and encouraging news: evils within a family can come to an end; also, by reading and hearing the story of Tamar, we had done her justice. "That is good news that someone hears her story," concluded a participant, and everybody agreed. We hereby achieved a happy ending that gave hope and encouragement. Because the group expected that the word of God would provide comfort, a happy or hopeful conclusion was looked for. That is why the group was convinced that God must be in the story. This was not only Tamar's story long ago in the Middle East, but also the story of battered girls and women in Amsterdam, India, Africa, and everywhere.

A number of questions remain as a result of this reading experience: How can God deliver and heal us from the damage done? How can this method create a realm where two opposite cultures can listen to and transform each other? Meeting through reports seems easier than meeting face to face. What might lie behind that? What will it take to make this method bridge the gap between objective and subjective readings and reflections on the same story?

## 13

## STORIES ARE CLOSE, REPORTS ARE FAR: THE LIMITS OF INTERCULTURAL BIBLE READING WITH HOMELESS PEOPLE (A DIALOGUE WITHIN AMSTERDAM)

*Luc Tanja*

Intercultural Bible reading assumes that one is able to see through the eyes of the other. The core question of the project regards what happens when small groups of readers of biblical texts from sometimes radically different contexts read the same Bible story and get involved in a dialogue about its meaning. Differing contexts are present not only in different countries but even among groups within the same city. In the present account, people familiar with living on the street were paired with a group of highly educated young Christians. These two groups from the same city, but with contexts far removed from each other, exchanged reports on how they read the story of the rape of Tamar.

In this essay I describe how this story was read with a group of the Street Pastorate and how an attempt to read through the eyes of another failed. In an explanation regarding this failure, I point out some of the limitations in the practice of intercultural Bible reading.

### Street Pastorate and Stroom

The Street Pastorate sponsored by the Protestantse Diaconie Amsterdam is set up for people familiar with living on the streets. Central to the Street Pastorate is the concept of presence: a way to be closely involved in the daily life of people for a longer period of time, without a preconceived message except getting to know the other. The philosophy group of the Street Pastorate, with whom the reading took place, can best be described by James's words: "I have seen it all." That is probably true, and it can also be said about the other individuals in the group. Most have slept on the streets in recent years. Although many of them now do have a place to sleep, their situation is still vulnerable. Those participating in the Bible reading were all men over the age of fifty. The philosophy group of the Street Pastorate meets weekly, always beginning with a short meditation: a half hour of becoming quiet.

The partner group consisted of members of a community of Christians called *Stroom* ("stream"). The members of this relatively new community were mainly aged twenty-five to forty-five, most of them with a degree in higher education. Stroom is associated with a Protestant church (Gereformeerde Kerk Vrijgemaakt). The group who read together with the Street Pastorate group met regularly for a meal and discussion.

### Reading the Story in the Street Pastorate Group

"This story is still happening like this every day," said James when asked to react after the story of Tamar had been read out loud in the group. "Women are repressed in this world. Specially in the Arab world, I know this, I've traveled there." This was the typical reaction to reading 2 Sam 13: the story was linked directly to situations in our present day world and directly connected to personal experience. Some had experienced situations of (sexual) abuse themselves. Other members of the group knew about women and men who are in the same situation in other countries or closer to home. The abuse in the Roman Catholic Church, at that time prominent in the media, was mentioned. For the group, the silence the church enforced upon the victims was the same as the silence imposed on Tamar.

Derk was troubled by reading the story: "Why do you take me by surprise with this story of things I did not experience myself? What can I do with this?" It is as if this story made a direct appeal to him to act. Being confronted with this situation of injustice, something needed to be done.

Simon said: "This story makes me think of the story of Jesus, who asks: 'Who is your neighbor?'" It struck Simon that in the story of the rape of Tamar, something was missing. There was an unsatisfying open end. By bringing up the story of Jesus and the love of one's neighbor, Simon resolved the situation. This story needed a hero, someone to take care of Tamar—she needed a good Samaritan.

Derk made remarks along the same line:

Will someone make clear to Tamar that she can overcome this, that she is no longer a victim?… So often people are in the role of the victim, without even knowing it.… She should not remain a victim, that is not how it should be among humans, not even among animals.… Fortunately there are people who can help those who are open for help.

The story of Tamar intersected here with the biography of Derk. He had been a victim, someone had helped him, and now he was free from assuming the role of the victim over and over again. Reading 2 Sam 13 made him wish the same for Tamar. The group members spoke in the present tense, as though this were a newspaper article, as though Tamar's need for help were here and now.

## Different Approaches

The most common way for this group to read the story was as if it were happening here and now. Some, however, had a different reaction. Karel refused to participate in the reading and discussion: "The story is too far away.… It makes me fall asleep, I don't know the intentions, I don't know what these people are going through, it is unknown territory for me. I have my own problems. I'm not interested, I would almost want to go for a walk, it is just not nice." Though he did not walk away, he did not take part in the discussion. A refusal to read along was to be expected: it is an understandable survival strategy. By keeping his horizons close by and making his world small, Karel was able to cope.

Johan took a variation on the position of Karel and refused to discuss the rape: "That is talking badly about sex, and I just won't have that." He refused to speak negatively about sex and did not want to condemn the rape. In the group he is known to talk freely, at times even excessively, about sex. For him sex is a joyful celebration of life. Johan has at times experienced a lack of acceptance from society, and at times people have labeled his behavior as criminal. Johan sees himself as a victim of his sexual hunger, and this role of being a victim has become part of his identity. A story of rape was a potential threat to this identity and was best kept at a safe distance. By keeping this part of the story away from him, he protected himself—it was his survival strategy.

For other parts of the story, Johan joined in the discussion. He related, for instance, the solitude of Tamar in her brother's house directly to his own experience of being left alone after his parents' divorce. In this he was in line with most of the group: the story functioned as a first speaker who opened up space for personal experiences.

## Reading the Report of the Other Group

The reading report of the Stroom group was discussed several weeks later. Because quite some time had passed since the Street Pastorate had discussed the story of Tamar and because some of the group were not there the first time, 2 Sam 13 was read again. Directly thereafter, the group read the report of the Stroom group. The comments of each individual of the Stroom group identified in the report were read by a different person in the Street Pastorate group. In this way, an attempt was made to make the report as lively and accessible as possible for the Street Pastorate group.

The members of the Street Pastorate group were asked to react to the report of Stroom. None of them did so in any substantial way. Some minor remarks were made like: "They read the story just as we do," indicating that they did not see the Stroom group as any different from themselves. Further comments on how the other group read were not made. Instead the group continued to speak about the story of Tamar. The discussion leaders intervened by asking direct questions and by giving their own reflections on the report of Stroom. It did not work. The reading report was not taken as a serious subject for discussion. The story of Tamar took center stage and, as at the first reading, opened up space to share one's own experiences of abuse and of being a victim.

This was not, however, a survival strategy. This second discussion was even more open than the first one. Several people dared to speak more personally. For instance, Mark remarked that in a way he could identify with Amnon: "I too would have had difficulty in restraining myself."

The report was not kept out of reach or placed beyond the horizon for safety's sake. This report was not a threat to the core values or identity of group members. The lack of response to the report did not come from an inability to identify with other personages, for the group members easily identified with characters in the story of Tamar. Furthermore, they commonly related well to guest speakers who presented a subject to the group. Whatever the subject, whether a spiritual journey or a hobby, the group was curious and asked questions. What the people of Stroom had to say, what they meant through this text, simply did not connect with the people of the Street Pastorate.

Perhaps the report by Stroom remained undiscussed because the contrast with the story of Tamar and Amnon was just too large. The story in 2 Samuel deals with taboos, dysfunctional families, sex, kings, and princes; few texts match this. The strength of the story of Tamar and Amnon has manifested itself also in other meetings between groups who read this Bible story. It proved to be difficult to stay on the topic of the reading experience itself, for again the story of Tamar took over. This fact plus the refusal of some people to read (a part of) the story could indicate that the choice for this particular Bible story had an unfavorable effect on the process of intercultural Bible reading. By looking at the reading strategies of the Street Pastorate group, however, one has another perspective on the difference between the discussion of the story and of the report.

The Street Pastorate group got no reaction on how the Stroom group read their report. Though this would have been interesting for the leaders of the Street Pastorate group, it is doubtful whether the members would have been interested, given the way in which they received the reading report by Stroom. They would have seen it merely as another continuation of discussing the story of Tamar.

## Reading Strategies

The Street Pastorate group kept the story close to their own experiences. The biblical text functioned as a starting point, as a first speaker. For some the story posed a question: "What can I do to help Tamar? She has been violated, she is in need." Solutions are given. Simon saw the need for a good Samaritan; Derk suggested helping in the way he had been helped before. The discussions offered a solution to the story. In doing so, the reader reconsidered his—in this case there were only men—own situation. It was like a test, a chance to find a new answer or to discover that the old way out was still the right way.

For others Tamar's story opened up a space for stories of their own. Because Tamar was left alone, there was room to tell about the times the group members had been left alone. The story brought a safe place in which the events of one's own life could surface. These events related to the events in the story, though not necessarily in a direct way. Johan, for instance, said: "I read this morning in the paper that a man went to visit his ex, and he found her in bed with the neighbor, and now they are both dead in the house." The story of one dysfunctional family brought up a recent story of another tragedy. The story gave room to tell of other matters, even if these seemed not to be directly related. The Street Pastorate group accepted these meanderings easily. What was most essential in the ramblings was that the path taken had roots in the present experience. Whether the meaning of the text itself could be linked to the path the discussion took was unimportant. Only when a line of discussion did not relate to recent personal events was it dismissed as irrelevant. Through these analogous stories, the text grew as it took on other present-day situations.

A third way to approach the story was to recognize a character in the story as being in the same situation as the reader. For example, "I too would have difficulty in restraining myself" functions as a warning to be careful in certain situations. Again the story gave a way to recognize situations and to learn from them.

The readers in the Street Pastorate group were aware that the story came from the Bible. They knew it was written a long time ago in a very different context. Still they read the story as if it were happening here and now. It was not at all a strange story. Who the author was, what the author wanted to say with the story, how the story has been read through the ages—all these questions were of no significance to this group. For them, the author was dead, and they did not search for what the author might have meant with this text, nor did they search for any other meaning in the text. They accepted the story as it was, no questions asked.

The report of the partner group asked for a different reading strategy. The report was intended to be read with questions in mind like: Who were these people who wrote this? What message is hidden in their words? What values are important to them? The report asked for an active reconstruction by the authors of the report. Those in the Street Pastorate, however, just did not read in this way. Within a text they searched for a story, characters, and events to which they could relate. A story opened up a space to talk about their own experiences, a way to put their lives in perspective; a story presented them with questions to resolve. The report from the other group had nothing that this type of reader could relate to and thus the report remained closed to them.

## Conclusions

We return to the questions raised at the beginning of this essay as to how the story of Tamar was read in the Street Pastorate group and how and why the attempt to read through the eyes of another failed.

The Street Pastorate group read the story of Tamar in a very direct way. The story opened a space for the readers where they could place their own experiences. In some ways this reading looks, at first sight, to be remarkably close to the way the Bible is read in certain evangelical circles. There too the stories are read without any distance in time or space, directly relating the text to present-day life. There is, however, one major difference between these two reading strategies. The readers of the Street Pastorate did not look for meaning in the text. The story functioned as a mirror or a starting point, but not as a vehicle to transfer meaning. Evangelicals, on the other hand, always look explicitly for meaning and search for God's word in the biblical text.

The Bible reading, and the detailed study of it afterward, opened new inroads for pastoral care. At first the experience seemed to offer few new insights. The stories told by the participants were already known. However, a more careful examination of the process gave a better understanding of the reading strategies used. For instance, during the discussion, mentioning the good Samaritan was not well understood, partially because the other remark that offered a solution was made at a different point in the discussion. Only on closer examination did it become clear that these readers were offering solutions and in doing so were also testing whether a solution like this would (still) work for them.

Reading the report of the Stroom group failed to bring about an exchange on reading strategies. Because the reading strategy of the Street Pastorate group did not include seeking after the author of a text, the authors of the report became irrelevant to the Street Pastorate group. There was thus no attempt to search for a meaning intended by the authors of the report, and the report became empty. The discussion by the Street Pastorate group took as its only starting point the story behind the report.

The report of the Stroom group was at a further disadvantage, because it had to compete with a powerful story. The story in 2 Sam 13 deals with taboos and strong emotions. At least for the Street Pastorate and Stroom, the choice for this story was unfortunate: Stroom was just no match for Tamar.

This failure to interact with a report points to limitations in the project of intercultural Bible reading. Groups who have a reading strategy in which there is no searching for meaning in the text and who do not reconstruct the author of a text—for whom the author is dead or nonexistent—cannot fully take part in intercultural Bible reading. The report of another group will not enable them to read through the eyes of another. Still the exchange might be of value to the partner group. Though we did not hear back from Stroom, it is quite possible that they were challenged by the Street Pastorate group's report to think about why they were so interested in academic issues, why they had less identification with the characters, and why they did not put their own experience into the story. Whether other ways of exchange (e.g., video, Skype, writing stories or plays) would have been more successful is presently but a matter of speculation.

# 14

## Making the Circle Safer:
## Intercultural Bible Reading
## in the Context of Sexual Violence
## (A Dialogue within South Africa)

*Charlene van der Walt and Kim Barker*

*Empirical research* as a term often conjures up images of strict clinical procedures and of painstakingly precise work conducted in sterile circumstances by a person wearing a white lab coat. Although certain types of research require such settings, in the present essay we trace a complex and often messy process that is characteristic of empirical qualitative research. Qualitative research has been described as messy, because it aims to account for the multiplicity of human experiences within a certain context:

> The role of qualitative research is not to determine which account is the more accurate or "truthful," but is rather to use these accounts as a resource in order to understand how "situated accounts" are told in a way that allows speakers to achieve a different purpose through emphasizing some aspects of their stories and de-emphasizing others. (Barbour 2008, 28)

In this paper we systematically and chronologically describe the research process designed to explore empirically the dimensions of the intercultural Bible reading process. The initial research process was developed as the empirical component of a doctoral project in Old Testament studies focusing on the distribution of power and the impact of ideology in the context of intercultural Bible reading.[1] The nature of participants' responses to the

---

1. The full project is described in Van der Walt's ThD dissertation, completed

process, analyzed as one component of the project, raised important ethical questions that contributed to our adaptation of the process. This essay is a reflection on empirical work in progress, as it is understood that qualitative research implies ever-evolving responses to the research context:

> The goal of qualitative research is to discover patterns which emerge after close observation, careful documentation, and thoughtful analysis of the research topic. What can be discovered by qualitative research is not sweeping generalizations, but contextual findings. This process of discovery is basic to the philosophical underpinning of the qualitative approach. (Maykut and Morehouse 1994, 21)

We describe the original research design and process in the first section. In the subsequent sections we explore why it became ethically necessary to adapt the process and how this was done.

## The Initial Space

The history of the interpretation of the Bible is one of power and control. In this regard Jeremy Punt argues:

> Attempts to say what the Bible "really means," to get the meaning, always stood in service of purposes determined by ecclesial, socio-political, ethical, nationalistic or other such concerns. Attempts to subvert existing claims to the Bible and its meaning often served similar, if opposing, interests.... The Bible as site of struggle involves, however, more than difference of interpretive opinion. The Bible is involved in the discourse of power and is drawn into a struggle for interpretive control as well as eventually ownership thereof. (Punt 2002, 425)

Looking back at the history of biblical scholarship, it is clear that a privileged position of power was long held by Western academic scholars. The language, themes of discussion, and focus of investigation were mainly determined by the few who had access to the academic environment. This privileged position is challenged by both feminist theology and African

---

March 2010 at the Department of Old and New Testament, Faculty of Theology, University of Stellenbosch, South Africa, under the supervision of Louis Jonker. For a full transcript of the dissertation and data collected, see http://irl.sun.ac.za/handle/10019.1/4019.

hermeneutics, which argue for a different space of conversation and different conversation partners.

Through the course of history different strategies have been applied to interpret biblical texts. Broadly speaking, four main phases of biblical scholarship can be distinguished, each focusing on a different aspect of the interpretation process:

(1) Historical-critical approach: the world behind the text. In this approach the focus is on the description of the text in terms of its process of development and the world in which the author(s) functioned. Louis Jonker (2005b, 27) describes this movement as: "The historical-critical approaches hold in common the presupposition that (biblical) texts can and should be understood only in the light of the historical context within which they originate."

(2) Literary approach: the world of the text. The text in itself became the main focus of biblical scholarship. "A text is a unique linguistic unit, constituted by the relationship of the parts to one another and to the whole. Whereas historical criticism regarded meaning as a function of origin, those who turned to the text itself regarded meaning as a function of the relationships among the parts of the text" (Lawrie 2005b, 68).

(3) The role of the reader in the interpretation process: the world in front of the text. In this approach the role of the reader is taken seriously. "The reader does not merely discover meaning, but plays an active part in the creation of meaning." Readers furthermore do not read the text in isolation, but as a function of the constant interaction between the text and the reader's personal context. The context of the reader becomes the key to the understanding of the text. "The specific context of the reader provides the horizon of understanding that enables the reader to make sense of the text" (Lawrie 2005a, 111).

(4) Hermeneutic of suspicion: the world under the text. "A number of influential approaches to the interpretation of texts are based on the suspicion that there are hidden factors at work in the production, circulation and reception of texts" (Lawrie 2005c, 167). Lawrie continues by describing a hermeneutic of suspicion: "The hermeneutics of suspicion suspects that what usually remains hidden is indeed a guilty secret. Neither authors, nor texts, nor readers are 'innocent' or neutral. They often work together to keep up the (false) appearance of normality and rationality" (167).

The intercultural Bible reading space constructed for this research was theoretically informed by the hermeneutical frameworks of feminist theology and African hermeneutics. Feminist thought argues for the importance of the contextually embedded voice of the individual. The importance given to the contextuality of individual voices grows out of one of the fundamental principles of feminism, namely, the central role of women's experience. Denise Ackermann describes the importance of this principle for a feminist hermeneutic as follows:

> A feminist hermeneutic, like all hermeneutics, is grounded in experience, and more particularly in women's experience of oppression.... It is essential to acknowledge that experience itself is interpreted and filtered through our cultural matrix, which in turn is formed by the race, class, time and histories of our lives. There is no universal experience for all people or even for all women. Yet, while accepting the particularity of experience as a hermeneutical category, we must acknowledge the universal fact of discrimination against and oppression of women. (Ackermann 1993, 21)

On the other hand, African hermeneutics theoretically offers a communal space where the voice of the individual can be heard. The term *African hermeneutics* does not imply a singular, all-encompassing movement or approach to theological issues. Africa is fragmented, and approaches to theological issues are numerous. Pluralism is, of course, not unique to Africa, but rather typical of postmodern reality, a reality that challenges the universalization of human experience.

> Resistance to this universalising and imperialist tendency, therefore, means an assertion of the radically, irreducibly plural nature of human existence. It implies a fundamental respect for the Other, one that does not and will not attempt to reduce the Other to the Same. Life is basically dialogical, like a good conversation. It is a relation that retains its distance; it is a face-to-face engagement that respects the "otherness of the other"; it is committed to hearing the voice of the other. Pluralism, thus, is a given fact of political, cultural, theological and religious life. (Peterson 1994, 223)

African hermeneutics takes diversity seriously and does not strive to create a new approach to biblical interpretation, but as Jonker (2005a, 637) rightly states: "An African hermeneutic is rather a hermeneutical stance or disposition according to which, and in service of which, a whole variety of exegetical methods or tools are used." The space that African hermeneutics describes allows for the transformation from a situation of multiculturality to interculturality, where the differences between various cultural agents are not merely tolerated but celebrated and brought into real interaction. African hermeneutics thus requires an ethic of hospitality. As Robert Vosloo proposes:

> The challenge posed by the moral crisis does not merely ask for tolerance and peaceful co-existence or some abstract plea for community, but for an ethos of hospitality. The opposite of cruelty and hostility is not simply freedom from the cruel and hostile relationship, but hospitality. Without an ethos of hospitality it is difficult to envisage a way to challenge economic injustice, racism and xenophobia, lack of communication, the recognition of the rights of another, etc. Hospitality is a prerequisite for a more public life. (Vosloo 2003, 66)

The praxis of the intercultural Bible reading process developed for this research, therefore, involves the coming together of diverse individuals from different cultural backgrounds within a safe space that allows for the interaction between these individuals and a biblical text. The intercultural connections take place on two levels. First, there are the differences between the various cultural frameworks that the participants bring to the interactions; second, there is the interaction between diverse modern Bible readers and the culturally removed biblical text. By allowing for the interaction between culturally diverse individuals, the intercultural Bible reading process theoretically becomes a safe space that promotes human dignity and facilitates social transformation.

In order to test these claims regarding the intercultural Bible reading space, an empirical study was conducted in the congregation of Grahamstown where Charlene van der Walt served as minister of the Dutch Reformed Church. As pastor, Van der Walt had contact with a broad spectrum of believers who could take part in the study. The empirical study explored the complexities of the intercultural Bible reading space by examining aspects such as the inherent power dynamics, as well as the role of individual ideological frameworks. Because of the dynamic complexities of terms such as *power, ideology*, and *culture*, a theoretical framework was required that would bring into play the hybrid identity of these terms. Power, ideology, and culture were critically analyzed in the intercultural Bible reading process by using the theories of Michel Foucault, John Thompson, and Geert Hofstede.

Foucault understands power as operating in all relationships, being in fact a relational strategy that functions in such a manner as to achieve more power. Foucault shows that where there is power, there is always resistance and that not all power is negative. He sees power as constitutive rather than destructive. Mark George (2000, 93) explains Foucault's thinking in this way: "Power, whether individual or institutional, always seeks to become more powerful and influential in society, and thus there is constant interaction, negotiation, and competition among forces. Frequently, forces combine in particular, complex arrangements or configurations in order to achieve more power." Foucault's ideas on power relate to the study of the intercultural Bible reading space in their focus on the relational nature of power and how it functions in particular social environments.

Thompson (1990, 56) claims that to study ideology is to be "concerned with the ways in which meaning is mobilized in the social world and serves thereby to bolster up individuals and groups who occupy positions of power.... To study ideology is to study the ways in which meaning serves to establish and sustain relations of domination."

Hofstede (2001, 9) describes culture as "the collective programming of the mind that distinguishes the members of one group or category of people from another." He identifies five universal depth dimensions of culture, "each rooted in a basic problem with which all societies have to cope":

(1) "*power distance*, which is related to the different solutions to the basic problem of human inequality";
(2) "*uncertainty avoidance*, which is related to the level of stress in a society in the face of an unknown future";
(3) "*individualism* versus *collectivism*, which is related to the integration of individuals into primary groups";
(4) "*masculinity* versus *femininity*, which is related to the division of emotional roles between men and women"; and
(5) "*long-term* versus *short-term* orientation, which is related to the choice of focus for people's efforts: the future or the present" (Hofstede 2001, 29).

The empirical Bible reading space and process that was constructed for the study brought together female Bible readers in Grahamstown in the Eastern Cape Province of South Africa. Four separate sessions took place, with a group of eight women from culturally diverse backgrounds taking part in each session. Cultural diversity was ensured in each group by the fact that participants were selected according to a profile constructed in such a way as to represent the cultural diversity that exists in the Eastern Cape region. Each group consisted of a young person, a skilled reader, a reader for the Dutch Reformed community, someone representing the Anglican community, a black/Xhosa-speaking woman, a nonbeliever, a reader between the ages of thirty and forty, and a participant who would enhance the group diversity in any way possible. The sessions were constructed in such a way as to optimize the meeting between the culturally diverse women and to allow for enough time to engage with 2 Sam 13:1–22, the biblical text chosen. The three-hour sessions consisted of ten phases that slowly led the participants deeper into the intercultural engagement. In phase 1, participants were introduced to one another and the process was explained. Each participant received a workbook in which all of the relevant data was collected for the empirical study, such as the research process, a number of different translations of the text, and enough space to make notes and comment on the process. During phase 2, participants filled in a demographic questionnaire and completed a free-writing exercise that was developed for the study to test the ideological starting point of individual participants. Phase 3 introduced a timeline exercise in which participants were given the opportunity to situate themselves temporally with regard to major world events. Participants were asked to indicate when they were born, where they were in 1994, the watershed year in the history of South Africa marking the end of the apartheid regime as the first general elections were held—it was this change that allowed for the possibility of intercultural engagement—and when they first became aware of rape as a social issue that threatened woman. This exercise allowed individual participants to get to know one another a bit better. Phase 4 consisted of a *lectio divina* reading of 2 Sam 13:1–22. The story was read meditatively in both Afrikaans and English. In order to place the biblical text within its own context, the participants were given some background information on the world behind the text in phase 5. In phase 6, participants were given the opportunity to spend some quiet time in personal reflection. Then, in phase 7, participants were paired up by the research team to allow for engagement between individuals who were as culturally diverse as possible; they were given the opportunity to share their responses to the biblical story with one another. The emphasis in this phase was not on dialogue, but on creating a safe space where one person could talk and the other participant would listen to the interpretations of their partner without interruption or challenge. Phase 8 consisted of an open group discussion, recorded and transcribed after the research process was completed. The discussions were introduced by the research assistant and continued freely for forty-five to sixty minutes.[2] The task of the research assistant was to guide the research process and to ensure that all the phases took place in the allotted time. During the open conversation, the research assistant facilitated the conversation but did not regulate it in any way: the discussions were directed by the participants. After the conversation, in phase 9, participants completed the free-writing exercise for the second time. They also filled in a questionnaire pertaining to the power dynamics experienced in the conversations and exploring the power dynamic depicted in the biblical story. In phase 10, participants were thanked for their participation and given the opportunity to remark on the process and to give relevant feedback.

The data collected was reworked into a digital format in order to simplify its analysis. After transcribing the recorded conversations, we conducted a detailed conversation analysis. The results of the conversation analysis formed the basis of an analysis of power dynamics in the research groups. The data collected in the free-writing exercise was analyzed with the help of a data analysis tool developed specifically for the research process; this allowed for an ideological assessment of the participants before and after the intercultural Bible reading experience.

The data collected and analyzed confirmed that the intercultural Bible reading space had the inherent potential to facilitate social transformation. Participants had the experience of being truly heard and of engaging with one another. The voice of "the culturally removed other" often challenged perceptions and helped individuals to comprehend the complexity of social situations. The discovery of the "other" and the everyday realities that others often have to face resulted in a greater awareness of the participants' personal position, especially when that position was one of privilege. However, the space could not avoid the problematic nature of inescapable power dynamics. Power functions in social situations and the inevitable forming of alliances between more powerful participants could not be prevented. When constructing groups for an intercultural Bible reading process, it is important to be aware of the realities of power in a social situation and to select participants based on dimensions of difference, as well as considering factors that promote the formation of alliances.

---

2. The research assistant was Kim Barker, a pastoral therapist with experience in qualitative research facilitation.

## A Space Discovered

It should be clear that the primary goal in setting up the intercultural Bible reading groups, as well as the process for this specific study, was not to create a space where women could freely and safely engage with issues of violence, rape, and abuse. We were taken aback, therefore, that it indeed became such a space.

In the very first research group, one of the research participants set the tone for the entire session by sharing her painful personal experience of rape within the confines of her marriage. This story was told in response to the timeline exercise question: "When did you personally become aware of rape as a threat to women?" She shared her disillusionment with the institution of marriage and with the vulnerable position in which she found herself. She could not deny her husband sexual intercourse, even though she knew that he had other sexual partners and was in fact HIV positive. We were moved by her courage to speak out in the group and by the fact that she felt safe enough to do so.

The facilitator was aware of the delicacy of the moment, but did not intervene as the group took up the challenge of responding with respect and care toward this participant. Indeed, again and again the courageous women who took part in the study claimed the safe space offered by the groups and enriched it both by sharing their own stories of pain and vulnerability and hearing the stories of the other in a caring and supportive manner. They held one another's stories with a sense of reverence and opened up possibilities of hope and resistance in spite of the real and painful reality of widespread sexual violence.

At the end of the Bible study group, the facilitator checked in with any participant who had disclosed experiences of sexual violence in her own life or in her family and offered further conversation and/or counseling when the participant felt that would be helpful. She also followed up with two participants within two weeks to determine whether they felt they could benefit from further support. While one participant welcomed the opportunity for a follow-up conversation, it was largely to share how she had coped with the experience of sexual violence and the measures she had taken to ensure recovery. No other participants felt the need for further support.

Already within this very first research group, we became aware of the possibilities that the intercultural Bible reading space held for creating a safe and supportive environment for women to speak about issues relating to violence, rape, and abuse. However, both as researcher and facilitator, we were aware that the responses and outcomes could have been different and that our commitment to ethical practice required us to reflect critically on the process we had developed and invited participants into (Guillemin and Gillam 2004; Gatenby and Morrison-Hume 2001).

This incident was an "ethically important moment" (Guillemin and Gillam 2004, 262) that, given the South African context, we might have anticipated but had not. The endemic nature of sexual violence against women and children in South African society cannot be denied. The South African Police Service estimates that 1 out of every 25 rapes is reported to the police. With 66,400 sexual assaults reported in South Africa in 2012–2013, this translates to a staggering 1.6 million sexual assaults occurring annually. Helen Moffett remarks in this regard (2006, 130): "These figures [referring to South African rape stats], as well as the failure of South Africa's overburdened criminal justice and health systems to respond appropriately to the crisis, suggest an unacknowledged gender civil war. The high rate of rape in particular is also fuelling South Africa's HIV and Aids pandemic." Marilys Guillemin and Lynn Gillam (2004, 262) define such moments as the "difficult, often subtle, and usually unpredictable moments" that almost inevitably arise in the practice of doing research, when the researcher's decisions and responses have important ethical ramifications. These may not necessarily be difficult decisions to make, and it may be clear to the researcher how to proceed, but there is "something ethically important at stake" (265).

The ethical concern that was at stake was whether the participant's disclosure of her experience of sexual violence in this context would prove to be beneficial or harmful for her. This question became all the more critical as comparable incidents were a recurring event in the research groups. Through evaluation it became clear that the research process held clearly identifiable risks: given the pervasiveness of sexual violence in South Africa, the possibility of eliciting strong responses of anger, sadness, or anxiety, or even triggering flashbacks and nightmares in participants in the Bible study groups was a real and legitimate concern. Although, as already mentioned, sexual violence was not the primary focus of the research and we were not actively eliciting the sharing of personal experiences of such violence, we had seen how the safety of the research context and the theme of the biblical text had invited sharing. We were challenged by Rachel Jewkes et al. (2000, 96), who caution:

Although many respondents state that they welcome the opportunity to talk to someone about violence in their lives, it should also be recognized that for informants, such an inquiry involves reliving extremely distressing events in their lives. This is a situation of vulnerability, which if not handled sensitively can lead to women being further traumatized with feelings of blame, hopelessness, and lack of self-worth being reinforced. The dangers associated with this are real—in a survey in Cambodia, a woman committed suicide after an interview.

This is a suitably sobering glimpse into the possible effects on research participants, and it highlights the importance of a carefully constructed research process. However, we also realized that the other side of the coin is that numerous studies have shown that participants in sexual violence research usually seem to find participation beneficial, whether or not they experience strong emotions in response to an interview or questionnaire (Draucker 1999; Priebe et al. 2010; Campbell 2002; Campbell et al. 2004).

At the completion of the initial research project, reflections on the group processes distilled the following key realizations. (1) The discussions within the Bible study groups went far beyond engagement with the biblical text: participants related the story to their own lives, and some participants shared painful stories (see Van der Walt 2012). So while the stated aim of the research was to observe the power relationships within the groups and to assess the effects of the intercultural Bible reading experience on participants' ideological positioning, what unfolded were conversations about sexual violence sparked by the biblical narrative. (2) Based on statistics and the experiences in the groups, we have to assume that every time a group of women gather in South Africa for almost any purpose, at least some percentage of the group will have experienced sexual violence themselves or within their immediate families. In the South African context sexual violence will never be a theoretical discussion—it is a painfully lived reality.

While keeping the risks in mind and following from the above-mentioned key realizations, we would like tentatively to consider the possible contribution that the intercultural Bible reading space can make in creating a supportive environment where women and men may reflect on issues of gender-based violence in the light of biblical stories. The remarks are a first exploration of the value of the intercultural Bible reading space for women's engagement with issues of violence, rape, and abuse. We understand that these are complex issues embedded within complex sociocultural and historical contexts and thus offer our remarks as troubling utterances rather than as conclusive arguments.

We are engaging in this reflection as the basis for the discussion of a new empirical study currently conducted in partnership with the Vrije Universiteit Amsterdam. The study, "Through the Eyes of Another II," involves Bible study groups from around the world engaging interculturally with regard to their interpretations of various biblical texts. The project facilitates the creative dialogue between Bible study groups from the first and two-thirds world by bringing into conversation Bible interpretations done in various contexts by a diversity of Bible study groups (see www. bible4all.org). The intercultural moment for the new project thus is not focusing on the cultural diversity within groups, but rather on the interaction between groups representing different cultural contexts.

Because of our previous engagement with the Tamar story in 2 Sam 13:1–22 and its particular relevance to the South African context, we have chosen this story again as the basis for the new process of intercultural Bible reading. The focus of this empirical research is to create a safe space where women and men can reflect on issues of power, position, and agency within the text and can engage with these issues in a creative dialogue with their own lived realities.

Considering the aim of the empirical research, special attention will be given, first, to creating a safe and supportive environment, and, second, to facilitating conversation around issues of power and privilege by asking specific probing questions. Research questions will initially focus on the dynamics within the narrative and gradually shift to the lived experience of the research participants. Attention will also be given to how the research process needs be constructed, taking into account the difference in dynamics for (1) groups of men, (2) groups of women, and (3) mixed groups. The research process will consist of two different sessions. In the first session the research groups will engage with the story of Tamar by using the constructed research process. After the first contact session a detailed summary will be made of the most significant moments in the process and this will be sent to the partnering group within a first world context. A follow-up session will then be conducted when the research group reflects on the response from the partnering group. If any further dialogue is sparked in the collaboration process, follow-up sessions will be organized when possible.

Sadly, sexual violence is a real part of the lived reality for significant numbers of women, children, and men in South Africa, and the feminist practical theologian Denise Ackermann (1997) has identified this as a pressing issue that should be central to women involved with theology, especially those in South Africa. Floretta Boonzaier and Cheryl de La Rey describe the unique complexities of South African society in relation to gender-based violence as follows:

> In South Africa, there are particular manifestations of violence against women that result in a unique interaction between race, gender and other forms of power to form complex dynamics of inequity and domination. The sociocultural context provides the boundaries through which women filter their experience of violence and through which men access preferred or devalued forms of gender identity. An analysis of woman abuse amongst South African women, therefore, cannot be accomplished without acknowledgement of multiple levels of analysis, such as the social, cultural, economic and historical contexts. (Boonzaier and De La Rey 2003, 1004)

Keeping these complexities in mind, Rachel Jewkes (Gender and Health Group, Medical Research Council, Pretoria) has developed a theory concerning the causality of intimate partner/gender-based violence. Her model for explaining these causes "presents it as a constellation or web of associated and mediating factors and processes which are centrally influenced by ideas about masculinity and the position of women in a society and ideas about the use of violence" (Jewkes, Leven, and Penn-Kekana 2002, 1615). Fundamental to the understanding of violence against women are two separate yet connected ideological concepts. The first is the ideology of male superiority, which

> legitimates the disciplining of women, often for transgression of conservative female gender roles, and often also the use of force in this. They construct women as legitimate vehicles for the reconfirmation of male powerfulness through beating since this is a demonstration of male power juxtaposed against the lesser power of women. They act to disempower women through denying equal access to education, employment and political roles. In so doing, they impact on women's perceptions of self-worth and self-efficiency, as well as reducing their social and economic ability to leave a relationship, return to family and/or live alone and thus severely curtail their ability to act against an abuser. (Jewkes, Leven, and Penn-Kekana 2002, 1615)

The second ideological factor that serves as an explanation for the high incidence of violence against women is the so-called culture of violence, where violence is deployed frequently as a tool for conflict resolution:

> Cross-cultural studies of intimate partner violence suggest that it is much more frequent in societies where violence is usual in conflict situations and political struggles. An example of this relation is South Africa, where not only is there a history of violent state repression and community insurrection, but also violence is deployed frequently in many situations including disputes between neighbours and colleagues at work.... Many cultures condone the use of physical violence by men against women in certain circumstances and within certain boundaries of severity. (Jewkes 2002, 1426)

> It has been argued that violence against women is much more common where interpersonal violence is generally common and it has been shown that childhood experiences of violence in the home serve to reinforce the normative nature of violence and thus increase the likelihood of women's acceptance of abuse. (Jewkes, Leven, and Penn-Kekana 2002, 1615)

## The Possibility of a New Space

In the light of the discussion of the ideological foundations for sexual violence and intimate partner abuse, we would like to propose that the intercultural Bible reading space, as discussed in the first part of the essay, can potentially be a life-affirming safe space from which alternative realities can be explored for both women and men. The potential of a new space is premised upon three possibilities that can be identified within the intercultural Bible reading space; these will be set forth below.

### Finding a Vocabulary to Name Experiences of Violence

Women and men most often do not report incidences of sexual violence or respond to probing questions about violence within the family or personal setting. The reasons for this are numerous and complex. They may be unable to name commonplace behavior as violent (Jewkes and Abrahams 2002) or to express in words the pain and suffering that they have endured in situations of violence and abuse (Herman 1997; McKenzie-Mohr and Lafrance 2011). They may choose to remain silent as a form of self-preservation, to protect themselves from further violation at the hands of the perpetrator or of the ones they choose to tell.

Most often in families, communities, and the broader society, including the policing and justice systems, the response to rape survivors speaking out about the violation they have experienced is one of horrified apathy, disbelief, or a not-so-subtle blaming—a questioning of where they were, what they were doing, what they were wearing, who they were with, the choices they made, and so on. In our country, opportunities for survivors of sexual violence to begin the process of naming the offense and then constructing coherent narratives about their experiences in a supportive receiving context are extremely rare. It is not surprising then that most survivors either attempt to disclose and then fall silent or never try in the first place.

In the intercultural Bible reading space, the individual's culturally embedded narratives are met by "the other," who may see things from a different perspective. This community of alternative viewpoints might offer a participating individual the tools and the language with which they could critically engage with their own life experiences and consequently begin to unmask "normal" behavior within a given context as violent or abusive. On a different level, the opportunity to critically reflect on the story of Tamar allows Bible readers a creative distance from their own lived experience. By speaking about Tamar's situation and the power dynamics that operate within the story, participants develop an interpretive key to their own, often unnameable, experiences.

## "Troubling" Ideologies of Male Dominance

In line with Bronwyn Davies, I choose to use the term *troubling* in this sense:

> The particular meaning of trouble that I am intending here is the same as when we say "the seas were troubled," where *trouble* means to agitate or to make rough. I use the word troubling, rather than "deconstructing" or "putting under erasure," since I find that too many readers of deconstructive texts take deconstruction to mean dismantling that obliterates the binaries and the boundaries between them. Binaries are not so easily dismantled, and deconstructive work often can do no more than draw attention to the binaries and to their constructive force. For some people, in some readings, deconstructive work may facilitate a different take-up of meaning, beyond the binaries. But this does not undo the continuing force of relations of power that operate to hold the binaries in place. I choose the word *troubling* to represent more closely what it is that deconstructive work can do. (Davies 2000, 14)

By bringing together critical biblical scholars and lay readers with a variety of interpretive tools to communally engage with the Bible text as a reflective surface, the possibility is opened for the "troubling" of ideologies of male dominance, which are often based upon exclusive practices of Bible interpretation. Within the process of contextual Bible reading, complex biblical narratives are often used as a so-called reflective surface. The text becomes the point of reference in a conversation where the singular reader, as constructed in the traditional bipolar model of biblical interpretation, is replaced by a more realistic diversity of readers around the biblical text in a multipolar model (see Kessler 2004). By using the Bible as a reflective surface in the process of intercultural Bible reading, the dominant or final nature of a biblical text is countered in that it is welcomed as one conversation partner among others. It is put on an equal level with the socially embedded narratives of the women and men taking part in the Bible reading exercise. Modern readers within these reading communities can be encouraged to ask critical questions of the Bible text and to read against the grain in order to unmask patriarchal ideas and practices.

## Countering a "Violent Culture" by Creating Safe Spaces

The primary contribution that the intercultural Bible reading space potentially could offer is the creation of a safe space where women and men can engage with the realities of a violent culture and its ramifications from within the confines of a caring and supportive environment. Michael White suggests that when people stand together in solidarity, however briefly and partially, it "provides us with the opportunity to look back on our taken-for-granted ways of thinking and being in the world"; he believes that this makes it possible for people to "think outside the limits of what we would otherwise think, to challenge aspects of our own participation in the reproduction of dominance, and to identify options for action in addressing disadvantage and inequality that would not otherwise be available to us" (1997, 141). By creating safe spaces where the voices of the individuals are embraced within a caring community of Bible readers, the possibility for "compassionate witnessing" exists. Kathy Weingarten (2003, 21–38) describes the ideal witnessing position in relation to violence as one of "awareness and empowerment" where we are able to acknowledge losses, to support mourning and grief, to humanize the enemy, and to witness individual and collective pain with as much heartfelt compassion as we can muster. In "compassionate witnessing" and a stance of solidarity the possibility of "reasonable hope" exists:

> Reasonable hope, consistent with the meaning of the modifier, suggests something both sensible and moderate, directing our attention to what is within reach more than what may be desired but unattainable. Reasonable hope softens the polarity between hope and despair, hope and hopelessness and allows for (more) people to place themselves in the category of the hopeful…. Reasonable hope is relational; consists of practice; maintains that the future is open, uncertain and influenceable; seeks goals and pathways to them; and accommodates doubt, contradiction and despair. (Weingarten 2010, 7–9)

By combining the insights from reflecting on the potential that the intercultural Bible reading space hold and the challenges posed by the ethically important moment described earlier, a new research process was develop for the new project.

## A Space Reconstructed

The process developed for the new project entails the elements presented below.

### Providing Information and Informed Consent

Before the intercultural Bible reading process with a new research group is initiated, participants are made aware of the potential risks and discomforts involved in the process. Most groups in the new phase of the project are established groups, made up of people that are well acquainted with one another. The intercultural engagement of the new project is not situated within the group that reads the text together, but between groups that share their respective interpretations. The aim and subject matter of the research was clearly stated in an informative letter. Before starting the process participants were asked to sign a letter of informed consent stipulating that they were participating in the process voluntarily. By having this element introduced before the start of the process, participants were also given the opportunity to withdraw if they were in any way uncomfortable. In each research group conducted thus far, there have been prospective participants who have opted not to take part in the process. From this we deduce that a moment of reflection and personal risk evaluation is important before starting the process, and this contributes to a greater feeling of safety and ethical responsibility.

## Welcome, Joining, and Being Present

The group session started with a moment of welcome, emphasizing the importance of being seen, acknowledged, and invited into the conversation. This moment also allowed the participants to perform identity claims upfront and to share some initial expectations of the process collectively embarked on.

## Establishing Safety

In this important moment, the so-called ground rules or house rules of the process were collectively constructed by the group; these rules were to serve as the guiding principles for the process. We chose to focus on the construction of a safe space and to invite the participants to help construct the values that would ensure this space. We offered a range of photographs that showed people in places of safety in the midst of what could otherwise have been dangerous situations. Participants were invited to select a photograph that drew their attention. As part of their introductory statements about themselves, they were then invited to say what drew them to the picture.

The goal of this exercise was to raise awareness among participants of their feelings or concerns about safety and about how to create a safe space before moving into a conversation about how the group could collectively create those same conditions required for safety within the group.

## Collective Time Line

One of the challenges in working with diverse groups of people is figuring out how to identify aspects of "unity" within the "diversity." Paulo Freire (1994, 157) calls this "the invention of unity in diversity." The aim of the timeline exercise was to generate "a rich shared sense of purpose, and also a diversity of memory and perspective" (Denborough 2008, 143–44). The timeline, physically constructed within the meeting space, offers a "visual representation of collective history" that stays as a reminder for participants during their time working together. It enabled participants to share powerful personal memories and history but in a way that linked them to a collective theme.

We put up the timeline, usually before participants arrived, and at the beginning of the exercise asked each person to consider the following questions:

- When did you first become aware of sexual violence as an issue that influences women's lives?
- Can you say a little bit about how it was that you became aware?

The person then wrote down the year involved and a sentence or two about what was happening to them at that time. They took turns in coming up and placing their pieces of paper at the relevant place on the time line, and, if they wished, shared with the group the story or experience involved.

The timeline "linked participants' stories and histories to a collective shared theme, a shared purpose" (Denborough 2008, 159). Rather than homogenizing history, it acknowledged and honored the rich diversity of history represented in the group. The timeline also showed a broader social history of the country and acknowledged that violence against women and South Africa's history as a nation are profoundly interrelated. The exercise placed individual stories against a broader societal and political landscape.

Rape Statistics

After much deliberation, especially taking into account the distressing or numbing impact that gross statistics can have on people, we decided to include in the process a component that reflected on statistical trends concerning rape and sexual violence in South Africa. Rape statistics in the South African context are both alarming and painfully complex. The main intention behind their inclusion was to contextualize rape as a larger societal and gender one rather than an individual issue. Louise du Toit (2005, 253) comments with regards to the value of statistics:

> Rape statistics have been powerfully used as a tool to shift the discourse on sexual violence from a "private" event, where sexuality as such is often still regarded as both shameful and private, to a political issue, where rape is seen as a "matter of political and public concern, because politics is about who has power over whom, and rape (and its threat) is one of the multiple ways in which people wield power over each other."

Michael White (1995, 88) agrees that "to assist people to establish an account of the politics of their experience helps to undermine the self-blame and the

shame that is so often experienced in relation to the abuse [or sexual vio-
lence] itself."

On another level, the use of statistics reflects one of the core values
of feminist approaches, namely, the insistence on the importance of context. Feminist theology is practical and contextual, as it acknowledges
and takes seriously the lived reality of people's lives. Feminist theology raises uncomfortable questions about practices taken for granted
that serve to marginalize or subjugate people. According to Ackermann
(1996, 34), the emphasis of a feminist theology of praxis is "collaborative, sustained action for justice, liberation and healing, empowered by
continuous struggle, hope and passion." The use of statistics and the
exercise devolved for the process thus aims at bringing the lives of the
most vulnerable into focus and to illustrate something of a communal
affectedness. In response to statistical statements concerning rape and
sexual violence in the South African context, participants are asked to
reflect on their own thoughts and feelings concerning the statements.

*Lectio Divina*

The story of Tamar was introduced to the group in the form of a *lectio
divina* reading process. The approach emphasized listening to the text
and to one's own responses to the text. Much of what is termed "Bible
study" in local churches takes place in an argumentative, logical, analytical style. Anticipating that participants might step into this mode,
we wanted to disrupt the discourses/binaries that suggest that there
can be a right and wrong, good and bad way of responding to the text;
we wanted instead to call forth an intensely personal, almost visceral
response through the *lectio*. One author had the experience of reading
the story of the rape of Tamar to a gathering of more than a thousand
young people who had just participated in an antirape protest at Rhodes
University in Grahamstown, South Africa. Many of the participants were
not churchgoers and would have had little knowledge of Scripture. Even
those who attended church regularly were unlikely to have ever heard
this passage read from the pulpit. The majority were therefore hearing the story for the first time. The word *visceral* aptly describes their
response. They groaned aloud, gasped, and groaned again as the events
of the story unfolded, caught up in the tragedy that was all too familiar
in their own contexts.

## Silence and Reflection

In order to give participants time to engage with the nuances of the story of Tamar, we included a time of silence and personal reflection. We were aware that the passage might evoke strong feelings, perhaps even triggering painful memories. The time of silence and reflection gave participants time to respect whatever the text invoked within themselves.

## Listening in Twos

After the time of personal reflection, participants were divided into pairs and encouraged to share their first response to the story of Tamar. The aim of the exercise was to allow participants to find a vocabulary for their initial experience of the story and to share this with someone who actively listened. Participants were encouraged not to ask questions or to interrupt each other, but to allow for reciprocal sharing and listening.

## Group Discussion

In contrast to the first process developed to explore power and ideology within the intercultural Bible reading space, where the aim was an open and unstructured conversation around the text, the new process involved a facilitated discussion with guiding questions. The guiding questions were developed in order to enhance a creative engagement with the narrative dimensions of the text and to make readers aware of the ideological dimensions and implications of the text. The line followed in the structured questions moved from narrative considerations, to ideological concerns, and ultimately to contextual reflection. The following questions are posed during the group discussion:

(1) Say something about the characters you encountered in the story and how they relate to one another.
(2) If you were investigating this event, what questions would you want to ask the characters?
(3) Is there anyone you would have expected to encounter in the story that is not there? Can you say some more about that?
(4) In the biblical text, whose experience is put at the center of the story? Why do you think that is?
(5) How do the men in this story avoid discomfort?

(6) Do you see anything similar to what we have witnessed in the story happening in your own community?

(7) Who in the story do you relate to? It can be a character that we meet in the biblical text or a character whose story has been overlooked or ignored.

Challenge to Action

In the final moment of the process, groups were challenged to reflect on the so-called "so what?" challenge. They were asked if there was any way in which they would like to respond or act in their particular contexts after this process of reading, reflection, and discussion. This invoked the agency of participants and encouraged a creative response to the often debilitating reality of sexual violence.

Conclusion

This essay has traced the complex realities of an empirical qualitative research process. Unexpected responses raised unanticipated ethical questions that needed to be addressed when the opportunity arose for the circle of intercultural engagement around the biblical text to be widened. The authors shared the action-reflection-action process that informed the introduction of measures to improve the safety of participants, their ethical accountability, and ultimately the life-giving impact of the process on all participants.

References

Ackermann, Denise M. 1993. "Meaning and Power: Some Key Terms in Feminist Liberation Theology." *Scriptura* 44:19–33.

———. 1996. "Engaging Freedom: A Contextual Feminist Theology of Praxis." *Journal of Theology for Southern Africa* 94:32–49.

———. 1997. "Forward from the Margins: Feminist Theologies for Life." *Journal of Theology for Southern Africa* 99:63–67.

Barbour, Rosaline S. 2008. *Introducing Qualitative Research: A Student's Guide to the Craft of Qualitative Research*. Los Angeles: Sage.

Boonzaier, Floretta, and Cheryl de La Rey. 2003. "'He's a Man, and I'm a Woman': Cultural Constructions of Masculinity and Femininity in South African Women's Narratives of Violence." *Violence against Women* 9:1003–29.

Campbell, Rebecca. 2002. *Emotionally Involved: The Impact of Researching Rape*. London: Psychology Press.

Campbell, Rebecca, Tracy Sefl, Sharon Wasco, and Courtney Ahrens. 2004. "Doing Community Research without a Community: Creating Safe Space for Rape Survivors." *American Journal of Community Psychology* 33:253–61.

Davies, Bronwyn. 2000. *(In)scribing Body/Landscape Relations*. Walnut Creek, CA: AltaMira.

Denborough, David. 2008. *Collective Narrative Practice: Responding to Individuals, Groups and Communities Who Have Experienced Trauma*. Adelaide: Dulwich Centre Publications.

Draucker, Claire Burke. 1999. "The Emotional Impact of Sexual Violence Research on Participants." *Archives of Psychiatric Nursing* 13.4:161–69.

Du Toit, Louise. 2005. "A Phenomenology of Rape: Forging a New Vocabulary for Action." Pages 253–74 in *(Un)thinking Citizenship: Feminist Debates in Contemporary South Africa*. Edited by Amanda Gouws. Burlington, VT: Ashgate.

Freire, Paulo. 1994. *Pedagogy of Hope: Reliving Pedagogy of the Oppressed*. Translated by Robert R. Barr. London: Bloomsbury.

Gatenby, Ben, and Karen Morrison-Hume. 2001. "Justice through Service: An Action Enquiry." Paper presented at the International Community Development Conference, Rotorua, New Zealand, April 2001. http://www.iacdglobal.org/files/gatenby.pdf.

Geertz, Clifford. 1975. *The Interpretation of Cultures: Selected Essays*. London: Hutchinson.

George, Mark K. 2000. "Foucault." Pages 91–98 in *Handbook of Postmodern Biblical Interpretation*. Edited by A. K. M. Adam. St. Louis: Chalice.

Guillemin, Marilys, and Lynn Gillam. 2004. "Ethics, Reflexivity, and 'Ethically Important Moments' in Research." *Qualitative Inquiry* 10:261–80.

Herman, Judith. 1997. *Trauma and Recovery: The Aftermath of Violence; from Domestic Abuse to Political Terror*. 2nd ed. New York: Basic Books.

Hesse-Biber, Sharlene Nagy, and Patricia Leavy. 2006. *The Practice of Qualitative Research*. London: Sage.

Hofstede, Geert H. 2001. *Culture's Consequences: Comparing Values, Behaviors, Institutions, and Organizations across Nations*. 2nd ed. Thousand Oaks, CA: Sage.

Jewkes, Rachel. 2002. "Intimate Partner Violence: Cause and Prevention." *The Lancet* 359:1423–29.

Jewkes, Rachel, and Naeema Abrahams. 2002. "The Epidemiology of Rape and Sexual Coercion in South Africa: An Overview." *Social Science and Medicine* 55:1231–44.

Jewkes, Rachel, Jonathan Leven, and Loveday Penn-Kekana. 2002. "Risk Factors for Domestic Violence: Findings from a South African Cross-Sectional Study." *Social Science and Medicine* 55:1603–17.

Jewkes, Rachel, Charlotte Watts, Naeema Abrahams, Loveday Penn-Kekana, and Claudia Garcia-Moreno. 2000. "Ethical and Methodological Issues in Conducting Research on Gender-Based Violence in Southern Africa." *Reproductive Health Matters* 18.15:93–103.

Jonker, Louis C. 2005a. "'Contextuality' in (South) African Exegesis: Reflections on the Communality of Our Exegetical Methodologies." *Old Testament Essays* 18:637–50.

———. 2005b. "Approaches Focusing on the Production of Texts." Pages 27–66 in Jonker and Lawrie 2005.

———. 2010. "The Global Context and Its Consequences for Old Testament Interpretation." Pages 47–56 in *Global Hermeneutics? Reflections and Consequences*. Edited by Knut Holter and Louis C. Jonker. IVBS 1. Atlanta: Society of Biblical Literature. http://ivbs.sbl-site.org/uploads/JONKER~1.PDF.

Jonker, Louis C., and Douglas G. Lawrie, eds. 2005. *Fishing for Jonah (Anew): Various Approaches to Biblical Interpretation*. Stellenbosch: Sun.

Kessler, Rainer. 2004. "From Bipolar to Multipolar Understanding: Hermeneutical Consequences of Intercultural Bible Reading." Pages 452–59 in *Through the Eyes of Another: Intercultural Reading of the Bible*. Edited by Hans de Wit, Louis C. Jonker, Marleen Kool, and Daniel Schipani. Elkhart, IN: Institute of Mennonite Studies.

Lawrie, Douglas G. 2005a. "Approaches Focusing on the Reception of Texts." Pages 109–66 in Jonker and Lawrie 2005.

———. 2005b. "Approaches Focusing on the Texts Themselves." Pages 67–108 in Jonker and Lawrie 2005.

———. 2005c. "The Hermeneutics of Suspicion: The Hidden Worlds of Ideology and the Unconscious." Pages 167–228 in Jonker and Lawrie 2005.

Maykut, Pamela S., and Richard Morehouse. 1994. *Beginning Qualitative Research: A Philosophic and Practical Guide*. London: Falmer.

McKenzie-Mohr, Suzanne, and Michelle Lafrance. 2011. "Telling Stories without the Words: 'Tightrope Talk' in Women's Accounts of Coming to Live Well after Rape or Depression." *Feminism and Psychology* 21:49–73.

Moffett, Helen. 2006. "'These women, they force us to rape them': Rape as Narrative of Social Control in Post-Apartheid South Africa." *Journal of Southern African Studies* 32:129–44.

Peterson, Robin. 1994. "Theological and Religious Pluralism." Pages 219–28 in *Doing Theology in Context: South African Perspectives*. Edited by John W. de Gruchy and Charles Villa-Vicencio. Maryknoll, NY: Orbis.

Priebe, Gisela, Martin Backstrom, and Mare Ainsaar. 2010. "Vulnerable Adolescent Participants' Experience in Surveys on Sexuality and Sexual Abuse: Ethical Aspects." *Child Abuse and Neglect* 34:438–47.

Punt, Jeremy. 2002. "From Re-Writing to Rereading the Bible in Post-Colonial Africa: Considering the Options and Implications." *Missionalia* 30:410–42.

Thompson, John B. 1984. *Studies in the Theory of Ideology*. Cambridge: Polity.

———. 1990. *Ideology and Modern Culture*. Stanford: Stanford University Press.

Vosloo, Robert. 2003. "Public Morality and the Need for an Ethos of Hospitality." *Scriptura*. 82:63–71.

Walt, Charlene van der. 2012. "Hearing Tamar's Voice: How the Margin Hears Differently. Contextual Readings of 2 Samuel 13:1–22." *OTE* 25:182–206.

Weingarten, Kathy. 2003. *Common Shock: Witnessing Violence Every Day; How We Are Harmed, and How We Can Heal*. New York: Dutton.

———. 2010. "Reasonable Hope: Construct, Clinical Applications, and Supports." *Family Process* 49:5–25.

White, Michael. 1995. *Re-authoring Lives: Interviews and Essays*. Adelaide: Dulwich Centre.

———. 1997. *Narratives of Therapists' Lives*. Adelaide: Dulwich Centre.

## 15

## THE BIBLICAL TEXT AS A HETEROTOPIC INTERCULTURAL SITE: IN SEARCH OF REDEMPTIVE MASCULINITIES (A DIALOGUE WITHIN SOUTH AFRICA)

*Gerald West*

I have used Michel Foucault's notion of "heterotopia" in an earlier essay to argue that space is an important component in enabling the poor and oppressed to forge an articulated response to domination (West 2009). There I argued that the question of whether the subaltern *can* speak (Spivak 1988) should be recast as a question that takes space seriously: "*Where* can the subaltern speak?" For, as James Scott so eloquently argues, subordinate classes are less constrained at the level of thought and ideology than they are at the level of political action and struggle "since they can in secluded settings speak with comparative safety" (1990, 91). Human dignity, I argued, even in the most damaged and denigrated subaltern, demands some form of "speaking." *How* the subaltern speaks depends almost entirely on the available space and the nature of that space. As Foucault (1967) has argued, "Our epoch is one in which space takes for us the form of relations among sites."

In this essay I probe other related dimensions of the notion "heterotopia" by interrogating ways in which the biblical text offers an intercultural heterotopia. First, I argue that Contextual Bible Study, the form of contextual Bible reading developed by the Ujamaa Centre over the past twenty-five years, is a heterotopia. I will probe in more depth how Contextual Bible Study as a process constructs or enables *the biblical text* to be a heterotopia. Finally, I will use a specific set of contextual Bible studies on 2 Sam 13:1–22 as resource for exploring how the biblical text might act, specifically, as an *intercultural* heterotopia.

## Contextual Bible Study as Heterotopia

In most cases Contextual Bible Study takes place within an already-secured site. In line with early forms of Latin American liberation theology (Míguez Bonino 1975), we have always emphasized the importance of working with organized groups of the poor and marginalized. Part of the reason for this is that the organized poor "have a shared interest in jointly creating a discourse of dignity, of negation, and of justice.... They have, in addition, a shared interest in concealing a social site apart from domination where such a hidden transcript can be elaborated in comparative safety" (Scott 1990, 114).

This is where Foucault's notion of the heterotopia is of use, for he identifies a heterotopia as a "counter-site," but in an unusual sense. Foucault is not, like Scott, contrasting marginal sites with dominant sites. For Foucault a heterotopic site is "counter" to a utopian site. "Utopias," argues Foucault, "are sites with no real place. They are sites that have a general relation of direct or inverted analogy with the real space of Society. They present society itself in a perfected form, or else society turned upside down, but in any case these utopias are fundamentally unreal spaces" (1967). Foucault continues,

> There are also, probably in every culture, in every civilization, real places—places that do exist and that are formed in the very founding of society—which are something like counter-sites, a kind of effectively enacted utopia in which the real sites, all the other real sites that can be found within the culture, are simultaneously represented, contested, and inverted. Places of this kind are outside of all places, even though it may be possible to indicate their location in reality. Because these places are absolutely different from all the sites that they reflect and speak about, I shall call them, by way of contrast to utopias, heterotopias.

Contextual Bible Study can quite usefully be reenvisaged along the lines of Foucault's heterotopic "principles." First, Foucault discerns that across cultures there are two main categories of heterotopias: "crisis heterotopias" and "heterotopias of deviation." Though Foucault sees a historical shift from the former to the latter in "modern" societies, in African societies these two forms reside side-by-side. "In the so-called primitive societies ... there are privileged or sacred or forbidden places, reserved for individuals who are, in relation to society and to the human environment in which they live, in a state of crisis: adolescents, menstruating women, pregnant women, the elderly, etc." (1967). In Africa, and, I suspect, elsewhere as well, sacred places, particularly among the marginalized, could be described as crisis heterotopias. The sites in which Contextual Bible Study as a methodology has been developed could certainly be characterized as such. Contextual Bible Study sites are constructed consciously as safe and sacred places in which the unutterable can be uttered.

Betraying a somewhat universalizing and totalizing perspective, Foucault believes that "today" such heterotopias are disappearing and are being replaced "by what we might call heterotopias of deviation: those in which individuals whose behaviour is deviant in relation to the required mean or norm are placed. Cases of this are rest homes and psychiatric hospitals, and of course prisons." He then adds—and this is particularly useful for my analysis—"and one should perhaps add retirement homes that are, as it were, on the borderline between the heterotopia of crisis and the heterotopia of deviation since, after all, old age is a crisis, but is also a deviation since in our society where leisure is the rule, idleness is a sort of deviation" (1967). This recognition of an intersection between these two forms of heterotopia is insightful, for this is how I would characterize the Contextual Bible Study site. In Foucault's language, the heterotopias the poor and marginalized force could be said to occupy "the borderline between the heterotopia of crisis and the heterotopia of deviation," since being poor or otherwise marginalized is both a crisis, from their personal perspective, and a deviation, from society's perspective, and, increasingly, from the church's perspective as theologies of prosperity and "well-being" gain ground across Africa.

Foucault's second principle offers a word of warning, cautioning us to recognize "that a society, as its history unfolds, can make an existing heterotopia function in a very different fashion; for each heterotopia has a precise and determined function within a society and the same heterotopia can, according to the synchrony of the culture in which it occurs, have one function or another" (1967). We in the Ujamaa Centre have understood that there is nothing self-evident about Contextual Bible Study. Indeed, as our South African society moves into a post(political) liberation epoch, the terrain in which a Contextual Bible Study site is constructed has changed. What José Míguez Bonino called the "the new poor" when he visited South Africa in the early 1990s are not the same as the organized poor of the social movements of the 1970s and 1980s, and even "the Bible" has a less stable identity. We—and this "we" is itself a shifting signification (Nadar 2012)—must work differently in order to construct Contextual Bible Study as a heterotopic countersite.

The third principle is that "the heterotopia is capable of juxtaposing in a single real place several spaces, several sites that are in themselves incompatible" (Foucault 1967). For example, and here I am drawing on the logic of Foucault's examples of the modern cinema and the oriental garden, Contextual Bible Study sites are often constructed on or into traditional Bible study or liturgical sites. While the traditional sites are characterized by individual and hierarchical patterns of leadership and group process, Contextual Bible Study sites are characterized by collaborative group leadership and processes. More importantly for this essay, the biblical text has the capacity to link or connect several spatially and culturally distinct sites, specifically the "cultural pasts" of the text's production and the "cultural presents" of the text's reception. This capacity of sacred texts to forge "lines of connection" between different "cultural source sites" and "cultural receptor sites" is one of their defining features, one I will explore more fully in the next section of the essay.

Fourth, "heterotopias are most often linked to slices in time—which is to say that they open onto what might be termed, for the sake of symmetry, heterochronies. The heterotopia begins to function at full capacity when men [and women] arrive at a sort of absolute break with their traditional time" (Foucault 1967). In terms of time, argues Foucault, heterotopias may accumulate (e.g., cemeteries, museums, and libraries) and/or distill (e.g., festivals) time. I will return to this principle more fully later, but for now it is important to recognize, first, how Contextual Bible Study as a practice embodies both, nurturing duration as a critical component of enabling an articulation of the hidden transcript, and discerning and isolating a particular moment of congruence or connection between the participants themselves and between the group and the biblical text. Second, it is important to recognize that just as the biblical text connects different places it also connects different times. Echoing the above, the biblical text has the capacity to link or connect several historically distinct times, specifically the "pasts" of the text's production and the "presents" of the text's reception. This capacity of sacred texts to forge "lines of connection" between an ancient text and a contemporary reader is another, related, defining feature, one I will explore more fully in the next section of the paper.

A fifth principle or feature of heterotopias, argues Foucault, is that they

> always presuppose a system of opening and closing that both isolates them and makes them penetrable.... In general, the heterotopic site is not freely accessible like a public place. Either the entry is compulsory, as

in the case of entering a barracks or a prison, or else the individual has to submit to rites and purifications. (1967)

The resonances with a religious "rite" such as Bible study are clear. As mentioned, Contextual Bible Study prefers to work with organized groups of the poor and marginalized, who "patrol" to some extent the participation in the sites they have sequestered. It is for this reason that there is a need for the socially engaged biblical scholar to be "called" or invited to participate in the group. This is why intellectuals, who are "organic" to a particular poor or marginalized community (Gramsci in Forgacs 1988, 301), are so important, as they already belong within the boundaries of the group.

The sixth and last principle of the heterotopia "is that they have a function in relation to all the space that remains." This function, Foucault goes on to elaborate, "unfolds between two extreme poles. Either their role is to create a space of illusion that exposes every real space, all the sites inside of which human life is partitioned, as still more illusory." The example Foucault uses for this first role is the brothel. "Or else, on the contrary," he continues "their role is to create a space that is other, another real space, as perfect, as meticulous, as well arranged as ours is messy, ill constructed, and jumbled. This latter type would be the heterotopia, not of illusion, but of compensation." The example Foucault uses for this second role is the colony (1967). In general terms, Contextual Bible Study is located in relation to all other space, for its processes acknowledge other spaces quite overtly. More specifically, Contextual Bible Study offers both heterotopias of illusion, where space is imagined as radically different from the constraints of "normal" (dominated) space, and heterotopias of compensation, where the configurations of participation and collaboration offer real alternative forms of ordering space. As I will argue in the next section, the biblical text plays the key role here.

Intracultural and Intercultural Lines of Connection

Because Contextual Bible Study has been foundationally shaped by the principle of the epistemological privilege of the poor and marginalized, the groups with whom we have worked have tended to be relatively homogeneous in terms of class and culture. Apartheid segregated "black/nonwhite" South Africans of various kinds into racial-cultural categories, assigning each racial-cultural "group" its own "group areas," through the notorious—biblically and theologically grounded (De Gruchy and

De Gruchy 2004, 32, 78)—"Group Areas Act" in three successive prom-
ulgations of 1950, 1957, and 1966. The effect of externally segregated
racial-cultural group areas, together with the internally sequestered sites
of the poor and marginalized within these areas, was and is that Contextual Bible Study groups tend to be homogeneous in racial-cultural terms.
In most cases Contextual Bible Study has been and is an intracultural site
in terms of the composition of the group. This has been the case, too, in
some of the other social locations in which the particular Bible studies
examined in this essay were done, for example, among largely Christian
Dalit communities in India.

That the 2 Sam 13 Contextual Bible Study I am reporting on here (and
which I facilitated) was effective in very different cultural spaces demonstrates that Foucault's third principle of a heterotopia holds for Contextual Bible Study: it "connected" quite different social spaces/places/times.
However, the connections between these various cultural spaces/places/
times were not constructed as intercultural sites, in the terms of the earlier
phase of this project (De Wit et al. 2004), though there was some intercultural "contact" via my presence as the facilitator across the African and
Indian contexts. During times of "report back" in the Indian contexts, for
example, when small groups shared their reports with the larger plenary
group, I would sometimes make "connections" between what they were
sharing and what I had heard shared in African contexts. Though this kind
of "informal" intercultural exchange can be a critical contribution in both
the general and technical sense, it has not been constructed as an overtly
intercultural encounter.

What I do want to designate as an overtly *inter*cultural encounter, an
intercultural heterotopic encounter, takes place in and through the biblical
text. This is a different order of intercultural encounter. For many African
readers of the Bible, and I suspect for faithful readers of the Bible in general, there is an immediacy of encounter with the Bible. African theology
has reflected on this dimension of African Bible reading quite specifically
and has developed a particular trajectory within African theology based
on the "recognition" between "primal" African culture and "primal" biblical cultures (see Mbiti 1978). As John Mbiti puts it, "The points of continuity between Biblical faith and culture and African Religion have been sufficiently strong for the Gospel to establish a strong footing among African
peoples" (1978, 311).

The immediacy of intercultural connection between the Bible and African readers is the more remarkable when it takes place through Contextual

Bible Study. This is because it uses the critical tools of biblical scholarship to create *distantiation*, in Paul Ricoeur's sense of the term, between the contemporary reader and ancient text. Drawing as it does on the resources and priorities of African biblical scholarship (Draper 2001), as well as on the interpretive resources and cultural capacities of ordinary African readers of the Bible, Contextual Bible Study incorporates a movement between three moments of reader-text engagement. The first moment is "in-front-of-the-text," a direct and unmediated encounter between text and reader. The second moment introduces or offers critical modes of reading into the process, beginning with literary analysis and followed by sociohistorical analysis. The third moment returns to appropriation, but now of a "different," distanced, text. The fact that intercultural encounter continues to take place in this third moment, albeit more critically, demonstrates the presence of Foucault's fourth principle in Contextual Bible Study as heterotopia. Through distantiation the text becomes "other" and, therefore, potentially another heterotopic site, one that is now "full" of time, where a recognition of its distance in time (and space) makes it "another" text. As Foucault observes, one of the features of a heterotopia is that they "are most often linked to slices of time," which "open onto what might be termed ... heterochronies" (1967). However, because Foucault believes, incorrectly, that time, unlike space, "was detached from the sacred in the nineteenth century"—betraying his European social location—he is unable to recognize fully that sacred heterotopias are sites that connect across sanctified time, so that, for example, a Contextual Bible Study can connect African masculinity (in the readers) and ancient Israelite masculinity (in a biblical text) interculturally, across time and space, though he does come close to some recognition of this sacred sense of time in his truncated discussion of Polynesian vacation villages (1967).

## An Intercultural Quest for Redemptive African Masculinities

The Ujamaa Centre has been working with 2 Sam 13:1–22 since 1996, in response to the request by African women for biblical resources with which to confront gender violence (West and Zondi-Mabizela 2004). The decades in which the Tamar Contextual Bible Study has been done around the world have produced a common refrain from the many women with whom we have worked. "The focus on Tamar, a young woman who is sexually abused, is important," they confirmed, "but what about a focus on men?" they asked. The Ujamaa Centre has endeavored to heed this call and has produced a range of Bible studies exploring a range of aspects of masculinity (Ujamaa 2009). We did not use the Tamar Contextual Bible Study in our emerging work on masculinity because of the gender sector with whom most of this work was done. We worked primarily with women's groups and groups where women formed a vast majority. This gendered space shaped the contours of the Bible study, resulting in a fairly fixed form where the textual and contextual focus was on the woman as the victim of rape and on the complicity of men in the gendered systems that perpetrate rape, as the format below demonstrates:

Second Samuel 13:1–22 is read aloud, preferably dramatically. After the text has been read, a series of questions follow.

> (1) Read 2 Sam 13:1–22 together again in small groups. Share with each other what you think the text is about.

Each group is then asked to report back to the larger group. Each response to question 1 is summarized on newsprint. After reporting back, the participants return to their small groups to discuss the following questions.

> (2) Who are the main characters in this story, and what do we know about them?
> (3) What is the role of each of the male characters in the rape of Tamar?
> (4) What does Tamar say and what does Tamar do? Focus carefully on each element of what Tamar says and does.

When the small groups have finished their discussion, each group is invited to present a summary of their discussion. After this report, the smaller groups reconvene and discuss the following questions.

> (5) Are there women like Tamar in your church and/or community? Tell their stories.
> (6) What resources are there in your area for survivors of rape?

Once again, the small groups present their reports to the plenary groups. Creativity is particularly vital here, as often women find it difficult to articulate their responses. A drama or a drawing may be the only way in which some groups can report. Finally, each small group comes together to formulate a plan of action.

(7)  What will you now do in response to this Bible study?

The plan of action is either reported to the plenary meeting or presented on newsprint for other participants to study after the Bible study.

When in 2007 together with a few other African male theologians I was invited to participate in the fourth Pan African Conference of the Circle of Concerned African Women Theologians in Yaoundé, Cameroon, to address the issue of masculinity, I returned to this text. My contribution was to tell the story of the Tamar Contextual Bible Study and to reflect on how we needed to include a focus on masculinity. As I prepared for the presentation, I reread 2 Sam 13:1–22, noticing really for the first time verse 2. My work had been strongly influenced by the pioneering work of Phyllis Trible on this text. Though she does not use the form of plot analysis, her analysis indicates that verse 2 is part of the plot's "complication." A common way of approaching a plot is to analyze how plots "move" from exposition to complication to resolution (Trible 1984). "Plots move," argues Jerome Walsh, "like an arc from a situation of (relative) stability, through a process of tension or destabilization, to a new situation of (relative) stability" (2009, 14). For Trible, verse 1, a situation of relative stability, is the exposition, and verse 2 is the beginning of the narrative tension. But what if, I now asked, verse 2 is in fact part of the exposition? What if the complication or tension only begins in verse 3?

Our problem with using this text in our work with men was that it portrayed men as perpetrators, with each of the male characters playing some role in the rape of Tamar. Indeed, question 3 above invites such an analysis. But if verse 2 can be considered an aspect of the narrative's exposition, then it portrays an Amnon who is full of desire but who does not act. The reason, argues Trible, drawing on historical and sociocultural resources, is that "as a virgin, Tamar is protected property, inaccessible to males, including her brother" (1984, 38). Amnon's state of constrained desire could be considered as a state of relative stability! We could then work with an exegesis in which verses 1–2 form the exposition, introducing the family (v. 1) and the initial tensive but "stable" state of the relationship between Amnon and Tamar. In this exegesis of the text, Amnon is a normal male! Like most males he experiences sexual desire, but does not initially act on this desire, because of a whole range of sociocultural constraints. It is Jonadab who ushers in the complication (v. 3), as the networks of patriarchal power become more apparent.

This exegetical insight offered us a way of working with this text with men. We have returned to this text and have begun to evolve a Redemptive Masculinity Contextual Bible Study using this text. At the moment the form of the study is somewhat flexible, but a relatively stable version of it is as follows:

Second Samuel 13:1–22 is read aloud, preferably dramatically. After the text has been read a series of questions follow.

(1) Have you heard this text (2 Sam 13:1–22) read publicly ... on a Sunday? Share with each other if and when and where you have heard this text read.
(2) Who are the main characters in this story, and what do we know about them?
(3) What is the role of each of the male characters in the rape of Tamar?
(4) How would you characterize Amnon's masculinity in this text? Consider:
   What prevents Amnon initially from acting on his love for Tamar (v. 2)?
   What is it that changes Amnon's love (v. 1) to lust (v. 2) and then enables him to act on his desire/lust (vv. 4–6)?
   How does he react to Tamar's arguments (v. 14)?
   How does he behave after he has raped Tamar (vv. 15–17)?
(5) What does Tamar's response to Amnon's assault tell us about her understanding of masculinity? Consider:
   What does she say (vv. 12–13, 16), and what do each of the things she says tell us about her understanding of what it means to be "a man"?
   What does she do (v. 19), and what do each of things she does tell us about her understanding of what it means to be "a man"?
(6) What are the dominant forms of masculinity in our contexts in various age groups, and what alternative forms of masculinity can we draw on from our cultural and religious traditions?
(7) How can we raise the issue of masculinity in our various gender and age groups?

The results are either reported to the plenary or presented on newsprint for other participants to study after the Bible study.

Question 1 performs a similar function to that of the first question in the Tamar Contextual Bible Study, but draws attention to the absence of the text in the male-dominated world of religious life, whether Jewish, Christian, or Muslim (this Bible study has been done by participants from each of these faith traditions at their own initiative). Questions 2 and 3, as in the Tamar study, draw attention to the details of characterization in the text and provide an overall orientation to the story. Questions 4 and 5 slow down the reading process considerably (Riches et al. 2010, 41), posing two related and quite difficult questions. We have wrestled with these two questions, often reformulating them, in order to devise a form of question that combines a careful reading of the text with the participants' own sociocultural understandings of notions of "masculinity." So far we have settled on a general question and then some prompting subquestions that focus on particular details of the text, such as the characterization of Amnon in verse 2. By introducing these prompting subquestions in question 4, we direct the rereading process to particular textual details and thus offer participants some of the fruits of the critical literary analysis of biblical scholarship, including the kind of detail Trible identifies in her exegesis of the central chiasmus (13:9d–18). By introducing the prompting subquestions in question 5 of the redemptive masculinities Contextual Bible Study, we again offer participants the opportunity to engage with the kind of literary detail discussed in terms of the Tamar Contextual Bible Study (above), but this time with a focus on masculinity. In addition, question 5 offers an opportunity to probe the sociohistorical and cultural dimensions of the text, as well as the distinctively intercultural appropriative opportunity to retell and relive Tamar's story by imagining with her what kind of masculinities she and we yearn for.

In addition to the Bible studies I did in African and Indian contexts from 2007 to 2011 (which served primarily, in terms of this intercultural project, to develop and establish the particular format of the Bible study), we also invited a colleague, Phumzile Mabizela, one of the pioneers of our work with women, to facilitate a series of Bible studies using this format. We decided to work with groups that had already participated in a "normal" Tamar Contextual Bible Study, so that we could measure to what extent the redemptive masculinities Contextual Bible Study constructed an intercultural heterotopia around ancient biblical and contemporary notions of masculinity.

Mabizela did some initial research to establish what groups had done the Tamar version of the Bible study and still retained a substantially similar set of participants. She identified three demographically different sites for comparative purposes and facilitated the Redemptive Masculinities version with each of these groups during November and December 2011. The first workshop was with an HIV and AIDS support group with whom the Ujamaa Centre has done extensive HIV-related work over the years. The Sibahle group, as they call themselves, is from the periurban/semirural area of KwaMpumuza, in KwaZulu-Natal, South Africa, not far from the Ujamaa Centre in Pietermaritzburg. As with most HIV support groups, this group consisted of women only. Of the eight women present, four had done the Tamar version.

The second workshop was quite different in that it was with a group of men. The Pietermaritzburg Agency for Christian Social Action (PACSA), an ecumenical activist agency with whom the Ujamaa Centre has worked for more than two decades, had established a men's group around issues of HIV and gender violence. This group invited Mabizela to do the Redemptive Masculinities version. Of the twelve men present, seven had done the Tamar version.

The third group was also quite distinctive. Mabizela was invited to facilitate the Redemptive Masculinities version in a consultation hosted by the Lutheran Church of Southern Africa (LUCSA) and the Lutheran World Federation (LWF) in Johannesburg, South Africa. The focus of the consultation was on mainstreaming HIV and gender in the work of these organizations. The fifty-five participants came primarily from the host organization (LUCSA), but also included church leaders and representatives from other Lutheran affiliated churches. As in the other workshops, the majority of participants were Africans, but here there was also a notable number of Europeans.

The responses in these quite diverse groups were remarkably similar. First, though the majority in each case had done the Tamar version, they were able to refocus on the new biblical detail in the Redemptive Masculinities version. The format of questions 4 and 5 did accomplish a greater critical distance by slowing down the reading process, with groups regularly returning to the Bible to reread a particular verse. Questions 4 and 5 also served to refocus the locus of appropriation in questions 6 and 7, with a sustained engagement with aspects of masculinity.

Second, in each case there was a clear intercultural connection between text and context. As is typical in contextual Bible studies, appropriation "encroaches" on the distantiation dimensions of the study (questions 2, 3, 4, and 5). Because most of the participants had done the Tamar version, questions 2 and 3 were dealt with rather quickly, but considerable time was spent on questions 4 and 5. Though there was sustained distantiation through questions 2–5, giving the text a distinctive voice, the groups found it difficult to remain detached. In discussing question 4, the PACSA male group used a local cultural term to describe Amnon: *isishimane*, a man who is not good at courtship and does not know how to approach women. The other two groups also described Amnon as a man who did not know how to act appropriately "on his own." To a limited extent, then, the first prompting question under question 4 did open up intercultural heterotopic space within which Amnon could be considered as a "normal" male.

A third similarity is that all the groups agreed that destructive and dominant forms of masculinity reside in men as a collective and in the systems that sustain male privilege. This is another indication that the textual detail invoked by question 4 enabled participants to consider Amnon as an ordinary man. Jonadab directly, and the other males in the narrative indirectly, enabled Amnon "to behave like an animal and just take Tamar's virginity," according to the PACSA men's group. In question 6 the sociocultural location of African masculinities was interrogated in some detail. In each case extremely negative characterizations of the dominant forms of masculinity were given, to the extent that the women of the Sibahle support group stated, "It is too late to work with the older men, but there is still a possibility of changing the attitudes of younger men."

A fourth similarity across the three groups emerged in their responses to question 5. Each in their own way assumed that women were the true repository of redemptive masculinities. Masculinity within a patriarchal system was the problem, but there were resources for a transformation of African masculinities from within the world and wisdom of women, both from contemporary women and from Tamar. The fundamental problem, they agreed, was the systems that retained power among males. The Sibahle women's group argued that both African culture and the Bible offered alternative forms of masculinity, but that "society condones" the dominant forms. The PACSA men's group offered a similar analysis, arguing that Tamar clearly reminded Amnon of "their cultural values" and that she had taken public action by tearing her clothes, in order "to expose his unacceptable behavior."

Though significant in their similarities, there were also distinctive responses from each group. First, the Sibahle women did not see any hope for older men. The PACSA male group saw a need for "more guidance from older men to younger men" and argued that this was needed in the various men's organizations within the churches. They agreed that this kind of formation was not structured into the life of the church. While the PACSA men's group saw some capacity for alternative masculinities in male role models, the Sibahle women's group allocated this task to peer educators in schools, trusting only younger groups of males for any kind of transformation. In contrast to both these responses, the LUCSA/LWF group concentrated on how women ought to be empowered, arguing that as "women suffer most from cultural, economic, religious, and social challenges as compared to those suffered by men," women should be empowered, as young adults, "to choose whom to marry." "Woman's needs," they insisted, "should be addressed directly to her" and not through some male, including her spouse.

Second, the PACSA men's group argued that church structures needed to "facilitate dialogues between men and women." They also saw the need to go outside the dominant forms of masculinity in order to find alternative masculinity models, and this included "facilitating an exchange between straight and gay men," as there "is a lot we can learn from each other." The dialogical dimension across gender and sexuality divides was a distinctive contribution of this group.

Third, the LUCSA/LWF group, reflecting perhaps the significant numbers of Europeans among the participants, seemed reluctant to turn to traditional forms of culture for resources. They also seemed reluctant to draw directly on the Bible for alternative masculinities. Instead, they envisaged transformation in terms of the empowerment of women and were not sure that traditional culture or the Bible was a source. They found Tamar too submissive to and constrained by patriarchy.

## Heterotopic Hermeneutics

It is clear from this analysis that the Contextual Bible Study process is a heterotopic space. While correct in asserting that "contemporary space is perhaps still not entirely desanctified," Foucault is wrong to imagine that time has been desanctified in African contexts, though he may be right in claiming that time "was detached from the sacred in the nineteenth century" (1967). The biblical text sanctifies both time and space, enabling faithful readers of the Bible to connect across both, finding and forging lines of connection between their own sociocultural sites and sacred "textual" sites within and behind the biblical text.

The critical resources of biblical scholarship open up additional lines of connection across time and space by enabling ordinary readers of the Bible to reread the same text differently through recognizing and appropriating different textual detail, whether literary or sociohistorical. The increased recognition of various details seems not, however, in most cases to hamper appropriation. The LUCSA/LWF group may be a case where critical distance generated a more cautious appropriation of the past, making the biblical past too different. Heterotopic space here has opened an intercultural gap. Discerning discontinuity, and not only continuity, seems to be a feature of intercultural heterotopias.

Finally, what is also clear is that heterotopias are

> real places—places that do exist and that are formed in the very founding of society—which are something like counter-sites, a kind of effectively enacted utopia in which the real sites, all the other real sites that can be found within the culture, are simultaneously represented, contested, and inverted.... Places of this kind are outside of all places, even though it may be possible to indicate their location in reality. (Foucault 1967)

Reading through the notes of Phumzile Mabizela concerning the three groups she worked with and drawing on my experience in a range of communities make clear that contextual Bible studies are moments and examples of the real places Foucault describes. Their location in reality is only part of their identity, as Foucault recognizes, for they also represent, contest, and invert numerous other places. The Bible's presence not only secures such places (the fifth principle), it offers both places of illusion and compensation (the sixth principle), juxtaposing sites and connections between sites that are incompatible (the third principle), which it does partly through allowing for the connection of places across sacred time (the fourth principle). By locating the Bible within an emancipatory paradigm like the Contextual Bible Study process, heterotopias of crisis and deviation—the dominant forms of heterotopia (according to Foucault's first principle)—become the primary sites of the Bible's presence. Finally, Foucault's second principle, that "each heterotopia has a precise and determined function within a society" (1967), is a reminder that heterotopic hermeneutics is profoundly contextual and profoundly fragile (the second principle).

References

Draper, Jonathan A. 2001. "Old Scores and New Notes: Where and What Is Contextual Exegesis in the New South Africa?" Pages 148–68 in *Towards an Agenda for Contextual Theology: Essays in Honour of Albert Nolan*. Edited by McGlory T. Speckman and Larry T. Kaufmann. Pietermaritzburg: Cluster.

Forgacs, David, ed. 1988. *An Antonio Gramsci Reader: Selected Writings 1916–1935*. New York: Schocken.

Foucault, Michel. 1967. "Of Other Spaces: Heterotopias." http://foucault.info/documents/heteroTopia/foucault.heteroTopia.en.html.

Gruchy, John W. de, and Steve de Gruchy. 2004. *The Church Struggle in South Africa*. 3rd ed. London: SCM.

Mbiti, John. 1978a. "Christianity and African Religion." Pages 308–18 in *Facing the New Challenges: The Message of PACLA (Pan African Christian Leadership Assembly); December 9–19, 1976, Nairobi*. Edited by Michael Cassidy and Luc Verlinden. Kisumu, Kenya: Evangel.

———. 1978b. "Christianity and Culture in Africa." Pages 272–84 in *Facing the New Challenges: The Message of PACLA (Pan African Christian Leadership Assembly); December 9–19, 1976, Nairobi*. Edited by Michael Cassidy and Luc Verlinden. Kisumu, Kenya: Evangel.

Míguez Bonino, José. 1975. *Doing Theology in a Revolutionary Situation*. Philadelphia: Fortress.

Nadar, Sarojini. 2012. "'Hermeneutics of Transformation?' A Critical Exploration of the Model of Social Engagement between Biblical Scholars and Faith Communities." Pages 389–406 in *Postcolonial Perspectives in African Biblical Interpretations*. Edited by Musa W. Dube, Andrew M. Mbuvi, and Dora Mbuwayesango. Atlanta: Society of Biblical Literature.

Riches, John, Helen Ball, Roy Henderson, Craig Lancaster, Leslie Milton, and Maureen Russell. 2010. *What Is Contextual Bible Study? A Practical Guide with Group Studies for Advent and Lent*. London: SPCK.

Sanneh, Lamin. 1989. *Translating the Message: The Missionary Impact on Culture*. Maryknoll, NY: Orbis.

Scott, James C. 1990. *Domination and the Arts of Resistance: Hidden Transcripts*. New Haven: Yale University Press.

Spivak, Gayatri C. 1988. "Can the Subaltern Speak?" Pages 271–313 in *Marxism and the Interpretation of Culture*. Edited by Gary Nelson and L. Grossberg. London: Macmillan.

Trible, Phyllis. 1984. *Texts of Terror: Literary-Feminist Readings of Biblical Narratives.* Overtures to Biblical Theology. Philadelphia: Fortress.

Ujamaa. 2009. "Redemptive Masculinity: A Series of Ujamaa Centre Contextual Bible Studies That Proclaim Life for Men and Women." http:// ujamaa.ukzn.ac.za/Libraries/manuals/Redemptive_masculinities_ series_1.sflb.ashx.

Walsh, Jerome T. 2009. *Old Testament Narrative: A Guide to Interpretation.* Louisville: Westminster John Knox.

West, Gerald O. 2009. "The Not So Silent Citizen: Hearing Embodied Theology in the Context of HIV and Aids in South Africa." Pages 23–42 in *Heterotopic Citizen: New Research on Religious Work for the Disadvantaged.* Edited by Trygve Wyller. Göttingen: Vandenhoeck & Ruprecht.

West, Gerald O., and Phumzile Zondi-Mabizela. 2004. "The Bible Story That Became a Campaign: The Tamar Campaign in South Africa (and Beyond)." *Ministerial Formation* 103:4–12.

Wit, Hans de, Louis Jonker, Marleen Kool, and Daniel Schipani, eds. 2004. *Through the Eyes of Another: Intercultural Reading of the Bible.* Elkhart, IN: Institute of Mennonite Studies.

PART 3

TOGETHER AT THE TOMB: CASE STUDIES ON JOHN 20

## 16

## "It Has Been Ordained by Our Ancestors That Women Keep Quiet": Intercultural Reading as a Challenge to Cultural Roles (A Dialogue between Indonesia and Bolivia)

*Batara Sihombing*

In this volume, this is the second essay analyzing the reading experience of an Indonesian group in interaction with a foreign partner group. The Rogate group in Pekanbaru, Sumatra, Indonesia, was linked with the Buenas Nuevas group in Santa Cruz, Bolivia.

The sharing of the story of John 4 gives rise to a remarkable growth of insights in the text. Here, it is shown how faith itself touches the heart of the other reader and transforms the attitude toward the text. Personal experience and engagement with struggle and resistance emerge as significant hermeneutical factors for transformation. Hermeneutical courage is stimulated; women in the Bible become a role model for change and transformation.

### Jesus Called Mary by Name

In John 20:16 when Jesus called out her name, Mary turned toward him and cried out in Aramaic, "Rabbouni!" ("my teacher"). The attention given to this verse by the Buenas Nuevas group touched the hearts of the Rogate members. Mary was alone and was crying outside the tomb, because she thought that the body of Jesus had been taken away. One brother from the Buenas Nuevas group explained that, in the midst of our confusion, crying, and sadness, Jesus is right close to us, but we are looking in a different direction. In spite of the fact that Mary did not yet recognize Jesus at the tomb, Jesus called Mary by name. He also calls us by our names and asks us why we are crying. This means that the Lord is always around us to help and protect us in the midst of our problems and difficulties.

The experiences of a brother and sister in Buenas Nuevas of God's protection in the dangerous times strengthened the Rogate members, assuring them that God is near us all the time, even though we are looking the other way and sometimes forget his presence. Especially in the Indonesian context, when in trouble, people ask for help from some power other than God, such as a shaman. One sister from the Rogate group confessed that the experiences and the understanding of verse 16 shared by friends from Buenas Nuevas strengthened her to face her own personal struggles, since Jesus called not only Mary by name but also everybody else by their respective names. Mary did not yet recognize Jesus in the tomb at that time, but after she was called by name, she was able to respond "Rabbouni" ("my teacher"). The insight of the Buenas Nuevas group that Jesus can call everybody by name shed new light on the verse for the Rogate group.

## Mary as Role Model

In John 20:18 Mary Magdelene reported to the disciples: "I have seen the Lord!" The Rogate members understood this verse to indicate that it was Mary, a woman, who was asked by Jesus to tell this news to his disciples: "I am returning to my Father and your Father, to my God and your God" (v. 17). Mary was the first witness of a meeting with the risen Jesus and was the first evangelist to proclaim the risen Lord. As a woman, standing alone and crying at the empty tomb, in the dark of the early morning, Mary showed courage and boldness. This is in stark contrast to Indonesian contexts where women would not dare to stay alone at a tomb in the dark for fear of ghosts. For the Rogate members, this text clearly supported the fact that their Batak Lutheran Church (Huria Kristen Indonesia) has ordained female pastors and elders. The women also have equal roles with men in Indonesian society since they have occupied offices such as president, minister, and governor. In spite of this, the women in the Rogate group felt that in their roles in the culture and the household they were still kept below those of their husbands. In the Batak cultural functions, women are expected to keep silent, and in the household they are to be submissive to their husbands. The women in the Rogate group voiced their opinion that women should have equal roles in the household and the culture. For several male members in Rogate, this verse served as an inspiration to respect their wives as equal partners in sharing responsibilities in their households.

The Buenas Nuevas group accepted that "Jesus gave the responsibility to talk about the resurrection to Mary, and in this we agree with you." According to them, "It is the responsibility of all believers to talk about the resurrection of Jesus." However, one person from Buenas Nuevas could find no similarities between the Rogate and Buenas Nuevas groups due to different cultures and values: while in Indonesia women are treated as a second-class citizens, in Bolivian society there is equality between men and women:

> Women have freedom to participate in all functions and activities of life. However, as we understand from the Bible, there are certain limitations to women's participation within the ministry of the church. For example, in our church women can participate in all ministry roles except being pastors or elders. Women also do not practice pastoral ministry or administer the Eucharist.

Though in this respect the two groups differed, in its final comment the Buenas Nuevas friends said that they learned many things about the culture and situation of the Indonesian group: "Though we have some doctrinal differences, in most aspects we believe the same thing. That faith in Christ saves us." They continued: "We are happy that women are able to participate in ministry within the church, though there remain challenges within the society and cultural functions." One brother from Buenas Nuevas comments that "it is great that women take responsibility so that men do not have the sole responsibility and that then men are not the only ones to receive the blame when things go wrong." In my opinion, the doctrinal teachings they believe in held them back from the transformation that could have come from the challenge contained in the Indonesian reading where the women argued for equal roles for women as ordained persons in the church (1 Tim 3:1–5; Titus 1:5–9).

## Mary's Role as an Evangelist

For both groups, verse 18 served as a clear commandment that all believers should share the good news about the resurrection of Jesus Christ. For brothers and sisters in Buenas Nuevas, who live in a predominantly

Christian country, this would be easier because they are free to share Christ to other people. One brother from Buenas Nuevas shared how he had asked his neighbor if he believed that Jesus had been resurrected, and he said that he did not. There is a clear need as believers to give evidence that they believe that Christ has really risen. In short, the Buenas Nuevas group stated that it is important to take the message of Christ to all creatures that do not know the Lord, because it is his command.

For the Rogate group the question was how they should share the good news of Christ in predominantly Muslim Indonesian contexts. Some Christians who verbally shared Christ to Muslim friends were physically attacked and tortured. For Muslim friends, religion is like gender, which is determined by birth: if one was born as a male, he will never become a female; those who are Muslim are never expected to become non-Muslim. Someone who approaches a Muslim to follow another religion must be punished. It is thus not easy to share the gospel in Indonesia; though one is eager to share the good news, one must do it wisely, carefully, peacefully. When the Buenas Nuevas group wanted to know more about the Indonesia situation, the Rogate members shared that they are not physically persecuted, but undergo mental and psychological persecution. For example, it is difficult to get permission from the surrounding Muslims to build a church. As a result, many Christians build a church without permission or license. Inevitably, this has brought conflicts between Christians and Muslims. Another harassment is that at work promotions are usually not granted to Christians. That only the Muslims are promoted to higher positions causes mental suffering and depression.

This insight into the Indonesian situation caused the friends in Bolivia to realize how very difficult and different their own situation was. This made them question whether they would be witnessing with as much enthusiasm and courage if they lived in the Indonesian context. They commended the Indonesians on their desire to share Christ with others: "it is a mark of a true believer to have faith in Christ in such difficult circumstances as you are living. This is something that truly touches our lives!" From this perspective we can discern that the friends in Buenas Nuevas gained a new appreciation of their partners in Rogate and in particular insight into how to share Christ with others. The difficulties and problems in Indonesia provided material for the Buenas Nuevas members to understand more clearly verses 17–18, which contain the proclamation of the gospel.

## Conclusion

The report shows that the intercultural reading provided the opportunity to experience transformation in the appreciation of the partner group and brought new insights in the text. The reading brought about a change of attitude toward friends within the same group as well as toward friends in the partner group. Apart from that, the reading also brought to light that differences both in doctrinal standpoints and in cultural contexts could form hindrances to accepting new ideas offered by the partner group.

17

# Ghosts, Women, and Evangelism
# (A Dialogue between Bolivia and Indonesia)

*Esa Autero*

The late Walter Wink stated in his book on the Bible and human transformation: "The model for students should be not the biblical scholar, but the biblical interpreter—a person competent to help any group of people understand the impact of the Bible in human transformation" (2010). He explains the reasons for the bankruptcy of traditional biblical criticism: "[it is] incapable of achieving what most of its practitioners considered its purpose to be: so to interpret Scriptures that the past becomes alive and illuminates our present with new possibilities for personal and social transformation" (2010). While everyone might not be as convinced about the bankruptcy of traditional biblical criticism, Wink's call for human transformation in relation to biblical scholarship is worth noting.

The intercultural Bible reading project is a partial response to this plea. This essay presents an empirical description and analysis of the intercultural exchange between the Buenas Nuevas group of Santa Cruz, Bolivia, and the Rogate group of Sumatra, Indonesia.[1] I look at the hermeneutical processes in both groups as well as the interactive process from the perspective of intergroup relations and conclude with a reflection on the role of the Bible in the process. In my analysis, I follow the sequence of the exchange between the groups.

1. Writing this essay was made possible by the support of *Missio Dei* International and a grant from the Agricola foundation.

## Transformation and Empirical Hermeneutics

One of the most difficult tasks in analyzing empirical reading reports is to define and measure transformation. In order to define and measure the hermeneutical processes and the potential transformative effects (or lack thereof) of the intercultural exchange, I used two basic approaches. First, to delineate the hermeneutical processes of the groups, I applied simplified codes to the text as developed initially by Ernst Conradie and Louis Jonker (2001) and further clarified by Hans de Wit (De Wit et al. 2004; De Wit 2008). I coded the text in respect to group composition and background, exegetical-hermeneutical processes (reading attitude, status of the text, and explanation strategies), and appropriation (appropriation strategy, context of appropriation, and praxeological effects). Second, to analyze the group interaction between the Buenas Nuevas group and the Rogate group, I took clues from social psychology, particularly social identity theory and intergroup relations. This helped me conceptualize the interactive process and enabled me to apply pertinent codes to the intercultural exchange. The interactive process was coded in terms of open/closed attitude, prejudice or in/out-group favor, labeling, perspective taking, empathy, and self-disclosure (see Tropp and Molina 2012; Abrams et al. 2005). Finally, transformation and freezing were measured simply by observing changes in the empirical reports with regard to intergroup interaction as individuals and/or the group moved toward openness and/or freezing. This process takes clues from de Wit's previous work on empirical hermeneutics (De Wit et al. 2004; De Wit 2008) and my own empirical work in Bolivia from August 2011 through June 2012.

Before I describe and analyze the empirical material, I briefly mention some critical issues that highlight the theoretical and practical challenges involved in intercultural Bible reading in general and in the exchange between the Buenas Nuevas and Rogate groups in particular. All conclusions need to be evaluated in light of these critical remarks.

The first concerns validity (see Babbie 2004). As De Klerk (2004, 173–74) noticed in regard to the earlier intercultural project, the empirical reports are of varying quality, and diverse methods are used in the reading process. In the present report, only the initial Bible study was constructed as a near verbatim report on the part of Buenas Nuevas, but this information is missing for the Rogate group, where the bulk of the data appears to be a concise summary rather than a verbatim report. Further, the composition of the Buenas Nuevas group changed during the process;

it is not recorded whether the partner group changed. It is undeniable that as groups change, the dynamics and interaction are affected. As De Klerk (2004, 173–74) suggested, for the purpose of validity, the use of a uniform reading method could be adopted, such as the Contextual Bible Study method. However, there are no guarantees that an imposed method would solve the problem. Also, imposing a uniform reading methodology on such diverse groups would be questionable. Thus the protocol of the current project was general and suggestive rather than prescriptive; it left room for improvisation and contextual adaptation. Much in this regard depends on the objectives of a given project.

The second and related issue concerns my role as facilitator and researcher. My initial plan was to recruit a Bolivian church group to participate in the project and to be only partially involved in the practical aspects of the process. As often happens during intercultural encounter, initial plans had to be modified. Perhaps due to lack of initial motivation on the part of the Buenas Nuevas group, they insisted that I lead and facilitate the whole process. In addition to my role as the facilitator, I was also perceived as the leader of the Bible study and treated as an "expert" to some extent. This does not mean that my comments were always uncritically accepted, nor that the questions I posed were answered. In general, my contribution was perhaps greatest during the initial study of the text, when, on a few occasions, in response to direct questions, I clarified the narrative development, gave some historical background information, and opened a way for participants to identify with the plight of Mary Magdalene. To my surprise, the latter led to the sharing of difficult experiences on the part of Buenas Nuevas participants and to a heartfelt response on the part of the partner group. I limited my comments to questions and clarifications of the partner group's response. Though I would see my own contribution as modest, I cannot discount my role even though I tried to maintain distance to the exchange while analyzing the very process I was a part of. This situation inevitably influences the reliability of the results.

Finally, two further critical issues surfaced. During my one-year stay in Bolivia, I had a chance to immerse myself in the culture, language, and customs of eastern Bolivia. I not only acquired detailed knowledge of the local culture but much extratextual information about "my group." Obviously, my knowledge and experience of the Indonesian culture, and particularly that of Batak, Sumatra, was nearly nonexistent, apart from the reports from the partner group. In that sense, the partner group could hardly receive as fair (or knowledgeable) a treatment as the Bolivian group

did. These factors, and perhaps others, undoubtedly affect the scientific
validity and reliability of the report and are to be kept in mind.

Group Profiles and Initial Reading of John 20:1–18

Group Profile and Background: Buenas Nuevas (Bolivia)

Buenas Nuevas is a conservative evangelical church, comprising about 120
members with an average regular attendance of 80; it is located in Santa
Cruz, Bolivia, and is part of a denomination called Union Cristiana Evangélica. The church was started about thirty years ago specifically to bring
this type of conservative denomination to Santa Cruz. The church is heavily focused on the Bible, and the inspiration and authority of the Bible are
held in high regard. The Bible is studied, meditated on, sung, memorized,
and held in high esteem by the congregation. The Buenas Nuevas church
is conservative in form and doctrine; the group members wanted to distinguish themselves from other evangelical denominations particularly in
their form of worship. As one of the participants stated, "most Bolivian
evangelical churches sing *alabanzas*[2] but we prefer hymns [accompanied
by piano and harmonica]." One of the participants also explicitly claimed
being "strong and traditional" in character.

From the report and from my dealings with the congregation, it is
evident that the people love one another deeply and that the communal
bonds are strong. Members call one another "brothers" and "sisters." Some
expressed concerns regarding the lack of membership growth in recent
years, while others surmised that it is perhaps partially due to the conservative nature of the church. The aspiration is to fill the congregation with
like-minded people who do not compromise the much-loved traditional
forms and doctrines.

As I discussed with some of the elders of the church the possibility
of facilitating an intercultural Bible reading project, I was given permission to present the project to the congregation. My more detailed presentation of the project during a regular Wednesday night Bible study met
with mixed responses. Some were positively inclined and primarily wondered how the process worked, while others were afraid a dialogue might

---

2. *Alabanzas*, or praise and worship songs, are popular among most Pentecostal,
charismatic, and evangelical churches. They are upbeat (pop or Latin type) songs with
popular rhythms with simple and repetitive choruses.

make some "doubt their faith" or "lead a weak brother astray." One even suggested that this might be a covert attempt to bring people under the authority of the pope! As the group comments became increasingly negative, even some of the elders started to doubt the possible benefits of the project. Finally, as the project was discussed with the leaders, they again gave the project a green light. Nevertheless, we agreed that I would be the one to try to find a group not too dissimilar to their group, and this group was not to be Catholic or Pentecostal.

The conservativeness of the Buenas Nuevas group is also reflected in the fact that some discussed the possibility of losing distinct cultural values and customs of *el Oriente* (eastern Bolivia). The rivalry and cultural clashes between the cultures of Andean region and *el Oriente* have a long history and have become more polarized after Evo Morales became the first indigenous president of Bolivia in 2006 (see Klein 2003). The group characterized the congregation as mainly middle class, but professions within the group ranged from artisans and unemployed single mothers to university graduates and leaders of medium-sized businesses.

## Group Profile and Background: Rogate (Sumatra, Indonesia)

Due to the lack of specific information, it is much harder to compile a group profile of the Rogate Bible study group. Incidental information was gathered from the exchange and from replies to the Buenas Nuevas group's questions. The Rogate Bible study group is part of the Batak Lutheran Church in Northern Sumatra, Indonesia, which celebrated its tenth birthday in June 2012. The small group gathers in houses every other week to learn more about Scripture. All participants apparently come from the Batak culture, though this was not explicitly stated in the report.

From the reports, it appears that the group is rather conservative in nature, though there are competing opinions within the group, especially concerning the status and role of women. There was little sharing of personal experiences and a lack of intimacy within the group, which might reflect Batak cultural practice, might result from the fact that the report was shared with another group, or have some other unknown cause. As a minority within a Muslim dominated country, the Rogate group faces psychological and mental persecution, restrictions of public expression of faith, and diminished opportunities in society, especially in employment. In general, the group members pose a number of questions regarding the relationship between their faith and local cultural practices. The pastor stated that they hold allegiance first to the gospel and then to *Adat*, or the customary laws of the Batak culture. He concludes, "We live under these two voices, and that is the fact of our obedience." However, the practical outworking of this relationship remains elusive due to lack of clarification and concrete examples. The social standings of the group members vary, though they consider themselves to be "ordinary people." Professions within the group range from bus driver and laborer to teacher and university lecturer.

Hermeneutical Processes of the Initial Reading of John 20:1–18: Buenas Nuevas

During the first reading report by the Buenas Nuevas group, the initial focus on the resurrection of Jesus led the group to discuss various textual details. This was followed by sharing personal experiences as group members identified with Mary's sorrow and the comforting attitude of the resurrected Jesus. Finally, the text provided encouragement to have faith and continue proclaiming the resurrection to people around them.

The reading attitude of the Buenas Nuevas group was pietistic and, on occasion, psychologizing; at the same time they focused on textual details and on the larger themes of resurrection and witnessing/evangelism. Some focused on the positioning of the grave clothes, while another commented on the location of the angels at the head and feet. It seems that for some group members the narrative flow was difficult to follow and needed clarification. Historical background information given by the facilitator seemed to have little effect on the reading process or understanding of the text per se.

It was probably the status of the text as the authoritative word of God that led at least some group members to take the narrative not only at face value but even as a sort of video portrayal of events. For example, Daniel insisted that Mary was unable to recognize Jesus due to having tears in her eyes.

The text also functioned as a source of comfort and spiritual guidance. For example, when the facilitator queried about the possibility of finding parallels between the way Jesus approached and comforted the grief-stricken Mary and the present-day experience of the participants, many group members wanted to relate their stories:

> Daniel: More than anything, I would say that we forget … because of problems, difficulties … most of the time we think that we are alone though it is not so. God is always here. I remember one situation … this

afternoon I was thinking about this problem … I could've been burned … and died … one possible accident. I remember when God protected me and God was here … many years ago. God is protecting even when one does not know it … even when we have gone away from God.

The sharing of these stories functioned as a key to a deeper and more personal reflection on life, spirituality, and God's involvement in one's lived experience.

The present-day implication of Jesus's resurrection and the need for witnessing surfaced toward the latter part of the study. Roberto reminded the group of the importance of telling others about the resurrection, taking his cue from John 20:17 ("Go to my brothers and tell them") and applying it directly to the group's experience. Others drew similar conclusions:

> María: as children of God we have to give good news to others because it is his command. That is what the Lord wants to say to us and that we are going to speak his word to all creatures that do not know.

> Daniel: we as believers need to say that he is resurrected … because many times, I, for example, one time asked my neighbor in my neighborhood: Do you believe in Christ? He said certainly, as one is supposed to believe, and then I asked him if he believes that Jesus has resurrected and he said that this not [i.e., he does not believe in the resurrection of Christ].

In addition to telling about Jesus's resurrection, one is encouraged to manifest resurrection in one's personal life:

> Daniel: so we as believers have to give evidence that Christ has really resurrected and that we have also been resurrected with him. We have to demonstrate new life, this change, a new birth. He who was dead now is resurrected and has transformed us … there has been a transformation in us.

Resurrection, evangelism, and changed lives seem to function as a heuristic key to unlock the meaning of the passage. A personal experience of transformation probably also is behind Daniel's comment on the insistence of changed lives.

It seems clear that the text prompted Buenas Nuevas to continue evangelistic efforts, proclaim the resurrection of Christ, and search for personal transformation. Transformed life in the present is proof of the resurrection of Jesus in the past, thus fusing the horizons from the perspective of present-day experience. Such witnessing and/or transformation are hardly new praxeological directions for Buenas Nuevas, but rather a reminder and encouragement to continue existing practices. The Buenas Nuevas group also utilized a loose identification with the grief-stricken Mary and the resurrected Jesus as a platform for sharing difficult personal experiences. This seemed to facilitate a communal process of discerning God's presence in the midst of life's uncertainties and struggles. It appeared to be a moving experience not only for the group members but also, as we will see later, for the partner group.

Hermeneutical Processes of the Initial Reading of John 20:1–18: Rogate

The Rogate group's reading focused on the resurrection, the question of women's role in church and society, and the relationship between faith and local cultural practices. The Rogate group maintained an open attitude throughout the study and, compared to the Buenas Nuevas group, focused more on thematic aspects than on details of the text. The resurrection of Jesus and Mary's role as the first witness to the resurrection were translated into the readers' present-day context and brought into dialogue with cultural practices of the Batak tribe.

After the pastor's initial summary and minisermon on resurrection, Ms. Lia posed a question based on Mary's role at the tomb and the resurrection of Jesus:

> My point is why in our culture, that is, Batak culture, the women still keep silence? When we have cultural functions we can see that only men have the rights to speak. How should we face this reality?

The ensuing discussion included a range of opinions regarding the position of women in the society and church, but finally the pastor was invited, or challenged, to give his authoritative opinion. He pointed out the need to discuss reasons for changes within the church as well as to open a discussion in the broader society concerning the role of women. Thus it seems that the text elicited a potentially emancipating discussion, though it is unclear whether this was followed by any concrete praxeological effects.

In addition to the thematic discussion of women's role, I found Ms. Lia's comments regarding why Mary was chosen to be the witness of Jesus's resurrection fascinating:

> Then the disciples went back to their homes.... Mary was the only one who kept remaining in the tomb. She was a woman but she had courage to be alone in the cemetery. Compared to our present time now, most people do not have enough courage to be alone in the cemetery because people are scared of ghosts.

It is interesting to note how the text and present-day reality were juxtaposed. The fear of ghosts within the Batak cultural context seemed to unlock the meaning of the passage in which Mary was alone at the cemetery and to promote a positive evaluation of Mary's faith and courage. By implication, it encouraged women's active participation in ministry and perhaps also gave further weight to earlier discussions regarding women's active participation within the society.

Similarly, the phrase "in the morning ... still dark" was compared to the local Christian practice of visiting cemeteries at 4 a.m. on resurrection day. This led to an explanation of the Christian practice by the pastor, which he concluded by saying:

> By visiting the cemetery we are reminded of our death as well as of our resurrection. So, being believers we are not afraid of death any more. This means that our death is not the end of life but it is the bridge into eternal life.

It is clear from these examples that the heuristic keys for the Rogate group lay in the present-day experiences of the group. Resurrection was thematically lifted from the text and applied to the group. Belief in Jesus's resurrection means eternal life, freedom from fear of death (and ghosts?), and as the pastor stated: "He is the Lord who is able to hear our prayer, and who loves to help us." Further, Mary's role as courageous witness of the resurrection was brought to bear as a challenge to conservative ecclesiastic and societal/cultural roles of women.

In conclusion, the Rogate group's reading of John 20:1–18 focused on broader themes of the text and prompted reflection on topics such as women, society, and culture. The Buenas Nuevas group's reading emphasized textual details and the theme of resurrection and witnessing, the focus being more individualistic and ecclesial, while omitting reflection on the broader societal aspects. Rogate's approach seemed somewhat more formal and intellectual, whereas the Buenas Nuevas group focused on the real-life experiences of individuals.

What happened as the groups attempted to make sense of each other's reading and tried to read the text anew "through the eyes of the other"?

## Mapping the Interaction

### Buenas Nuevas Responds to the Rogate Reading of John 20:1–18

The members of Buenas Nuevas found it difficult to imagine what life is like in Indonesia, since nobody had visited that part of the world. One individual imagined that all women are covered from head to toe, and many reasoned that this was why the partner group focused so closely on women's liberation.

One individual concluded that the partner group's study was not very deep like "ours" due to its primary focus on women. A woman participant agreed with this, but saw the reason for the superiority of their own reading to lie in the focus on textual details. Another person was of the opinion that it is impossible to interact with the partner group, because they had such different views on the status of men and women: "we have equality and you see women as second-class citizens." The same participant insisted strongly that the resurrection is the main point of the text and that there is no negotiation on this point.

Nevertheless, there were more nuanced perspectives in the Buenas Nuevas group as well. One of the leaders observed that the Rogate group exhibited a range of opinions regarding women and their participation in church and society. Some also noted the pastor's comments on equality between men and women in Christ and within the church. In general, it seems that the Buenas Nuevas group considered it strange that Rogate had devoted so much space to reflecting on the relationship between their culture and faith. In response to this, one of the ladies in Buenas Nuevas group commented that "cultures pass away with people, and so do women, but the Word of God remains forever." This seemed to me like a dismissive and negative comment; but, to my surprise, some Rogate women regarded it as a word of comfort. This issue of perception demonstrated how vulnerable to misunderstanding intercultural communication is, whatever the reasons for initial misunderstanding here might be.

From this brief description of the Buenas Nuevas group's response to Rogate, one can discern a range of attitudes. From the perspective of social psychology (Tropp and Molina 2012) and intergroup relations (Tindale et al. 2005; Abrams et al. 2005), there is a mixture of prejudice, labeling, and generalizations as well as some openness on the part of a few group members. There was little decategorization, or attempts to see individual faces, though some Buenas Nuevas group members saw past the stereotypes. Perhaps a sharing of personal experiences might have helped the Buenas Nuevas group see why the Rogate group focused so much on women's status and role and the cultural practices in their reading, though this remains purely speculative. One's own group was seen as superior to "the other" in many respects. The societal structure as well as the hermeneutical practice of the partner group were seen as inferior and unintelligible in many respects. There were few attempts to understand the plight of women in the partner group or "the other" in general. Hermeneutically, there was only a superficial recognition of the relationship between culturally oppressive practices of Batak society and the longing for liberation, especially on the part of the women in the partner group. This loose connection did not lead to empathy or concern for the women's plight by the Buenas Nuevas group. Finally, there were few attempts to read or understand the text "through the eyes of the other." The only thing that the groups seemed to agree on, according to Buenas Nuevas comments, was that "it is the responsibility of all believers to talk about resurrection."

On the positive side, in the end the Buenas Nuevas group wanted to pose questions to understand the Rogate group's life and experiences better. It seems that the Buenas Nuevas group truly had difficulties imagining the situation of the partner group. In this endeavor to understand further, one of the questions concerned the real-life situation of persecution and opened up a fruitful conversation. The other question, concerning whether all Rogate participants were (mature) Christians, was partially seen as hostile by some Rogate members.

## Rogate Responds to the Response of Buenas Nuevas

The Rogate group's report started with an informative response to the Buenas Nuevas's queries regarding the status of women in Batak society, in the family, and in the Indonesian Lutheran church. The group (pastor?) made clear that "we have no differences regarding the role of women in ministry," but that women's status in society is unequal. Rogate also clarified that all participants had been Christians for many years.

A new dimension of Rogate's experience emerged as the group told about the persecution and oppression they face in their sociocultural context. Though the Rogate group members had not experienced physical violence, they reported mental and psychological persecution, frustration, and marginalization at work, conflicts with the Muslim majority, and their inability to construct churches. In regard to marginalization at work, they reported that "mentally we are full of depression."

After the cordial and rather informative answers, Rogate confronted some of Buenas Nuevas's earlier comments and questions. Buenas Nuevas's query regarding the partner group's Christian commitment and/or level of maturity prompted a strong reaction. One participant responded that "you tend to look at us as a primitive people." This statement seems to be a paraphrase; it would have been interesting to know a bit about the discussion that surrounded this comment. In addition, some Rogate women said that men within Buenas Nuevas are unable to understand "the suffering of women in our place." However, the women within the Buenas Nuevas group were attributed a more sympathetic stance, as one of the women quoted a Buenas Nuevas woman's comment: "the cultures pass away with people, and so do women, but the Word of God remains forever." As mentioned earlier, to me this comment seemed unsympathetic, but the women in the Rogate group evidently took it to be positive.

Finally, Rogate concluded the report by posing questions to Buenas Nuevas. They inquired about the level of religious freedom in Bolivia and particularly about the role of women in society, church, and family. It is unclear whether the latter question was an informative inquiry or an implicit challenge to the Buenas Nuevas group regarding the status and role of women.

The Rogate group's response to Buenas Nuevas was rather formal and informative. Questions were answered, though the polyphony of voices that came across in Rogate's initial report regarding the status of women was not addressed. The strong reaction to Buenas Nuevas's query regarding the status of group members as Christians was, in my opinion, quite understandable. This reflects perhaps what social psychologists would call a symbolic threat to the group's identity (Tropp and Molina 2012, 12–13). Later the Buenas Nuevas group modified this statement, and their opinion of "the other" grew in both understanding and affection.

Buenas Nuevas Responds to the Response of Rogate

The Buenas Nuevas group reiterated their difficulty in understanding the partner group's culture and situation, though they reportedly had gained much from the Rogate group's response. Buenas Nuevas also wanted to clarify that they did not see the partner group as "primitive" or doubt the sincerity of their Christian commitment.

Buenas Nuevas explained their ability to practice their religion freely and were clearly touched by the difficult situation of their partner group:

> Very sad to hear about the persecution that you are experiencing in your country. Discrimination in the work place and society must be depressing as you mentioned … [and] not being able to construct churches must be frustrating.

From these comments one can see a movement toward empathy and a positive appraisal of "the other." The Buenas Nuevas group encouraged the Rogate group to stay strong and promised to pray for the Rogate group members.

In regard to the status of women, the Buenas Nuevas group's answer to Rogate is somewhat ambiguous:

> In our society women have freedom to participate in all functions and activities of life. However, as we understand from the Bible, there are certain limitations to women's participation within the ministry of the church.

According to the Buenas Nuevas group, women are excluded from the roles of pastor and elder. The theological justification is based, for example, on 1 Tim 3:1–5 and Titus 1:5–9, as well as on the way Paul organized male elders according to Acts. This is seen as a "clear biblical teaching." In society, however, women have full freedom to participate in all functions. The Buenas Nuevas group also sees the husband as "the head of the household" according to "biblical teaching." Nevertheless, they wanted to qualify the term "head of the household" by giving a practical example from daily interaction between a husband and wife:

> We do not think that this means that the woman is tied down or has no place in societal functions or that she obeys all of the wishes of her

husband.... [There is also] a passage in Proverbs and other sections of
the Bible which indicate that women have independence especially if the
husband does not live a godly life.

It is unclear to which biblical passage this more qualified statement refers to
in Proverbs (Prov 31?) and elsewhere in the Bible; however, there seems to
be some unresolved tension between the "clear biblical teaching" and these
statements. The Bible is used here to construct theological statements and
to justify actual practices of the church. Based on an earlier analysis of the
group's Bible study, it is not strange that the reading horizons are fused or
that there is lack of awareness regarding genre, history, or the cultural gap.
It is perhaps noteworthy that the women were most vocal within the group
to restrict women's participation in certain ministry roles. Finally, some
in Buenas Nuevas appeared to be sincerely happy regarding the increased
freedom of women in Indonesia.

Overall, after somewhat negative and "frozen" initial comments
during the first exchange, it is clear that the Buenas Nuevas group began
to take first steps toward understanding "the other." They exhibited empathy toward the plight of persecution, grew in knowledge, and initiated
perspective taking (ability to see issues from more than one perspective).
Knowledge, empathy, and perspective taking, among other things, are
aspects that, according to recent research in intergroup relations and social
psychology, are contributing factors in reduced prejudice and better cooperation between groups (Tindale et al. 2005; Abrams et al. 2005). Rogate's
stance as (mature) Christians was no longer queried. Instead, there was
respect for the partner group: "Despite the fact that we have differences
in this respect [ministry roles of women], we do see that you are sincere
Christians because you believe in the Lord Jesus Christ, and he is the one
who sees the heart above all."

The Buenas Nuevas group seemed able to move from prejudice to a
more open stance toward the partner group to the extent that they saw
both groups as part of a larger group who believe in Jesus Christ. This
process, which the social psychologists call recategorization (Tindale et al.
2005), enabled the Buenas Nuevas group to create a category that included
both groups despite their differences. The Buenas Nuevas group was also
able to make positive comments regarding the fact that women were
enjoying more freedom in Indonesia than before. This, however, did not
translate into a reassessment of women's roles within the Buenas Nuevas
group or to deeper reflection of status of women within Bolivian society.

Response of Rogate to Buenas Nuevas's Initial Study of John 20:1–18 and Their Final Comments

The Rogate group's response to the initial Bible study of Buenas Nuevas was sent together with the conclusion to the exchange. They began the report by expressing heartfelt gratitude for their prayers. They considered the Buenas Nuevas group as part of their spiritual family:

> We are so happy to have you our brothers and sisters who pray for us. In spite of the fact that we are a minority in Indonesia, we have you as our family in God who pray for us, as we also pray for you always.

Judging from the many comments and questions the Rogate group had about the Buenas Nuevas reading, some were impressed by the attention to textual details. Rogate found that as they themselves focused on certain details in the text, they discovered new questions and tended to frame the queries to Buenas Nuevas from their own sociocultural perspective. Thus, as Rogate explored Buenas Nuevas's commentary for the reason why Jesus did not allow Mary to touch her, they commented: "It seems … that Jesus is not the real Jesus. Is that the reason why we are not allowed to touch or to communicate with spirits of our ancestors? Or is there another reason?" Here it appears that the risen Jesus and his refusal to allow physical contact[3] is likened to the spirit of the ancestor. The prohibition of physical contact with Jesus in the text then prompted a query about the present-day prohibition regarding communication with the ancestral spirits. This conclusion is based on the importance of ancestral spirits and communication with them (see, e.g., Waddington 2002). The emphasis on the spirits, cemeteries, and ancestors come across also in the Rogate's earlier reports. Nevertheless, the query was left unanswered within the Rogate group, nor was it touched on later by Buenas Nuevas.

One lady was impressed by the Buenas Nuevas group's reading and particularly the way they had applied the message to their daily life: "after you explored the text you also applied the message of the text for the daily life." The group was also encouraged by the sharing of personal stories during the Bible reading: "some of you shared their horrible experiences

---

3. It seems that the physical contact per se is the issue here. Whether the original Greek present imperative (μή … ἅπτου) is meant to convey mere touching, holding on or clinging, or something else is beside the point here.

and how God was with them. The sister confessed that your experiences have comforted her in her personal struggles."

Connecting the reading of the text to real-life experiences by the Buenas Nuevas group seemed to prompt potential praxeological effects in the Rogate group as well. Although they had agreed on the importance of resurrection, Daniel's (Buenas Nuevas group) practical example of sharing Christ with his neighbor and the enthusiasm of the Buenas Nuevas group on the topic led Rogate to a question: "Do you have any suggestion what should we do in telling non-Christians about the resurrection of Jesus?" Rogate acknowledged the difficulties involved in this endeavor and the potential consequences of such practices in a Muslim country.

Finally, the Rogate group expressed gratitude to Buenas Nuevas for the exchange. They were particularly touched by the personal nature of Buenas Nuevas's reading and stated the importance of their comment that "we … always forget that God is next to us at all times.… God knows our cry and problem, and he calls us by name."

It is interesting to note the manifold changes in the Rogate group's understanding and perception of the Buenas Nuevas group and even how they experimented with the hermeneutical approach of Buenas Nuevas. Rogate embraced Buenas Nuevas as part of their "spiritual family" and appreciated that Buenas Nuevas was praying for them. The self-disclosure of Buenas Nuevas seemed to open a point of identification on the level of lived experiences and brought the groups closer together. According to intergroup research, self-disclosure is one of the most important avenues to reduce intergroup conflict, provided that the timing is correct (Tropp and Molina 2012, 17–34).

Rogate was also impressed by Buenas Nuevas's hermeneutical approach. Rogate seemed to experiment with the detail-oriented exegesis but approached the passages with their own questions in mind. Thus a number of cultural practices of the Batak people were again brought into dialogue with the text, this time with more attention to smaller units of the text. Perhaps the most surprising issue was the praxeological effect of the Buenas Nuevas group's hermeneutics on the Rogate group. The Rogate group was willing to adopt a new and potentially dangerous practice of telling their neighbors about Jesus's resurrection. Thus it is probably not an exaggeration to say that the Rogate group moved through two stages: first, to experiment with the hermeneutical stance of their partner group though adapting it to their liking; second, they (potentially) adopted a new praxis. It is difficult to say whether the praxeological effect of witnessing about resurrection truly took place or merely remained an ideal that the group would like to practice. It is also difficult to pinpoint whether it concerned witnessing verbally or/and by means of transformed personal lives, as Buenas Nuevas suggested both. Finally, perhaps surprisingly, Rogate did not comment in their report on Buenas Nuevas's view of women. The issue of women's status in church and society receded into the background. Instead, their focus seemed to have shifted to topics where both groups found common ground and probably to what was new and of interest to the Rogate group. In light of previous negativity between the groups, the positive appraisal of the Buenas Nuevas group and the willingness of the Rogate group to ask for advice are truly remarkable.

Buenas Nuevas's Final Response and Conclusion to Rogate

The final response from Buenas Nuevas showed a new level of appreciation of the partner group and a move toward self-evaluation that was notably absent from earlier comments. The Buenas Nuevas group started by stating that they had gained many new insights about the way Christians live in Indonesia and that they had come to appreciate the freedom in Bolivia. They also commented on how essential application to life is in their study of the Bible.

When the Buenas Nuevas group considered the eagerness of the Rogate group to share their faith despite opposition, the Buenas Nuevas members raised self-critical comments: "[Would we] be witnessing about our faith with as much enthusiasm and courage if we lived in your situation?" They also wanted to openly commend Rogate for this.

The Buenas Nuevas group acknowledged the difficulty of giving advice about witnessing to a group living in such a hostile environment. Nevertheless, older group members recalled the time when Protestant Christians were harassed and persecuted for their faith in Bolivia. They mentioned prayer and a confident trust in the Lord as the main ingredients in their struggle: "true prayer from the heart is the most important thing." In addition to prayer, Buenas Nuevas shared practical advice on "how ... [to] share Christ creatively and discreetly."

Finally, as Buenas Nuevas concluded their report, they confessed that the exchange had "opened our eyes to a reality very different from ours." It is possible that at least partially the group was able to translate the intercultural experience into their own context. One group member compared the intercultural dialogue to the difference between denominations in Bolivia and concluded that "there are reasons for different Christian denominations and beliefs."

The Buenas Nuevas group's final report reveals a shift toward transformation as well as areas where change was not considered. Buenas Nuevas openly confessed to gaining a new perspective on how Christians in Indonesia live and by extension an appreciation of their own religious freedom. Additionally, they were challenged to reflect on their own spiritual practices of prayer and evangelism as they compared their situation to that of their partner group. Thus the Buenas Nuevas group gained new perspectives on these aspects regarding the self and "the other." This even led to a degree of self-criticism in regard to their spiritual fervor. Perhaps most importantly, they were able to move from a negative and stereotyped understanding of the Rogate group to a new perspective and even to admiration of the partner group. As the Buenas Nuevas group gave their final advice on evangelism to the Rogate group, they were aware of the differences between the sociocultural and religious contexts and proceeded with empathy and caution.

Despite these positive developments, after the initial confrontation and exchange of ideas, the role and status of women were not considered further. One is left with the impression that in Bolivian society women and men are treated equally. There was no mention of the pervasive machismo or subjugation of women in Latin America or (eastern) Bolivia.[4] Similarly, dialogue between culture and faith that featured so prominently in the Rogate group found no echo in Buenas Nuevas's discussions apart from few (dismissive?) comments. Drawing explicitly from the eastern Bolivia's cultural heritage could have potentially opened new insights into the text.[5] This possibility was not entertained even after Rogate's examples. Finally, there seems to have been no praxeological effects apart from a reiteration of already adopted praxis. The foundational hermeneutical insights and methods of Buenas Nuevas were neither challenged nor reflected on in any way. In conclusion, the greatest gain for the Buenas Nuevas group was in the perspective

---

4. While gathering my empirical data in Bolivia, one Pentecostal church openly acknowledged machismo and the need to change existing practices both inside the church(es) and in society.

5. Admittedly, there is little hermeneutical work done on enculturation of Christian faith and/or biblical hermeneutics in the eastern Bolivian lowlands. However, the Andes region's situation is quite different in this regard; see, for example, Estermann 2006.

on the self, increased insight in the "other," and a renewed attitude including empathy toward the partner group. Even if there was no praxeological effect, I consider these aspects to be quite positive, given the strongly conservative nature of the Buenas Nuevas group. Perhaps more surprising is the overall influence of the Buenas Nuevas group's comments on their partner group.

## Transformation and Stagnation

It is difficult to be certain of the reasons for transformation and for the freezing of perspectives for both groups, that is, why the Rogate group was eager to adopt, at least potentially, a new praxis of witnessing despite the risks involved and why the Buenas Nuevas group was unwilling to entertain a new perspective on issues such as their hermeneutical method, the status of women, and culture.

From the perspective of social psychology, some factors that affect intergroup relations and reduction of conflict are useful here. According to Linda Tropp and Ludwin Molina (2012, 14–35), self-disclosure, empathy, shared activities, and cross-group friendship are factors that reduce prejudice and increase perspective taking (the ability to see issues from more than one perspective) between groups. This in turn has a potential to reduce intergroup conflict and leads to transformation of individuals and groups. The Buenas Nuevas group started the process with a low level of motivation and a high degree of prejudice, a stance that would not predict success in an intergroup conflict. This stance was observable in the earlier part of exchange in the form of negative statements and attitudes. As the understanding of the partner group's culture and life situation grew, more positive comments and attitudes emerged. I would see that this change is linked at least partially to the fact that Rogate chose to disclose its status as a persecuted minority. A statement like "mentally we are full of depression" was a bold self-disclosure and was surprising since in the same report Rogate queried whether Buenas Nuevas considered the Rogate group to be true Christians. In the next report the Buenas Nuevas group became empathetic and exhibited a desire to pray and encourage the Rogate group.

Similarly, it was the ability of the Buenas Nuevas group to see "human faces"[6] and the practical implications that enabled the Rogate group to

---

6. That is, they practiced what social psychologists call decategorization and stopped viewing the group as a homogeneous unit.

experiment with the hermeneutical and praxeological aspects of Buenas Nuevas's reading. The Rogate group was particularly impressed by the self-disclosure of difficult life experiences and the appropriation of the text (e.g., "God is next to us at all times") on the part of Buenas Nuevas. Rogate also valued Daniel's practical example of sharing the resurrection with a neighbor. Here as well one can see the importance of self-disclosure, and perhaps, more specifically, the sharing of profound personal and communal experiences of suffering and struggle that resonated with the partner group.

It is perhaps even more difficult to give reasons for freezing or a lack of willingness to consider the perspective of the partner group. On the part of Buenas Nuevas, the lack of initial motivation and prejudice certainly played a part, but this does not explain the change in attitude that did occur. It is perhaps important to note that Buenas Nuevas group did not remain intact throughout the exchange and the time span between the different phases of the dialogue was lengthy. The lack of willingness on the part of Buenas Nuevas to reflect on, for example, the relationship between their culture and faith or the status of women is probably to be attributed to their deeply held theological convictions as revealed particularly in their comments on the role of women. Here I believe self-disclosure in the form of real-life experiences on the part of Rogate might have opened up valuable avenues for further discussion. Also, the Rogate group did not interact on the level of specific biblical texts that would probably have been the preferred method of the Buenas Nuevas group as conservative evangelicals. Though some of these comments are suggestive and speculative, I do think that they point to directions that may provide provisional explanations. Causality is impossible to prove, and correlation remains difficult to demonstrate here.

Finally, I would like to pose a question about and reflect on the role of the Bible in the intercultural exchange process: Is the Bible an integral part of this intercultural dialogue, or is it merely the lowest common denominator that all groups agree on? In other words, does the Bible hold merely an instrumental status in the dialogue?

Both groups in this investigation held the Bible to be authoritative, and the Buenas Nuevas group openly shared their high regard and love for the Bible in principle and practice. Perhaps not surprisingly, neither group explicitly discussed the authority or doctrine of the Bible in the exchange. It remains a mystery whether these two groups would have agreed to embark on an intercultural dialogue that did not include the Bible. Throughout the exchange, I detected that the Bible was more than just an instrument. Even for the Buenas Nuevas group, which some scholars might label fundamentalist, the resurrection story in John 20:1–18 became more than a prescriptive list of doctrine and ethics. A feature that caught my attention was the parallel development between the Buenas Nuevas group's understanding of their partner group's status as Christians and the theological perspective of John 20:1–18 and John's Gospel in general. At the beginning of the exchange process, Buenas Nuevas seemed unsure whether some members of the Rogate group were true or mature Christians: "Are all who are part of your Bible study group Christians or are some unsure of their faith?" After hearing about the difficult and oppressive life situation of the Rogate group, the Buenas Nuevas group embraced the partner group as "sincere Christians" and started to empathize with them and pray for them. In the final report, Buenas Nuevas not only embraced the partner group as "brothers and sisters" but admired their faith and perseverance. While the parallel is not exact, John 20:1–18 also exhibits a similar development in understanding on the part of Mary toward the resurrected Jesus. She moves from weeping and desperation (20:2, 11, 13–14) to a surprising recognition of Jesus as "Rabbouni" (20:16) and to becoming the herald of the resurrected Lord (20:17–18).[7] In addition to this, in Buenas Nuevas's rhetoric, intertextual echoes of the biblical texts can be detected as Buenas Nuevas encouraged their partner group to stay strong despite difficulties: "[we] bless you, encourage you to stay strong and move forward in the strength of the Lord," in which can be heard echoes of 1 Cor 15:58 and Josh 1:9. Thus the text, alongside intercultural dialogue, becomes a window and mirror of the community experience of self and the partner group and, by extension, of their manifold use of biblical texts. Sadly, Buenas Nuevas was unable to take distance or to reflect critically on their hermeneutical practices and core doctrines. Indeed, it seems that their hermeneutical stance reflects broadly what Néstor Míguez considers the received "missionary theology" (2004, 334–47), even though the group thought that their interpretation was unequivocally "biblical."

In the case of Rogate, the text prompted a critical evaluation of cultural practices in the surrounding society. However, as Rogate experimented with Buenas Nuevas's exegetical approach, the issue of the status of women

---

7. This pattern of growth in understanding and faith is a major theme in John's Gospel and obviously is in reference to Jesus (see, e.g., John 1:35–51; 4:1–42; 9:1–40; 11:17–44; see Acts 10–11 for similar development from difference perspective).

receded to the background, though the dialogue between biblical text and culture remained intact. The transformation process of the Buenas Nuevas group seemed to touch their attitudes toward and impressions of the partner group rather than their own deeply held theological convictions. This is perhaps both the danger and the beauty of the intercultural project: it allows the groups to decide for themselves which aspects they choose to discuss, engage, omit, or push to the background.

Walter Wink (2010) pointed out that one of the goals of biblical interpretation is to so "interpret the Scriptures that the past becomes alive and illuminates our present with new possibilities for personal and social transformation." Though Wink's vision was not fully attained during this exchange, I do see the intercultural exchange as a process that sowed seeds of transformation, and the Bible played a role in it. Even with a group like Buenas Nuevas, I detect a degree of positive transformation, though they froze in the very area that could have breathed life into their small congregation. As social psychologists Tropp and Molina stated, "positive outcomes of contact can still be achieved even among those most resistant to cross-group relationships" (2012, 26). Those who believe that a positive transformation process involves not only group dynamics and social psychology, but also the movement of the Spirit, cannot stop until the seeds of transformation have been spread far and wide.

## References

Abrams, Dominic, Daniel Frings, and Georgina Ramsley de Mours. 2005. "Group Identity and Self-Definition." Pages 329–51 in *The Handbook of Group Research and Practice*. Edited by Susan A. Wheelan. Thousand Oaks, CA: Sage.

Babbie, Earl. 2004. *The Practice of Social Research*. 10th ed. Belmont, CA: Wadsworth.

Conradie, Ernst M., and Louis J. Jonker. 2001. "Bible Study within Established Bible Study Groups: The Results of an Empirical Research Project." *Scriptura* 78:381–98.

Deaux, Kay, and Mark Snyder, eds. 2012. *The Oxford Handbook of Personality and Social Psychology*. Oxford: Oxford University Press.

Estermann, Josef, ed. 2006. *Teología Andina: El Tejido Diverso de la Fe Indígena*. 2 vols. La Paz: ISEAT.

Klein, Herbert S. 2003. *A Concise History of Bolivia*. Cambridge: Cambridge University Press.

Klerk, Jilles de. 2004. "Through Different Eyes: Indonesian Experiences with an Intercultural Reading of John 4." Pages 161–75 in De Wit, Jonker, Kool, and Schipani 2004.

Míguez, Néstor. 2004. "Reading John 4 in the Interface between Ordinary and Scholarly Interpretation." Pages 334–47 in De Wit, Jonker, Kool, and Schipani 2004.

Tindale, R. Scott, Amanda Dykema-Engblade, and Erin Wittkowski. 2005. "Conflict within and between Groups." Pages 313–29 in *The Handbook of Group Research and Practice*. Edited by Susan A. Wheelan. Thousand Oaks, CA: Sage.

Tropp, Linda R., and Ludwin E. Molina. 2012. "Intergroup Processes: From Prejudice to Positive Relations between Groups." Pages 1–84 in *The Oxford Handbook of Personality and Social Psychology*. Edited by Kay Deaux and Mark Snyder. Oxford: Oxford University Press.

Waddington, R. 2002. "The Karo Batak." In *The Peoples of the World Foundation*. http://www.peoplesoftheworld.org/text?people=Karo Batak.

Wink, Walter. 2010. *The Bible in Human Transformation: Toward a New Paradigm in Group Bible Study*. Kindle Electronic Reading Edition.

Wit, Hans de. 2004. "Codes and Coding." Pages 395–434 in De Wit, Jonker, Kool, and Schipani 2004.

———. 2008. *"My God," She Said, "Ships Make Me So Crazy": Reflections on Empirical Hermeneutics, Interculturality, and Holy Scripture*. Translated by Henry Jansen. Nappannee, IN: Evangel Press.

Wit, Hans de, Louis Jonker, Marleen Kool, and Daniel Schipani, eds. 2004. *Through the Eyes of Another: Intercultural Reading of the Bible*. Elkhart, IN: Institute of Mennonite Studies.

# 18

## EASTER AT CHRISTMAS:
## READING FAMILIAR TEXTS IN UNFAMILIAR WAYS
## (A DIALOGUE AMONG GHANA, COLOMBIA,
## AND THE NETHERLANDS)

*Eric Nii Bortey Anum*

John 20 is part of the familiar Easter story. "Familiar" refers to what is common, well known, household, or proverbial. It represents the traditional, typical, or frequent ways that John 20 is interpreted. "Unfamiliar" represents that which is different, new, and foreign in interpreting the text.

In the context of intercultural Bible reading, a text is not going to be read within the specific, well-instituted, and practiced traditions; rather, it is to be read specifically as a tool for exchange of meaning across different communities of readers. This method takes up the question, "Can intercultural reading of Bible stories result in a new method of reading the Bible and communicating faith that is a catalyst for new, trans-border dialogue and identity formation?" The components of such an undertaking are explained by asking: "If (1) ordinary Bible readers from radically different situations and contexts (2) read the same Bible story and (3) enter into conversation with each other about this reading, (4) what will happen?" (De Wit 2004, 4).

The intercultural dimension of this project aims at "comparison, exchange, confrontation, meeting, conversation." The intercultural concept was adopted, because it gives "the opportunity for finding a grid, a number of calibration points, which are necessary for discovering and converting differences between interpretations" (De Wit 2004, 25). A common assignment is agreed upon, and the participants interact with one another after processing the text within their own location, using their own distinct methods or means to do so. Most importantly, an attempt is made to involve participants in conversation with one another in order to arrive at a deeper understanding of the text. In this regard, "There is, in every true manifestation, an intrinsic, that is dialogical, interaction between the object's disclosure and concealment and the subject's recognition. The interaction is conversation" (Tracy 1987, 28).

This kind of conversation makes room for multivocal texts, contexts, and methods. The question is how the process is to be formalized so as to qualify as an interpretive methodology. Concerning this type of conversation, David Tracy (1987, 28) says, "Once the results of that conversation are communicated to others, it enters into another dialogue, in principle, with the whole community of competent readers." In terms of the connections it makes, the intercultural Bible reading project fits into the framework of what Tracy proposed in terms of hermeneutics, since the outcome of the conversation is used as data for the composition and compilation of interpretation.

Specifically, the purpose of the project is to contribute toward empirical hermeneutics using the experiences of ordinary users of the Bible as the basis. With specific reference to this particular project, the space is that of empirical hermeneutics within an intercultural perspective. It has to do with the question of whether reading Bible stories jointly by groups from radically different cultural and sociopolitical contexts can contribute to transformation and changed perspectives (De Wit 2012, 5). A key aim of this project is transformation both of the community of readers and of the academy by expanding the perception by means of the intercultural dimension in biblical interpretation.

Here what I term "hermeneutical risk" is being taken as the project ventures into the realm of transactions in its approach to biblical interpretation. The participants need to contend with the back-and-forth process of reports, clarifications, questions, queries, agreements, disagreements, disappointments, fascinations, and resolutions. Out of these risky transactions between different contexts, interpretations are expected to emerge that eventually affect all stakeholders. The focus of this essay is on the total effect of such a reading process, including its major function as an instrument of change through navigating between familiar and unfamiliar factors.

## Introduction

The data for this essay is based on the following groups from Ghana, which I coordinated, and their partner groups in other countries:

- First-year Bible School Secondi with a group from Hoorn 2, the Netherlands
- Second-year Bible School Secondi with Latin American Pastoral Biblical Institute (IBPL), Bogota, Colombia
- Takoradi Bethel Methodist Young People's Service with Mensen met een Missie group, the Netherlands
- Dodowa Adventist Youth Group with a group from Hoorn 1, the Netherlands

Questions and comments that arose during a preparatory meeting with the first- and second-year Secondi Methodist Bible School groups and the Takoradi Methodist Youth Group included:

- How can we read in a different manner a part of the Easter story that we know so well?
- Are our partners going to read and get something else from this story other than what we all already know?

These questions confirmed to me the topic to be explored; the topic was further confirmed by the first report from the Pastoral Biblical Institute, Bolgota, Colombia, in which was stated:

> The Intercultural Reading of the Bible is a new and fascinating way to read the Bible. Through it, biblical accounts acquire a previously unknown depth. The participants, who come from sometimes radically different cultures, read together the same biblical account. They are challenged to try out new and unknown approaches to the biblical text.

This statement is in line with what Hans de Wit (2004, 4) calls "the core question of the project": "what happens when Christians from radically different cultures and situations read the same Bible story and start talking about it to each other?" Interpretation and meaning evolve during the interchange of readings and are therefore not predictable. Even though the text was familiar to the reading groups, it was read not for the purpose of celebrating Easter, but deliberately to gain unexpected insights through the interchange with another group.

## Leading Questions

The following questions were used to guide us in our approach to the text:

(1) To what extent did the familiarity with the text affect the reading?
(2) How did the intercultural reading process create unfamiliar readings among the groups and their partners?
(3) In what ways did the familiar and the unfamiliar interact to produce transformation in the intercultural reading process?

## Observations

In observing the process of the exchange of reading reports, the following factors came to the fore and will be treated separately in the sections below: (1) the influence of familiarity; (2) the contribution of the group process to unfamiliarity; (3) the development of more unfamiliarity from the reactions from partner groups; (4) the effect on unfamiliarity of the season in which the text was read; and (5) signs of transformation.

The Influence of Familiarity

The groups revealed their familiarity with the text in the titles they gave to the text:

- Jesus's resurrection
- The death and resurrection of Jesus
- The empty tomb
- The appearance of Jesus to Mary Magdalene: "it is about Mary's encounter with the resurrected Lord"

Interestingly, the Dodowa SDA group had a title for the entire study: "The Inspection of the Tomb," but they also stated that the text is about the death and resurrection of Jesus Christ. So within the familiar, that is, the Easter story, the Dodowa group of Southern Ghana isolated the inspection of the tomb as their specific focus for this study.

In the Ghanaian context, during the whole Passion Week in preparation for Easter, there are evening services during which the Easter story, compiled from the Gospels, is read in local dialects and Easter hymns and songs are sung. This culminates in the Easter Sunday services; Monday is normally a picnic day in which the churches go looking for Jesus in a celebration of what is called *Emmaus*. In most churches, therefore, the text of John 20:1–18 will normally be part of the readings on Saturday night, but this would not be accompanied by discussion.

The story is read and few or no comments are made, because the carefully compiled stories are self-explanatory. Further light is thrown on the stories by the locally composed songs that provide contextual explanations to the stories.

This assumed clarity of the intention of the text came to be challenged during the intercultural exchange. For instance, all the groups from Takoradi read the story with the firm conviction that John is the disciple described as "the disciple that Jesus loved." The first-year Bible School Secondi group, for instance, stated that "John—the disciple whom Jesus loves, runs to see Jesus in the tomb but couldn't wait after seeing the empty tomb." Their partner group from the Netherlands wondered how they were so sure that the disciple that Jesus loved was John. When they were discussing the reaction from their partner group, they indicated that it is "obvious," meaning that they know this from their tradition.

The Secondi and Takoradi groups read the texts in the languages Fante, Nzema, Ahanta, and English. The Hoorn 2 group, who read with the first-year Bible School Secondi group, wondered how possible and feasible it was to read the text in so many languages: "we noticed that your group used four different languages, three Ghanaian and English. Is it difficult for you to communicate in this way? Or is there one language spoken by everyone?" The response was that "the people in the group bring different Bibles to the discussion and these are the languages in which they are familiar with biblical texts, as most often those are their mother tongue."

In the Ghanaian context, even though most people are educated, their familiarity with their mother tongues and the ease with which they express themselves in these make it preferable to use different languages in the discussion. This is to ensure a meaningful discussion that will allow people to freely read and contribute to Bible discussions in the language they are comfortable with. Not all are at home in English. In the Western Region of Ghana the four languages mentioned are used by most people, and many understand and use more than two or three of the languages mentioned. When a participant uses an expression that is not understood, clarification is provided by others in the group.

The groups from Ghana use the entire Easter story known to them without paying particular attention to the text in John. Their familiarity with the narrative is due to the custom in their churches of reading a Synoptic compilation from the four Gospels every Easter.

The Contribution of the Group Process to Unfamiliar Readings

The timing of the reading project contributed to unfamiliarity. One of the Dutch groups that read with the Dodowa SDA group in Ghana remarked, "We read this commentary together a week before Christmas. It felt rather odd to be studying the Easter story during the Christmas festivities." Reading an Easter story and analyzing it during the Christmas season seemed strange. It is likely that many groups with church traditions would read this story during the season allotted to it in the Christian calendar and would find the study and discussion of this text to be out of place at a different time, particularly one marked by other stories and traditions.

All the groups from Ghana were brought together specifically for the project; this created a context in which the group dynamics with the potential for generating unfamiliar readings needed to be developed. The Hoorn 2 group form Holland remarked: "We have observed that you have proceeded systematically. This has perhaps been done so because that is the method you use at the Bible school?" As it turned out, the approach had nothing to do with the Bible school, but that the group felt that for the sake of the reading project they needed to read the text more meticulously than they normally would do.

Upon reflection one cannot fail to notice that the participation in an international reading project changed the modalities for reading the text for the Ghanaian groups, particularly for the second-year Bible school students who read with the Hoorn 2 group from Holland. An explicit effort was made to probe deeper into the texts to pick out issues that in the habitual readings were not looked for or that were even teased out of the text. For instance, the attribution of positive and negative traits to the characters in the text was normally not done within the context of the Easter reading. Surprisingly, the Dodowa Seventh-day Adventist Youth Group even attributed negative traits to the angels and to Jesus. With regard to the two angels, the positive traits included:

- Loyalty: they were loyal to duty by guarding the body of Jesus and remaining in the tomb after Jesus was resurrected.
- Secrecy/confidentiality: they kept the news about Jesus's resurrection a secret to be announced by Jesus himself.
- They represent the presence of God.

The negative traits included the fact that they kept the truth away from Mary.

With regard to Jesus, the positive traits included:

- He was faithful: he kept his promise to resurrect.
- He was respectful: he reported back to the father who sent him.
- He showed humility and simplicity: he did not show off but rather appeared simply to be thought of as a gardener.

The negative trait was that he delayed in revealing himself to Mary.

Attributing character traits to the figures in the story does not normally happen while reading this text. No wonder their partner group, Hoorn 1 of the Netherlands, reacted by saying that they "wondered (aside from John 1) if it is possible or wise to make positive and negative lists of people around you to the way they react to certain circumstances?" Normally, it is those like Judas Iscariot and Peter who are critiqued. The partner group of the Dodowa Seventh-day Adventist group of Ghana, Hoorn 1 of the Netherlands, found it rather strange for the Ghanaian group from Dodowa to read in this way. Perhaps reading the text without the usual Easter atmosphere gave the Ghanaians the freedom to do such creative analysis of the characters in the text.

## The Development of More Unfamiliar Readings from the Reactions from the Partner Group

Certain reactions challenge the partner group to look more closely at aspects that are not familiar to them in reading the text. The Hoorn 2 group considered it strange that the first-year Bible School Secondi Ghanaian group related Mary Magdalene to prominent and successful women in political and national life in Ghana. Mary Magdalene was identified as a "messenger," in the Ghanaian context to be identified with Yaa Asantewa, who led and fought for the Asante Kingdom against British colonial suppression; with Samia Nkrumah, the daughter of late President Kwame Nkrumah and the chairperson of the Convention Peoples Party (CPP); with Konadu Agyeman Rawlings, the former first lady and presidential aspirant; with Mrs. Moore, the Women's Fellowship national president of the Methodist Church; with Mrs. Georgina Baiden, the first vice president of Methodist Church Ghana; and with Georgina Woode, the chief justice of Ghana.

Though they found the Ghanaian suggestions unexpected, the Dutch group began looking at how they could find such models in the Dutch context and share them with their Ghanaian partners: "Because you used Maria Magdalena as the most important character in this story, we also searched for more facts." Thus, though the Dutch group found the Ghanaian suggestions strange, it encouraged them to do a more unfamiliar reading of the text.

Issues related to hierarchies between the disciples—that is, John and Mary giving Peter a higher prerogative—that were raised by the Mensen met een Missie group caused the Secondi Bible School first-year group to discuss the ranks of the various people mentioned in the text. Because when John and Mary got to the tomb they waited for Peter and gave him the honor of entering the tomb first, Peter is given a place superior to the other two. The question as to whether there was a hierarchy between the men, and between men and women, was also discussed. This caused the Ghanaian readers to look at status and social class as it comes out of the text, something they would not normally do. They also looked more closely at why some people were mentioned by name, but others merely described by phrases like "the pupil that Jesus loved." Their conclusion was that it was the personality traits rather than hierarchical rank that was the basis for the attitude of the characters. For instance, Peter is known for his courage and bravery, while John is described as timid and passive. The Mensen met een Missie group accepted the fact that the story presented a reversal of the hierarchies that existed in Jesus' time, for Mary Magdalene, not the male disciples, was the one who saw and recognized Jesus first.

## The Effect on Unfamiliarity of the Season in Which the Text was Read

As indicated earlier, for the Hoorn–1 group of the Netherlands, the time of reading this Easter story coincided with Christmas. They made the following observation: "We read this text together a week before Christmas. It felt rather odd to be studying the Easter story during the Christmas festivities." Indeed, it is strange and unfamiliar to be reading an Easter story of death and suffering at Christmas, which is about joy and happiness.

All the groups I dealt with read this text outside the Easter season. This gave them the opportunity to escape from the "Lent-like" feeling and from over spiritualizing the text. They were able to connect better with the text than they usually would when reading it during Lent as part of the Easter story. Not only was more gathered from the story, but it was also possible to relate the story to the present secular context. Even though some groups found it strange that the title of resurrection was given to the text, the reading itself paid little attention to details of the story in terms of the death and resurrection of Jesus. The familiar scene was given an unfamiliar reading.

Signs of Transformation

The unfamiliar reading led to the highlighting of virtues like patience, role models, humility, respect for others, caring for and sharing with others, and not holding things back from others. These were mentioned in two poems that the Dodowa group composed, to be found in the appendix: "The Resurrection" by Lord Lugard Webu and "I Have Seen the Master" by Ebenezer Quaye.

According to the Latin American Pastoral Bible Institute, they "experience this as a tremendously enriching process. The Intercultural Reading of the Bible is fascinating, but it is also a complex process." They continue: "to see individual Mary's role applied to Ghana's context and its contributions for woman actuation and value in that context" is transformative. According to the Dutch group in response to the modeling of Mary Magdalene:

> We have started thinking about Dutch women of who you could say this. We came across the first female minister in the Netherlands (Marga Klompe), a well known [sic] of [sic] television personally [sic] who liked to dedicate herself to the disabled (Mies Bowman), and the woman who was for years was the face of the Dutch Branch of the Salvation Army and who felt completely at home in the toughest neighbourhoods of the capital, between vagrants and prostitutes (Major Bosshardt).

Transformation is evident in this indication of the awareness raised by the reading process among the Dutch partners regarding the search for role models in their society, taking note of their achievements within the Dutch context: "spontaneous reading of the Bible gives us contributions [sic] to know some social values in which those brethren are immersed," and these serve as lessons.

The Takoradi Youth Service indicated that Mary was not "following the crowd"; this was picked up by the Mensen met een Missie group of the Netherlands. The Mensen group responded to what the Takoradi people stated concerning "what do we set our hearts on in the morning?" The possibility of opening yourself up to what the day has to offer was further elaborated on by the Dutch group by sharing with the Ghanaians that, "We feel it also refers to the fact that it is always possible to start anew." This dimension made a real difference to the Ghanaians, who indicated that "it is still important in times of economic hardships and failures to still make a fresh start." The life-negating elements were listed, including bad attitudes toward work in the secular context like the civil service, and the attitude to governmental policies. The group pledged to make a fresh start and to reappraise such matters, looking for how they can see light in them instead of the darkness they saw most of the time. The issue of punctuality at work and appointments was dealt with in the context of making a fresh start. On the other hand, the Dutch group indicated that sometimes their problem was that they could be "too punctual." Thus the kind of transformation that the intercultural reading brings is culturally relative: an element from the exchange could bring about transformation for one group, while for another group this aspect might not even appear to be related to the exchange.

The Hoorn 1 group made connections between some of the characters who participated in the Christmas story in order to extract more meaning out of the text, thus indicating that:

- The presence of angels is an important component in the Christmas story, relating to the revelation to Mary and to the shepherds the night of his birth.
- The announcement to the shepherds was at night and involved a bright light; in John the visit to the gravesite was at daybreak and there was darkness in the grave.
- The suffering of Jesus was also revealed in the Christmas story in his humble birth, but with this came also the same hope for a totally new beginning as in the Easter story, for the heavens opened and there was light in the darkness.

The Hoorn 1 group who read the text at Christmas were able to make connections between angels, darkness, and light and ended up relating this to the Dutch context. They looked at a painting from the late Middle Ages by a Dutch artist named Geertgen van Sint Jans. The theme of the painting is glory and suffering. In the painting, light as well as darkness present glory and suffering. This made them aware of how in the midst of darkness light can penetrate and make an impact. The life-affirming elements were identified and highlighted as the reading process provided the impetus for hope to emerge in a contemporary context where life-negating elements like economic recession were magnified and projected.

The critical look at the essence of Easter caused some groups to reevaluate what they did at Easter. Merely going through the rituals and not paying attention to real-life issues was discussed. The Hoorn 2 group indicated that Easter ought to signify "new beginnings." The resurrection, according to them, "brings a breaking off (a change). It is synonymous with clarity. If there is no breaking off there is no clarity and without clarity there is no newness." The follow-up discussion of their partner group from the first-year Secondi Bible School evaluated their own perception of Easter. Even though it did not completely fall in line with that of the Hoorn 1 group, they ended up by stating that Easter ought not to be a routine celebration, but that values like courage, forgiveness, and hope that they saw in the text ought to be projected in the life of the church.

## Conclusion

In sum, the presentation focused on three main concepts—familiarity, unfamiliarity, and transformation.

The familiarity with the text makes it easier for the groups to proceed from the known to the unknown in the reading process. To start out, they could easily read in front of the text.

An unfamiliar platform for the reading process was created by the intercultural process involving proper recording of meetings for discussions, reflecting on different reading methods and meanings extracted from texts, reading a familiar text in an unfamiliar time of the Christian year, and the necessity of clarifying and seeking clarification. Some of the groups from the same context also had the opportunity to interact with one another differently through this project.

The familiar and the unfamiliar nature of the project contributed to the emergence of new ideas and ideals from John 20. The issue of looking at the Easter story differently was emphasized in the reading process. The interrelationship between Christmas and Easter came to the fore. The importance of clarity, as understood as being metaphorically referred to by light coming out of darkness, was a striking and challenging insight.

Lastly, with regard to transformation, issues arose concerning making room for changes or new beginnings in our global context where gloom is projected instead of glory. Awareness was created concerning the relevance or significance of role models within the sociocultural and religious contexts of nation states in the readers. The intercultural readings of the groups therefore specifically call for developing one's lifestyle so as to be, like Mary Magdalene, a role model for one's nation.

Appendix: The Two Poems of the Dodowa Seventh-day Adventist Group

1. *The Resurrection*, by Lord Lugard Webu

> The waiting is over
> The fact itself had been
> Unto her like a night she had seen
> Two dark nights
> Became days in themselves
> Packed with strict anticipation
> How? Why? So soon?
> Hard to believe indeed
> Hard to tell to another
> Who had not had a taste of it
> She must find Him
> Yes!
> She must find her master
> Her savior
> Her redeemer
> The thoughts of it
> The shock
> The amazement
> The inception and obsession to find Him
> Did blind her
> Who has the answers?
> Are there possibly more than one answer?
> Or more than one bearer of the good news?
> The news of His whereabouts
> May be
> Just may be
> One option was obvious
> The powers that be
> Could have an answer
> But she dared not mate with that
> Let alone fertilize
> And hatch it

Her status
Her social standing
Her branded role
If otherwise
Would have sparked
A bit of well lit conviction
Breeding the appropriate actions
The master's ministerial connectedness
A closely obvious idea
Passed the test, making way
For an option worth pursuing
For an unusual earliest morning visit
The mention of it
Made it impossible to keep away
A rush to the scene
Engulfed with mixed feelings
Was realized in proficiency
The complete search party
Dual headed
With one stretching out
As far as the eyes could reach
Saw what was supposed to be
A reason to keep calm
The other seemingly sure head
Ploughed through the gloom bear and cub
Saw much evidence
Could this mark the defeat of finite reality?
An unopposed unbelief was revealed
Leaving the heavy cloud still hanging
The overwhelming answer
Came away finally
Initiated by a divine touch
Good news at last
He has risen
He is alive
Victory all the way
Free forever
The well-crafted redemption plan for man
Is manifested

Jesus Christ, the victor
Just believe
And be saved.

## 2. *"I've Seen the Master!"* by Ebenezer Quaye

She comes to the tomb early
Will darkness blind her gaze?
The stone removed from the tomb
Amazing! The seals of the powers broken
The hand of the Almighty has spoken
Napkin folded? Job well done
But where is the Lord?
Stolen, taken, carried away
Her dominating thought
But did the two angels signal any hope?
When they asked
"Woman, why are you crying?"
Not so immediately hearing again
"Woman, why are you crying?"
"Who is it you are looking for?"
Engrossed in grief
The same voice of the Master
Became the voice of a gardener
Then recognizing the Savior
Exclaimed, Rabbouni!
She'll never let him go
Although he must go
"I've seen the Master!"
Was the message of the preacher
The herald of hope, the first evangelist
Women have a place in ministry
Her patience, commitment, compassion …
Shall be the hallmark of a preacher
She found him, showed the way
Women can lead us
To see the empty tomb, the rolled away stone
The risen Lord!
"I've seen the Master!" has been her message
The message through the ages
And so shall it be
"I've seen the Master!"

References

Tracy, David. 1987. *Plurality and Ambiguity: Hermeneutics, Religion, Hope.* London: SCM.

Wit, Hans de. 2004. "Through the Eyes of Another: Objectives and Backgrounds." Pages 3–53 in *Through The Eyes of Another: Intercultural Reading of the Bible.* Edited by Hans de Wit, Louis Jonker, Marleen Kool, and Daniel Schipani. Elkhart, IN: Institute of Mennonite Studies.

———. 2012. *Empirical Hermeneutics, Interculturality, and Holy Scripture.* Intercultural Biblical Hermeneutics 1. Elkhart, IN: Institute of Mennonite Studies.

# 19

# "We Are So Beautiful": Reading the Bible and Transforming Life (A Dialogue between Colombia and the Netherlands)

*Ignacio Antonio Madera Vargas*

The context in which the intercultural reading of John 20:1–18 took place is that of four grassroots ecclesial communities (CEBs; see Iriarte 1996).[1] Three of these communities have been meeting in their homes around the word of God every week for eighteen years to help clarify the reality in which they live, in their families and neighborhoods, in their country, and in the real world. The most recent of these communities has existed for two years to date. The participants are of various ages: the eldest of them are about fifty years old and belong to the oldest communities, and the youngest belong to more recently formed communities. The newer communities attest to the participation of young people and children as active members. In these neighborhoods, the level of education is that of elementary school; in the most recently formed communities, some young people have achieved a grade in high school or a technical degree, but this is exceptional.

---

1. As is well known, these CEBs reflect the Latin American church's pastoral choice following the Second Vatican Council and the guidelines of the Episcopal Conferences in Medellín, Colombia, in 1968 (II General Conference of the Latin American and Caribbean Episcopate); in Puebla de los Angeles, Mexico, in 1979 (III General Conference of the Latin American and Caribbean Episcopate, nos. 155, 619); in Santo Domingo, Dominican Republic, in 1992 (IV General Conference of the Latin American and Caribbean Episcopate, no. 54); and in Aparecida, Brazil, in 2007 (V General Conference of the Latin American and Caribbean Episcopate, nos. 178–80).

Like most men and women in Colombia, the people of these communities are working class and earn the minimum wage (around three hundred dollars per month). The eldest are already retired without the benefit of a pension, which makes them dependent on their families for maintenance.

The neighborhoods involved are located in the Resurrection parish to the south of Bogotá and and have an average population of 35,000. Four neighborhoods were selected for participation in the intercultural Bible reading project: Las Lomas, Puerto Rico, Madrid, and Mirador 1–2. These areas take part in the social conflicts of the working-class neighborhoods of the great Latin American cities: overcrowded homes, a lack of educational opportunities, gangs, street violence, and unemployment (see Aguilar and Escamilla 2011).

## Features of the Bible Reading

When reflecting on the text, the participants use direct, informal language, and resort to narrative and to spontaneous and suggestive expression (cf. Katz 1971). They favor the use of metaphors (cf. Ricoeur 2001) and do not employ rationalizations, induction, or deduction, though this does not imply that they are not simultaneously capable of recognizing and identifying the diversity of languages that come from other cultures. This points rather to, on one hand, the acknowledgment of difference, and, on the other hand, to the assertion of their own identity.

The following expressions illustrate the previous statement from the Francisco Jordan group coupled with the Zaandam group in the Netherlands:

> Our reading of the Bible goes more to life, the reading of other people from other cultures is more about understanding, they bring up problems that don't come up in popular sectors, it's curious that such different interests exist, but at the same time it's very nice to sense the way other people from other countries see the Word. Our group has people of all ages, including children, in contrast to groups in other countries which are comprised mainly of elderly people.

The difference in the perception and analysis of the text between groups made up of teachers or intellectually trained people and groups made up of members of the lower class is clear and easily discernible. It is reflected, first and foremost, in that the groups that belong to grassroots ecclesial communities in Colombia in their reflections refer directly to life and do not give priority to interpretive details that are not relevant or imaginable in the way of thinking of the common people, for example, the relation between Jesus and Mary Magdalene and its possible affective connotations or other features such as the comment from the Francisco Jordan group:

> To us, what the Bible leaves behind is a message, a message for our life that wants to be put into practice. They have to investigate, investigate, and investigate why that is written there. Well, honestly, many questions remain unanswered to me, because in our life, nothing is like that.

The grassroots ecclesial communities meet in the houses of their members, and thus the place of meeting fits with the type of reading that takes place in a homelike context. It is a reading outside the temple, the official places, and the churches; consequently, there is an appreciation of the house, the *oikos*, as a meeting place for the community around the Word. This is the reason why these communities prefer not to meet in a temple hall or in the parish house, but in a warm family environment, even when they must accept the typical inconveniences of small houses or find they are short of furniture to accommodate everybody. Let me quote the following comment: "A question: is it also going to be far for them to go meet at the houses? Because, it would be nice that they do it like us, to meet at everyone's house. Oh yes, let's go to Holland!" They speak of going to Holland to emphasize the significance of meeting in their homes.

## Intercultural Reading: Has It Generated Change?

The men and women who participated in the intercultural reading of John 4 (see De Wit et al. 2004) concluded that reading the text generated change in their lives at two levels.

At a personal level, there was transformation of the manner of being and reacting. This transformation became apparent in their characters and in the way they related to the members of their families—their sons and daughters, their wives, and their brothers. The word made them change the assessment they had of themselves and of other people. Reading John helped them internalize, think, and share their own experiences with their families. This sharing also facilitated the process of transformation: "our understanding is broadened, the way of comprehending and understanding is changed because aspects that weren't noticed before the confrontation with the other readings are now assumed."

On a social level, it has helped open people's eyes to the need of getting involved with the real-life situations in the neighborhoods and the need of developing leadership, thus becoming aware of the country's situation, the youth's situation in the neighborhoods, and the causes of the problems. "Reading with other people has made us see the differences that exist in this world, the diversity of our personalities."

Concerning the political situation and the influence of the word in the liberation processes, they assert:

> We relate the political situation that was lived at that time to ours, they [our partner group] recognize what we do. Because, in spite of being Latin and not having as much experience as they have, we took that subject. That is what impacted me the most. Unfortunately one or two things hide the beautiful things we have, we set a beautiful example: us, our community. We are the ones that work, preach the gospel, try to support others.

The Colombian participants see the communitarian reading experience as contrasting with the violence and division in the country. They dislike the stereotypes or false and negative images people of other cultures have about their country. They think that establishing a more direct contact with all of the realities of cultures of the Global South is necessary to have a more realistic vision of their virtues and values. "Colombian women are beautiful spiritually and physically. We are beautiful!" they pointed out with pride in one of the communities that participated in the project. That is why they question why others think that

> Colombia is a horrible thing, the worst, they believe there's only a lot of violence. That is only a part of the truth, because we are also a country with a beautiful geography, joyful and party-loving people that find the ability to strengthen and increase that joy and sense of hope in the Word. Even the country might be better tomorrow than today.

They express with clarity that the intercultural reading provides a great opportunity to change the image of the neighborhood and of the country and to feel proud of their social conditions rather than underrating it:

> The beautiful thing of this cultural exchange is that we were presented through the priests with the opportunity that a group of people, that meet in different homes, can change the image of a neighborhood, of a community, of a society, and make them change the concept and perception

they have of us as a humble people, a third world people. It's a step that we're taking as a community, it's a step we take today and that can be improved every day to change the image and thought they have of us. Not every person is violent, not every person is a thief, and we have to keep working on this to change that image they have of us.

## The Relationship between Cultures

An important element of the experience of knowing the way other cultures approach the biblical text is understanding that, in another culture, the reading is perhaps done with greater care, noticing the details that were not considered important or perceptible in one's own group reading. Likewise, noticing the organization of the meetings of the partner groups, the punctuality, and the order of the meetings deserves attention.

Since the Colombian communities are Catholic, an aspect they highlight and find interesting is that people of Protestant denominations read the Bible in community in the same fashion they do. The fact that in the experience of other cultures the reading of the word is linked to missionary activities also caught the attention of the participants. They recognized that both have the assistance of the Holy Spirit to fill one with power to interpret when listening to the word:

> As people from other countries—Holland, Peru, Germany, Bolivia—are capable of comprehending and understanding, also one from another culture is capable of the same, in spite of having no theological studies.... We are people from different countries and are still able to see the same things in relation to the Word—the way we feel it, the way we live it, how we analyze it. In spite of not having biblical or theological studies, we comprehend and understand. We don't notice the details that those who have made studies consider important, because we implement the Word directly to everyday life and its burdens.

The communities were happy at having their reports read and of reading the experiences of other cultures. That pleasure enriched them and gave them a feeling of proximity:

> We would like to go to Holland to see the way they live with our own eyes, because they have come here and they have seen how we live,[2]

2. Some members of the Dutch partner groups visited the Colombian group in Bogotá.

although they haven't always had a real vision of our country and city, it
seems as if some negative experiences have branded too much how they
see us—no more than a violent and very inequitable country. They exag-
gerate and then, to them, all is negative.

The cultural differences are an opportunity to learn to know and appreciate one's own culture:

What happens is that over there, they are part of a very disciplined culture, which is why they're like that, while over here we have a lot more
fun than them. We here are more loose, like it said over there in the reading, we are more for partying, we don't get involved so much in church
affairs as they do because they are more disciplined.

The process of reading the word and the intercultural exchange enhanced
the awareness of the circumstances of impoverishment, as became evident in a statement referring to a visitor from the partner group: "The rich
are rich because of us." Before visiting our group, the visitor knew nothing about the neighborhoods of Puerto Rico or Lomas. Instead of being
shocked by the circumstances, she was happy with us; she was charmed
by us; she wants to come back here; she wants to come back to Lomas.
Her mentality, regarding what she thought about these neighborhoods
changed a bit too. We can imagine she will tell her group what she saw in
our midst.

The exchange challenges us to keep progressing in the knowledge and
appropriation of the Word as an engine of transformation: "Let's learn
more and be able to match our ideas with theirs." Likewise, some of the
details of what the Colombians were able to know or perceive from their
partner groups have encouraged them to make changes, even in the course
of their meetings. They hope the other party also makes changes due to
what has been shared:

We are going to try to implement the introductory song and the farewell
song, and it would be very nice if they also pick up something from us,
some of the things that go on at the community meetings. That is, not
only the warmth of meeting in a home, but also the warmth of human
contact. Because, in Colombia, something we are known for is human
warmth, warmth of home, isn't it?

## References

Aguilar, Adrian Guillermo, and Irma Escamilla. 2011. *Coordinadores, Peri-urbanización y sustentabilidad en grandes ciudades*. Ciudad de México: Universidad Autónoma de México UNAM, Instituto de geografía.

Iriarte, Gregorio. 1996. *Qué es una comunidad Eclesial de Base?* Bogotá: San Pablo.

Katz, J. 1971. *Filosofía del Lenguaje*. Barcelona: Martínez Roca.

Ricoeur, Paul. 2001. *La metáfora viva*. Madrid: Trotta.

Wit, Hans de, Louis Jonker, Marleen Kool, and Daniel Schipani, eds. 2004. *Through The Eyes of Another: Intercultural Reading of the Bible*. Elkhart, IN: Institute of Mennonite Studies.

## 20

# LOOKING BEYOND SECULARISM AND COMMUNISM: EXPERIENCES FROM EASTERN CUBA (A DIALOGUE BETWEEN CUBA AND THE NETHERLANDS)

*Ricardo González Kindelan*

Reading the Bible is setting God free from the finiteness of the text.
Reading is an exercise of freedom and liberation. Reading is to re-create.
—José Arregui (2009, 4)

In this essay we offer a brief survey of the experiences of two reading groups, one from Utrecht, the Netherlands, and the other from Santiago de Cuba, Cuba, under the auspices of the international project "Through the Eyes of Another."

Our essay is focused on the most important aspects of change occasioned by the exchange between these two partner groups as they read together John 20, using the method of intercultural Bible reading. It is necessary to include some background information, such as a description of the social and religious context in eastern Cuba, as well as some details about the Cuban group of readers and their involvement in the reading project. We describe different moments in the exchange process, and highlight the main topics that emerged from the interaction of the groups in response to the reading reports. An analysis of the testimonies of the two Cuban women and the resulting challenges arising out of the contextual and intercultural Bible reading exercise are also included. The unabbreviated versions of these two life histories are included at the end of the next to last section. After reflecting on the process, we present some conclusions confirming the transforming character of this exercise as a powerful tool in the promotion of reconciliation and transformation at a personal and social level.

## Preceding Experiences

### Contextual Bible Reading in the Cuban Context

The exchange between Dutch and Cuban readers has some antecedents. The first experiences with the intercultural Bible reading method in Cuba dates back to 2005 (see Rufin 2010), when several groups took part in the "Through the Eyes of Another" project. Due to the positive results of those experiences, it was suggested that the exchange could be extended so that new groups of readers would be able to participate. In general terms, this background helps us explain the nature and further development of the process and illustrates the outcomes as shown in the testimonies of two female members of the Cuban group.

### Eastern Cuba: A Sociotheological Challenge

That the group of readers who participated in this phase of the project were from eastern Cuba necessitates that some relevant details be emphasized. Historically, the eastern part of Cuba manifests both social and theological differences from the rest of the country.

Without dealing with other contrasts, we refer here particularly to the fact that the level of biblical and theological education is lower in the eastern region than in the rest of the island. The main core of the Cuban ecumenical work as well as the national institutes for theological training are located in the west. Consequently, citizens in the east have fewer opportunities to access up-to-date biblical and theological knowledge. The distance also sometimes has hindered those interested from attending and completing courses and workshops on biblical and theological topics. Similarly, when visiting Cuba, theologians and Bible experts from abroad deliver their lectures to the nearer and more immediate audience, namely, in the western part.

It is within this context that the intercultural Bible reading took place. Developing contextual reading of the Bible that generates a real analysis of the social and religious reality demanded an extra effort and greater awareness in the eastern region. For example, the hermeneutic process of appropriation (see Conti 2000) often remained incomplete due to a failure to analyze the reality of one's actual situation. Though the analysis of the social situation was included in the process, it did not accomplish the intended purpose, because many ecclesial communities considered themselves not to be the proper place for this type of debate.

The urgency and relevance for increasing the level of theological education in eastern Cuba was one of the primary stimulants that resulted in the emergence some eighteen years ago of an ecumenical project currently known as Bartolomé G. Lavastida Christian Center for Social Service and Pastoral Training. As part of its thematic areas of work, the Field of Bible and Theology emerged, from which regular meetings of contextual Bible reading have been held for more than a decade. These formative encounters for Bible reading were articulated within the Bible Program of the Cuban Council of Churches. Participants were invited to analyze and reflect on their immediate context, starting from the reading of challenging Bible texts related to social and religious issues.

Nevertheless, the process of contextual Bible reading was itself a big challenge, because of the diversity of social, political, and religious backgrounds interacting through the participants. Another factor was the resistance to this new way of reading the Bible shown by some churches, as it raised questions on the effectiveness of the more traditional method of Bible study. By putting aside the fundamentalism present in several communities, a new type of Bible reader was emerging, making the difference by a constant application of the method.

The Intercultural Exchange between the Dutch and the Cuban Group

The Cuban Partner Group: Composition and Initial Difficulties

Like other groups, the Cuban and the Dutch groups read together John 20, which tells of Jesus's resurrection and the events immediately following, namely, the appearance of Jesus to Mary Magdalene and the rest of the disciples and the story of how Thomas would not believe the good news until he could "see and touch" the resurrected one.

One of the first signs that the exchange between the two groups would be a challenge had to do with technology. The Cuban group was unable to develop a web-based exchange with its Dutch partner group because of the current economic difficulties in Cuba regarding the free use and access to information and communication through the Internet. The Cuban group was sincerely thankful to the members of the Dutch group for their kindness and understanding in this matter and their willingness to exchange the reading reports and further information through e-mail, which was the only available service.

The Cuban group was ecumenical, composed of members who already had contact with the contextual Bible reading method. Furthermore, in one way or another, many of them were coordinating small groups of Bible reading in their churches, prayer cells, or Bible study groups.

Despite the diversity of church traditions present in the group, it was possible to perform the contextual Bible reading exercises and become involved in the dynamics of the intercultural exchange, starting from reflections and analysis that challenged one to look beyond the narrow frame of individual interpretations of the text and the theological denominational systems represented in the group.

Characteristics of the Intercultural Exchange: Expanding the Horizons

The exchange with the Dutch was characterized by mutual and deep respect between the two groups, making the exchange process positive and fluid.

That the text of John 20 is full of interpretive possibilities came out clearly in the exchange. Both groups started out from their own respective contexts to tackle questions and concerns in the light of the text. The reports showed how the groups could establish an open dialogue, a real movement between the text and its readers, confirming what is known as the hermeneutical circle.

In several aspects the emerging readings of both groups evidenced surprising similarities. The identification of the members with the roles of characters in the story, like Thomas and Mary, was remarkable, highlighting mainly the perspective of gender. Although the majority of the men identified themselves with Thomas and the women with Mary, not all did so. The participants from both groups were able to establish both similarities and differences with respect to the roles played in the narrative by Thomas and Mary. This all was nuanced by gender aspects, that is, by the distinct manner in which men and women react to challenges and experiences like those related in the text.

Differences in the approach to the text include that the Dutch group approached the interpretive exercise, in their own words, from a more "reserved" or more intellectual perspective, while the Cuban group proposed an interaction with the story that would take more advantage of the emotions and experiences related by the story.

The relationship between religion and society assumed an important place in the exchange. Both groups could identify with some indications of opportunities and limitations in relation to the free and public exercise of the Christian faith. A common challenge emerged having to do with finding creative ways for effective dialogue between scientific thought and religious beliefs, since in both latitudes these fields appear to be categories that tend to exclude each other mutually.

The Cuban group included some valuable data in their reaction that allowed the partner group to become more familiar with the current situation in Cuba. Among other things, they mentioned how churches and religious organizations all over the country united to help the people from the eastern provinces that were severely affected by Hurricane Sandy in October 2012, which destroyed large parts of the eastern region of the island, including almost the whole city of Santiago de Cuba, in less than four hours.

## Intercultural Bible Reading and Transformation: The Stories of Two Women

As illustration of the possible transformation that this method of exchange can bring about, we share the stories of two members, and it is not by accident that these two are women. In itself, that they are women is loaded with meaning and opens the door to numerous possibilities and reflections.

The path that we traveled hand in hand with the intercultural Bible reading process allowed us to identify phenomena that were already known but that had not been sufficiently examined in the light of biblical and theological perspectives from other cultural contexts. Specifically we refer here to gender-based violence that is officially combated but has not been completely eliminated from the cultural and psychological structures and whose observable expressions affect the day-to-day relationships between men and women.

Furthermore, we could also discern signs of gender-based violence within the church. This violence is legitimated by means of public declamations based on a fundamentalist doctrine, which in turn emanates from closed, completely decontextualized readings of the Bible. This manner of reading the Bible always leads to the same results: privileges for men and the disqualification of women, or at least the concept that women are at a different or inferior level in relation to men.

This is why it was so important to have two women talk about their life experiences and the personal transformation they experienced through involvement with the intercultural Bible reading project. Their testimonies are but examples of an impact that takes place more often, and they help us examine to what extent this exercise can lead to transformations not only at a personal level but also at the level of society.

To summarize their experiences that indicate the presence of a transformation process and to record these here, we used the life histories as a tool for sociological research. At the end of this section, we include the two life histories as recorded by the women themselves.

Their life experiences are quite different, and they also came to be acquainted with the Bible reading method in diverse ways. The first life history is of a school teacher and the second of a lady evangelical pastor. The first one was raised in a traditional Catholic family, and the other one came from a family without a religious background. In both cases the first encounter with the Bible was within a strongly fundamentalist context, which had a negative influence on their lives. In the first case, this led to a total abandonment of individual and social responsibilities; and in the second, such closed, dogmatic, and decontextualized readings of the Bible contributed to a distorted image of God, resulting in feelings of guilt and of low self-esteem. Two lives had been obstructed by biblical readings that had little to do with the promotion of values such as integrity and social responsibility and that were devoid of critical reflection on the reality of their immediate situation.

In time, these two women were linked up to the method of contextual Bible reading and consequently expanded the horizons of their theological interpretation. They became important participants within the Cuban partner group. The whole process had a significant impact on them, which in turn gave them the tools to give a new direction to their lives. In our opinion, at this point we can speak of transformation in the two lives presented here.

The first woman relates that, thanks to the encounter with the method of contextual or intercultural Bible reading, she was encouraged to rebuild her professional life. She returned to the university to complete the career she had abandoned and got a new job after having been unemployed. Before this turnabout, she had been following some interpretations of Bible texts regarding the last times, focusing in the idea of an imminent return of Jesus.

In our second case, the view of God as unfair, who legitimatized inequality and patriarchy, changed into one of a liberating God whose desire is fulfilled in a society where men and women have equal rights and possibilities. In this case, the remarkable changes in theological and sociological paradigm resulted in a new concept of how family life and pastoral ministry should be developed. She has included the gender perspective and the results of Bible reading as the liberating key in every area of her life.

Both women emphasize the importance of the reading method used, which permitted them to identify structures oppressive to women, structures that are being legitimated by biblical readings full of discrimination and marginalization. At present, both women are currently fighting for the rights of women in churches and more broadly in Cuban society.

First Case History

My first contact with the Bible goes back to my teenage years when an uncle of mine repeatedly told me that it was a sacred book that contained God's holy word. It was a Bible written in an ancient language; I started reading many times, but could not go beyond the first pages of Genesis because of a lack of understanding of what I read. I was raised in a family with a Catholic tradition, but with no direct relationship to the sacred Scriptures. We came to know what the Lord said in his word only through what was told to us in masses.

In 1994 I decide to approach an evangelical church since I felt myself far away from God. There, for the first time, I received biblical training, which happened to be completely fundamentalist in its theology. This approach influenced my life in a negative way and cut short the best years of my youth. Those were six years of relentless anguish in my life. I devoted myself to reading and studying the Bible on my own, and I found things that seemed absurd to me, even though I was forced to believe them because of my faith. According to the stigmatizing teachings I had received, everything was evil and woman's position was unfavorable in relation both to men and to society. I quit my studies, dropped out of college, and stopped the construction on my own house, thus trying to follow the teachings that Christ would return soon. Six years passed and I decided I could not continue that way. I separated from that group and spent a whole year without attending any church.

Later, I returned to a church with a different tradition, with a vision closer to liberation theology. I was offered a course given by the Martin Luther King Centre, which gave me, for the first time, an opportunity to participate in spaces of sociotheological training following the methodol-

ogy of Bible reading by ordinary people in Havana. I admit I was fasci-
nated because it was precisely what I needed. My evolution was slow and
gradual, but decisive.

Today I am not a graduate in theology, only because I live in a part of
the country where there is no seminary I can graduate from. Texts like the
one of the Samaritan woman, which I could not understand before and
which was used merely to condemn women, as well as the one of the adul-
terous woman and so many others from the Gospels, such as John 20, have
now been revisited with the intercultural Bible reading approach. These
have helped me to realize I wanted to be an autonomous, independent
woman and to have an intimate and direct relationship with Jesus. I told
myself I did not want to continue being the outcast and excluded woman
I had been until then. I had a life project waiting for me that had been
severed by fundamentalist readings of the Bible. Since then I resumed
the same college major I had abandoned fourteen years previously and
managed to obtain my degree. I trained as a popular educator and started
working at the Bartolomé Gregorio Lavastida Centre as coordinator for
the ecology department. I feel like a completely fulfilled woman, and I am
very happy doing what I love.

Second Case History

In my youth I used to believe that God was evil, and I blamed him for not
bringing justice to this world despite his being all-powerful. I actually did
not think much about him, but was indifferent. The first time I visited a
church, it turned out to be one with a conservative theology. There I was
given the image of a God that could send you to hell simply for having a
manicure or doing your hair, and, at the same time, a God that would send
you to paradise if you kept the commandments and the regulations given
by that church. I felt, and believed myself to be, a second-class product,
only a helpmeet for a man, one who had to obey the decisions of the husband simply because he was the head of the family, and I used to wonder
why God was so severe to us women. I lived for two years with these doubts
and thoughts, not daring to express them.

Then I moved to a different faith community, and there little by little
I was able to deconstruct that image of God. It was not easy since it had
become a part of my life, despite my feeling uneasy about it. It was the
Bible reading by ordinary people and later the intercultural Bible reading
that provided the tools that allowed me to pursue this deconstruction. The

thorough analysis of the text made me see that the Bible was written by and for a specific context, and therefore it needed to be contextualized. I understood that in many churches women are victims of violence, as I was at one a time, being made slaves by discriminatory and narrow-minded readings. All this new learning produced a change in my life, both in the church context and in the social spectrum, both in my speech and in my theology.

This methodology allowed me to know the liberating God, the God of love. I understood that God's call to women to teach and to be active in their communities overcomes the patriarchal authority that limits them to the life cycle of home and children. Today and every day I try to have gender equity at home, and that is what I teach in my church. I read the Bible through the eyes of a woman, because I am a woman, so that every verse becomes good news and carries a liberating message. Although the masculine image of God has prevailed, women have initiated a movement of reinterpretation of the presence and the action of God in their own stories. We see him as a God who identifies with our cause and promotes equity between men and women.

Reflections and Conclusions on the Theme of Transformation

Without a doubt this exercise in intercultural Bible reading has broadened our vision and comprehension of the biblical text and its transformative potential. Reading the same Bible text along with a group from another country, in an almost completely different reality, and perceiving in the reading reports and subsequent exchanges signs of confluence as well as aspects that distinguished the groups from one another meant being challenged to enlarge our perspectives and to look beyond our theological and sociological boundaries. It impelled us to take a step forward into a fresh and new stream of interpretive possibilities.

It made us look beyond the interpretations usually given to certain texts and challenged us to examine Scripture from the perspective of others who likewise approached the Bible looking for a message of hope and for guidance for their lives. The process of intercultural Bible reading also made us realize how interpretations of biblical texts are heavily influenced by the culture and the political and socioeconomic conditions of those engaged in the interpretation.

With the same text as the basis for the exchange, both groups were mutually challenged to reconsider the commonly held interpretations. The biblical text has much more to say about the respective real-life situations of each group, but these are only unveiled when we accompanied one another in experiencing the text. As a result, the two groups were no longer the same, nor was the text the same for them: the hermeneutic circle had expanded. There has been a qualitative process of transformation of concepts and interpretations that positively influenced the adoption of a new attitude toward life and toward the Bible.

Nonetheless, transformation was not always desired. In some cases, the intercultural Bible reading process was considered risky, and its invitation remained unheeded. Such people did not want to undertake a process that would question their traditional interpretations, since they felt secure and saw these as the only valid alternative.

Both the similarities and the particularities of the contexts in which the readings were produced led in most cases to a closer identification with the partner group. To see oneself reflected in the struggles and dreams of another group led to greater solidarity and empathy, which in turn allowed the groups to grow and expand their interpretive spectrum.

In our particular context, the Bible maintains its strength as the source of meaning. In some cases, it is used to justify fundamentalist positions and interpretations that do not properly promote justice and social responsibility. Nevertheless, a growing sector of Christianity in our country comes to the Bible with their concerns and desires for a more genuine process of personal and social transformation. Historically, Cuban Protestantism has been deeply fragmented. The fact that there are people, in spite of the diversity of traditions that they represent, who manage to look beyond these differences and search for a greater role and responsibility in their immediate ecclesial and social environment on the basis of a shared Bible text, represents an encouraging sign of transformation. The possible, necessary, and irreversible transformation will continue as a viable option in the theological context of the communities these people represent.

## References

Arregui, José. 2009. "Por una lectura crítica de la Biblia." *Éxodo* 99:4–11.
Conti, Cristina. 2000. "Hermenéutica Feminista." *Alternativas* 5.11–12: http://servicioskoinonia.org/relat/225.htm.
Rufin, Daylins. 2010. "What We Are, What We Want to Be." Report presented to the organizing committee of the International Conference on Contextual Bible Reading. Utrecht.

## 21

# LOOKING FOR THE BODY OF JESUS: MARY MAGDALENE THROUGH THE EYES OF AN ANCESTRAL PERUVIAN CULTURE (A DIALOGUE BETWEEN PERU AND INDIA)

*Marisol Ale Díaz and Manuel Obeso Perez*

A few decades ago, José Ortega y Gasset, a Spanish-speaking philosopher, argued that beliefs are like the firm ground on which we tread (2007; published originally in 1979). He was right, because we go through life—here, there, and everywhere—on the basis of our beliefs. We usually do not think out our beliefs; we live them: we are guided by them and move toward them. To feel accompanied, to feel motivated, to feel that what we do is important, to be sure that everything will go well for us—this all inevitably has to do with our beliefs.

Life is lived best when we are in harmony with our beliefs. Our beliefs draw life's horizons and link past and future horizons. When horizons darken it is, because, at the level of our beliefs, we have entered into a crisis. Such times are not only the product of concrete events, but are also experienced as a crisis because our belief systems leads us to interpret them as such. That is our "objectivity."

The different degrees of instability in the face of the loss of a loved one have to do with the strength of the ground on which we stand. That strength does not prevent us from passing through "the valley of the shadow of death" without being battered and, many times, shocked. It does not liberate us from the existential question of what one should do, for there is no quick or easy answer even on the basis provided by beliefs. It is a process of reweaving life from the tatters left by the pain of loss and absence.

In our work with intercultural reading groups, we are constantly "bumping" into the beliefs of people, and through this we "bump" into people themselves. This confrontation is much more critical when beliefs

are being subjected to pressure or are in a crisis as a result of the impo-
sition of other faiths. The Christianity that arrived in our countries did
the latter: it demonized the ancestral beliefs surviving in our midst. This
happened as well to our concern for and veneration of our deceased, the
ancestral cult of our dead.

The text of John 20, with which the Peruvian group read together with
our partner group from India, tells of the resurrection of Jesus of Nazareth. Due to a huge cultural and geographical distance between us and our
partner group, the reading took us along a road initially not foreseen. The
presence of the different other influenced our group and prepared us to
read and see in the text aspects not previously seen. A "virtual" dimension
was given to the reading dialogue, which opened us to concerns about our
identity and the existential preoccupations shared with the other.

However, something else also happened: we started talking with the
geographically distant other one, and it turned out that we were dialoguing with our own "other," the one that was existentially linked with us in
the world of beliefs. The journey we initiated with the text appeared to be a
struggle, because before rationalizing it, we first "felt" it. We sensed the life
and the pain hidden behind the text; we sensed the lives of others in our
context. We started to feel that deep inside us, and it was a feeling of being
fractured. The tears of Mary Magdalene and her heart-rending lament,
"we do not know where they have laid him," became the desperate cry of
the "other" from Peruvian society: the men and the women of the Andes
and the Amazonia who pilgrimage for years with their pain in the relentless pursuit to find the body or the remains of their loved ones who were
taken from them by force.

To dialogue with the other and with the text, in the presence of
another, our partner group, allowed us to be enlightened and understand
our own reality better, because becoming involved in the lives of others, we
became "the others" of the "other." At the same time, when we started to be
aware of our cultural practice, we could shed new light on the text, with a
real dialogue as a result. In imaginal form we embraced those who make
the devotion to their dead a generator of life, of integration; we embraced
those who despair "when they don't know where their dead are" and only
find comfort and strength when they have them "with them." To know
where the loved ones are buried is extremely comforting and mitigates
their total absence. Without that, there is no rest: rest comes only when
the remains of the deceased are where the family placed them. This was
humanly enriching and integrative.

The reflections we share here are the result of the exchange with our partner group, which has been initiated but is not yet finished. They represent our journey through a world of beliefs that we thought we had lost, because we had buried it a long time ago "so it could not harm us or offend God." However, it never disappeared: it was always before us, though we had not been able to "see" it.

Briefly formulated, there are three issues that we should consider when talking about the resurrection. These will be presented in the following three sections.

## Discussing the Resurrection amid a People Who Venerate Their Dead

With us, to talk about the resurrection does not necessarily imply talking about revivification itself. Although the testimony of the Gospels to the resurrection of Jesus of Nazareth, which gave rise to these reflections, leads us to encourage the hopeful confidence that mitigates the desperate desire to recover what was "lost" and fill "the emptiness" that was caused by death, what remains is the concrete, real, and unbearable fact of "loss" and of "emptiness,"[1] which rips apart the most sensitive of human fibers.

The "hereafter" with all its beauty and fullness has failed to solve the impotence and the feeling of absurdity we experience in the here and now when faced with the loss of a loved one, with the emptiness it leaves in us, and the impossibility to return to the situation prior to the arrival of death that took one of our loved ones away behind its impenetrable borders. However, facing those impassable borders, we start the battle to care for that—with the body as a token—which will allow us to transform grief into a celebration of the continuity of life.

The experiences in our country, for a long time tormented and repressed in its beliefs, make us understand the desperate feeling of Mary Magdalene that makes her cry out: "They have taken the Lord out of the sepulcher, and we know not where they have laid him" (John 20:2). To her grief over the death of the Lord is now added a pain much more intense: the disappearance of his body. An empty tomb is a most desperate situation. The loss and emptiness is double and more unbearable.

We understand Mary Magdalene's despair because we experienced it close at hand during the war in the interior at the end of the previous

---

1. See http://www.revistadelauniversidad.unam.mx/4307/4307/pdfs/43kraus.pdf.

century. Many families suffered the disappearance of parents, husbands, wives, and children; to this day, there is despair over not knowing where the bodies were placed. The families still weep over them and can only stop weeping after they can bury the bodies or what is left of them. Only then will they find consolation and fill the void of their absence (Yoffe 2009, 6).

The body of a loved one, even after death, remains important, because it is the only means left to "hold" him or her and thus to quell the emptiness. From this point of view, a tomb without a body is meaningless. For those who have suffered such loss, an empty tomb does not work at all. Even if it is true that the tomb is for the dead, those who are most in need of a tomb are the living, in order to fill the void. The dead do not need a tomb: it is we, the living, who need the tomb to rest the bodies of our dead, a tomb where we can "house them" so they can remain among us, so they can allow us to fill the void, to stop there being an unrecoverable loss. It seems that this deeply felt need is the origin of the desire to give our dead a place and to honor them.

To have them in our midst and to honor our dead ancestors is an ancient custom in our land. The Christian calendar prescribes that the dead have to be remembered every November 2, an imposed and impossible reduction: they are remembered on that day and every other day of the year. To give an impression of how deep the veneration of our dead is, this day is a national event that does not go unnoticed because of the huge movement of people toward the cemeteries throughout the entire country.

"Visiting" them, "seeing" them, or "being with" those who "used to be" is important both because of what they meant during their short or long existence and because of what they mean to those living today. What they gave to their families has not finished, and the presence of the family is evidence of this recognition. The "visit" does not have to wait until the date set by the Christian calendar. Nowadays it is difficult to find a cemetery that is just a place of rest for the dead, for Sunday after Sunday families are mobilized to "see" their loved ones, and the deceased must be "prepared" for scheduled visits as well as for unexpected events that result from family emergencies.

The old "eradicators of pagan idols,"[2] whose main task was to discover where the communities had hidden the mummified bodies of the ances-

---

2. The writings of the time highlight the Cusqueño priest Francisco de Avila as one of the major "eradicators of idolatries." See Arriaga 1920.

tors they wanted to venerate, should be concerned about the return of the worship and veneration of ancestors, a practice they so eagerly sought to eradicate. They sought to win a more important war, not against the dead but against the living (Martinez de Codes 1990), but they did not succeed. Caring for the bodies of the dead remains a community, a family, responsibility. The veneration of the *malqui* (Quechua: "tender plant to plant") is there again, as a mechanism to ensure prosperity and well-being among the living (Gareis 2004).

The families of Andean roots that ascended socially, rather than abandoning this "antiquated" habit, have strengthened it among new generations. Prosperity and the growth as a family is felt as the fruit of respect and loyalty to the dead. No wonder that illness, family misfortune, or failure is related to the negligence of the members of the family in the veneration of the dead. Strange signs or incidents will be identified as the protest of the deceased for leaving them abandoned in the cemetery: "No one comes to 'see' him or her."

The expressions "I am going to see " or "let's go visit " mean that people feel or think that the departed one is really there. Therefore, respect for "your dead" cannot be mediated or replaced by just remembering him or her or sending presents: such is justified only if the person is unable to do so or lives in a faraway place. The obligation of "being with " on holidays when the dead are remembered is almost compulsory. The dead are honored in your presence and by your presence. The idea that the dead person is not there is unthinkable: he or she is there, in his or her "new home."

The loss and vacuum that death caused is mitigated in devotion, in the veneration of the dead, especially of fathers and mothers, the elders of the community. It can be said without exaggeration that through the veneration of the dead the relationship that characterized the lives of the departed is restored, maintained, and kept alive, that is, both their relationship as providers and caregivers as well as the devotion and respect for family roots.

The veneration of the dead seeks to meet the needs of those living in the here and now. Life expectancy and enjoyment in the hereafter[3] are not

---

3. "For the Andean man the soul is not definitively separated from the body, it returns each year on the day of all the saints from their long trip by interstellar space and families must wait for them rejoicing, and with a feast. There have to be meals and drinks, so that the souls are happy and not sad when nobody has gone to wait for them at their tombs or places where they died, either by day or by night. It is believed that

at stake, the time to share that can wait. What is at stake here is how we solve the present of the descendants with the decisive support of those who are no longer here but who do influence the present in order to maintain the unity of prosperity of the family. If the dead continue to intervene, is that perhaps a form of resurrection in the here and now?

## Discussing the Resurrection: Restore the Links to the Dead through Food and Drink

In the face of the abrupt fact of death, it is nearly impossible to imagine the subsequent process of the restoration of the links with the deceased. The "rescue" of the body of the dead loved one is an odyssey that takes place in a state of numbing emotional shock, of bewilderment, as a result of the intense and exhausting pain. At such times and afterward, related to the wake and the funeral, more than one family member has the experience of being accompanied by the dead, of being comforted, and even of hearing them talk to them in the moments they are overwhelmed by pain and tiredness and have become drowsy. The suffering of the bereaved causes them to think much about the deceased, and in the evenings they have dreams in which they see and talk to the deceased. There comes a time when the deceased talks and says, "I am alright, don't worry about me." Then the person who dreamed wakes up and feels calm. For other people, the silhouettes and the images of the deceased reappear, not in a direct way, but only from the side or the back, not the face. He or she can be seen entering a room, but when one tries to address the deceased, there is nothing. For others the deceased is like an angel who approaches them and whispers in their ear: "Where I am, I am peaceful, good," or "The being about whom you think is well." After this, tranquillity is given

---

while the dead and buried body still has some meat on it and has not turned into bone, 'the soul is seized within the body until it becomes bones,' and then will be released to continue its final journey. Usually this rotting of the body takes a period total of three years and then after the exhumation of the bones and a second burial the soul embarks on its ultimate road trip. In the case of Cayma in the second burial the *tocka* is not included: the skull is left with the devout. It will be materialized and not spiritual form that the 'soul' stays at home in order to take care, and help, as if the person to whom it belonged is still alive. For this reason many people express in the feast: 'I have a little soul in my house, garden, farm.' Because the little soul will ask God for them, and that gives it the aspect of holiness and something miraculous, in line of the Christian style" (Pacheco 1999).

to the living, the sadness is relieved, and a firm belief in a God is established (Pacheco 1998).

Except for that unforgettable first moment, characterized by desperate grief and despair when the "change of residence" was confirmed, gradually the "new residence" changes from a meeting place for meditation into a festive family room with color and music. Currently many cemeteries look more like parks, but that is not true in all cases. The colorfulness of the cemeteries of the marginal urban areas is a product of the initiative of those who revere their loved ones with colorful flowers. The process of adapting to the new situation is not uniform throughout. For some it is harder than for others to "solve the loss and emptiness" that covers everything like a suffocating mantle.

One of the rituals observed when "retrieving" those who had gone before is that the family table is used to offer the deceased person a banquet of the best dishes on the Day of the Dead:

> When the month of November, which in Quechua is called *aya marka* or *aya killa* (month of the dead) comes near, there are many preparations of meals, liquor, candles, flowers, selection of those who will pray, and invitations to the family. Late in the afternoon of the first of November, when the birds chirp before they go to rest, and when the shadows begin to cover the valleys with their dark and somniferous mantle, there is much hustle in each house: they are setting the table (which can be made from wood or a mantle lying on the floor) on which they serve varied and exquisite meals, liquors such as *chicha* and *cañazo* (liquor made from cane), they light the candles and the whole family meets to perform the rites. After dinner, speaking about the date and recalling the deceased relatives, who have to be convened, all are directed to the room where the table is set. There, at the announcement of the beginning of the rite, all become silent, remove their hats and caps, become serious and begin singing the songs following the directions provided by those who pray, who read their notebooks that contain prayers transmitted from generation to generation. These are copies of other previous copies. But those who already know them by heart demonstrate their experience. A dialogue starts between those who pray and the others, or between men and women, or between two heterogeneous groups of all ages that surround the table. After the singing comes the moment of silence. All, without distinction as to gender and age, formulate from the depth of their hearts the invitation to their preferred deceased to try the food prepared and served to them. During these approximate five or ten minutes of solemn silence—time of communication with the dead—the candles flicker, all

keep their heads lowered out of respect for the guests of the other world who would be inside the room or very close to it. The living and the dead are seen from different dimensions. The *picante de papa* (spicy potato), the *cuy frito* (fried guinea pig), the *mazamorra de maíz* (gruel of maize), the *cancha* (corn nuts), the *frituras* (fried dishes), and the *guisos de carne* (stews of meat) are steaming at the table. The *chicha*, the *coca*, and tobacco are also there with their unmistakable fragrances and colors. It is not necessary to leave them any cutlery because "the souls" do not need them, they "eat" only the smell, the essential or elementary part of the food. An elderly person, in a low but audible voice, orders that all will leave and the lights are turned off. Finally the father or the mother spreads ashes on the floor and then exits and locks the door with a key. All will leave to sleep quietly, thinking about the visit of the souls to the feast prepared for them by the living. This long night sharp and sporadic howls of dogs are heard who tell one another what they are seeing and feeling. Those howls are stabs that rip apart the delicate and dark cloak of the night and hurt the ears of those who sleep and dream about their deceased. The next day, when the door is opened to the night banquet, you can see the traces of visitors from the other world. Then you know how many and who came to the invitation. (Carranza Romero 2013)

The table functions as the center of the family communion where food and drink are shared, and the new situation serves to reestablish the link with the one who died and to bring him back and reintegrate him into the family. Nobody finds it strange that the family table is put in the cemetery during those special dates and that the family goes there and eats with their relatives who reside there.

In the new neighborhoods that surround Lima there is high population of Andean origin. There the Andean people continue to celebrate the rite for their dead. But in the cemetery of the new village Nuevo Perú [New Peru], which is on the heights of the Rimac district, on 2 November there is a festive atmosphere because not only do they offer food to the dead but they also hire a band of musicians to play the music most preferred by each deceased. With food, drinks, and music the cemetery gets a more cheerful atmosphere that certainly even pleases those who rest there. (Carranza Romero 2013)

The "rule" to meet with your loved one is that you can invite him or her to come to the table to share what was to his or her liking. The taste in food and drink of the deceased remain the criterion for the families when it comes to eating with the loved ones in their new place of residence. It

brings the family satisfaction to be able to share together the food that
the deceased loved ones liked. The best of every piece of food in terms of
quantity and quality will be for the deceased loved one. The starting point
for the sharing of food is the toast in the deceased's honor; this toast is not
only on the occasion of his or her birthday.

In matters related to the preparation of the food, women definitely
play an important role, for their traditional skills in the culinary arts
enable them to satisfy the good taste of the honoree. It is not unusual to
find among the family those who guard the regulations, who do not overlook possible shortcomings in how food or drinks are prepared, and who
consider what might become a source of annoyance to the loved one who
will be visited. Comments like the following are not uncommon: "Take
care because he or she does not like low salted food," or "It does not have
enough chili," or "He or she never liked this," although many would question whether such knowledge concerning the tastes of the deceased was
correct.

In these meals new generations learn to recognize and to acquire the
tastes or preferences of those who represent their family roots and who,
despite the "change of residence," continue to influence their family life.
Eating and drinking are no longer mere mechanical actions, but become
the fundamental elements of building the adequate atmosphere to allow
experiencing the presence of the revered loved one. With food and drink
one tries to ensure their presence at the family reunion at the "new home."

Amid eating and drinking, the life of the deceased is brought on stage
in front of the family. Remembering is inevitable, and through shared
remembrance the family deals with the dark spots in what is left as memory
of the deceased. Those who knew the deceased provide new insights into
his or her life; and, recognizing those, the deceased is reincorporated into
the life of the family in new ways. In many cases, these meals in front of
the father, the mother, or some other respected relative in their new home
makes reconciliation and family cohesion possible.

### Discussing the Resurrection:
### Linking the "Corporality" of the Dead to Here and Now

Jesus was embodied in a community, and, therefore, we find in the Gospel
of Mark after the death of Jesus the invitation to his followers to go to
Galilee to see him and meet with him. The body of Jesus takes on a new
dimension: it is not only a part of the community that comes together

to celebrate its presence—the community *is* "his body," the community *is* Jesus's presence.

Among us corporality and the earth have an inseparable relationship when it comes to the veneration of the dead. In the past, the dead guaranteed the possession of the land for the community or family and their right to remain on it. The strategic presence of the dead ensured protection to the community and constituted the fundamental argument to sustain their right to the land. However, not all of this has been lost. These beliefs remained; they are like roads on which people walk again, roads that get people moving once more. The corporality of the deceased in their abode remains vital to the families and relatives.

When families move to the cemetery, the new residence of the dead relative, they go looking not for absence but for a vitalizing presence. Where the dead body was given its last resting place becomes the "place of presence." Just as our body is the place of our vital presence, the place where the body rests is the place par excellence for encounters to celebrate together with this vitalizing presence.

The tomb embodies the dead and shows the deceased to be present; it permits one to localize and venerate the deceased and appeal to his or her protection on the basis of the deceased's privileged position. The tomb, as the place of presence, is a convener, not only for the family reunion. It calls for celebratory remembering. The memory becomes celebratory, because it does not invent a motivating presence but, on the contrary, this presence is fully assumed. The use of verbs like "visit," "view," "talk," which we noted above, indicate something that is beyond doubt: a real objectified presence. You cannot worship the dead just anywhere: it has to be where he or she is.

The corporealization of the dead or, in other words, the materialization of memory faces threats related to the influence of beliefs that propagate the removal of the body. Such is the case in the cremation of the dead. A few years ago this was not an option, but now it is gaining ground even among the common people. The pressure ranges from the economical to the suggestion—and we should not forget that the common people are highly suggestible—that, to avoid the spread of the evil that caused the death of the loved one, it is best to cremate the body. In the long run, one can see that this will not be an impediment to venerate one's dead. The families that cremate their dead generally keep with them the container that contains the remains. It is not unusual that within the house a kind of altar is made for the container, accompanied by a photo. There they place flowers and light a candle as a sign that at that home the dead are remembered. The habit of throwing the ashes in the river or in the sea, practiced in other cultures, has not been able to establish itself in a society that venerates their dead by "materializing them."

In evangelical circles the prohibition to visit the dead is widespread. This prohibition is based on the fact that the dead relative "is no longer there, he or she is with the Lord," that he or she is departed. Therefore, it is totally unnecessary to make all this effort to recover the bond with the deceased, and because of certain alleged matters of faith, it is urgent to "dematerialize memory." Interestingly, in these sectors one can observe the special care and attention given to certain parts of the house and to the place at the table that are identified with the one who has departed. It is not surprising that their place at the table is left open, as if somehow he or she were still present, and no one is allowed to sit in the place that belongs to the dead: "Here dad sat and he continues to sit at the table"; "This is my daddy's or mommy's chair." In each house there are places that are clearly identified with the dead, and when at certain times something moves or a sound is heard that is felt to be familiar, expressions are heard like: "It's my dad," or "It's my mom," who is not happy, because they touched his or her things, or he or she wants to say something to the family, because they did not fulfill what was promised.

Places that "belonged" to the deceased are respected and then, as a result of the oral tradition of the family, are easily identified and acknowledged. Besides keeping the body in the house that belonged to him or her, a whole ceremony is added before taking the body to the cemetery. The body is carried to the church where the deceased had attended, reenacting the itinerary of the deceased's life by making a series of bows with the coffin in certain places supposedly significant to the deceased. This is just an example of the adoption of rituals to stay connected to the one that has gone.

Urban planning processes have led to hollowing out the importance of the home. It is not possible for an extended family to live there together, even less that the fathers or mothers, the respected loved ones who died, live there. The modernization of cemeteries allows families living in urban areas to see the cemetery as the continuation of their homes. Fathers and mothers renew their bonds with their dead relatives by visiting them in the cemetery Sunday after Sunday. When the children hear that they will go to see their grandfather or grandmother, it is the opportunity to spend a pleasant day. In the context of the worship of the dead, it is vitally important for the family to link up again with the deceased, since their house is no longer a place of memory and no longer allows the family to feel the departed as being part of family life.

## Conclusions

With this brief nonacademic approach to belief in the resurrection, we wanted to show how many shared matters appear in the discourse of the resurrection and that these come from the custom of honoring and revering the dead. The language used, such as "see" and "visit," is an indicator of a real experience that curiously seems to have disappeared from worship in many churches.

The emphasis on the corporality of the dead to confirm their presence and revitalize the link with those who recognize and revere the dead is a strong element to be reckoned with in periods when disintegration and breakdown of family ties plagues entire families. When we compare the festive nature of sharing food and drinks in the presence of the dead to church services celebrating the Lord's presence in the bread and wine, we are invited to think that in the latter the tension between absence and presence has not been elaborated in depth.

Another issue that also appears as provocation is that Protestant/evangelical Christianity failed to attach importance to the practice of venerating the dead. Rather than fight this practice, it should have reflected more on this link as a foretaste of what is to be in the future. Clearly the veneration of the dead is a constant looking to the past, to how the past accompanies the future in a productive way. Looking toward the future has somewhat diluted the horizon because the present is not lived sufficiently as an evocation of the past and anticipation of the future.

Here the intercultural Bible reading process favors the rapprochement of life and its world of beliefs with the Bible. The people we work with embark on a process of reconciliation with their culture and with their beliefs that were combated by theologies supposedly based on the Bible.

Intercultural Bible reading makes a great contribution to transformation of the spirituality of the people: the experience of a faith more linked to everyday life than to a body of doctrine nurtured by schemes and reasoning. In our opinion intercultural reading of the Bible is an important instrument for recovering the connections in a reality that appears fragmented and menacing. The brightness in the eyes or the relaxed faces when people read the Bible in an intercultural way is indescribable. Showing emotions and affection becomes a learning mechanism. Emotional healing processes that start appear today more like an illusion than a completed process.

## References

Arriaga, Pablo José de. 1920. *La extirpación de la idolatría en el Perú.* Lima: Imprenta y Librería Sanmarti. http://www.cervantesvirtual.com/servlet/SirveObras/57961663656463163754491/index.htm.

Carranza Romero, Francisco. 2013. "El mundo de los muertos en la concepción quechua." *Ciberayllu* 23 April. http://www.andes.missouri.edu/andes/Especiales/FCR_Muertos.html.

Gareis, Iris. 2004. "Extirpación de idolatrías e identidad cultural en las sociedades andinas del Perú virreinal (siglo XVII)." *Boletín de Antropología* 18.35:262–82. http://nuevomundo.revues.org/3346.

Martinez de Codes, Rosa Maria. 1990. "La Reglamentacion sobre idolatría en la Legislacion Conciliar Limense del siglo XVI." http://dadun.unav.edu/handle/10171/4794.

Ortega y Gasset, José. 2007. *Ideas y Creencias.* http://new.pensamientopenal.com.ar/12122007/ortega.pdf.

Pacheco, Edgar Chalco. 1998. "La muerte en la ciudad de Arequipa: Comportamiento de una población heterogenea." Pages 493–505 in *Anales de la XII Reunión Anual de Etnología, La Paz Bolivia, MUSEF (Museo Nacional de Etnografía y Folklore), 26–29 Agosto 1998.* Vol. 1. http://edgarchalcop.blogspot.com/2008/10/la-muerte-en-la-ciudad-de-arequipa.html.

———. 1999. "El escarbo de huesos en Cayma y el culto a las almas." *Revista Sociales* 6:151–64. http://edgarchalcop.blogspot.com/2008/10/el-escarbo-de-huesos-en-ca-yma-y-el.html.

Yoffe, Laura. 2009. "El duelo por la muerte de un ser querido: Creencias culturales y espirituales." http://www.palermo.edu/cienciassociales/publicaciones/pdf/Psico3/3Psico%2009.pdf.

## 22

## THE COMPLEX ROLE OF VIEWS ON THE
## BIBLE IN INTERCULTURAL ENCOUNTERS
## (A DIALOGUE AMONG CUBA, COLOMBIA,
## GHANA, AND THE NETHERLANDS)

*Hans Snoek*

In the past fifteen years a small miracle has happened: dozens of reading groups, thousands of miles apart, have read the same Bible text and corresponded with one another about it. This gives the impression that the Bible is a universal book that, despite differences in cultures and beliefs, can stimulate readers to look at a text differently. Although the success of the project of intercultural Bible reading has been surprising, it would be too simple to state that the exchanges have always led to transformation. Sometimes the distance between groups was too great, which showed up in traces of incomprehension, distancing, and in some cases even a strengthening of prejudices and caricatures.

All in all there has been little research on the question of which preconditions allow the intercultural reading of the Bible to bring about transformation. As a result of a case involving the text of John 20, in the following I seek to analyze how the view of the Bible held by Protestant reading groups in the Netherlands and their partner groups abroad have contributed to transformation. By "view of the Bible," I mean the level to which readers attribute authority to the Bible. In the first part of the essay, I focus on the reading and exchange of reports. After that I go into the background of the Dutch view of the Bible, and trace in which way it is important to scrutinize one another's suppositions.

## Ordinary Dutch Readers Read John 20

In the Netherlands, three Protestant groups I was involved with read John 20. The group in Hoorn has a Mennonite background; the groups in Utrecht and Zaandam are affiliated with the Protestant Church Netherlands, the largest mainline church in the Netherlands. Hoorn was partnered with Methodists from Ghana, Utrecht with a Cuban group consisting mainly of Baptists, and Zaandam with a Roman Catholic reading group from Colombia. When reflecting on the reading reports, it became apparent that the participants from Hoorn had few difficulties with the story of John 20, as a selection of the reactions from Hoorn show:

> I don't have any difficulties with resurrection: Jesus was resurrected, as well other people. Moreover, in Lourdes [France] you can see all kind of miracles.

> Jesus truly arose because he shares his experiences and troubles with the disciples. This kind of exchange with Jesus is perhaps difficult to understand for others, but he just believes.

> Why should we question this passage so much since there are no answers anyway? We don't know the author's reasoning for writing it but it does stimulate our imagination so that we're interested in it two thousand years later. For me it is not very relevant if it actually happened or not. The story has a great symbolic value for me anyway.

The participants from Utrecht and Zaandam had more doubts concerning John's description of the empty grave and the appearance of Jesus:

> The story is important to my belief. It is essential that it happened. Jesus died for our sins and that means you always get a second chance if you mess up. For me that is more important than knowing that it does not end with death.

> The historical aspect is far less important than the symbolic dimension of resurrection. In my view the text of John 20 focusses on overcoming evil with good.

> It is essential for Christianity that death is not the end. The importance of Christ's death is that it is a comfort in your life and death. Though it is very essential, I do not understand it.

> If I had read this text in high school, I would have thought it really hap-
> pened, but I have learned along the way that there is a lot of symbolism
> in the Bible.

It is not easy to detect why some Dutch readers would like to read the text from a symbolic point of view, but the expression "I have difficulties understanding" stands out, as it is repeated several times in the reports from Utrecht and Zaandam. Furthermore, the reading reports show that in these two groups only a few participants feel comfortable saying that they can only believe in the physical resurrection if there is a scientific explanation for it. Apparently they want to maintain John 20 as a symbolic story in order to let the resurrection remain a significant event.

All in all the Dutch reading reports offer various indications to help reconstruct which view of the Bible the Dutch ordinary readers employ. In Hoorn the participants appear to have little trouble accepting the text as a sound historical resurrection story. The reports from Utrecht and Zaandam show a different view of the Bible, in the sense that participants pose difficult questions when reading John 20. Though they acknowledge that the resurrection is an essential element in the Christian faith, they hesitate to call it a historical event. In line with this, some advocate a more symbolic reading of the text.

### Partner Groups in Ghana, Colombia, and Cuba Read John 20

The Ghanaian report, which mainly consists of concise statements, shows that after reading John 20:1–18, the reading group concluded that Jesus had indeed risen again. Ghanaian participants point out in the discussion of the different characters in the story that John showed his unbelieving side by not entering the tomb. Maybe this was his way to show that he had difficulty believing that Jesus would die and rise again. According to the Ghanaian readers, this disbelieving disciple is opposite to Mary Magdalene, who took it upon herself as an evangelist to report the good news.

The Cuban group did not stop reading at John 20:18, but read the entire chapter, which led them to evaluate the role of Thomas as well. One of the participants underscored that she recognized herself in Thomas: "His attitude is a portrait of us as humans. We have the right to think using our own senses. But also disbelief is currently a part of human nature. His attitude was open and sincere." The other participants also emphasized that they recognized themselves in Thomas's attitude of "seeing is believing." Nonetheless, not everyone agreed; one of the participants accentuated the exact opposite: "The expression 'Blessed those who didn't see, and yet believed,' is a reflection of our faith. Friendship between Jesus and Mary Magdalene makes me feel happy and excited, as he models a behavior for me when it comes down to fight prejudices. This text awakens my hope and clearly states that timing is God's, not ours."

Compared to the Cuban report, the Colombian partner group has strikingly few doubts. Once again the phrase "seeing is believing" is brought up, but in a negative sense. Multiple participants emphasize that God asks them to believe in him, even when they cannot see him. As one of the participants puts it: "Some disciples have been guided by what they saw. Christ challenges us to believe that he came to rescue us, even when we cannot see that." Another participant adds: "The Bible calls for us to believe, because belief can move mountains. And that means we are called to believe in God."

## Views on the Bible and Their Backgrounds

The contents of the six reading reports show that the intercultural Bible reading groups have read John 20 from different perspectives. In the next section, I would like to examine which views of the Bible form the basis for the differences between the readings groups, using the hermeneutics of Paul Ricoeur.

Ricoeur bases his philosophical hermeneutics on two encompassing principles: the world of the text and the world of the hearer. Ideally these two worlds are in dialogue with each other, which creates an interplay of question and reply. It is fundamental that this dialogue is conducted on the basis of equality, in the sense that the world of the text is not above the reader, nor is the text subject to the rule of the reader.

The interesting part of Ricoeur's hermeneutics is that he approached it not only from a philosophical point of view, but as a Protestant thinker also paid attention to views of the Bible. He emphasizes that in the Christian tradition

> the founding role attached to the sacred texts and the founded condition of the historical community do not designate interchangeable places. The founding texts *teaches*—this is what the word *torah* means. And the community *receives* instruction. Even when his relation surpasses that between authority and obedience to become one of love, the difference

in attitude between the word that teaches with authority and the one that responds with acknowledgment cannot be abolished. (LaCocque and Ricoeur 1998, xvi–xvii)

Such a view of the Bible implies that the authority of the Bible is above the reader. In the following paragraphs we will describe that way of dealing with texts as "an obedient attitude toward the Bible."

When we look back on the six reading reports, we see that the groups from Hoorn, Bogotá, and Ghana have familiarized themselves with John 20 in the sense that they listened to the teaching, and this resulted in an obedient attitude toward the Bible. Put differently, at no time did the participants from Hoorn, Bogotá, and Ghana show the need to question the authority of the resurrection story. Such an obedient attitude toward the Bible has very old roots. For instance, for centuries the people of the Netherlands (and of other parts of the world!) have presumed without doubt or discussion that the Bible is the word of God. In the seventeenth century, in reaction to the era of Enlightenment, several movements added that the Bible is the *infallible* word of God.

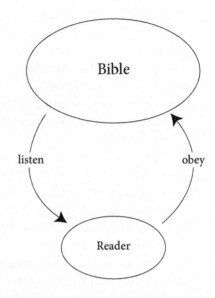

A second view of the Bible that has an equal right to exist, according to Ricoeur, is the mirror image of the view of the Bible just outlined. Ricoeur (2013b, 143–50) stresses that the reading of texts in which God reveals himself may be

accompanied by critical reflection because the texts were written by witnesses. According to Ricoeur, the role of the witnesses in the Bible can be compared with a law court in which one has to differentiate between true and false witnesses: the reader can approach the Bible with a certain reserve or suspicion. Such a view of the Bible resembles more the way the groups from Utrecht, Zaandam, and Cuba read the text: the Dutch readers were doubtful of the solidity of the witnesses in John 20 who professed that they had seen Jesus truly risen again. Furthermore, one notices that some participants from the Cuban group identified themselves with the suspicious attitude of Thomas, who did not instantly believe that Jesus had been resurrected.

This suspicious attitude toward the Bible grew in Western Europe during the Enlightenment when a number of scholars began to notice some apparent contradictions in the Bible. In the Netherlands, it has only been in the second half of the twentieth century that this view of the Bible has seeped through to the church, especially within the Protestant Church Netherlands. For instance, one of the well-known ministers of this church, Nico ter Linden, has emphasized his difficulties with the bodily resurrection of Jesus. According to him, the story of Easter should be read not literally but figuratively: "The crucifixion of Jesus is representative of the triumph of evil over good. The so-called resurrection and the empty grave the apostles found illustrates that in the end all will be right" (Koelewijn 2011, 7).

## Was There Transformation of the View on the Bible among the Six Groups?

When looking at the different views of the Bible that are introduced in the six reading reports, it is interesting to trace whether and in which way the intercultural Bible reading participants noticed that the partner group read the text in John 20 in a different way. If a difference was noticed, it is interesting to see whether this led to a transformation in the view of the Bible. In the correspondence between the groups, concepts like "view of the Bible" or "relationships of authority between text and reader" do not occur, which may not be a surprise. After all, for many ordinary readers these terms would be too abstract; however, some participants did notice that the partner group had a different way of approaching the text than they themselves did.

The clearest difference can be found in the correspondence between Bogotá and Zaandam. The Spanish group noticed that their partners from

Zaandam read John 20 less from their heart and more based on intellect. A Colombian participant asked a critical question: "Would it be possible that by digging so much in a text, you have the chance to keep the text away from yourself?" Another participant from Bogotá says it even more poignantly: "We believe what is written in John 20. For us the Bible is a message of life, which is to be respected. They [the Dutch] need to dig in it, and dig and dig." Another Colombian participant adds. "We read the story of John 20 as it has been handed down to us by Jesus and we live accordingly. They are more focused on the research of what happened in Jesus's time."

The correspondence between Cuba and Utrecht lacks any suggestions that a difference in the view of the Bible was noticed in the partner group. Possibly the realization of the differences only occurred to the Cuban group later on. During the conference in Amsterdam, February 2013, the mentor of the Cuban group noted that the approach of the Dutch group was "demur and intellectual, ... while the Cuban group proposed an interaction that would take more advantage of the emotions and experiences related to the story." The Utrecht group did respond to this comment by the Cuban partners, but there is a possible difference in the view of the Bible that was not articulated.

Finally, in the letter from the Hoorn reading group, one notices that the participants greatly appreciate the way in which their Ghanaian partners have read the text. Keeping in mind that both groups seem to have an obedient attitude toward the Bible, one is not too surprised that in their correspondence the theme of the view of the Bible is not discussed.

As we then look at the ways in which the exchange between the six groups has led to transformation in the view of the Bible, we find a mixed picture. The clearest traces can be found in the correspondence between Zaandam and Colombia. The Dutch group seems to have much respect for the way in which the Colombian partners read the text, especially for the fact that they read it in their very own way: "Indeed, they [the Colombian group] have the idea that we are studying in the Bible.... I think, however, stay close to yourself, do it in your own way." In addition to that a Colombian woman who emigrated to the Netherlands and took part in the Zaandam reading group said: "People in Bogotá differ from people in Zaandam; they have another mentality and another culture." These words give the impression that the Zaandam reading group learned more or less to respect the view of the Bible of their Colombian partners, more along the lines of agreeing to disagree.

The exchange between Utrecht and Cuba shows no traces of a possible transformation of the view of the Bible, maybe because, as we have seen, the difference between the groups was not that great. The reading groups in Ghana and Colombia did not respond to the Dutch reading reports. It is therefore not possible to trace in which way the view of the Bible of the partner groups in Hoorn and Zaandam, respectively, stimulated them to change their own view of the Bible.

From the survey above, it seems that ordinary readers in Utrecht and Zaandam implicitly acted from a suspicious attitude toward the Bible, placing the authority of the reader above that of the Bible. It is possible that for the reading groups in other continents it was difficult to understand such a view of the Bible, especially when they themselves had a more obedient attitude toward the Bible. In the rest of this essay, I want to examine the presuppositions of the more suspicious attitude toward the Bible whereby difficult questions are posed to the biblical text. I hope this analysis will help to understand better the background of this attitude within the society and culture.

Behind the Dutch Reports: Statistics on the
Ambiguous Authority of the Bible in the Netherlands

As far as we know there has been no longitudinal research on the influence of Protestant doctrines in the Netherlands. However, Jos Becker and Joep de Hart (2006, 64) look into the way Dutch Protestants and Roman Catholics give their assent to a number of classic Christian doctrines. Their investigation renders the follow picture, focusing on three statements that could influence a reading of John 20. The table below reports the percentages of those assenting in a given year:

|                              | 1966 | 1980 | 1991 | 2002 |
|------------------------------|------|------|------|------|
| Bible as the word of God     | 77%  | 65%  | 65%  | 62%  |
| Reality of life after death  | 83%  | 75%  | 69%  | 72%  |
| Reality of heaven            | 94%  | 90%  | 86%  | 92%  |

The percentages show that in the second half of the twentieth century the number of Christian Dutch who view the Bible as the word of God has diminished. Almost as significant is the fact that belief in an afterlife and the existence of heaven have diminished over the same period of time as well. The fading importance of these three convictions will at the very least not have stimulated Dutch Protestants to believe that Jesus rose from the dead and that he thereafter took his place next to his heavenly Father.

A second set of statistics that could be interesting comes from Heijme Stoffels (2004, 164). Building on earlier surveys, he looked at how Dutch people in 2004 thought about eight different statements, which are closely related to the question of what kind of book the Bible is. Over a thousand randomly chosen Dutch subjects participated in Stoffels's survey. As in earlier surveys, participants could choose more than one statement, which results in the totals not being 100 percent. (See table below; statements 2, 6, and 8 were not surveyed in earlier research by Stoffels.)

|  | 1989 | 1996 | 2004 |
| --- | --- | --- | --- |
| 1. The Bible is God's message to humanity. | 61% | 51% | 38% |
| 2. The Bible is a book full of myths and legends. | — | — | 33% |
| 3. For belief in God the Bible is a necessity. | 40% | 35% | 25% |
| 4. The Bible is a guideline for my actions. | 41% | 36% | 23% |
| 5. The Bible is God's infallible Word. | 33% | 28% | 18% |
| 6. The miracles in the Bible really happened. | — | — | 16% |
| 7. The Bible inspires me in my daily life | 26% | 28% | 15% |
| 8. Everything in the Bible has happened historically as it is written | — | — | 13% |

Stoffels (2004) shows that the Dutch population has been ascribing less and less authority to the Bible over the years, which corresponds to the trend noted by Becker and De Hart (2006). Furthermore, Stoffels's calculations offer points of contact with the reports from Utrecht and Zaandam. As we have seen, the intercultural Bible reading participants in these two groups have a suspicious attitude toward the Bible, in the sense that they do not automatically see John 20 as God's infallible word (statement 5), have a hard time believing that the miracles truly happened (statement 6), and do not accept that everything in the Bible is an exact reference to historical facts (statement 8). All in all Stoffels's statistics give the impression that the view of the Bible in Utrecht and Zaandam, as revealed in their reading of John 20, is closely related to a Dutch trend to look more suspiciously at the Bible's authority.

## Behind the Statistics: The Influence of Culture

Charles Taylor, a Canadian philosopher, has tried in the past decades to survey what a "modern person" is. We are unable here to do justice to Taylor's body of thought, but a sketch of a few of his insights could be helpful in further interpreting the remarks of the participants in the Utrecht and Zaandam reading groups and in explaining the statistics above.

Taylor points out that the Western world has changed dramatically during the past few centuries and that this has consequences for the world of ideas people have. For instance, the erosion of social relations in the 1960s has produced a generation of young people who stood against "a 'system' which smothered creativity, individuality and imagination" (Taylor 2007, 476). More and more Westerners were making a personal search for their deepest source, in which keywords like "self-realization" and "authenticity" play an important part: "Everyone owns an original way to be human and must therefore discover what it means to be himself" (Taylor 2002, 68). Because of this view of humanity, using the self as a primary reference, the full weight of the individual comes to lie on oneself. As a result, one attaches more importance to personal opinions than to the opinions of anyone else. Closely related to the "shift towards the Man," a process has been taking place for a long time in Europe, is one that Taylor calls "subjectivization," a phenomenon that has a certain logic. As the "enlightened Man" has freed himself from various authorities, such as the church, the Protestant teachings, and the Bible, a void is created in which one can only rely on one's own subjective notions. For instance, there is a radio program in the Netherlands ("Position NL") where anyone can give their opinion on the most complicated problems in society, for everyone has one's own authority.

Taylor's vision could help to understand the discussion on John 20 in Utrecht and Zaandam. For readers who approach texts from a subjective angle, it is logical that when they themselves do not have experiences of people rising from the dead, they find the empty grave of Jesus difficult to comprehend. Furthermore, the phenomenon of subjectivization can help one understand why some participants are critical toward Jesus's remarks to Thomas. Jesus asks Thomas to believe something that is not easily understood. Thomas's attitude coincides with the reference frames of some ordinary readers in Zaandam and Utrecht. Apparently Jesus has no a priori authority to these ordinary readers, but he would have to earn that authority by being in line with the frame of reference of the reading groups in Zaandam and Utrecht. Earlier studies have shown that some Dutch intercultural Bible reading participants have a critical stance toward Jesus. With regard to John 4, the story of Jesus and the Samaritan woman, some Dutch participants thought that Jesus was acting strangely and was almost snappy toward the woman (Snoek 2004, 195). In a culture of subjectivization, there is a certain logic to ordinary readers putting their own critical questions to the text and to their feeling themselves to be above the Bible when the answers are unsatisfactory. Strikingly, Johan Roeland (2009), a Dutch sociologist of religion, has shown that the phenomenon of subjectivization is not only present in historical churches like the Protestant Church Netherlands, but also influences the evangelical movement in the Netherlands.

However interesting Taylor's vision is, strictly speaking a subjectivized reading of the Bible is not a particularly recent phenomenon. From the beginning, the Bible has had to deal with readers who used the filter of their own experiences and opinions when reading the texts. However, there is a difference with the past in the sense that a diminishing percentage of twenty-first-century readers in the Netherlands see the Bible as the word of God (Becker and De Hart 2006; Stoffels 2004) and that they therefore are able to ask more critical questions. A view of the Bible based on suspicion raises the question of what exactly the Dutch readers are expecting from the Bible. On the one hand, the Bible is, as the Dutch-Brazilian scientist Carlos Mesters said, "a flower without protection": any reader can do with it what he or she thinks is right. On the other hand, the Bible is and remains an intractable book, even when read in the twenty-first century by people who may not be hearing the story they had hoped for.

## The Importance of Perceiving the Other's View on the Bible

One of the ideals of the intercultural Bible reading project is that the exchange of reading experiences can stimulate people from different cultures toward transformation in their thinking and/or doing. At a conference in Amsterdam (February 2013), a number of examples were presented in which this ideal was realized. At the same time, much work needs to be done to enlarge the transformative power of the Bible. In the remainder of this essay, I want to examine in which way intercultural Bible reading can contribute to that.

Characteristically, in the international Bible reading project, reading reports play a crucial role in the exchange between readers from different cultures. However valuable this written correspondence is, it is and remains the tip of the iceberg in which the larger part remains under the surface and is hardly visible to the partner group. Many factors that have led to a certain way of reading can hardly be found in the reading reports and the correspondence, because ordinary readers are often not aware of the very different world their partners live in. One of the factors we have explored in this essay—the view of these groups on the Bible —has left a deep mark in the way the six groups read John 20. At the same time, it showed that views of the Bible most often belong to the submerged part of the iceberg, as a result of which the reading reports offer too few indications to comprehend fully the differences in approaching the text. A hiatus like this makes it that much harder to think about one's own view of the Bible and even more difficult to transform it.

The phenomenon "view of the Bible" is only one of the invisible, subconscious elements in the intercultural Bible reading project. Reading reports hide even more elements that could be crucial to reading groups to empathize with and understand the partners. Some of these elements involve differing ultimate beliefs like images of God, Jesus, or the world, as well as of spirituality, ethics, and eschatological questions. One by one these ultimate beliefs influence the way people read John 20. Each of the six reading groups had to implicitly, and sometimes explicitly, ask themselves questions such as: Does God rule over life and death? Is Jesus man and/or Son of God? Do I believe that miracles can truly happen? Does the resurrection show that believers should hope for a life after death?

Answers to such questions are part of the ultimate beliefs people develop over the course of their lives, and these cannot be changed when intercultural Bible reading partners in other parts of the world apparently do have different opinions. The ultimate beliefs of intercultural Bible reading participants will be built on the foundation of their own view of the Bible. This view of the Bible not only plays a crucial role in the reading of a text, but it will also be the driving force of the ultimate beliefs that hinder transformation. These issues require more attention within the intercultural Bible reading project because of the complex role that the view of the Bible plays in the intercultural exchange. To put it more concretely: facilitators who guide the reading groups should be more attentive to making the view of the Bible and the related ultimate beliefs explicit.

It will be clear that a role like that is hardly simple. To develop an antenna for the view of the Bible within one's own reading group and within that of the partner group requires that the facilitator have both knowledge and reserve. For instance, it would be unwelcome if facilitators were to evaluate the view of the Bible of the partner group, or of one's own reading group, from a normative standpoint. The Bible is too rich and too complicated to be read from a single view of the Bible. For this reason, it is certainly legitimate not to sanctify a single view of the Bible. A Bible text will more likely come to its full potential from an obedient, a suspicious, and a dialogical standpoint. Maybe the approach of intercultural Bible reading creates space to start a conversation between the bountifulness of the text and one's own ultimate beliefs and to experience that old attitudes toward faith can be given a new life.

## References

Becker, Jos, and Joep de Hart. 2006. *Godsdienstige veranderingen in Nederland. Verschuivingen in de binding met de kerken en de christelijke traditie.* The Hague: Sociaal en Cultureel Planbureau.

Koelewijn, Rinskje. 2011. "Ik ben een matige vaster. Interview met Nico ter Linden." *NRC Handelsblad* (23 April). www.nrc.nl/handelsblad/van/2011/april23/ik-ben-een-matoige-vaster-12012312.

LaCocque, André, and Paul Ricoeur. 1998. *Thinking Biblically: Exegetical and Hermeneutical Studies.* Translated by David Pellauer. Chicago: University of Chicago Press.

Ricoeur, Paul. 2013a. *Hermeneutics.* Vol. 2 of *Writings and Lectures.* Cambridge: Polity.

———. 2013b. "Hermeneutics of the Idea of Revelation." Pages 111–52 in *Hermeneutics.* Vol. 2 of *Writings and Lectures.* Cambridge: Polity.

Roeland, Johan. 2009. *Selfation: Dutch Evangelical Youth between Subjectivization and Subjection.* Amsterdam: Amsterdam University.

Snoek, Hans. 2004. "Biblical Scholars and Ordinary Readers Dialoguing about Living Water." Pages 304–14 in *Through the Eyes of Another: Intercultural Reading of the Bible.* Edited by Hans de Wit, Louis Jonker, Marleen Kool, and Daniel Schipani. Elkhart, IN: Institute of Mennonite Studies.

Stoffels, Heijme. 2004. "Onderzoek Bijbelgebruik. Volksboek of vergeetboek? Steeds minder bijbels in huis." Pages 163–200 in *De Bijbel opnieuw vertaald.* Edited by Henriette Bonarius. Trouw Dossier 34. Amsterdam: Uitgeverij Maarten Muntinga.

Taylor, Charles. 2002. *De malaise van de moderniteit.* Kampen: Kok Agora.

———. 2007. *A Secular Age.* Cambridge: Harvard University Press.

# PART 4
## AM I MY SISTER'S KEEPER?
## CASE STUDIES ON OTHER TEXTS

## 23

## AM I MY BROTHER'S KEEPER? JUSTICE AND TRANSFORMATION IN A MALAGASY-NORWEGIAN DIALOGUE (GENESIS 4)

*Knut Holter*

The plot of the Cain and Abel narrative in Gen 4 seems quite problematic. Each of the two brothers brings gifts to the Lord, who—to my mind, rather disturbingly, even quite unjustly—"looked with favor" on Abel and his offering of the firstborn of the flock but "did not look with favor" on Cain and his offering of the fruits of the soil (vv. 4–5). I would have preferred a narrative where God looks with favor on both the shepherd and the gardener, a narrative in which my ideas of divine and human justice would be more easily discerned, a narrative that would have a more obvious potential as a transformative facilitator among contemporary readers.

So to my male, middle-class, white, northern European, and Protestant mind, the narrative is quite problematic. I realize that these sets of interpretive qualifiers could mean that the problem is not necessarily in the narrative but precisely in "my mind," reflecting my own political, social, ethnic, cultural, and religious situation. What is more, in spite of my disappointment about a God who does not fit my theological and ethical frameworks, it could be that the narrative still has potential as a transformative facilitator among contemporary readers. To explore this, I have challenged two Bible study groups—one in my own congregation in Stavanger, Norway, and one in Fianarantsoa, Madagascar, a city I occasionally visit—to read and reflect upon the Cain and Abel narrative, and to dialogue with each other about its meaning.

## Reading Contexts

For this project, groups were sought for that shared some basic character-istics in spite of coming from different parts of the globe. A crucial point in this selection was the aim of reducing the number of variables, so as better to be able to recognize differences. First, both Bible study groups, which each existed prior to this project, recruit their members from urban contexts (industry, business, universities) and from typically middle-class and tertiary educated layers of their respective societies. This means that the members of both groups were used to communicate with people from other cultures and countries and that they were able to relate to theoretical questions arising from written texts. Second, both Bible study groups were of mixed gender with members in their forties to sixties. Thus the group members shared some of the challenges facing the in-between generation, such as caring for elderly parents as well as children and even grandchil-dren. The latter factor is important when reading a text like Gen 4, with its plot of complex family relations. Third, both Bible study groups are affiliated with a Lutheran church. This too is of some importance, as the Evangelical Lutheran Church of Madagascar and the Lutheran Church of Norway have a history of interaction dating back to the 1860s, when Nor-wegian missionaries began work in Madagascar.

The historical interaction between Malagasy and Norwegian Luther-ans deserves some further attention. One aspect is the role of the Old Tes-tament in their respective Sunday services. The Norwegian missionaries who started their work in Madagascar in the nineteenth century simply transferred the Church of Norway lectionary to Madagascar. At that time the Norwegian lectionary for Sunday sermons included only texts from the Gospels. The Malagasy Lutherans have kept this lectionary until today, whereas the Norwegian Lutherans have introduced a lectionary for Sunday sermons that includes Old Testament texts. As a result, Lutherans attending Sunday services in Norway occasionally hear a sermon on the Cain and Abel narrative in Gen 4, whereas Lutherans in Madagascar never do, in spite of being part of a church that, generally speaking, shows more interest in the Old Testament than is the case in Norway.

Another aspect of the interaction between Lutherans in Fianarantsoa and in Stavanger is an academic collaboration between the Fianarantsoa-based Lutheran Seminary, now a graduate school of theology, and the Stavanger-based Mission School, now a specialized university. This col-laboration dates back to the 1880s when the first Malagasy student came to study theology in Stavanger. In spite of more than a hundred years of collaboration between Fianarantsoa and Stavanger and between Malagasies and Norwegians reading the Bible and being involved in theological training, no dialogue on a particular biblical text or motif has been undertaken prior to this point. There have been a few instances of Norwegians investigating the role of the Bible in Madagascar (Munthe 1969) or providing textbooks in biblical studies for a Malagasy audience (the most recent example is Holter 2012), but there has been no previous attempt to facilitate and study an actual Malagasy-Norwegian dialogue on a particular biblical text or motif.

The two Bible study groups accepted the invitation to participate in the project and agreed to dedicate two group meetings to the project. In the end each devoted three group meetings to the project, from late 2011 to early 2013. The two project coordinators, Olivier Randrianjaka in Fianarantsoa and Knut Holter in Stavanger, did not participate in the group discussions. The correspondence between the groups was done in the form of letters written in Malagasy and Norwegian, translated into English by the project coordinators and sent by e-mail. Before the first meeting, the groups were given a brief written presentation of the project, including: (1) some general textual perspectives, locating the text within the primeval history, and noticing some societal and religious patterns reflected in the text; and (2) some applicative perspectives, asking whether it is possible to make connections between the text and contemporary family relations.

## Analytical Contexts

Although there had been no previous example of a Malagasy-Norwegian dialogue on a particular biblical text or motif, the present dialogue on Gen 4 forms part of a broad spectrum of interpretive webs. Two nodes of these webs should be briefly addressed here—the dialogue and the text.

The first node concerns the dialogue. The Malagasy-Norwegian dialogue is but one of many examples of dialogues between African and European readers of the Bible, "ordinary readers," without formalized training in biblical interpretation, as well as "professional readers," theologians and exegetes with formalized training in biblical interpretation. Such dialogues are, however, a rather recent phenomenon. For centuries, any interaction between Africa and Europe with regard to the Bible was characterized by the colonial context, with the Europeans seeing themselves as the interpretive subject of a monologue vis-à-vis Africa rather than having a dialogue with Africa, thus viewing the Africans as a receiving object rather than as an interpretive subject (Holter 2008). This conceptualizing of the dialogue/monologue was fundamentally wrong: from the very moment the Bible became available, African readers developed their own interpretive strategies in relation to the book and/or text (West 2000). Nevertheless, due to the colonial past with its shadow stretching far into postcolonial times, it is probably only in the last generation that African and European readers of the Bible have been able to meet as equal interpretive subjects. A couple of research projects might illustrate this new situation. One is the mid-1990s "Bible in Africa Project" (Ukpong 2000), which also included surveys of popular biblical interpretation in Port Harcourt, Nigeria, and Glasgow, Scotland (Riches 1996). Some differences with regard to how the Bible is used in the two contexts are highlighted without any value-based assessments of these differences. Another project is the 2006 conference on "African and European Readers of the Bible in Dialogue" in Stellenbosch, South Africa, searching for ethically accountable ways of relating the biblical texts to what is increasingly acknowledged as our—African and European—common context (De Wit and West 2008).

More directly, however, the present Malagasy-Norwegian dialogue on Gen 4 is part of yet another research project initiated in Amsterdam, "Through the Eyes of Another: Intercultural Reading of the Bible" (De Wit et al. 2004). The aim of the project is to develop an empirically based understanding and interpretation of what happens when small groups of readers of biblical texts, sometimes coming from radically different contexts, read the same text and get involved in a dialogue about its meaning. The project initiator and director, Hans de Wit (2004, 488; 2012, 17–32), points out three distinct elements of intercultural Bible hermeneutics: (1) an analysis of the interaction between culture and the process of interpreting biblical texts; (2) an exploration of the conditions that make possible the communication about the meaning of biblical texts across cultural boundaries; and (3) an emphasis on questions of liberation and of truth across cultural boundaries.

In the intercultural Bible hermeneutics that develops from such elements, the concept of the "other reader" plays a key role (De Wit 2012, 47–58). The communication of the meaning of biblical texts across cultural borders and the implicit potential of revealing culturally biased and oppressive readings requires people or groups who can serve each other as the "other reader," that is, as a reader who reflects and represents social and cultural experiences and concerns other than our own, hence being able to offer a critical rereading of our reading of the text.

The second node of the interpretive webs of the Malagasy-Norwegian dialogue on Gen 4 concerns the text itself, as this particular text is involved in various interpretive discourses. Such discourses are historically, culturally, and ideologically interdependent, and many of them probably have little to contribute to the current dialogue. Still, a couple of "African" discourses on Gen 4 from a generation ago deserve attention, as they focus on interpretive strategies for transformation. One is the potential of reading the Cain and Abel narrative from enculturation hermeneutical perspectives. An example here is the Nigerian linguist, Modupe Oduyoye, who in his commentary on Gen 1–11 argues that the Cain and Abel narrative reflects a conflict between settled civilization (Cain) and pastoral nomadism (Abel), a conflict that has counterparts in traditional Africa. The sympathy of the text is with the nomadic side, Oduyoye argues, and may thereby help contemporary African readers to see their cultural and political experiences from a nomadic perspective (1984, 63–74). Another is the potential of reading Gen 4 from liberation hermeneutical perspectives. Examples here are the South African theologians Allan Boesak and Itumeleng Mosala, both of whom use the Cain and Abel narrative to illustrate the struggle against apartheid, the former from a literary perspective (Boesak 1984), the latter from a source-critical and materialistic perspective (Mosala 1989). These "African" readings of Gen 4 from the 1980s received significant attention in the 1990s. In South Africa, Gerald West analyzed the interpretation of Boesak and Mosala, noticing the need for a biblical hermeneutics that has an explicit commitment to the community of the poor and oppressed (West 1995). In Ethiopia, Mark McEntire, an American missionary and biblical scholar, together with his Ethiopian students read Mosala, Boesak, and Oduyoye, noticing the need for a biblical hermeneutics that allows for various, and potentially contending, readings in various contexts (McEntire 2000).

I cannot go into all aspects of these two nodes of the interpretive webs of the Malagasy-Norwegian dialogue on Gen 4. Nevertheless, the discourses around the two nodes should be able to raise some questions relevant to the present search for transformative potentials in the dialogue. One question would then be to what extent the dialogue allows for an understanding of the two Bible study groups as equal interpretive subjects, irrespective of the colonial and missionary past. Another would be to what extent the dialogue enables the group members to see and be challenged by the interpretive perspective of the culturally "other reader." A third would be to what extent the dialogue encourages the groups to look for enculturation and liberation potentials in the encounter between biblical text and experienced life.

## The Question of Justice in the Dialogue

In proceeding to the Bible study groups and their dialogue, we concentrate on one particular motif, namely, the question of justice. The term *justice* is not used in the Cain and Abel narrative, neither did it occur in the presentation of the project. This was intentional, so as not to influence the discussion. Still, concepts of justice are clearly present in the narrative—both as divine justice and as human justice—and the question of justice could therefore be fitting as an illustrative case.

In relation to Gen 4, the question of divine justice can be phrased: Does God really represent justice in a narrative where he is portrayed as looking with favor on the shepherd Abel and his offering from the first-born of the flock, while not looking with favor on the gardener Cain and his offering from the fruits of the soil?

This key plot of the narrative proved problematic to the members of the Stavanger group. In their first report they argue that God appears to act unfairly to people, and they ask—intended, I think, as a rhetorical question—whether it is actually better to be a shepherd than a gardener. The problem that Gen 4 seems to portray God as unjust continued to challenge the Stavanger group, and throughout the dialogue this was not resolved. On the one hand, the biblical portrayal of a God choosing some people—such as Jacob (a liar), Moses (a murderer), and Rahab (a prostitute)—does make sense, they argued, as God looks on the heart and knows all things. On the other hand, the parallel portrayal of a God rejecting others, such as Cain, does not make sense, and it can only be accepted from the perspective that God's thoughts are higher than ours. Therefore, in their third report the Stavanger readers concluded somewhat hesitantly by simply clinging to their conviction: "We know that God is not unjust."

The Fianarantsoa group saw no difficulty with this key plot of the narrative. In their first report, they argued that the rejection of Cain and his offering not only made sense when read from a traditional Malagasy perspective, but it was actually an obvious consequence of the kinds of offerings brought forward by the two brothers. Malagasy tradition distinguishes between bloody and nonbloody, that is, agriculturally based, sacrifices. The former is the more expensive and prestigious, is offered to the creator god, Zanahary, and is performed for the atonement of sin. The latter is cheaper and less prestigious, and although it can be offered as a first crop offering to Zanahary, it is more often offered to ancestors and other spiritual beings. To the Fianarantosa group, therefore, it is not surprising that God favors the more expensive and prestigious offering of Abel, intended for and fitting the expectations of the Creator. The decision of Abel to bring the most valuable offering also corresponds, the Fianarantsoa group argued, with the testimony of the New Testament: "By faith Abel offered God a better sacrifice than Cain did" (Heb 11:4).

Another aspect of the portrayal of God in Gen 4 is the extent to which the Bible study groups expected God to intervene in their lives. The Fianarantsoa group expected God to intervene here and now in reaction to evil. This means, they argued, that victims of oppression and murder are not to react against the injustice they undergo but to wait for God, who will avenge them. He did so in the case of Cain, who, according to Malagasy culture, received the most terrible punishment of all, namely, that of being expelled from his own land. The Stavanger group had quite a different understanding of the punishment of Cain: that God continued to take care of him was interpreted positively and related to the saying at the end of the chapter: "at that time men began to invoke the LORD by name" (v. 26).

The diverging interpretations as to whether God is portrayed as just in this narrative had consequences for how the two groups understood the relationship between the human actors in the narrative. Interestingly, both groups acknowledged that the human actors were not only the two brothers but also their parents, though they are somewhat hidden beneath the surface of the narrative.

The conflict between the two brothers was easily recognizable to the two groups. The Fianarantsoa group pointed to the Malagasy tradition that the older son is normally responsible for the cultivation of the fields, whereas the younger son is responsible for the animals. Since the older brothers therefore become more familiar with the family fields, they might use their knowledge for personal benefit when the inheritance is distributed, and this might result in conflict among brothers. The group also pointed to the Malagasy tradition that a younger brother is not allowed in any way to supersede the older one. In this sense Cain's anger is justified: Abel had taken a position belonging to Cain, and what Cain experienced is the behavior of an excluded or marginalized family member.

The Stavanger group, too, recognized the conflict between the two brothers. Like their peers in Fianarantsoa, they referred to experiences of conflicts among siblings. Some cases have to do with family property, others with different religious affiliations. Most attention, however, was given to the problem of general mistrust among siblings, with bad feelings as a result. Several of the group members told about sibling jealousy and not being able to talk together, and they tried to find signs in the Cain and Abel narrative of corresponding experiences. Perhaps Abel was arrogant; perhaps Cain invited him into the fields to make up to him, but then his anger took over. Generally speaking, the Stavanger group preferred psychological explanations. They emphasized that each has a responsibility for controlling one's feelings, even when wronged by others. It is better to address conflicts and talk about them, rather than sweeping them under the carpet. When this perspective was related to the Cain and Abel narrative, a point of contact was the narrative's focus on sin: "it desires to have you, but you must master it" (v. 7).

Both groups also asked about the role of the parents. Although the parents played marginal roles in the narrative—the father is mentioned in verses 1 and 25 only, the mother additionally in verse 2—both study groups gave them key roles in the relationship between the two sons. Already in the first report, the Fianarantsoa group criticized the parents for being too passive in a tense situation. According to Malagasy culture, the parents should be reconcilers: the parents should have intervened and solved the conflict before it got so serious. The Stavanger group noticed the parents' absence. In their first report, they suggested that the conflict resulted from something the parents had done. When sibling jealousy increases, parents are often more part of the problem than of the solution, they argued.

The second and third rounds of reports demonstrated that the two groups at this point had basically divergent views. In Madagascar, the Fianarantsoa group argued that the parents are indeed not the problem; they are the solution. Parents are responsible for their children even when they have grown up and have their own families, and as such the parents are entitled to intervene in the lives of their children. The Stavanger group, on the other hand, had as ideal that parents should not interfere in the lives of their grown-up children. As parents, they argue, we can say what we feel and think about certain issues, but we should not give advice. If we interfere with the lives of our grown-up children, they will be offended.

## A Potential for Transformation

As briefly mentioned in the introduction, my interest in Gen 4 grew out of curiosity as to whether the Cain and Abel narrative might have a potential to facilitate some kind of transformation—personal, spiritual, or political—among contemporary readers. I admitted my prejudice against the narrative's portrayal of a God "disturbingly, even quite unjustly" looking with favor on Abel and his offering and not on Cain and his offering. Nevertheless, I decided to ask whether an intercultural dialogue on this narrative might reveal some transformative potential. During the process of working with the dialogue, it became clear that this was the case. I note three examples, following the three questions I raised in the conclusion of the section on analytical contexts.

My first question related to the extent to which the dialogue allows for an understanding of the two groups as equal interpretive subjects, irrespective of the colonial and missionary past. The background for this question is the historical interaction between Malagasy and Norwegian Lutherans, where the Norwegian Mission Society strongly influenced the development of the Malagasy Lutheran Church for more than a century. A reference to "Stavanger," the home city of the mission society and of the Mission School used to train its missionaries, is in such a context more than a geographical reference: it symbolizes the theological, organizational, and economic power of the mission agency that founded the Malagasy Lutheran Church.

There are no signs in the reports from the Bible study group in Stavanger that they were aware of this historical context or tried to be sensitive in that respect. On the contrary, in a couple of cases they asked questions that could easily have seemed somewhat patronizing to their partners in Fianarantsoa. One case was when the Fianarantsoa group, with reference to Malagasy tradition, argued that Abel's offering was better than that of Cain. This interpretation, and even more the rationale for it, came as a surprise to the Stavanger group. They asked with some concern, I think, whether Christians in Madagascar were still influenced by traditional Malagasy religion. Although this question could have been seen as an example of Western patronizing, the Fianarantsoa group responded in a friendly manner, explaining to the Norwegians some of the enculturation hermeneutical experiences of Madagascar. Pre-Christian thoughts do indeed continue to influence Malagasies, both Christians and non-Christians. However, the Fianarantsoa group emphasized, one should acknowledge that not all aspects of pre-Christian religion are unbiblical. Another case was when the Fianarantsoa group—again with reference to Malagasy tradition—argued that we can expect God to intervene here and now in reaction to evil and that he will avenge those who have suffered harm. The Stavanger group was hesitant and asked with a critical undertone whether this point of view represents traditional Malagasy concepts or Malagasy Christian concepts as well. The Fianarantsoa group responded by noticing the many parallels between Malagasy and Old Testament concepts of God's retribution and judgment.

I would tend to argue that these two cases are indicative of interpretive equality between the two groups. In neither of the two cases were there any signs that the Malagasies felt inferior in their interpretation. On the contrary, in both cases the intercultural dialogue allowed the Fianarantsoa group to take the lead vis-à-vis their partners (even "Stavanger"!), and in both cases they referred to biblical motifs to legitimize their use of Malagasy traditions as interpretive resources for the Cain and Abel narrative.

My second question concerned the extent to which the dialogue enabled the group members to see and be challenged by the interpretive perspective of the culturally "other reader." The background for this question was the need to confront all biblical readers with their culturally biased readings. An effective way of doing so, Hans de Wit has argued (2012, 47–58), is to let a certain biblical reading be confronted with another reading representing other social and cultural experiences and concerns.

From the beginning, the two Bible study groups approached the biblical text quite differently. Whereas the Stavanger group read the Cain and Abel narrative in the light of their own personal experiences with siblings and parents, the Fianarantsoa group used their first report to give a survey of some general, religiocultural traditions in Madagascar in relation to the biblical narrative. The Norwegians were somewhat upset by this: in their second report they asked whether the groups had been given the same project presentation, and they criticized the Malagasies for presenting an academic lecture on traditional culture and religion rather than describing how they would apply the text to their lives as Christians. The Fianarantsoa group responded to this criticism by arguing that since their report was supposed to reflect the discussion of the group, they had wanted to communicate their thoughts in a "harmonized way."

In the final report from the group in Stavanger, this topic was addressed once more, but this time in a more relaxed manner. They said that initially they had wanted to read the text as Christians, not as Norwegians;

however, indirectly confirming De Wit's model about the "other reader," in retrospect they understood that they too were influenced by the culture in which they live. As examples they mentioned their egalitarian culture as opposed to more elitist cultures elsewhere, and the role of the family, which in the Norwegian context is of less importance than among the Malagasies. It would probably not be difficult to find other examples of how their interpretation of the Cain and Abel narrative was influenced by the Norwegian culture, such as their preference for psychological explanations and the individualism characterizing their interpretation, which allowed individual experiences to be presented on behalf of the group, as opposed to the "more harmonized way" of the Malagasies.

My final question had to do with the extent to which the dialogue encouraged the groups to look for enculturation and liberation potentials in the encounter between the biblical text and life experiences. Behind this question lies in the memories of the European colonization of Africa, a colonization that was expressed not only in political oppression and economic exploitation of the continent but also in the oppression of culture, religion, and language. The Bible played an important but ambiguous role in the history of colonial and postcolonial Africa. Certainly the Bible was used to legitimize the European oppression and exploitation, but eventually it was also used to nurture the African resistance, not the least from various enculturation and liberation theological perspectives (Holter 2008).

Turning to the material of the Malagasy-Norwegian dialogue, we notice a clear difference with regard to these two interpretive perspectives. On the one hand, enculturation theological perspectives are clearly visible in the dialogue. The Fianarantsoa group repeatedly refers to Malagasy cultural and religious tradition, partly as a general interpretive context but partly also as an explicit interpretive resource, such as in the interpretation of the two types of offerings, or in the interpretation of Cain being expelled from his country. The Stavanger group eventually acknowledged that their reading to some extent reflected their own cultural situation. Whereas the dialogue situation encouraged the Fianarantsoa group to look for interpretive resources in their cultural context, their Stavanger partners did not use their contextually based experiences and concerns explicitly as a means of reading the narrative.

When it came to the question of a liberation theological perspective, however, there was almost nothing to be found in the dialogue material. This could have been for several reasons. One is that both being typically middle class, neither of the groups seemed to see a need for "liberation." Another is that the Malagasies, who actually have been colonized, have a history of half a century of independence after liberation. Whatever the reason, it corresponds with the observation by De Wit in his empirical analysis of three thousand pages of popular readings of John 4 that such material often reflects little of the more explicitly sociopolitical concepts of liberation theology (2012, 63).

In a previous section on the analytical contexts of the present dialogue, I referred to a particular interest in reading Gen 4 from "African" perspectives back in the 1980s, particularly Modupe Oduyoye's enculturation hermeneutical reading and Allan Boesak and Itumeleng Mosala's liberation hermeneutical reading. I also noticed that these "African" readings of the Cain and Abel narrative received some significant attention in the 1990s. With this background, one would assume that Gen 4 might still be used to illustrate certain key experiences and concerns within "African" biblical interpretation. Nevertheless, more recent, explicitly "African" interpretive surveys of Genesis, such as those by Barnabe Assohoto and Samuel Ngewa (2006) and Rodney Sadler (2010), unfortunately neglect the enculturation and liberation hermeneutical experiences and concerns of Oduyoye, Mosala, and Boesak. I tend to think that these recent readings of Genesis are fairly representative of the current interpretive situation.

The material on the present Malagasy-Norwegian dialogue is by no means sufficient to challenge the current interpretive situation. Still, the reading of Gen 4 by a Bible study group in Fianarantsoa, who intuitively makes use of enculturation hermeneutical perspectives, might be taken as a sign that the concerns for justice and transformation expressed by leading African professional interpreters of the Bible a generation or so ago still deserve attention.

## References

Assohoto, Barnabe, and Samuel Ngewa. 2006. "Genesis." Pages 9–84 in *Africa Bible Commentary*. Edited by Tokunboh Adeyemo, Solomon Andria, Issiaka Coulibaly, Tewoldemedhin Habtu, and Samuel Ngewa. Nairobi: WorldAlive.

Boesak, Allan A. 1984. *Black and Reformed: Apartheid, Liberation, and the Calvinist Tradition*. Maryknoll, NY: Orbis.

Holter, Knut. 2008. *Contextualized Old Testament Scholarship in Africa*. Nairobi: Acton.

———. 2012. *Fandalinana Testamenta Taloha mihatra ami-konteksta aty Afrika sy Madagasikara*. Antananarivo: FLM Trano Printy.

McEntire, Mark. 2000. "Cain and Abel in Africa: An Ethiopian Case Study in Competing Hermeneutics." Pages 248–59 in West and Dube 2000.

Mosala, Itumeleng J. 1989. *Biblical Hermeneutics and Black Theology in South Africa*. Grand Rapids: Eerdmans.

Munthe, Ludvig. 1969. *La Bible a Madagascar: Les deux premières traductions du Nouveau Testament malgache*. Avhandlinger utgitt av Egede Instituttet 10. Oslo: Egede Instituttet.

Oduyoye, Modupe. 1994. *The Sons of the Gods and the Daughters of Men: An Afro-Asiatic Interpretation of Genesis 1–11*. Maryknoll, NY: Orbis.

Riches, John. 1996. "Interpreting the Bible in African Contexts: Glasgow Consultation." Pages 181–88 in *"Reading With": An Exploration of the Interface Between Critical and Ordinary Readings of the Bible: African Overtures*. Edited by Gerald O. West and Musa W. Dube. Semeia 73. Atlanta: Scholars Press.

Sadler, Rodney S. 2010. "Genesis." Pages 70–79 in *The Africana Bible: Reading Israel's Scriptures from Africa and the African Diaspora*. Edited by Hugh R. Page Jr. Minneapolis: Fortress.

Ukpong, Justin S. 2000. "Popular Readings of the Bible in Africa and Implications for Academic Readings." Pages 582–94 in West and Dube 2000.

West, Gerald O. 1995. *Biblical Hermeneutics of Liberation: Modes of Reading the Bible in the South African Context*. 2nd ed. Pietermaritzburg: Cluster.

———. 2000. "Mapping African Biblical Interpretation: A Tentative Sketch." Pages 29–53 in West and Dube 2000.

West, Gerald O., and Musa W. Dube, eds. 2000. *The Bible in Africa: Transactions, Trajectories and Trends*. Leiden: Brill.

Wit, Hans de. 2004. "Intercultural Bible Reading and Hermeneutics." Pages 477–92 in de Wit, Jonker, Kool, and Schipani 2004.

———. 2012. *Empirical Hermeneutics, Interculturality, and Holy Scripture*. Intercultural Biblical Hermeneutics Series 1. Elkhart, IN: Institute of Mennonite Studies.

Wit, Hans de, Louis Jonker, Marleen Kool, and Daniel Schipani., eds. 2004. *Through the Eyes of Another: Intercultural Reading of the Bible*. Elkhart, IN: Institute of Mennonite Studies.

Wit, Hans de, and Gerald O. West, eds. 2008. *African and European Readers of the Bible in Dialogue: In a Quest of a Shared Meaning*. Studies of

Religion in Africa: Supplements to the Journal of Religion in Africa
32. Leiden: Brill.

## 24

## BREAKING DOWN THE BOUNDARIES THAT APPEAR TO MAKE US ENEMIES (A DIALOGUE BETWEEN DOMINICANS AND HAITIANS ON RUTH)*

*Digna María Adames Núñez*

The present essay presents the results of an intercultural Bible reading process in the Dominican Republic in 2009. This project was meant to generate face-to-face encounters between two populations—Haitians and Dominicans—who do not tend to associate with one another. What each population supposedly knows about the other is affected by images influenced by the social media and by groups with economic and political power on both sides of the island of Hispaniola, groups who propagate the idea that each of these two countries is a threat to the other.

As a result, the social imaginary[1] in each country regarding the other is based on prejudice and rejection, which creates a particularly tense relationship between Haitians and Dominicans. We believe that sitting at the same table, using the Holy Scriptures as a link, offers the possibility of breaking the imaginary boundaries that appear to make us enemies. That way, a new perception is born, one that grants freedom and allows us to meet the other as he or she wishes to reveal himself or herself, with all his or her mystery and treasures, like a gift that can help and guide our own processes of personal growth.

For this reading experience, the first chapter of Ruth and the topic of immigration were chosen. The project included a group of Dominicans and

---

* This essay has been translated by Alaí Reyes-Santos and Liomarys Reyes-Santos.

1. "Social imaginary" refers to those schemes, socially constructed, that allow us to perceive something as real, explain it, and intervene operationally on that which each social system considers as reality.

a group of Haitian immigrants, all residing in the city of Santo Domingo. The Jesuit Services for Refugees and Immigrants[2] based in Santo Domingo held all the meetings. I designed and coordinated the project. I consider myself a Dominican, and it is is from that perspective that I participated in the intercultural Bible reading process and analyzed the reality of the island.

## The Fertile Soil of the Intercultural Bible Reading Project in Santo Domingo

In order for the reader to have an idea of the concerns that motivated the project, I share a series of stories extracted from everyday interactions between Dominicans and Haitians in the Dominican Republic. The narrative, along with the metaphors, imagery, and parables, are in my view special ways of approaching the reality of intercultural perspectives. We are engaging a reality that is polysemic and dense, that surpasses all conceptualization, analysis, and system.

It is difficult to forget the astonished expression of a Haitian young man when a vehicle of the public transportation system stopped to pick him up, but suddenly accelerated after stopping right in front of him. A white-skinned woman inside the vehicle had told the driver that if he let that dirty Haitian get on, she would get off without paying her fare. This event occurred in 1996 in Santiago de los Caballeros, the second most important city of the Dominican Republic. Along with the growth of the construction industry, Haitian immigration in this city increased at the end of the 1980s. Up until that decade, there was not a significant presence of Haitians in that area.

This event reminds me of an experience from my childhood. When my mother tried to make my younger sister stop sucking her thumb, she threatened her by saying that the Haitian would eat her. I had often seen

---

2. Jesuit Service for Refugees and Immigrants in the Dominican Republic is part of an international network belonging to the Companñía de Jesús, whose mission is to boost processes of change aimed at the improvement of the sociopolitical, economic, and cultural conditions of immigrants, refugees, forcibly displaced people, and their descendants in the Dominican Republic and the Caribbean and to promote intercultural dialogue, respect for human rights, and solidarity among peoples. They operate on the principle of participative democracy, inspired by the mission of Companñía de Jesús: "Serve in faith and the promotion of justice." The Companñía was founded in the Dominican Republic in 1997.

Chago, a Haitian, walking and carrying a hatchet on his shoulder, and I imagined him chopping my sister up to eat her. I grew up believing that Haitians ate people, even though I did not even know what Haiti was. Back then I did not understand that the hatchet was the tool Chago used to make a living, working all day in the hot sun on the rice plantations in the northern part of the country. In reality, the idea that Haitians were wild cannibals remained with me throughout my childhood.

Sadly, these kinds of stories were not limited to my childhood. The last weekend of October 2012 I attended a family lunch. After we finished eating we started singing and joking. One of the "jokes" asserted that Haitians "stink" more than pigs. The joke told the story of a group of scientists that had complained about pigs' bad smell, but the pigs had complained about Haitians' body odor.

That same month, on October 1, 2012, I had read the following story in a national newspaper:

> The administrator of the green space, Ensache Evaristo Morales, known as Andrés, has denied the free use of this space to the Haitians who live or work in the zone of the Dominican capital; this decision is not protected under any law or regulation. The location has space to play baseball, football, and other sports. Andrés, who says that he has dedicated his whole life to promote sports among youth, expresses his rejection toward people from the neighboring nation. "The Haitians, I do not accept them here," he said during an interview. (Sosa 2012)

These and many other stories that could be told testify to a social imaginary in the Dominican Republic regarding Haitians that ascribes to them the following characteristics: Haitians are ugly, cannibals, dirty, stinky; they do not know how to speak; they are invading the country, stealing jobs from Dominicans; they are criminals, illegal immigrants. In short, the Haitian is someone to be feared, someone from whom one needs to defend oneself. On the other hand, to Haitians and especially to Haitians living in the Dominican Republic, the Dominican is an abuser, an oppressor, someone who may require Haitians to defend themselves, meaning that one must be extremely careful.

The intercultural Bible reading gathering of Haitians and Dominicans had a practical goal that arose from resistance to making the other into a monster, an enemy to be feared. Our reading process hoped to create a space where it would be possible to meet each other on equal terms, assuming that we shared the same human dignity and rights. The proj-

ect was aimed at transforming perceptions of the other in order to begin
to create new social relations that respect the dignity and rights of all
human beings. Therefore, it hoped to accomplish the transformation of
old imaginaries so that we could understand each other and be capable
of knowing each other as equals who together could construct a shared
existence. The latter was the motto from the campaign of the Jesuit Services for Refugees in the Dominican Republic advocating intercultural
relations (2008–2011).

## Location: Island of Hispaniola

The Island of Hispaniola is the only island in the world shared by two
independent countries. The Dominican Republic and Haiti share a 76,192
km² island, of which the Dominican Republic covers 48,442 km² and Haiti
27,750. The countries are divided by a 276-km frontier containing four
access points between the two countries; the rest of the border is made up
of sparsely populated mountains.

The relationship between the two countries has frequently been tense
due to political and social issues; however, both the commercial relations
and the movement of people from one side to another have been fluid
throughout the history of the two nations. Haitian migration to the Dominican Republic resembles that of other movements in the world today: it is
brought about by profoundly exclusive systems that drive humans out if
their homelands in pursuit of a better quality of life. Often the migrants
have to defy seemingly impassable frontiers.

Due to its geopolitical location, the Island of Hispaniola is a common
layover for many travelers and migrants. The Dominican Republic is well
known as a site where migrants are in transit to other locations. It is cal-
culated that more than two million Haitians live in the diaspora, mainly
in the Dominican Republic, Canada, and France. There is also a large
Dominican population abroad, mainly in Puerto Rico, the United States,
and Spain.

The migrant Haitian population in the Dominican Republic has
grown in the past years due to a number of factors: the growth of the sugar
industry in the Dominican Republic, Haiti's economic and political situation, and the earthquake in January 2010. Around three hundred thousand people lost their lives and approximately one million lost their homes
during the earthquake. It is estimated that around one million Haitians
reside in the Dominican Republic.

The majority of this population are vulnerable, since they do not possess the required legal documents to remain in the Dominican Republic. In many cases, they also lack identity documents from their country of origin. The vulnerability of the migrant Haitian population in the Dominican Republic is augmented by their being in a country where blackness is rejected, where their history reinforces the idea of conflict and of a Haitian invasion.[3]

In its 2007 report, Amnesty International pointed out that the way that laws and immigration policies in the Dominican Republic have been applied has not been consistent with international human rights. Amnesty International denounces the government employees who frequently apply immigration laws and birth registration rules in a discriminatory manner. The Dominican Republic was condemned in 2005 by the Inter-American Court of Human Rights for denying a birth certificate to two young girls of Haitian descent (the Yean and Bosico case). Amnesty International also revealed that, even though the position of Haitian migrant workers in irregular situations are more threatened, Dominicans of Haitian descent and migrant workers in regular circumstances are constantly exposed to human rights violations as well.

Along with these components of exclusion and vulnerability regarding documentation, a strong expression of anti-Haitian sentiment continues to exist and has frequently produced violence between the two populations. Daily interactions between Haitians and Dominicans are influenced by prejudices expressed through gestures, verbal language, legal discrimination, physical abuse, and even murder. Those Haitians who manage to keep a job in the Dominican Republic are subjected to abuse, insults, and physical violence by their employers; occasionally they are repatriated in order to avoid paying them their salaries.

---

3. This topic is extensively complex and cannot be explained in the present essay. However, as illustration, it has been a year since the Dirección General de Migración has issued residence papers to Haitian immigrants, without any legal or logic reason. The General Migration Law 185-04 states in article 151 a plan of regularization for immigrants, but eight years after this law was issued, the plan is yet to be implemented. The case is no less difficult for the children of Haitians, since access to Dominican nationality is practically impossible for them in the present judicial framework. Furthermore, the discriminatory laws aim at taking away the nationality to those who have legally acquired it.

Anti-Haitian prejudices also affect the sons and daughters of immigrants in the Dominican Republic. A young Dominican of Haitian descent who had difficulties with his documents told us the following: "We, the bateyeros,[4] have been taught that whenever we talk to a white man we need to look at the ground, we can never look them in the eye." Here the word *white* was a synonym for Dominican. We who spoke with him were Dominican, and there were Dominicans in the group with skin color as dark as his. Belonging to an identity rejected in the social imaginary generates an environment of permanent hostility and mistrust. The worst thing that can happen is the internalization of this discrimination, as in the previous example.

The Intercultural Bible Reading Project in the Dominican Republic

Since 2007, the Jesuit Refugee Service includes in its strategic framework at a national level the promotion of intercultural relations between people (see Jesuit Refugee Service Strategic Framework 2007–2011, line 2). This proposal is especially challenging in the case of Dominican-Haitian relations. Jesuit Refugee Service's strategy aims at transforming minds through face-to-face encounters with the other who is different but who also shares the same human dignity and rights.

To achieve this objective, we have developed programs for positive encounters with the other in order to create relationships of mutual enrichment. In this endeavor, we became acquainted with the intercultural Bible reading project and considered it to offer a promising prospect. With this in mind, a pilot project was developed from the Dominican Republic's Jesuit Refugee Service (Centro Bonó) from July 2008 to May 2009 with two groups of fifteen individuals each, one group of Dominicans and one of Haitian immigrants, in Santo Domingo.

As previously discussed, the topic of migration was proposed, and we selected the book of Ruth for our reading. This choice of text involved a deviation from the global intercultural Bible reading process. Obviously, we chose this topic because of the importance of migration in the Dominican society and because the Jesuit Refugee Service had invested particularly in improving the popular mutual perception of the two groups. The

---

4. Name given to people who live in a *batey* (sugar company town), generally Haitians and their descendants.

topic was not articulated at the beginning, but rather the selected reading allowed the topic to surface on its own, in all its complexity.

The book of Ruth was not chosen by accident: it offers a fresh look at the identity of God's people. In a postexilic context with strong religious, political, and cultural powers and with a clear exclusion of groups, especially of women, the book of Ruth, with its metaphorical, open narrative, offers a quest opposed to the established order. It takes the most human aspects from the history of law (levirate law, the role of the gō'ēl, the ears of grain) and places the salvation of totally ignored and discriminated groups, such as foreign women, squarely in the middle.

We set forth with the objective of generating profound changes in the way one relates to those different from oneself through a process of understanding, unmasking one's own prejudices, and having face-to-face encounters with the purpose of mutually enriching and widening the perspective toward new social relationships influenced by respect, dialogue, and acknowledgment.

During the months of July and August, the groups were composed. Later during the month of August, it was possible to start working on the first phase of the project, the reading of the text. The Dominican group could not be organized until September, at which time they began reading the selected text.

The Haitian group comprised fourteen individuals, two women and twelve men, who met every fifteen days during a period of seven months. The Dominican group had twelve members, one man and eleven women, who also met every fifteen days for nine months.

In the first semester of 2009, the intercultural Bible reading project reached an important qualitative level: the groups produced reading reports belonging to the last three stages. These reports were translated into both languages (Haitian Creole and Spanish) with the purpose of supporting interculturality. The confrontation stage opened a path that created space for the encounter with the other group, including all the prejudices and biases. This allowed for a true face-to-face dialogue to take place, a true encounter between the migrant community and the host community.

At the end of the process, there was a day-long intercultural celebration with these first two groups. We reflected on the first part of the encounter, and the members of both groups became acquainted. The celebration also included an academic analysis about migration and interculturality and an intercultural party, in which all the cultural groups from both countries participated. Hans de Wit, the coordinator of the global intercultural Bible project, was also present at the celebration. His expertise in the topic helped contextualize the discourse produced by both Haitians and Dominicans in the reading reports. We were able to have a dialogue: once again we faced our own biases until we were able to reach a real change in perspective in our view of the other.

## The Balance of the Process: A Qualitative Reflection

When the reading process takes place among a small group of friends, the conversation flows freely, without censorship. That is a privileged space for prejudices to become evident and for us to confront ourselves with them. When facing someone unknown, there is an ethical imperative to change our perspective. It is the thesis of the intercultural Bible reading project that, through processes that may take a long time, comparable to the kingdom of God profoundly penetrating a person, it is possible to change a negative image of another that turns the other into a threatening and uncomfortable presence. This assumption was proven to be true in this short pilot project.

The change in perspective for the Dominican and the Haitian groups regarding the other produced remarkable comments and changes in attitudes. We compile here a list of the ones we considered to be the most important.

## Sitting at the Same Table

The image of a group of Haitians and Dominicans sitting around the same table is probably the most powerful symbol of a change in the social imaginary of the relationships between Dominicans and Haitians living in the Dominican Republic.

A young lady from a province of the Dominican Republic who began to participate in the intercultural activities from Centro Bonó spontaneously said: "I used to only know the Haitian that sells nuts, avocado, and ripe bananas in the street, but now I am with them in the groups and we talk, normal." The word *normal* reflects a definitive change in the place that the other occupies in one's social imaginary. The image of a Haitian selling fruits in the streets stands for someone living in poverty, in need of help, barefoot, covered in dust, and wearing old, dirty clothes.

The image the Dominican group had of Haitians was often based on their image of Haitian migrants living on the *bateyes*, who came to work on the sugar plantations, who sell fruit or beg in the streets, or who work in construction. In an abstract way, they knew that Haitians deserved a fair treatment at work, and they were aware that Haitians were exploited: "In construction you work with Haitians because they are easily exploited; they settle for anything" (Ana, Dominican group).

This is why Haitians need help and solidarity. Many in the Dominican group had participated in projects that were aimed at assisting "poor Haitians." Luisa (Dominican group) tells of a time in front of a library when she saw a homeless Haitian with her children in the streets. To go from there to sitting at the same table and to dialogue with each other required a Copernican revolution in the way the Dominicans conceive of the place the other occupies. The dialogue revealed that the Dominican group was not communicating with the group in front of it, but it spent considerable time dialoguing with the "poor Haitian from the *batey*" who needed their charity. In the confrontation stage, an impasse took place in the Dominican group, because they were not used to being questioned directly by a Haitian immigrant.

On the other hand, the group of Haitians residing in the Dominican Republic felt uneasy. Sometimes they reacted by contradicting the statements made about them by the Dominican group; sometimes they defended themselves or became inhibited. In this case, since the members of the group were middle-class Haitian students, their intention throughout the process was to position themselves as different from the Haitians who work at the sugar cane plantations or sell fruit: "what catches my attention is that I observe that everyone in the Dominican group sees and psychologically understands the Haitian migration phenomena *very badly*" (Jan, Haitian group).

That is why sitting at the same table to discuss carries such symbolic value. A face-to-face encounter with the other—not from a higher perspective that minimizes the other but looking at and being looked at without any masks, in one's own vulnerability—generates a new liberating encounter. It is from that vulnerability that human beings find each other, not from a defensive mask of wanting to be stronger and better. Sitting together at the same table created more equality, more understanding, and a more familial perception.

## A New Look at Migration

One of the most controversial topics on the island is that of Haitian migration to the Dominican Republic. The intercultural Bible reading process allowed the topic to emerge freely, reaching a profound level of analysis.

The Dominican group started to recognize that their ideas about Haitian migrants were limited by mainstream representations of "poor Haitians" who work in the sugar cane plantations and live in *bateyes* and that instead Haitian migrants are a diverse population. Recognizing the limitations of their understanding, the Dominicans changed their perception of Haitians. The Dominican group was able to conclude that:

(1) The causes for Haitian migration are numerous: there are financial reasons, but also political, cultural, and social motivations. This opens up a new horizon of understanding for a much more complex reality that rules out simplistic analysis.

(2) Haitians are a diverse people with a vast cultural wealth and distinct social classes and ideologies. As a people they need to be understood in all their complexity.

(3) The Haitian who migrates is not necessarily representative of the Haitian people as a whole.

(4) It is necessary to go to Haiti and learn to know its language, geography, and people (a profoundly transforming idea coming from the Dominican Republic).

(5) The Haitian immigrants are not inferior; they do not beg for charity. Like Dominicans, they want to be treated with respect, and to live with dignity in their own country. When living in a foreign country, they need their human rights as migrants protected: they have a right to migrate.

(6) The Haitian individuals with whom the Dominican group met have hearts, their own histories, wounds, hopes, and faith. This recognition of the Haitians' full humanity brings the previously abstracted prejudices against them into question. It is an invitation to promote face-to-face encounters with the other. We meet each other with the same vulnerability and with the same desire for justice and peace.

The Haitian group also had to rid themselves of their own perception of Dominicans as oppressors. They learned to differentiate among Dominicans: the group they had in front of them were not the immigration agents, border soldiers, or the Junta Central Electoral staff members who denied their children documentation. This generated new possibilities for the encounter that consequently generated profound changes in their perception of Dominicans as a group, including:

(1) The Dominicans are not homogeneous. They do not form a huge, evil, anti-Haitian population. Like Haitians, Dominicans are diverse human beings; though there is much injustice, there is also a great desire to open spaces for fellowship.

(2) By showing themselves to the Haitian group as they are, with their prejudices and vulnerabilities, the Dominican group was open for a change in their own biases, and this created room for a change in the Haitian group's perception of Dominicans.

(3) The Dominican group expressed the desire to welcome and respect Haitians and their human rights, to get to know the immigrants, to learn their language, and to learn more about the people in the process of dialogue.

(4) The Dominican group could represent an existing history of Dominican solidarity with the Haitian people, of Dominican attempts to offer companionship to Haitian immigrants who dream of a decent life.

(5) The Dominican group could become an accomplice of this "agonizing attempt for a decent life." That is why they received an invitation from the Haitian group to join in the struggle and fight for the rights of Haitian immigrants in the Dominican Republic.

The Dominican group invited the Haitian group to see the Haitian reality in all of its complexity. Just as not all Haitian immigrants work in the sugar plantations in the Dominican Republic, so not all Haitians are private college students who can be financially supported by their parents:

> Mercedes (Dominican group): A Haitian at UNIBE[5] is not the same as a Haitian who sells oranges in the street. It [Haitian migration] needs to be seen from all angles and perspectives. There are people with big interests. They [some Haitian migrants] see themselves as well-educated people and others as ignorant, so they do not feel like they belong to that group.

This kind of questioning is important for the Haitian group. It invites them to transform their own representation of Haitian migrants. They were invited to recognize that:

---

5. The Universidad Iberoamericana is one of the most expensive universities in the Dominican Republic, mostly attended by upper-middle and high-class students, as well as a great number of foreigners. It is practically bilingual.

(1) Social inequality exists within both countries.

(2) Each group needs to analyze their own realities with higher levels of complexity, not restricted to what pertains specifically to one's own group.

(3) It is necessary to open up to higher levels of solidarity with those who suffer the most, such as the Haitians living in poverty and the orphans of both nations.

(4) This also implies greater efforts for unity in the immigrant community in the Dominican Republic. These efforts would require the members of the intercultural Bible reading Haitian group not to be ashamed of Haitians living in poverty but to accept the challenge of fighting together for their rights.

(5) In order to share the common longing for better living conditions for all, it is necessary to overcome the tendency to divide the communities and the tendency to create excessive distinctions between "others" and "us."

Many devices have managed to create a social imaginary of fear and rejection toward Haitians in the Dominican Republic. Images such as "peaceful invasion," "labor invasion," "unification of the island," "unstoppable post-earthquake avalanche," create the idea that having Haiti as a neighbor is a constant threat to Dominicans, that Haitians make it harder for Dominicans to find employment, to have access to services, to live in peace, and even to have autonomy as a country.

The intercultural Bible reading process demonstrates that the Haitians who participated in the reading of Ruth 1 simply want to live in dignity in their own land and home: "I want to go back home, I would like to see change in my country, for all Haitians to come together and show the rest of the nations that we can unite" (Roudy, Haitian group). Returning to Haiti becomes a sort of dream, a return to the promised land where they will no longer suffer discrimination or oppression: "One day we too, the Haitian people, will be liberated from all the humiliation that many Dominicans put us through" (Roudy, Haitian group).

There is hope that all Haitian people will unite to achieve a change. Being an immigrant is a temporary phase to them and overcoming that stage is a dream. This is interesting since one could think that a person who migrates does so to find a better life and would find it difficult to return, but the Haitian intercultural Bible reading group had different expectations: "We used to be a country like any other in the world; we need to put an end to this political crisis that is destroying our country. I wish we could go back to our home just like Naomi did," Zenon reiterates.

The Dominican group realized that the members of the Haitian group wanted to return to their land and their people more than anything else. The solution is not as simple as helping them in the Dominican Republic, but it is about a real change taking place in Haiti so that Haitians do not need to migrate in the pursuit of a decent life, but can stay in their home country if that is what they want.

That is really the immigrant's dilemma. While the conditions that pushed one out of one's country remain unchanged, the immigrant cannot return. But the dream is to live in dignity in one's own country. This revelation unmasks the Dominican fear of a peaceful invasion. What Haitian migrants truly want is to live in their own homes in peace. What needs to be attacked is the unfair economic and political conditions that drive migrants out of their country and away from their people.

Another important aspect of the intercultural Bible reading experience is that the Haitian group questioned the Dominican group about their passive attitudes when they see Haitians discriminated against and exploited in the Dominican Republic:

> I congratulate the Dominican group for attempting to get closer to the Haitian immigrants who are struggling. If we work together to fight poverty, if we participate in small group activities—in other words, if the rest of the Dominican people had good faith—they would help migrants, because they could be immigrants too. (Antoine, Haitian group)

The Haitian group asked the Dominican group for solidarity to work on a common cause. This was an important transformation of their initial perception of Dominican-Haitian relations. They concretely request the Dominicans to:

(1) Approach migrants and get to know what affects them in the Dominican Republic.
(2) Advocate for migrant's rights.
(3) Bear witness to the injustices experienced by immigrants.
(4) Join efforts with the Haitian migrant community so that Haitians are treated fairly in the Dominican Republic.

The specific composition of each group produced differences in perspectives on social matters, gender issues, and spirituality; however, the groups did discover numerous things in common. Why then put so much emphasis on the differences? For example:

(1) The Bible is held sacred by both groups. In the Bible, they found a resource that allows them to reflect on their own reality and the reality of the other. It also provided an opportunity to ask questions and open new, more hopeful paths to transform Dominican-Haitian relations.

(2) By studying the passage, both groups recognized that migration is a common reality for both Haitians and Dominicans. Therefore, Haitians and Dominicans must see each other "as two wings of the same bird," as two good neighbors who share a common concern, in order to explore together why their peoples migrate, as well as to pay attention to the struggles of Haitian, Dominican, and other diaspora populations who claim their human rights as migrants.

(3) There were references of shared historical processes. Javier, for example, referred to the French and Spanish colonization and to the plantation system on both sides of the island.

(4) Both countries on the island have the same geography and are exposed to the same risks. When this intercultural Bible reading experience took place, the earthquake in Haiti had not occurred yet, but after this experience there was a heightened awareness of the need to work together to find solutions to the problems held in common. Also, there has been an increase in the amount of initiatives that try to establish ties between the two communities, and there is a higher demand for Creole courses since the Dominican population has a greater need to communicate with its neighbors.

Finally, both groups made a commitment to work for a change in the social imaginary of Dominican-Haitian relations. The following statements were shared by the participants:

1) "We need to ask ourselves what we are doing to improve our situation, because someone is critiquing you to help you move forward" (Jan, Haitian group).

(2) "I wonder if the reality they see would be the same reality we would see if we lived there" (Javier, Dominican group).

(3) "Our education system makes us drag along the racial problem from childhood. Historically, we have been influenced by those

beliefs [the Dominican is white, the Haitian is black], we always want to refuse the reality that, as a nation, we are black. The drums are our true identity. We need to reflect upon how we manage our interaction with Haitians in a different way and resist discrimination" (Javier, Dominican group).

(4) "This process, especially the second stage [confrontation] has made me reflect about how we relate with people from our personal perspective and [that we need] to *look with the other's eyes*, to wonder and ask before acting: how do you feel about this situation and how do you experience it. First, reach a consensus instead of going forth based on the ideas we regularly believe and take for granted" (Leticia, Dominican group).

(5) "The process needs to be expanded in order to have a 'conversion' and to change stereotypes. We have a different posture and more sensibility, but how would a different group react to this?" (Ana, Dominican group).

(6) "I am curious, it is a culture that is so close to us but I do not know a lot about it, and I now feel motivated to learn about it and understand it" (Alina, Dominican group).

(7) "One understands discrimination when one experiences it; discrimination is not experienced the same way when one lives in one's own homeland as when one is away from it" (Luisa, Dominican group).

## Conclusion

The hegemonic discourse of rejection of Haitians in the Dominican society has been built up throughout history, and it is within that same history that it can be changed. The intercultural Bible reading groups are small and insignificant in number in comparison to all the Dominican and Haitian people who should go through this process, but we believe that this experience slowly produces deep changes within the participants. The lives of the people who participated were shaken up several times during the process. We are convinced that the project is an initiative that opens multiple roads for social change, especially in the social imaginary, where changes operate slowly.

The intercultural Bible reading experience coordinated from the Jesuit Refugee Service at Centro Bonó offered an intercultural encounter with the other, destined to meet him or her, to unmask one's own prejudices, and to proceed toward new modes of relating to each other through newly acquired intercultural perspectives. It produced "a life-changing experience for those who assumed it as a step towards a learning process that integrates the other through dialogue and face-to-face encounters" (De Wit 2009, 11).

The intercultural Bible reading experience aims to produce changes not only at the level of reasoning but in daily attitudes and relationships. Therefore, the project is aimed at producing profound changes in the everyday life of the participants and new social relationships that would make possible the development of a culture of peace.

The intercultural Bible reading project has achieved its purpose in the pilot experience of Dominican-Haitian relations:

> The intercultural reading of the Bible places the biblical readers in a space where it is not possible to stop questioning and attempting to answer questions asked by others, questions about one's life history in light of the biblical text, questions about one's context in relation to others, questions related to one's responsibility for the other, for the world and the great asymmetry that characterizes it. This is why the intercultural Bible reading has everything to do with identity, the encounter, responsibility, and the common search for truth and liberty. (De Wit 2009, 11)

If the first experience already generated such results, it is to be expected that the project has a profoundly liberating potential in many other relations where reconciliation is needed. Thus it continues to be valid, and the challenge to continue its implementation remains open. This proposal was expressed by the participants themselves: "Carmen wants us to expand the space and for it not to be shut down, wanting for us to have an encounter at least every trimester"; "Antonia states that reading the Bible in this way has enriched her life" (report by the Dominican group).

## References

Adames, Digna María. 2012. *Interculturalidad como horizonte y praxis.* Revista Estudios Sociales 155. Santo Domingo: Centro Bonó.

Cook, Elisabeth. 2011. *La Mujer como Extranjera en Israel: Estudio Exegético de Esdras 9–10.* San José: Universidad Bíblica Latinoamericana.

Esquirol, Joseph. 2005. *Uno mismo y los otros.* Barcelona: Herder.

Fornet Betancourt, Raúl. 2001. *Transformación intercultural de la Filosofía: Ejercicios teóricos y prácticos de Filosofía Intercultural desde Latinoamérica en el contexto de Globalización.* Bilbao: Desclée de Brouwer.

———, ed. 2006. *La Interculturalidad a Prueba.* Revista Concordia. Serie Monografías. Aachen: Missio.

———. 2009. *Tareas y propuestas de la Filosofía Intercultural.* Revista Concordia. Serie Monografías 49. Aachen: Missio.

Freire, Paulo. 1970. *Pedagogy of the Oppressed.* Translated by Myra Bergman Ramos. New York: Herder & Herder.

Jesuit Refugee Service Strategic Framework. 2007–2011. Unpublished paper. Santo Domingo: Centro Bonó.

Ramírez, José Enrique. 2004. *El Libro de Rut. Ternura de Dios frente al dolor humano.* San José: Universidad Bíblica Latinoamericana.

Santo Domingo Intercultural Bible Reading Reports. 2009. Centro Bonó.

Sosa, Mario Esteban. 2012. Acento Newspaper October 1. Santo Domingo. www.Acento.com.do.

Wit, Hans de. 2009. "Intercultural Bible Reading Handbook." Unpublished manual. Vrije Universiteit Amsterdam.

## 25

## ON BECOMING A FAMILY IN SOUTH AFRICA: INTERCULTURAL BIBLE READING AS A TRANSFORMATIVE POWER IN SOCIETY

*Louis Jonker*

Introduced with the liberation of Nelson Mandela from prison in February 1990, the new political dispensation in South Africa has brought an acknowledgment of the diversity of cultures, languages, and religions. The infamous success of the apartheid ideology as a social engineering process lay exactly in the area of cultural refutation in which the social interaction was regulated in terms of four "racial" groups—so-called white, black, colored, and Indian people. More recently, the acknowledgment of the diversity of culture, language, and religion has become one of the building blocks of the new democracy. Generally speaking, South Africans have come a long way since 1990 in the acceptance of the *multiculturality* of society.

An empirical-hermeneutical research project conducted in the Western Cape of South Africa during recent years, however, argued that a move toward *interculturality* has not necessarily taken place alongside the acceptance of multiculturality. Although there are small-scale examples that disprove any generalization, it can be confidently stated that the South African nation does not see themselves as a "family" (see Tutu 2004).

In a small-scale project, researchers at the University of Stellenbosch intended to make a contribution to this situation (see Jonker 2007).[1] The present essay provides a description of the empirical process followed and a report on the results. By our mode of reporting, we also intend to

1. The project was funded by the National Research Foundation of South Africa (NRF), a fact we gratefully acknowledge here. Views expressed here are, however, the responsibility of the author.

contribute to the development of the fairly new field of empirical herme-neutics, particularly advocated by Hans de Wit at the Vrije Universiteit Amsterdam (see De Wit 2004b). The essay concludes with some observa-tions on how intercultural Bible reading can function as an alternative transformative power in the process of fostering interculturality in (South African) society.

## A Small-Scale Observation

### The Participating Groups

The empirical study in this project was conducted as case-oriented qualita-tive data analysis: "the non-numerical examination and interpretation of observations for the purpose of discovering underlying meanings and pat-terns of relationships" (Babbie 2004, 370). A case-oriented analysis aims at an in-depth understanding of the role of variables in a limited number of cases.

Eight groups were identified to participate in the empirical phase in 2008–2009. Although the sampling in this qualitative research did not have the intention of being representative of the cultural diversity in South Africa, the groups were chosen to establish at least three kinds of cultural interaction that are representative of the Western Cape Province. The dis-tinction made here between "White Afrikaans" and "Colored Afrikaans" still reflects the racial past of this country and indicates that differences or variations in culture exist between the "White" population and the "Colored" population. Although the majority of these two groups share a common mother tongue, the apartheid ideology has engineered social differences between them that exist until today. This reality was, therefore, taken into account in the selection of groups. The following sections pres-ent the "cultural pairs" involved in the study.

### Xhosa–White Afrikaans

Two pairs—groups 1 and 2 and groups 3 and 4—participated in this cate-gory. The following biographical information for each group was included in the computer analysis.[2]

---

2. The qualitative analysis of the empirical data was done using computer soft-

## Group 1

Cultural group: Xhosa

Language: isiXhosa

Group size: > fifteen members

Gender: mainly male

Age distribution: majority thirty–fifty years

Group history: < five years

Reason for existence: need for teaching (all being lay pastors in their churches)

Association in congregation: place of teaching/education; Bible study group; place of training for mission

Place of meeting: school in township

Denomination: majority African Independent Churches, a few Methodist or Pentecostal Churches

Education: on average between primary and secondary school level

## Group 2

Cultural group: White Afrikaans

Language: Afrikaans

Group size: six–ten members

Gender: female and male (equal distribution)

Age distribution: majority > fifty years

Group history: newly established

Reason for existence: for the purpose of the project

Association in congregation: desire to cross borders to other believers

Place of meeting: home of participant

Denomination: all Dutch Reformed Church of South Africa

Education: on average tertiary level education

## Group 3

Cultural group: Xhosa

Language: isiXhosa

Group size: six–ten members

Gender: female

Age distribution: majority twenty–forty years

## Group 4

Cultural group: White Afrikaans

Language: Afrikaans

Group size: six–ten members

Gender: female and male (majority female)

Age distribution: majority < thirty years

ware Atlas.TI Version 5.0.66. For more information on this software, which was especially designed for qualitative analyses, see www.atlasti.com.

| | |
|---|---|
| Group history: > ten years | Group history: newly established |
| Reason for existence: women's association in congregation | Reason for existence: a previous group disbanded, and some of those group members started with a new group |
| Association in congregation: place of teaching/education; Bible study group; place of training for mission | Self-identification of group: pastoral support group for one another |
| Place of meeting: in church of their congregation | Location: home of one participant |
| Denomination: all Uniting Reformed Church of South Africa | Denomination: majority Dutch Reformed Church of South Africa |
| Education: on average between primary and secondary school level | Education: on average between secondary and tertiary level education |

## White Afrikaans–Colored Afrikaans

One pair—groups 5 and 6—participated in this category.

| **Group 5** | **Group 6** |
|---|---|
| Cultural group: White Afrikaans | Cultural group: Colored Afrikaans |
| Language: Afrikaans | Language: Afrikaans |
| Group size: six–ten members | Group size: eleven–fifteen members |
| Gender: female | Gender: female and male (majority female) |
| Age distribution: on average forty–sixty years | Age distribution: on average forty–sixty years |
| Group history: group established over twenty years ago; although membership has changed, the original core of the group is still present | Group history: < five years |
| Reason for existence: need for Bible study | Reason for existence: initiative of congregation to give spiritual support in difficult times |

Association in congregation: Bible study group; place of learning/education; pastoral support group for one another; outreach to community

Association in congregation: pastoral support group; prayer meeting; outreach to community

Place of meeting: home of a participant

Place of meeting: in church building

Denomination: majority Dutch Reformed Church of South Africa

Denomination: majority Uniting Reformed Church of South Africa

Education: on average tertiary level education

Education: on average between primary and secondary school level

## *Xhosa–Colored Afrikaans*

One pair—groups 7 and 8—participated in this category.

**Group 7**

Cultural group: Xhosa

Language: isiXhosa

Group size: eleven–fifteen members

Gender: female and male (majority female)

Age distribution: on average > fifty-five years

Group history: <five years

Reason for existence: need for training/education; initiative of church

Self-identification of group: place of training/education; Bible study group

Place of meeting: public hall

Denomination: mixed but majority African Independent Churches

Education: on average between primary and secondary school level

**Group 8**

Cultural group: Colored Afrikaans

Language: Afrikaans

Group size: six–ten members

Gender: female and male (equal distribution)

Age distribution: > fifty-five years

Group history: > ten years

Reason for existence: after spiritual experience during Pentecostal services

Association in congregation: prayer group; pastoral support group; outreach in community

Place of meeting: church building

Denomination: mixed but mainly from Protestant tradition

Education: on average between primary and secondary school level

The eight groups functioned individually in three of the four phases of the empirical study (see below). An intercultural experience was present in phase 3 when the groups met their partner groups for a joint discussion of the biblical text they had studied in the previous phase.

Procedure

*Initial Meeting with Group Leaders*

In order to facilitate ownership and participation by the different groups, the group leaders were invited to an initial meeting where the aims of the project were explained. It was emphasized to the group leaders that the aim would not be to investigate intercultural Bible reading as such, but rather to establish whether intercultural Bible reading contributes to the development and facilitation of the prerequisites for a successful intercultural exchange.

Although the broad outline of the procedure was communicated to them by the project leader, the group leaders had the opportunity to work out the fine details and were also involved in the final selection of the biblical text to be studied. After the project leader had suggested five different texts from the Old and New Testaments related to the themes of family and hospitality (see below), the group leaders chose Luke 11:1–13. The group leaders found it fascinating that Jesus's parables of the friend visiting at midnight and the father providing for his son are connected in the Gospel of Luke with the Lord's Prayer. They were used to reading the Lord's Prayer in isolation from the parables and therefore thought that this text would provide a stimulating discussion. This initial and preliminary reaction of the group leaders to the text was later confirmed in almost all the group studies.

Another matter that received attention in the initial meeting with the group leaders was the ethical aspect of the research. The group leaders confirmed their group's consent to participate in the project and made an agreement with the project leader that no individuals or groups would be identified in the reports of the research results. Group leaders were assured that all group members would be invited to a concluding meeting where the results would be presented to them before any publication thereof. The concluding meeting could provide as well the opportunity to celebrate their interculturality jointly.

## Training of Research Assistants

In order to achieve comparable results, three research assistants were trained to assist the project leader with the semistructured interviews and reporting. The assistants finalized the questionnaires for the interviews together with the project leader and agreed on a protocol for reporting on the group sessions (see explanation of phases 1 and 4 below). It was agreed upon that the coding of the reports in Atlas.TI would be done by the project leader alone in order to ensure consistency.

## Phase 1: Semistructured Interview

As explained in the previous publication on the project (Jonker 2007), two concepts served as axes around which the semistructured interviews could be designed. The concepts of "family" and "hospitality" were chosen because: (1) the concepts are often metaphorically related to fundamental issues in the Christian faith; (2) they are well known in all three cultural groups involved in the project; and (3) they can be applied to different spheres of life, from personal to ecclesial and public spheres.

The first semistructured interview was conducted by a research assistant (or project leader) and took place in the venue where the respective groups normally met. In a few cases groups decided to do phases 1 and 2 during one extended session. The structure described below was followed.

Introduction/Biography/Self-Identification

Start off by sharing something about your group. Who are you? How do you see yourself?

Family
(1) What do you understand under the term *family*?
(2) How does a "family" function?
(3) Would you describe your church as a "family"?
(4) Would you describe the South African nation as a "family"?

Hospitality
(1) What is "hospitality"?
(2) Do you think your group/the church should show "hospitality"?

(3) Do you think that "hospitality" is a characteristic of the South African nation?

The discussions took place in the mother tongue of the group members, either Afrikaans or isiXhosa. Two of the assistants who could speak isiXhosa—one as a mother-tongue speaker and the other as a fluent second-language speaker—were asked to conduct the sessions of the three isiXhosa-speaking groups.

The research assistant (or project leader) summarized the reactions according to the guidelines agreed upon during the training session. Key words and/or phrases were noted and a thorough description of the reactions of group members was provided. These reports were then prepared for inclusion in the Atlas.TI database as a first set of primary documents; for ethical reasons they were not shared with the partner groups. In order to make them accessible for other researchers, the two isiXhosa-speaking assistants prepared the reports of the three isiXhosa groups in either English or Afrikaans.

*Phase 2: Bible Study of Luke 11:1–13*

The groups were requested to convene a second meeting to read or study Luke 11:1–13 in the way in which they usually would conduct their meetings. The newly established groups were asked first to have a short discussion to agree on how to structure their meeting and how to treat the text. Groups were also asked for permission to videotape the sessions for the purpose of showing their respective partner groups in phase 3 how they conducted their session. All groups consented to this.

There was a rich variety of modes of handling and interpreting the biblical text in the group sessions. The mode of engaging with the text correlated with the biographical self-description provided by each group. Those groups who focused on Bible study as such employed various methods of textual analysis and made use of different Bible versions, commentaries, and other reference works. Groups who saw themselves primarily as prayer groups used the text as a starting point for their prayers and supplications. Support groups scrutinized the text to find suggestions for how they should support one another or reach out to the community.

Although those readings and/or interpretations of the biblical text documented in the video recordings produced interesting results, they did not form the focus of the present analysis (see above and Jonker 2007), and transcriptions were therefore not included in the Atlas.TI database.

## Phase 3: Intercultural Meeting with Partner Group

The groups linked as "cultural pairs" were required to convene at the home or the usual meeting place of the other group. In this way the groups were exposed to one another's cultural environment and had the opportunity to experience the hospitality of the host group. All cultural groups acted as hosts as well as guests. The hosts were asked to receive the partner group in their usual manner of receiving guests.

At these meetings each group had the opportunity to share with the partner group their biographical and self-identification information. Thereafter, they shared their readings of the biblical text orally, with some excerpts of the video recording shown by the assistant (or project leader). In cases of isiXhosa–Afrikaans pairs, the conversation took place in the common language, English, or an interpreter assisted to bridge the language barrier. Two of the four meetings were followed by a social event.

## Phase 4: Semistructured Interview

In the fourth phase another structured interview was conducted with each group individually according to the following protocol, with the tested aspects mentioned in parentheses in each case:

(1) What was your experience of the joint meeting? Do you think it was successful or not? What do you mean when you say it was successful or not? (*experience of interculturality*)

(2) In which respects are you similar to and/or different from the other group? (*experience of continuity and/or discontinuity*)

(3) Did your knowledge of and insight into the other group change through this contact? If so, how and why? (*change of knowledge and/or insight*)

(4) Did your attitude toward the other group change during the contact? If so, how and why? (*change of attitude*)

(5) Did you experience hospitality during the meeting? If so, describe this. (*changes in understanding of hospitality*)

(6) Do you think that you belong to the same "family" as the other group? (*changes in understanding of family*)

(7) What was your experience of the whole process followed in this project? (*evaluation of participation in project*)

The reports were again compiled by the assistants similarly to phase 1 and included as a second set in the Atlas.TI database.

## Concluding Plenary Meeting

A final plenary meeting of all participants was organized at the Faculty of Theology, University of Stellenbosch. Transportation was provided for those members who needed it. Nearly 70 percent of the participants attended the meeting. Only one group was not represented at all.

The plenary meeting had three aims: (1) to celebrate the intercultural experience by a short devotional, a major part of which was devoted to singing in the different languages and styles of the cultures represented; (2) to inform the attendees of the research results of the analysis of the interview report; and (3) to join in socializing afterward.

In general this last meeting was perceived as positive by all participants; many groups requested to continue the contact with one another on different levels. Unfortunately, it was not possible to conduct a follow-up investigation into whether further contact across cultural boundaries indeed took place. However, from some personal conversations, it appears that individuals encountering one another again outside the context of the project felt a bond, because they had this shared experience.

## Coding of Reports

### Coding Strategy

Based on the experience in a similar project (see De Wit 2004a), a deductive and an inductive approach were applied. The main categories of codes, as well as the first sublevel, were preconceived according to the research design of the empirical study. The codes used within each category were formulated during the process of coding. The richness of the material, therefore, guided the heuristic process interactively.

Sixteen reports (two sets of eight each) were analyzed. A comparison within each set revealed interesting continuities and discontinuities between the groups. However, the main aim was to compare the reports from the first set with those from the second set (interviews before and after the intercultural meeting, respectively). Based on the theoretical discussion provided in the previous essay (Jonker 2007), the following "before/after" patterns were regarded to be significant: (1) a change in knowledge of the other; (2) a change in motivation to cross boundaries; (3) a change in skills to communicate across boundaries; (4) a change of attitude toward the other; and (5) prominent and recurring themes.

*Codes and Code Clusters*

The list of codes provided in the appendix gives the main and first sublevels of the coding process. Coding was done by the project leader alone in order to ensure consistency. The categories—in capital letters—and codes were originally formulated in Afrikaans. The English version provided in the appendix represents a translation of the original category and code list. The following main code clusters were distinguished:

01 BIOGRAPHICAL DATA
02 UNDERSTANDING OF "FAMILY"
03 UNDERSTANDING OF "HOSPITALITY"
04 ROLE DURING INTERCULTURAL MEETING (PHASE 3)
05 EXPERIENCE OF INTERCULTURAL MEETING (PHASE 3)
06 (DIS)CONTINUITY WITH PARTNER GROUP
07 KNOWLEDGE OF THE OTHER
08 ATTITUDE TOWARD THE OTHER
09 EXPERIENCE OF "HOSPITALITY"
10 EXPERIENCE OF "FAMILY"
11 GENERAL EVALUATION OF PARTICIPATION IN PROJECT

The responses coded in clusters 01, 02, and 03 were gained from the first semistructured interview held with each group before the intercultural exposure; those coded in clusters 05 through 10 were the outcome of the second semistructured interview after the intercultural exposure. Apart from the two key concepts "family" and "hospitality," those prerequisites for intercultural communication highlighted in the theoretical reflection were used as heuristic keys for the analysis of the amount of transformation that took place (see particularly code clusters 07 and 08). Code clusters 05 and 06, which documented the reaction to the intercultural meeting, were cross-checked against the role of the group (see code cluster 04, either as host or guest) in order to see whether the context within which the meeting took place influenced the outcome in any way.

*Cross-Tabulation*

The biographical data were not cross-tabulated with the other reactions since the present qualitative analysis was not concerned with those correlations and since the sample size was too small to make any meaningful observations. The interpreters of the data had no intention of arriving at conclusions about the typical experiences and/or reactions of different cultural groups.

## Summary of Observations

The qualitative analysis of the data delivered interesting and variegated results. The exercise confirmed again that a small-scale qualitative study does not necessarily deliver representative data, but it does facilitate a deep understanding of community dynamics. Before summarizing our findings in the next main section, we will first list some noteworthy observations.

Prominent and Recurring Themes

The reports on the first structured interviews produced a rich understanding of the terms *family* and *hospitality*. Thirty-two different codes were used to describe the groups' understanding of "family"; the majority of these codes occurred more than once. The definitions of "family" offered most frequently included:

- It is a place where we support one another. (5 responses)
- It is a place where we share our problems and support one another. (5 responses)
- It is a place where diverging views are possible. (5 responses)
- It is a place where individuals live and act for the benefit of one another. (5 responses)
- It is a place where the relationships are built by means of love. (5 responses)
- It is a place where blood ties bind us together. (4 responses)

Only twelve codes were needed to describe the groups' understanding of "hospitality"; a discernible repetition of themes occurred, the most prominent including:

- It means that we care for one another. (8 responses)
- It means that we make space for one another. (8 responses)
- It means that you are prepared to sacrifice something of yourself to others. (7 responses)
- It is related to love and acceptance. (7 responses)
- It requires trust among people. (4 responses)

These responses in the first interview confirmed that the key concepts of "family" and "hospitality" were well suited to this empirical research. Participants related well to these concepts, and the concepts proved to be useful heuristic tools to investigate the participants' experience of interculturality in South African society. The following subsection provides a description of how they analyzed the South African situation in terms of these key concepts.

Experience of the South African Nation in Terms of "Family" and "Hospitality" before the Intercultural Meeting

Before the intercultural exposure, when the participants were asked whether they experienced the South African nation as a family, they responded overwhelmingly negatively. Only three codes were needed to mark the few positive responses. Across the spectrum of biographical profiles, five responses noted the South African nation to be a family, because the common faith in Christ crosses over divisions and boundaries. One person found South Africa to be a family on account of shared experiences in this country, while another isolated response indicated that it was because of being welcoming toward foreigners and outsiders. Two further positive codes were needed to capture two responses that expressed the dream of South Africa being a family ("it should be an ideal for the South African nation to be like a family"; "prayer can bring reconciliation"). Nonetheless, the discussions on this topic were overwhelmingly negative. Ten codes were necessary to express the fact that the participants mostly did not see the South African nation as a family:

- The South African nation is not a family. (5 responses)

- The apartheid past still causes division. (4 responses)
- Cultural differences cause division. (3 responses)
- Internal relationships among people should improve. (3 responses)
- The present government again causes divisions. (2 responses)
- Some people still think in racial categories, and this causes division. (1 response)
- Some still do not trust black people. (1 response)
- Mind shifts are necessary. (1 response)
- We do not have enough commonalities. (1 response)
- We do not know one another well. (1 response)

The same pattern of response emerged from the discussions on whether the South African nation is hospitable. Only four out of fifteen codes marked positive responses ("normally, tourists experience South Africans to be hospitable"; "there are examples of hospitality despite poor circumstances"; "knowing one another eliminates fear"; "to be prepared to help one another eliminates fear"). Two of these positive responses referred to the issue of fear, which will be discussed further below. The negative responses to this question were coded as follows:

- Fear impedes hospitality. (10 responses)
- Distrust impedes hospitality. (10 responses)
- A lack of *ubuntu*[3] impedes hospitality. (3 responses)
- People do not want to be challenged. (2 responses)
- Individualism impedes hospitality. (2 responses)
- Hospitality should have boundaries! (2 responses)
- Hospitality is not expressed in deeds. (2 responses)

---

3. The term *ubuntu* reflects a Southern African ethic or humanist philosophy. The term is often connected to the Nguni proverb *umuntu ngumuntu ngabatu* ("a person is a person through other persons"). Many different definitions of the term exist, and many different traditions of its origin are given. See the good summaries in Gade 2011, 2012. Desmond Tutu once described *ubuntu* as follows: "One of the sayings in our country is Ubuntu—the essence of being human. Ubuntu speaks particularly about the fact that you can't exist as a human being in isolation. It speaks about our interconnectedness. You can't be human all by yourself, and when you have this quality—Ubuntu—you are known for your generosity. We think of ourselves far too frequently as just individuals, separated from one another, whereas you are connected and what you do affects the whole World. When you do well, it spreads out; it is for the whole of humanity"; see Ubuntu Women Institute 2012.

- Poverty impedes hospitality. (2 responses)
- Socioeconomic differences impedes hospitality. (1 response)
- Politics impede hospitality. (1 response)
- Hospitality is often experienced exclusively within one's own culture group. (1 response)

The above examples show how prominent the role of fear was in the responses of participants. The concerns of people on this issue are reflected in the following statements:

- Fear keeps people apart.
- Somebody told about something that happened near the "Bantu" township of Khayelitsha where her car broke down. She was terrified when that happened. Everybody passed her until a car with two black men stopped to help.
- Many colored people still fear black people.
- It seems as if white people also fear others, because almost every house has a high wall built around it.
- Hospitality would require that we break down all these fears and that we start trusting one another.
- There are unfortunately some examples of xenophobia.
- We fear our neighbor rather than care for him.
- Refugees come to South Africa due to their bad circumstances, but we also treat them badly because we fear that they will take our jobs.
- Many people are security conscious, and high fences separate us from one another.
- Presently, it is very difficult to act hospitable in South Africa, because it is simply too big a risk, for example, to give somebody a lift or allow somebody whom you do not know into your home.

The interviews conducted before the intercultural experience reflected a high level of multicultural awareness but a low level of intercultural appreciation. The prominence of fear and distrust confirmed our hypothesis that South Africans have come a long way since 1994 in acknowledging the multiculturality of our society. Though the acceptance of multiculturality is an asset, the fostering of interculturality is still a desideratum. The past is still with us, and cultural differences still cause divisions in our society.

Experience of Intercultural Meeting

In the next phase of the project, intercultural exposure was experienced on three levels: (1) exposure to one another; (2) exposure to one another's reading of Luke 11; and (3) exposure to one another's context (four out of the eight groups crossed boundaries to be hosted by their partner group). Some of the guest group members reacted negatively to the exposure—ranging from initial hesitancy to staying away from the intercultural exposure meeting. Although members who were opposed to the intercultural exposure, and particularly to the idea of visiting their partner group in their context, did not explain their attitude and responses to the research team, the personal interviews with the group leaders revealed some of the motives for staying away. Again, the issue of fear featured strongly in those instances. Nonetheless, the majority, including even some who were very hesitant, responded positively when asked in phase 4 about their experience of the joint meeting. A rich variety of reasons was provided for their positive experience, as summarized in the following:

- There was spontaneity in the meeting.
- We were enriched by their being different from us.
- We could go and visit them.
- We experienced love and affection.
- We experienced unity/faith/love across boundaries.
- They came to visit us in our context.
- The joyful tone in our partner group.
- We could share our interests and life stories.
- It was a real meeting.
- We experienced community.
- We developed respect for the other group's Christian witness.
- We could pray for one another.
- We could trust one another.
- The meeting encouraged us.
- There was open discussion.
- We could meet one another as equals.
- It was a very nice conversation.
- We could get to know one another.
- We could learn from one another.
- The Spirit was among us.

What was remarkable in these responses is that they occurred across the cultural spectrum of participating groups and that they were independent of the role of the group as host or guest.

(Dis)continuities Noticed

The groups were asked to analyze their own positive experiences in terms of the similarities and differences between themselves and the other group, and they noted the following:

- We could connect with one another.
- We all love the Lord.
- We all take God's Word seriously.
- Our zeal for the Lord.
- Love for one another.
- Communal supplication in prayer for the needs of society.
- We discuss the same issues.
- We have a shared sense of humor.
- We share a common language (coming from the cultural pairing of "Colored Afrikaans" and "White Afrikaans").

The list of dissimilarities noticed by participants is long:

- Differences in socioeconomic circumstances
- Different approaches
- Different ways of engaging with the world of our experiences
- Different type of venues for group meetings
- Different ways of sitting in the group (coming from the cultural pairing of "Colored Afrikaans" and "White Afrikaans")
- Different levels of spontaneity
- Their childlike commitment to God
- Differences in self-understanding as a group
- Different cultures of singing
- Differences in clothing
- Different compositions of groups (in terms of male and female)
- Differences in race
- Differences in body language
- Language differences
- Different compositions of families

- Prayer has a different function

What is not reflected in these coded responses, however, is the appreciation of and even fascination with the differences reflected in the body language and tone during the feedback sessions. Differences were acknowledged and listed, but with appreciation and respect for "the other."

Changes Noticed

The second structured interview probed the groups for changes. Two
questions were to prompt feedback on this matter:

- Did your knowledge of and insight into the other group change
  through this contact? If so, how and why? (*change of knowledge
  and/or insight*)
- Did your attitude toward the other group change during the contact? If so, how and why? (*change of attitude*)

The questions relate to indications in literature that intercultural communication is facilitated by these factors. Marlene Kool (2004) has, for
example, identified certain conditions for a change of perspective in intercultural communication on the basis of her analysis of reading reports
compiled in the intercultural Bible reading project, "Through the Eyes of
Another," initiated by the Vrije Universiteit Amsterdam. The first factor
Kool mentions is "Attitude toward the partner group," observing: "The
most important condition for successful intercultural communication is
the attitude people have when they enter the process. This attitude can
make or break the process" (363). De Wit (2004c, 506–7) also presents a
brief summary of basic conditions found to facilitate successful intercultural Bible reading:

> Attitude: Successful interaction requires a basic attitude of openness,
> trust, vulnerability, and willingness to criticize oneself and to see one's
> own faith insights as relative. This attitude applies to the reading process
> of the group itself as well as to the interaction with the partner group.
> Confrontation is allowed, but it must be based on trust. Not every type
> of motivation is productive. Motivation especially focused on acquiring
> new knowledge, focused on challenges, turns out to be enriching.
> Knowledge: The group needs basic knowledge of how cultures oper-
> ate. Differences between groups soon become apparent, but it requires

knowledge to see how these cultural differences can be identified and understood.

Insight: Insight into the group's own reading attitude and interpretation method is also important. This insight enables participants to discover the connection between the method and the results of their interpretation and that of the partner group.

All groups responded overwhelmingly positively to the two questions. In terms of "attitude," the following codes were used to express the richness of the responses:

- Our appreciation for them increased.
- We got to realize the similarities between us.
- The Bible changed our attitude.
- The contact brought greater spontaneity and openness among us.
- It brought a sense of closeness.
- Our misconceptions of the others changed.
- There was more trust among us.
- We also realized the differences between us.
- We can learn from them.

The changes of knowledge and insight were described as follows:

- Our biases disappeared. (8 responses)
- Our knowledge of their life world increased. (5 responses)
- Our respect for their dedication increased. (4 responses)
- We got to know one another's ways of life.
- We discovered our shared (spiritual) needs.
- We gained more insight in their faith and how they worship.
- We need more time together and exposure to one another.
- Our appreciation for their integrity increased.
- Knowledge of one another made us more confident in the presence of one another.
- We discovered one another as human beings.
- We can now communicate with others.

The code that attracted the most responses was the one that acknowledged that the members' biases toward their partner group disappeared:

- Although some of us thought that the white people will always try to show off their cleverness, we discovered that we were quite comfortable to communicate with them.
- Exposure to the white people helped us to break down our biases.
- We always think of crime when we think about townships, but there are good people as well.
- They did not show over self-confidence which can be intimidating. We expected them to be overly self-confident.
- They seemed to be a bit shy to talk during reporting, while we thought they would be saying a lot of things that we should learn.
- We did not really know how white people think about God and their faith. We always thought that they were very different from us and that they do things and believe things that we don't.
- We got to know them as sincere and they didn't just pretend in their response to us. They were not "whitewashed."
- All of us have stereotypes of other people. Our knowledge of them and therefore our expectations of them were mainly formed by the relationships we have with black people in a work situation.[4] Even if they are equal to us, we normally still experience distance between us. But the trouble the group took to come and visit us on a Sunday afternoon and the way they dressed brought a totally different impression.

Experience of the South African Nation in Terms of "Family" and "Hospitality" after the Intercultural Meeting

In the second structured interview, the groups were again probed as to their experience of the South African nation in terms of the concepts "family" and "hospitality." Interestingly, a significant shift had taken place from their initial understanding of and responses to these concepts. After the intercultural meeting, the following expressions of the experience of hospitality were given:

- We experienced love and friendliness. (8 responses)
- Our meeting created openness toward one another. (8 responses)

---

4. The reference here is to the context of having domestic servants, mainly from the black communities, working for white people in their homes.

- Our common faith creates hospitality. (4 responses)
- The others opened their world for us. (4 responses)
- The meeting created the feeling that we fit into the South African nation.
- We discovered our commonalities.

In response to the question why they experienced a sense of family, the following codes emerged:

- We share Christ with one another. (8 responses)
- We are coworkers for Christ.
- The meeting strengthened our sense of family.
- Our church ties make us a family.
- There are more similarities than differences.
- We all bear the image of God.

These positive responses contrast dramatically with the negative understanding of the South African nation in terms of "family" and "hospitality" observed before the intercultural exposure. Although the project included only a single intercultural Bible reading meeting, one may state with confidence from the data presented above that a significant transformation took place in all groups, as well as in the individual group members, in their openness toward and understanding of "the other."

## Summary of Findings

A Lack of Interculturality in South African Society

The hypothesis that this research took as a point of departure—that although there is an awareness and even an acceptance of multiculturality in South African society, interculturality is still lacking—was clearly confirmed in this study. I have argued that the concepts of "family" and "hospitality" could serve as instruments to probe into the understanding and experience of interculturality in society. Although all participating groups had a multifaceted understanding of these concepts and valued a sense of family and hospitality highly in their own spheres, they found these concepts incongruent with how they perceived the South African nation. The data described above have shown that the experiences of participants before the intercultural exposure were dominated by fear and a lack of knowledge of "the other." The rich quotations on these issues revealed that fear manifested itself in all cultural groups who participated, albeit in different forms: "fear that foreigners will take your job"; "fear that your property may be stolen by others"; "fear that others may endanger your life"; "fear that you will be humiliated by others"—all facets of a dominant factor that impedes interculturality in society. Furthermore, it emerged that fear is often associated with a lack of knowledge of "the other." Many misconceptions of "the other" emerged during the process of intercultural exposure. It was established that exposure to "the other" on the basis of a common Bible reading and an increase in knowledge of "the other" break down fear. Breaking down fear in turn facilitates an experience of interculturality.

A Common Denominator

Reading the Bible together should not be underestimated in this process. This exercise was not merely utilized as a research tool in the empirical research, but served as well as an instrument that underlined the common denominator of a shared Christian faith.[5] In the planning phase of the project, the value and potential of this common denominator among all cultural and racial groups in South Africa was sensed. The mutual sharing of the groups' interpretations of Luke 11 was therefore deliberately included in the intercultural exposure. The participants' discovery of a shared faith provided the condition within which interculturality could be facilitated. Without this common denominator, the experience of intercultural exchange might have been very different. This point underlines how important it is to realize that the Bible as the holy Scriptures of the Christian community is a powerful transformative instrument in South African society. Intercultural Bible reading exercises should therefore be considered as an alternative way of facilitating interculturality in South Africa.

---

5. According to the 2001 census, 79.7 percent of the South African population confesses to the Christian faith. One may postulate that the same potential for interculturality might be found in other faith traditions in South Africa. However, Islam (with 1.5 percent) and Hinduism (with 1.3 percent) have their constituencies in specific racial and cultural groups, and they do not cut across boundaries in the same significant way as Christianity does.

## An Inclusive Hermeneutic

In the first contact, the groups were informed that they would read Luke 11 in their own manner of conducting a Bible study, but that they will then also have to share their reading with a partner group at an organized meeting. This strategy was deliberate in order to create interaction between what Rainer Kessler (2004, 452–59) called bipolar and multipolar understanding. The readings within the groups took place according to the conventions and theological convictions of the group itself. The intercultural meeting created the opportunity to share that reading and to give account of it in a multicultural environment. The hermeneutical dynamic created by the interaction changed the inner or exclusive hermeneutic of each group into an inclusive hermeneutic. The group members responded in terms of continuities and discontinuities of their respective readings of the text within the context of a shared Christian faith. Intercultural interaction within the context of a common denominator created the space within which an inclusive hermeneutical understanding could start developing, and within which a movement from bipolar to multipolar understanding could take place (see also Jonker 2001, 2005, 2008).

## The Importance of Crossing Boundaries

It has become clear how important the issue of crossing boundaries was in this exercise. Crossing boundaries was achieved not only by means of the multicultural pairing of Bible study groups, but also by the physical crossing of boundaries when one group visited the other in the latter's context. This was particularly significant in the South African context, where, if not political realities, economic realities still keep people apart. People are not acquainted with the physical world of "the other." It has been described above how important the factor of fear was in the act of crossing boundaries. In one case, only three members of the guest group turned up to accompany the research team to their partner group's context that was in one of the "black" townships. Interculturality has a physical dimension. The impact of the intercultural experience was so much greater for those who crossed boundaries and left their own safe spaces to enter into the world of "the other." An increase in knowledge of "the other" and changes of attitude were facilitated tremendously by the physical crossing of boundaries, which was part of this empirical study (see also Riches 2004).

On Becoming a Family

The metaphor that guided this research was the rich understanding of "family" and "hospitality" present among group members. Remarkably, in the first interview, groups were more than willing to admit they experience the dynamic of family and hospitality in their own personal spheres and in their churches. The overwhelmingly negative response to whether they also thought of the South African nation as a family was indicative of the lack of interculturality in society. The changes in knowledge of and attitude toward "the other" facilitated by the project at least opened the perspective that the South African nation may indeed show traces of becoming a family. The common denominator within the Christian community, the discovery that many of their fears were unreal and irrational, and their realization of a common fate, brought the awareness of the South African nation becoming a family into view.

## Conclusion

Although this project harvested its data from a small-scale observation in a limited number of Bible study groups, the qualitative analysis of the rich feedback from the two structured interviews enabled the researchers to penetrate those feelings and attitudes reflecting the participants' experience of interculturality. With the help of the two concepts "family" and "hospitality"—concepts whose understanding cuts across cultural boundaries and that can be extended from the family sphere to church and society—the research team was able to describe the "before" and "after" patterns in terms of knowledge of, insight in, and attitude toward "the other." Whereas there was a prominent awareness of the multiculturality of the South African society before the intercultural intervention of the research project, this multiculturality was mainly experienced in terms of differences from "the other." The intercultural meeting on the basis of a shared Bible study created significant changes. The changes observed in the responses emphasized not only how important intercultural exposure is, but also how valuable it is in South African society that the Christian faith cuts across cultural and racial boundaries.

There was certainly no pretension in this project that the research changed society significantly. Only a small number of people were involved, and, apart from the plenary feedback session, no follow-up was organized. One may even doubt whether the transformations observed in this project are sustainable. However, the project confirmed clearly that the tool of intercultural Bible reading has transformative power. It also confirmed the importance of a statement made in the initial theoretical phases of this project: "Interculturality is ... a personally driven strategy to overcome 'othering'" (Jonker 2007, 483). Churches, but also other governmental and nongovernmental stakeholders, should take note of this valuable tool for changing South African society into a "family."

## References

Babbie, Earl R. 2004. *The Practice of Social Research*. 10th ed. Belmont, CA: Wadsworth.

Gade, C. B. N. 2011. "The Historical Development of the Written Discourses on Ubuntu." *South African Journal of Philosophy* 30:303–29.

———. 2012. "What Is Ubuntu? Different Interpretations among South Africans of African Descent." *South African Journal of Philosophy* 31:484–503.

Jonker, Louis C. 2001. "Towards a 'Communal' Approach for Reading the Bible in Africa." Pages 77–88 in *Interpreting the Old Testament in Africa*. Edited by Mary Getui, Knut Holter, and Victor Zinkuratire. Nairobi: Acton.

———. 2005. "'Contextuality' in (South) African Exegesis: Reflections on the Communality of Our Exegetical Methodologies." *OTE* 18:637–50.

———. 2006. "From Multiculturality to Interculturality: Can Intercultural Biblical Hermeneutics Be of Any Assistance?" *Scriptura* 91:19–28.

———. 2007. "On Becoming a Family: Multiculturality and Interculturality in South Africa." *ExpTim* 118:480–87.

———. 2008. "Living in Different Worlds Simultaneously; Or: A Plea for Contextual Integrity." Pages 107–19 in *African and European Readers of the Bible in Dialogue*. Edited by Gerald West and Hans de Wit. Leiden: Brill.

Kessler, Rainer. 2004. "From Bipolar to Multipolar Understanding: Hermeneutical Consequences of Intercultural Bible Reading." Pages 452–59 in De Wit, Jonker, Kool, and Schipani 2004.

Kool, Marlene. 2004. "Intercultural Bible Reading as a Practical Setting for Intercultural Communication." Pages 360–76 in de Wit, Jonker, Kool, and Schipani 2004.

Riches, John. 2004. "Intercultural Hermeneutics: Conversations across Cultural and Contextual Divides." Pages 460–76 in De Wit, Jonker, Kool, and Schipani 2004.

Tutu, Desmond. 2004. *God Has a Dream: A Vision of Hope for Our Time.* Johannesburg: Rider.

Ubuntu Women Institute USA. 2012. "Ubuntu: A Brief Meaning of the African Word 'Ubuntu.'" http://uwi-usa.blogspot.be/2012/01/ubuntu-brief-meaning-of-african-word.html.

Wit, Hans de. 2004a. "Codes and Coding." Pages 395–434 in De Wit, Jonker, Kool, and Schipani 2004.

———. 2004b. "Intercultural Bible Reading and Hermeneutics." Pages 477–92 in De Wit, Jonker, Kool, and Schipani 2004.

———. 2004c. "Epilogue." Pages 506–7 in De Wit, Jonker, Kool, and Schipani 2004.

Wit, Hans de, Louis Jonker, Marleen Kool, and Daniel Schipani, eds. 2004. *Through the Eyes of Another: Intercultural Reading of the Bible.* Elkhart, IN: Institute of Mennonite Studies

## Appendix: Code List

01 BIOGRAPHICAL DATA
    01.01 DENOMINATION
    01.02 CULTURE GROUP
    01.03 LIVING AREA[6]
    01.04 REGULAR PLACE OF MEETING
    01.05 SIZE OF GROUP
    01.06 GENDER OF PARTICIPANTS
    01.07 AGE PROFILE OF PARTICIPANTS
    01.08 AGE PROFILE OF GROUP
    01.09 REASON FOR INITIAL GROUP FORMATION
    01.10 SELF-DESCRIPTION OF GROUP
    01.11 LANGUAGE USED IN GROUP
    01.12 LITERACY LEVEL
02 UNDERSTANDING OF "FAMILY"
    02.01 DEFINITION OF "FAMILY"

---

6. In order to ensure anonymity, the area names are not included here. The area numbers do not necessarily correspond to the group numbers given above.

02.02 CHURCH / CONGREGATION AS "FAMILY"?
02.03 SOUTH AFRICAN NATION AS "FAMILY"?
03 UNDERSTANDING OF "HOSPITALITY"
    03.01 DEFINITION OF "HOSPITALITY"
    03.02 CHURCH / CONGREGATION AS HOSPITABLE?
    03.03 SOUTH AFRICAN NATION AS HOSPITABLE?
04 ROLE DURING INTERCULTURAL MEETING (PHASE 3)
    04.01 Guests
    04.02 Hosts
05 EXPERIENCE OF INTERCULTURAL MEETING (PHASE 3)
    05.01 INITIAL EXPECTATIONS
    05.02 GENERAL EXPERIENCE
    05.03 REASONS FOR GENERAL EXPERIENCE
06 (DIS)CONTINUITY WITH PARTNER GROUP
    06.01 CONTINUITIES
    06.02 DISCONTINUITIES
07 KNOWLEDGE OF THE OTHER
    07.01 CHANGES OBSERVED
    07.02 TYPES OF CHANGES IN KNOWLEDGE OBSERVED
08 ATTITUDE TOWARDS THE OTHER
    08.01 CHANGES OBSERVED
    08.02 TYPES OF CHANGES IN ATTITUDE OBSERVED
09 EXPERIENCE OF HOSPITALITY
    09.01 EXPERIENCE
    09.02 REASONS FOR EXPERIENCE
10 EXPERIENCE OF FAMILY
    10.01 EXPERIENCE
    10.02 REASONS FOR EXPERIENCE
11 GENERAL EVALUATION OF PARTICIPATION IN PROJECT
    11.01 EVALUATION
    11.02 THE FUTURE

# 26

# AN INTIMATE REVELATION:
# READING LUKE 15:11–32 WITH ADOLESCENTS

*Taggert E. Wolverton*

In 2009 a pilot project was launched to determine whether adolescent readers could benefit from the process of intercultural Bible reading in ways similar to those reported by adult readers. The focus of the research with the adolescents also attempted to measure whether the reading process would be catalytic to the spiritual growth of the participants. For the purposes of the study, the concept of spiritual growth was originally defined along axes that included a deepened sense of belief, an observable increase in theological knowledge, and an increase in the amount of Christian activities. Due to the small size of the study, the expectation was not to prove a causal link between intercultural Bible reading and spiritual growth as defined in this way, but to open an investigative space that would allow a snapshot to be taken of adolescent participants and any changes which might appear within these dimensions. In 2010 the research was expanded to include fourteen participating groups from Europe, North America, South America, and Asia, and by February of 2012 ten of the groups had completed their exchanges to the point that the data could be examined for signs of spiritual growth along the lines of the project's focus. The project generated over 173 primary documents of backgrounds, transcripts, and other reports, many of which were multiple pages in length. The materials from each group were compared along the time line of the group's participation to look for signs of change in the participants' spiritual maturity.

It soon became apparent that in several instances the participants in the adolescent study revealed clear signs of spiritual growth, even though those signs did not readily line up with the originally proposed, more structured methodological construct based on Stark and Glock's dimensions of religiosity (1968, 14–16). In the following, I will elaborate on the presence and the power of these documented revelatory moments that appeared in the experience of the majority of the groups. These will demonstrate how engagement in the intercultural Bible reading process moved the participants further along the axis of spiritual maturity, not by increasing their theological vocabulary or the frequency of activity in their local communities of faith, but by leading them into new insights about the text, themselves, and the other groups.

## Learning to Read the Bible Differently

One of the characteristics of intercultural Bible reading is that it opens up the interpretive process such that there is space for other voices to be heard. The normally individualistic procedure of constructing meaning necessarily changes when practiced in the presence of others. Because at the beginning of the process each group must have an initial interpretation decided upon and owned by all members, the opportunity arises for new insights from the other participants even before the first reading report is exchanged. In some groups, in this initial process the members already saw a change in their understanding of the biblical text as they talked with their fellow group members.

In one group from the Netherlands, two members experienced how, even in the discussions at this initial phase, there is the possibility of changing perspective toward the text:

> M: That it doesn't matter how far you stray from the path, that's … if you come back and are truly sorry for what you've done then you can always be welcomed back into open arms.
> B: But it could be that you're always welcome back with open arms anyway because definitely the kid was repenting, but before he even got there to tell his father he felt sorry for what he did the father was already welcomed him back.
> T: How, what do you mean?
> B: Well it says here … [reading] when he finally came to his senses he said to himself at home even the hired servants have food enough....
> And then it says so he went to his father and while he was still a long way off his father saw him, his father saw him coming. Filled with love and compassion, he ran to his son and embraced him and kissed him. That's already there, that already shows that he really welcomed him back even

though he didn't even know about the repentance. He wasn't even told, the son didn't even tell him that he was sorry about it.[1]

The statement of the first adolescent initiated the response of the second, and moved him from a suppositional stance ("But it could be") to a more definitive statement ("That's already there, that already shows"). Later on in that same group's first meeting there is another instance of a shift due to one of the members' questions. It is clear that the discussion motivates the different participants to interpret the text in a way other than they had before:

Ti: I'm wondering why does he come back, is it for, because he understands that he needs food or something?

T: Yeah, that's right because when you're talking about forgiveness, is that, because your question I think is that … why he, what does he come back for, is it for the food, for, right, is that your question?

Ti: Yeah, because he decides to go back when he has nothing and he sees that at home they, well, I don't know how to say….

Tr: Nah, it's a good question. You have to ask, I think you're asking the right question, why is it now that he's gone back? You know, I mean, we know why he's where he's at today, why he's lost everything we know what he did, but why is he going back? Is he going back for forgiveness or is he going back simply because it looks like a better place than he is now? That's a great question.

M: It doesn't even matter why he goes back as long as he does go back. Well….

B: He realized he was better off there.

T: No, I think that's legitimate too. Does it matter? In this parable, what's it speaking to? Because it is presented where he's not, he's not saying….

M: He threw away his pride so that he would go back so he loses something as well. He doesn't only gain from it.

Tr: Yeah, I think that's right as I think about more because of what he says in verse 21. I think he says it further up too. But I think he gives us an indication of what, of why he's going back. Not, it's not simply, "Oh it's better for me" but probably that as well but he realizes that he's sinned. And he says it to himself and he says it to his, I think he says it further up….

Ti: Yeah, he says it to himself.

T: I know but that's a good question though, Ti, because….

---

1. Crossroads Group, 2009. "Crossroads Reading 1 Transcript" (Amsterdam).

Tr: It could be he's just trying to play him.

T: Because he says in 17 at home, when he finally came to his senses he said to himself at home even the hired servants have food enough to spare. And here I am dying of hunger. I will go home to my father and say....

Tr: Yeah, not "and feel."...

T: Father I have sinned I'm no longer ... please take me on ... so here I am dying of hunger is his last thought.

T: Hmmm. That's interesting. So then that makes me go back and wonder again about, since it finishes with the sticking point on the older son, you know, what does that mean? In other words, it's not focused, I think by what you're saying, it's not focused on just that front, right, the story could have stopped right there. So it goes on to the older son.

Tr: I think maybe for us to understand it we need to, it says in the, at least in my translation, the beginning of chapter 15 it says now the tax collectors and sinners were all gathered around to hear him but the Pharisees and the teachers of the law muttered, "This man welcomes sinners and eats with them." Then Jesus told them this parable and he tells three different parables of lostness. So if you think about it in that why did he tell this parable of the lost sons to tax collectors and Pharisees, what was he, what message was he trying to tell them specifically?

B: That ... come back to God or Jesus, then be forgiven.

T: Everyone has equal treatment.

M: Especially in this case if the group also left and then came back he would also receive these....[2]

Many shifts are apparent as the group moves through discussing the younger son's motivation; the end result is that the participants end up with a different interpretive perspective on the text than that with which they began. A group of adolescent girls from Vietnam and China asked a similar question during their first meeting; that question became an important catalyst for several later discussions as they continued to wonder about the younger son's motivation for coming home:

> S: Well and I know that, we're done with questions, we're really done, but it may have been you who said that it was also about forgiveness and that's an interesting, you said, but was he really ... he was asking for forgiveness but was he just hungry? And at the same time we may not know that, but

---

2. Crossroads Group, 2009. "Crossroads Group Reading 1 Transcript" (Amsterdam).

I'm, in my heart it makes me thankful that if I've done something wrong I can try to make it right and go to God to do it. I may not be able to fix it by myself, I may need his help, but at least there's a place to make a turn to try to make it right. And the only thing, because I've never thought about, you know, was he just hungry, but he's at least having to admit where he said I have sinned against both heaven and you and I'm no longer worthy to be called your son. So he's at least saying I've done this wrong and I need you to help me. And so that apparently was enough.[3]

A group from Malta also saw that their discussion in preparation for the first exchange allowed them to learn from each other's perspectives as they talked through their ideas on meaning of the passage:

G: The younger son is the good one.
R: It's like he's a hero.
M: But in God's eye, every sin is the same if the older son sinned and the second one sinned. If the second one like, for example, make a big sin it's still the same like the first son did.
G: The younger son realized his mistakes. The older one didn't.[4]

While it must be admitted that these are subtle shifts, at the same time they are significant as they demonstrate a change in perspective and an opening of understanding. In one group, one of the participants expressed his awareness of how the process of changing perspectives on the meaning of the parable was a nuanced progression:

T: Did you learn anything from them though, did you think anything different when we talked with them? I think y'all did. There were some different things, some different perspectives … so what does that mean?
J: Well, like with anything, it might even be like subtle changes.[5]

In other cases the shift in perspective on the passage was more obvious and explicit. When a different or new question was offered by a partner group, the receiving participants typically openly acknowledged the new viewpoint and then directed the course of their conversation to consider

---

3. Ben Lippen Girls Group, 2011. "Ben Lippen Girls Reading 1 Transcript" (Asia/International).

4. Malta Group, 2009. "Malta Reading 1 Transcript" (Malta).

5. Gateway Boys Group, 2012. "Gateway Boys Reading 3 Transcript" (South Carolina).

it. When a group of adolescent girls from the United States reviewed the transcript of the group of girls from Vietnam and China and read that their partner group wondered about the younger son's motivation for returning home, their questioning of his impetus became a focal point.

> T: So they're wondering why the younger brother came home—was it just because he was hungry or did he really want the forgiveness?
> A: The fact that they were wondering, the younger brother, if he came home just for food, not really for forgiveness. I thought that was a really good point because I never really thought of that. You just kinda think, yeah he was sorry and all that kinda stuff but like....
> T: It doesn't really say does it?
> A: No. So there like wondering what the younger son's motives really were....
> S: I think she said if he wasn't hungry would he have come home?
> T: So here's my question then ... I guess my question is though if Jesus didn't tell this part of the story, why would that not be part of the story, the parable?
> EG: Because it wasn't really relevant, or it was relevant ... what was relevant was how accepting his family was in taking him back....
> T: So now I'm having another thought. So think about this—so if Jesus didn't make clear what the motivation was, so is it enough to come back for whatever reason, whether it's spiritual, physical need? Never really thought about that before....
> S: Cuz isn't that what the word *repent* is? Turning?
> T: So does it really matter why you come back as long as you come back?
> A: God can use physical, like if you're really sick or something that can get you to turn back to God rather than ... it's however God decides to do it.
> S: I do, well, it was a whole brand new thought to me of would he have come home? So I don't know if that's worth a reply back....
> S: To just say that was a neat thing we had never thought of, having heard the story many times growing up. I mean I've heard this story all my life and never heard that. That's a whole new ... and I have thought of that a lot.[6]

Sometimes the prompting came because someone in a partner group reacted to a small phrase or description in the passage that the receiving

---

6. Gateway Girls Group, 2012. "Gateway Girls Reading 2 Transcript" (South Carolina).

group had not noticed; in the resulting discussion the participants end up validating the new understanding.

> T: How did the group see themselves in the passage? What would you say?
> B: Mostly as the younger son.
> T: Yeah, mostly as the younger son. A lot of pressure. Feeling responsible.
> B: Yeah. Stress with the family.
> A: Like one of the guys expressed it when he said the servant....
> An: He said he'd just kinda go with whatever.
> A: I'd never thought about that.[7]

In another group:

> GB: Something that stood out, the brother was like you've been out with prostitutes. I think that stands out because how he didn't say anything about that one part about how he knows, you know?
> T: Right, so when he comes back, that the older brother says, "Yeah, but dad, he's been hanging out with prostitutes," so how would he know that?
> T: Interesting! I don't know—I don't know if I've ever thought about that.[8]

Finally, a mixed gender group of Japanese adolescents exhibited the clearest example of a change in their understanding of the text after they interacted with their partner group. In their background report they expressed that they were interested in reading the Bible as a piece of Western literature and that they were not affiliated with any church or religious group. In their initial interpretation, they discussed how the main themes for them were endurance, kindness, "love for family," change, and doing good things. After the exchange with their partner group in the United States, however, their thoughts about the passage began to shift, and they remarked several times about the differences between their initial understanding and their new viewpoint that came after reading their partner group's report:

---

7. Gateway Boys Group, 2012. "Gateway Boys Reading 2 Transcript" (South Carolina).

8. Greene Group, 2010. "Greene Group Reading 1 Transcript" (South Carolina).

E: They said the story is about forgiveness, without hesitation … this was very interesting for me; it was not in our report, it was very innovative for me.

E: Firstly they say the central message is God's mercy and forgiveness, and only later they add jealousy and greed … but I do not think jealousy and greed are so central in the story.

[As. reads further on p. 2; when As. reads the sentence "I think the dad kinda represents God," E. is completely amazed.]

E: So the father from the story is God?

A: Yes, this is one of possible, and in this case a highly probable, interpretation.

E: But how do they know it?

A: The leader asks them to focus on the heading, on the title of the story … they say it is called parable.…

E: Do they know how to read the story just because of its title?

A: A parable is one of the genres of biblical narratives. In this kind of stories the reader would look for something … hidden beneath the literal surface. We could say that a parable is a short story with some lesson to be learned, you see? So when they read the title, they know.… However, we were unable to find what is under the surface. I tried to push you in that direction, but you could not see anything. So what we did instead was a literal reading.

E: But I think it is a completely different story now. If the father represents God, you know we said that father is very kind. I think what we should understand from the story is the kindness of God and not the forgiveness!… And how can the father be God when he runs to meet his son?

E: To find out that father represents God was certainly the most shocking thing for me.

Ta: It was definitely the forgiveness, when we read it together I did not think about it at the beginning. Now I can agree with them, but there are definitely more things besides that in that story.[9]

This group's response typifies the kind of opening and maturing in perspective toward the biblical text that indicates spiritual growth and also highlights why a more structured tool, such as Stark and Glock's measures of religiosity, would have difficulty in pinpointing the processes at work in intercultural Bible reading (1968, 14–16). The responses of the participants when examined in detail reflect their developing understanding of

---

9. Yamato Group, 2011. "Yamato Reading 2 Transcript" (Japan).

the plurivocity of the Bible, a component of spiritual maturity. Yet because they do not, and perhaps cannot, express this in exact terms, their finalized understandings—their spiritual growth—become difficult to place on a clearly defined scale that measures a change from one point to another. Several of the participants changed their understanding of the text, and, while at times their expressions of these changes intersected with specific empirical categories, ultimately the measure of their spiritual growth from the intercultural Bible reading process could not be limited to how well they were able to match their expressions of growth to predetermined categories. Rather, it was in the communal and conversational space that intercultural Bible reading creates where these changes in perspective about the text surfaced.

### Learning to See Oneself Differently

Another indication of spiritual growth that manifested itself more easily in the spaces between the fixed categories was the way in which the participants gained insight into themselves through their participation. As they read and exchanged their interpretations, the adolescents expressed that they were learning things about themselves and how they relate to God, the Bible, and the world around them.

Sometimes the differences with the partner groups highlighted a deficit in their own approach to spirituality and commitment to change, such as these comments from a group in the Netherlands show:

> Th: They compare the story to their own life, to their own family lives more than we did. We just look at the part in the Bible and we thought how it had a meaning at that time....
> Y: So it's more interesting for them....
> Y: Well, what I feel right here is that we read texts, we talk about it, we think about it, but we don't really ask ourselves how we can change it in our real life, in our own life. We say, "Well, this is how it happens over here, this is how it goes in Holland," but we're not keen on changing ... and I don't know if they are keen on changing stuff....
> Tr: It makes a connection ... a lot of them said the same thing, why they were there ... to help one another. Maybe their whole focus is more ... if you can call it application-based versus cognitive (knowledge). It's more than "how do I make this real, how do I turn this into an activity."...

Y: Which makes sense though, actually, why would you go to a place to learn stuff if you can't really use it?[10]

That the following participant's partner group was not composed of Christians gave a new insight into how God can use anything or anyone to bring fresh awareness and understanding:

S: But I think for me personally, that question you just asked, does that change anything knowing that now they're not Christians, is.... I still learned from them and their questions really actually changed some of my whole thinking about that story that I'd never thought of before. So it just shows me just to be open to new ideas and learning from whoever God wants me to learn from.[11]

In other instances, when the participants applied the specific dynamics of the parable's story to their own life situations, they gained insight and perspective on their own circumstances and attitudes due to the catalytic influence of the text. Quotes from several groups show this dynamic:

GIR: I feel like I fit the older brother, too, because I get extremely jealous of my little brother. He's home-schooled so he's with my parents all the time he gets special attention. I mean I don't know if it's the fact that I'm a little bit older but I mean the thing is I don't get to spend time alone with my parents and my little brother N. gets to spend every day alone. I think it's special when I get to spend that alone time and I don't get that very much. So he's just a perfect student, he does all this stuff, and I feel like I have to try really hard to match up with that.[12]

Tr: Because ... I see myself in here. I don't know if you see yourself in here, but I see myself in here a bit. When you're working hard for something, you're trying to do the right thing and someone else gets rewarded not for what you've done but for what they've done and you're thinking, "I'm over here working my tail off," and then you're so, I'm so prideful, angry, upset about it I can't even go in to the party. I don't even care, I can't even be part of that. I'm not going to do that.[13]

10. Crossroads Group, 2009. "Crossroads Reading 2 Transcript" (Amsterdam).
11. Gateway Girls Group, 2012. "Gateway Girls Reading 3 Transcript" (South Carolina).
12. Brookwood Group, 2009. "Brookwood Reading 1 Transcript" (South Carolina).
13. Crossroads Group, 2009. "Crossroads Reading 1 Transcript." (Amsterdam).

One of the girls compared it to an everyday situation at school. She worked hard to finish a certain assignment on time, even though it meant that she had to make long hours and skip some social activities. Later at school she found out that not all students had finished the piece. The teacher reacted mildly and gave them more time to work on the assignment. This girl got angry both at her fellow students who did not work as hard as she had done and at the teacher for not punishing the "lazy" students. She could feel why the eldest son got angry at his father.[14]

> Al: I can think of an instance when I was younger, I'm talking like second grade, and I'm in this class. These two kids were always doing bad stuff. They're always getting the class in trouble and they would get the whole class in trouble instead of just those people and so then our teacher wanted us to, wanted the class to, decide if we should forgive them or not. And I remember me specifically saying I don't think we should let them because this is what they did and this is what they deserved. And then now I think about it…. Yeah, I remember that, I remember the two kids' names—T. and F. Yeah. I remember how I wasn't showing God's love and grace….
> T: Why do you think that made such a mark?
> Al: Because how God has shown us grace and forgiveness us for everything we've done and then it's like that one thing, oh, I know the parable but I forget, it's in the back of my mind, how God loves us and how we should show the same love and forgiveness to other people.[15]

Finally, when the participants were given an open-ended opportunity to describe their experience of the project through the means of a second survey, several of their comments reflected the fact that they had changed due to their involvement. Responses included the following:

> "Cool, interested, help me to be more open."

> "Very interesting, and fun to see their perspectives in life and God. Also helps me understand their cultures and life. Do it again!"

---

14. Oldemarkt Group, 2012. "Douwe Reading 1 Transcript" (Oldemarkt, Netherlands).

15. Gateway Boys Group, 2011. "Gateway Boys Reading 1 Transcript" (South Carolina).

"AWESOME! I have learned a lot of new things and it has been great to gain another perspective that I have not even thought about before."

"Helpful understanding the Bible."

"Interesting and eye opening to see how something I always thought of in one way can be thought of in a different way."

"Interesting. It really changed my view on how I view things in the Bible/ world."

"A culture shock."

"Informative and wonderful for me."

These statements highlight that the intercultural Bible reading process served as a medium through which self-insight and transformation became possible for many of the participants. Regardless of whether they ultimately chose to completely internalize the new ideas or perspectives with which they were confronted, which would involve an investigation beyond the scope of this study, it was in this opportunity for a clash between their view of self and the principles in the parable or their partner group's interpretation that they experienced greater insight into their own spirituality and so demonstrated spiritual growth as they responded with openness to these fresh realizations.

## Learning to See Others Differently

Another indicator of spiritual growth that came to the fore in several of the groups was an increasing ability to see from the perspective of their partner group members and to factor that new awareness into their experience of the exchange. In many instances, this ability came through the recognition that their partner group had a different approach to reading the text than they did, and ultimately this realization moved them to try to understand why those differences might be there.

T: Is there is a difference in the way the group in Bolivia reads the Bible … or does it feel similar?

M: I think … they question more … when we discuss we say what we think about it we don't ask questions … [we say] what we think is the right answer.
Tr: Why do you think that is? Is that cultural or … ?
Th: They compare the story to their own life, to their own family lives more than we did we just look at the part in the Bible and we thought how it had a meaning at that time….
Y: So it's more interesting for them….
Tr: Maybe it's … a different time … maybe here there's still very much … an expectation that the land gets divided and they could really identify….
T: So you see that they do more of looking at the text, interacting with their life with the text and circumstances and we tend to do more of … this is just what it means…. Which way do you like better?[16]

Sometimes the circumstances of the other group prompted a sense of identification. For a group of boys in the United States, the discovery that church attendance was mandatory for their partner group, made up of boys primarily from China who were studying in the United States, created a feeling of empathy and awakened a sense of injustice:

B: Well it's almost like, it's kinda like a complicated situation because they're being forced to do something that they, that's like, when you're forced to go to school you don't like going to school. If you're forced to go to church you're not going to like it. You know, if it's like a mandatory … like you have detention afterwards, of course you just want to get it over with, you're not….
A: I don't like that at all, especially when you're, like B. said, being forced. Even if you might like it if you're not being forced it puts a damper on things and you get that rebellious kind of feel because you just don't want to.[17]

Another striking result was the way that the adolescents frequently saw themselves as similar to their partner groups who were actually from a significantly different culture. Several of the American groups, the Maltese group, and the Asian groups identified with their partner groups on the basis of their perceived similarities, and that identification was then

---

16. Crosroads Group, 2009. "Crossroads Reading 2 Transcript." (Amsterdam).
17. Gateway Boys Group, 2012. "Gateway Boys Reading 3 Transcript." (South Carolina).

woven into the groups' discussions when it came time to compare their interpretations of the text:

> T: Problems that they wrestle with, what did you hear?
> A: Jealousy and issues between family, like maybe brothers and sisters.
> T: Yeah, which, I think that sounded pretty familiar. Which is interesting that teenagers from a completely different culture, it's not American culture because it was done, the gals are from China and Vietnam … but sounds similar….[18]

> We felt the partner group interpreted the passage in much the same way as we did … we think they interpreted the text in the same way as us because they are not so very different from us, culturally or socially.[19]

An exchange between an American and a Japanese group, however, shows the most dramatic instance of how the adolescents learned to see their partners differently through the process. When the American adolescents discovered that their partners were not Christians, this became a major source of discussion. In the exchange that followed, there was a definite tension as they sought to understand their Japanese partner's point of view:

> M: But what do you guys think about what we've just read on that page?
> G: They're just blind.
> M: Yeah. They didn't see it. They didn't see what *you* saw.
> B: I'm surprised they didn't see, like, any forgiveness. I was waiting for that when we read the last part. Not any kind of forgiveness … they just concentrated on….
> HF: Remember, guys, that Buddhism is a lifestyle of works, working and working and working so there's so much pride, there's so much honor, you know, these are the things that you hear about when you hear about Japanese lifestyle. You don't hear about forgiveness, you don't hear about second chances or those kinds of things. We … view the world from our viewpoint, from the viewpoint that there is a God in heaven who loves us and cares about us, and so that's why it would be so difficult for them because they don't. Their god is not a god of second chances.

---

18. Gateway Girls Group, 2012. "Gateway Girls Reading 2 Transcript." (South Carolina).

19. Brookwood Group, 2009. "Brookwood Reading Final Letter" (South Carolina).

B: So is that their, is that why she's so amazed? Because she associates Buddha with God? And so she's thinking, whoa, Buddha is actually on earth.
Bo: Buddha's not really a god....
B: But is that what she's associating ... that's what she's thinking....
Bo: Buddha's the enlightened one.
F: He's a teacher.
M: I think B, though, that you're right. That they're starting to understand that the God that's in this Bible that you read is a forgiving God. And that's why you got forgiveness out of the story and that's just not something that they had ever heard before.[20]

Interestingly enough, the Japanese group as well goes through a similar process as they seek to come to grips with their American counterparts' interpretation and perspective:

A: Why do you think they are praying at the beginning?
E: Because they are taught to do it this way? It seems to be important for them, but personally, I do not know how would this influence their reading ... it can be just some kind of a ritualized behavior?
Ta: Perhaps they are showing respect to the Bible this way....
Er: For me it was just a story, but for them it is a holy book, so they definitely must take it differently.
A: Do you think that when they read the Bible it makes them to stop and contemplate about it?
Er: I think they must receive something from it, otherwise they would not do it ... but it is questionable what it is ... and it would be interesting for me to find out what is it....
E: Umm,... their opinion is very ... firm ... they immediately knew what is the story about.... I don't think they will change it because of reading the Bible with us ... they have the access to the Bible for a very long time ... and ... they have somebody else to tell them what is this story about ... I mean authorities from church, their families ... so I do not think they want to be challenged.... I hope they will not be deeply shocked when they find out that we were unable to identify father with God.
T: Maybe they want us to change ... maybe this is the reason they are in the project ... or they are simply searching for a different feeling ... as E. said, they know the Bible by heart, so maybe it is difficult for them to find any novelty there ... and this way our reading may be interesting for them....

20. LaBelle Group, 2011. "Labelle Reading 2 Transcript" (South Carolina).

A: Do you think they will find our reading valuable?
Er: Our opinion does not have much significance for them ... and they maybe become angry with me as I said that the father is a fool.
Ni: Our opinion depends on feelings, emotions—their opinion is based on Christian knowledge, they certainly won't change it because of us....
A: So, you think their reading is very much influenced by who they are, from what background they are coming....
A: Can you find anything in their report to support it?
Er: Prayer at the beginning, background knowledge of Bible, they recognize the type of story.[21]

One of the signs of spiritual maturity is the ability to develop a compassionate understanding and identification with others who hold a perspective different from one's own. Through the process of intercultural Bible reading, a significant number of the group members found themselves challenged to undertake exactly that course as they attempted to see the Bible "through the eyes of another." The resulting changes in their perspectives (and the empathetic ways in which they responded) during the course of this project points to the ability of intercultural Bible reading and exchange to assist in spurring on the spiritual growth of adolescents as it provides the opportunity to mature by means of a significant and meaningful dialogue.

## Conclusion

Spiritual growth is a complex and multifaceted phenomenon, to be sure, and the reality remains that the picture that has emerged from this project's research is admittedly but one facet of an elusive process. Yet at the same time, the above examples are hopeful indications that speak to the ability of intercultural Bible reading to move adolescents further along in their journey of spiritual maturity and to do so in a manner that incorporates their full enthusiasm and energy.

While a more highly structured measurement tool may not have been able to capture accurately the subtle processes at work, the shared space that intercultural Bible reading creates still proved fruitful for the adolescent participants and their spiritual growth. Many of the participants' responses indicated an opening up and maturing in perspective toward the biblical text as they changed their understanding of its possible mean-

---

21. Yamato Group, 2011. "Yamato Reading 2 Transcript" (Japan).

ings. Also, as they read and exchanged their interpretations of the text, they expressed how they were learning new things about themselves and how they relate to God, the Bible, and the world around them. Several of the participants demonstrated their willingness to adjust their own interpretive lenses in order to see the text from their partner group's perspective. Through such shifts as these the adolescent participants demonstrated that they were taking observable steps on the path toward spiritual maturity.

More thought and research is needed to prepare the church's theologians of both the systematic and practical type as they seek to lead in partnership with this next generation of Bible readers, but how comforting to know that even in the uncertainty of today's world, God's word is still accomplishing his desire to bring in a plenteous harvest.

> As the rain and the snow come down from heaven, and do not return to it without watering the earth and making it bud and flourish, so that it yields seed for the sower and bread for the eater, so is my word that goes out from my mouth: It will not return to me empty, but will accomplish what I desire and achieve the purpose for which I sent it. (Isa 55:10–11 NIV)

## Reference

Stark, Rodney, and Charles Y. Glock. 1968. *American Piety: The Nature of Religious Commitment.* Patterns of Religious Commitment 1. Oakland: University of California Press.

# 27

# SHARING MEMORIES, OVERCOMING SOLITUDE: READING THE STORY OF THE WIDOW AND THE UNJUST JUDGE IN SITUATIONS OF IMPUNITY IN LATIN AMERICA (LUKE 18:1–8) (A DIALOGUE AMONG PERU, COLOMBIA, EL SALVADOR, AND GUATEMALA)

*José Vicente Vergara Hoyos*

In this essay I take a brief tour of contextual situations in which Latin American people live in the face of impunity; I also cover some interpretations of the biblical text, taking as a starting point the life of believing communities in our continent. It brings together the sincere and supportive interaction between those who share the same reality of pain, suffering, and the need to make claims so that impunity does not reign, but justice. I deal with three aspects: the impunity in Latin America, the struggle for justice, and the transformation toward an attitude of solidarity.

## Impunity in Latin America

Some realities cannot be covered up by Latin American countries, which have a structural weakness when it comes to administering justice. There have been few or incomplete investigations of persecution and capture, with slow and insufficient hearings that do not give clarity concerning those guilty of the killings and the abuse of human rights. In this context it becomes evident how impunity becomes instituted at both legal and moral levels. In this regard, the commitments of nongovernmental organizations are overshadowed by the accusations from political sectors, who charge them with serving groups of outlaws.

Our project on intercultural Bible reading within the context of impunity reflects that the struggle against the violation of the rights of individuals is overshadowed by factors having to do with their socioeconomic situation. The majority of the victims of violence are poor, economically marginalized, and socially excluded; they are ignorant of their rights as citizens and are among those despised because of ethnic differences, as in the case with indigenous communities. Often peasant and indigenous communities are accused of being in league with the insurgence; this has not only endangered the guarantee of their safety, but also precluded the full backing of their rights. Thus the agencies responsible for achieving justice are continually faced by distortions of evidence, lawsuits, and other vicissitudes on the part of those who expect that crimes and violations will not be prosecuted.

To achieve justice in our continent means that judges should be confronted with the problems involved in providing and ensuring justice. The difficulties undermine the professional sense and honorable task for which the legal system was instituted, but this confrontation in itself complicates achieving the intended objective. Sometimes not only are the judges faced with such problems, but they themselves have also been involved in corruption scandals, having been favored by political or bureaucratic patronage for approving a biased legal process, which not only blemishes the respect for the dignity and memory of the victims, but also raises questions as to the ethical and moral commitment of the authorities themselves.

The success of justice is dependent on the professional and moral responsibility of the judges; otherwise processes end up promoting injustice for future generations to inherit, in which hatred and violence open new breaches in the possibility of a full restoration of socially recognized rights. These breaches breed distrust in the democratic institutions of our Latin American countries, and in turn, discredit the legal order and the consistency of the rule of law.

Thus, in the face of the private interests and hidden powers which for centuries have dominated the region, our Latin American states have discovered that they are unable to fight criminals and masterminds of massacres and of human rights violations of defenseless populations. The power of the state persistently quarrels impotently or finds itself in the contradictory situation of existing parallel to the power held by the mafia in service of drug trafficking, networks of money laundering and arms trafficking, paramilitary groups or terrorists who finance themselves by the kidnappings, as well as existing parallel to right-wing or left-wing political forces who reject and kill opponents.

Amid such contexts, the request for the longed for and hoped for justice takes different paths. One, among many, is that of the suspicions of links between judges and the networks connected to unjust enrichment, to political corruption, to government interests, to state authorities who suppress those of the judiciary power committed to the truth, whose exercise of their work and the fulfillment of their duty is jeopardized by the fear of being raped or murdered by these same groups.

As our research in Guatemala (see Amnistía Internacional 2002), in Salvador (see Asamblea Legislativa de El Salvador 2010), in Peru (see Asociación Paz y Esperanza 2008), and in Colombia shows, the interference in trials for violations of human rights are dependent on powers parallel to the state authority. This has not only brought about the weakening of democratic structures but also the increase in levels of poverty, displacement, and illegal invasions in suburbs in the big cities, in places where services and plans for urban development do not get into the city's budget plan.

Furthermore, both in the villages and in the marginalized zones of our cities, the clamor of women and orphans for justice continues to resound despite the fact that the lawsuits have been filed away in the court system. Not without reason do our people not only complain about the judges who do not want to do them justice, but they in turn tend to associate justice with the responsible institutions, with the incumbent government, or with the state before whom the victims say that they are not being heard—their claims and cries fall on deaf ears. This in turn not only depletes the confidence that an effective resolution would come from such institutions, but it also proclaims the depletion of hope in a turnabout of justice in our societies.

This goes to the point that freedom, one of the promises that shaped the democracies in Latin America and in Western societies, today runs the risk of being diluted into a fight for justice. However, "the truth will make us free" (John 8:31–32) has been vetoed in courts and tribunals. In this regard, the efforts of truth commissions of our nations in recent decades have made significant and proper progress against the assassinations and human rights violations, such as occurred in Peru in particular with the imprisonment of former president Alberto Fujimori. Nonetheless, such efforts lapse in other lawsuits in other countries of the continent.

In this way, the struggle for justice turns out to be incomplete when it is about calling to memory. The intercultural Bible reading has led us to contemplate a painful spectrum that reveals the other side of the story of the struggle for justice on our continent. Latin American people who are *"crying in the wilderness"* (Isa 40:3–5) testify to their own sufferings and cries, prayers and longings, hopes and deep desires that such situations not be repeated in future generations.

According to Hans de Wit, intercultural Bible reading has become a reading out of pain, "from the wound, from their traumas, like the story of this widow" (De Wit and López 2013, 315). Furthermore, this method accommodates to the reading of the other one, it helps us to learn to know the other one, and especially to discover the true strength of the biblical stories. Centered on readers who may not be erudite, but ordinary readers, in contexts of their personal and community lives, intercultural Bible reading faces us with alterity as a relevant aspect, and with the overcoming of cultural boundaries, seeking an opening for the encounter with the other. It is precisely to these encounters that they refer when sharing about the impunity practiced in their places of origin.

## The Struggle for Justice (Luke 18:1–8)

Taking the text in Luke as point of departure, the participating groups not only ask for the meaning of what is read, but accompany the questions to the text by questions relating to their own particular situations. Thus, the judge in the text may be understood to refer to the state and the agencies directly responsible for the protection of fundamental rights and the administration of justice. In this sense, the support of the community for institutions becomes complementary to the promotion of justice, instead of support that it is obliged to impart.

The interaction of such communities dialoguing about justice and violence suffered becomes an experience of communication between groups within the same continent, a dialogue transcending the cultural, ideological, religious, and contextual boundaries to which they belong. Thus the biblical story of the widow and the judge, besides being an invitation to persevere in prayer, makes them aware of the disinterest of the judge who was apathetic to the cries of those who suffer. The cries of the widow in Luke can bring to mind their own cries. The biblical passage restores the reminder of the extreme necessity of one's rights and warns that justice cannot become the charity of the judge, as one of the groups interpreted.

As shown by the various reports of the groups involved in the dialogue about the text in Luke, the stories of the women participating in the groups resemble the attitude of the widow, who, despite the difficulties, perseveres to obtain for her family the benefits that were due. From this perspective the interpretation of the text allows a woman a better understanding of her own situation, which in turn comforts and inspires women who identify themselves with the widow.

The text not only causes the participants to interact with contexts similar to those narrated in the Gospel, but also allows them to identify with the two characters in the story. In this manner, the dialoguing communities bring the story close by; it relates to their own lives; they reenact it when they, on the basis of their faith, read into it the rights denied and thus arrive at a continuous and persistent claim for achieving justice.

Nonetheless, for some groups this dialogue points out their inability to draw out internalized, vivid experiences of pain. The group from Peru, for example, warned the group *Semillas del Reino* (Seeds of the Kingdom) in Bogotá that they interpreted the text by taking as point of departure different categories than their own, with which they could not agree; besides they had formulated additional questions and of delayed in giving response to the reports (De Wit and López 2013, 158–59). This presents a situation in which the confrontation of interpretations suggests that the delay in sending the reports was related to the need to "process the history of violence in their own lives before being able to communicate about it with strangers" (2013, 160). This demonstrates that reading a text together equips those who participate in this communitarian reading for an articulation of the process of pain and suffering, but which in turn counts on a believing community that will accompany them and listen to them.

For one of the paired groups, justice is part of the commitment of their own actions:

> God gives us justice through our actions.
> We have to insist on action for justice so that, having hope, we do not go crazy.
> Do we wonder today how we challenged the structures of impunity?
> What kind of justice do we seek?
> When is the right moment for pardon? (De Wit and López 2013, 163)

With these questions to the text, they identify the action of the widow as God's action (prayer action), as if God himself were offering a complaint because of the lived and experienced situation.

This got the attention of the readers of Peru when they realized that life helps to interpret the parable of the widow. De Wit assures that, unlike the *Semillas del Reino*, the group from Peru had associated God with the judge "imparting to the parable the function of showing the unfailing and unconditional love of God, and thus making a call not to lose hope and not to become disheartened" (De Wit and López 2013, 163).

The Colombian group agreed with its partner group: "There is a rereading focusing on the priority of God and not on reality.... We need to take the reality of violence in Peru more into account; besides, there is no reference to the severe struggles for human rights that occurred there" (De Wit and López 2013, 167). This comment tries to answer the group from Peru, thanking them for their contributions and making the group of Peru a partner that will look back on themselves to establish and identify threats, despair, and how to respond out of faith to this danger.

The richness of the dialogue between these two groups displays a panorama of questions about justice; furthermore, the relationship between the text and reenacting of the same does not impoverish the biblical passage; instead the questions and additional comments expand the sense and understanding of what the text means by justice. They ask in response: "What justice do we demand? When is justice done?" They comment:

> Justice remains as a debt. With all that we are experiencing ... there cannot be a promise of God's justice unless human action is fair.... The Lima document does not ask for justice. It appears to be a text produced by a group of intellectuals, and precisely not by those who have suffered in their own flesh; living the reality of violence is not the same as being far away from it. (De Wit and López 2013, 166—*Semillas del Reino* group, second reading report)

Nonetheless, as is apparent in the reports of the groups, in the second reaction to the Colombian group, the participants of the *Bartolomé de Las Casas* Institute of Peru recognize how, in spite of the distrust that they often had toward such institutions, they did not want to lose having expectations of them. The Peru group members felt called to participate in movements like "Para Que No Se Repita" (so that it is not repeated) from a church committed to battling the inequality and violence that dehumanize the lives of Latin American people. From this idea they justify their own position in relation to what they understand justice to be.

In another dialogue corresponding to the Centro de Formación y Orientación groups from El Salvador and catechists of Colombia, the concept of justice appears as a possibility that might be realized as a result of their own efforts. This is a justice that relates as well to a concept of a revengeful God: "We young people must entrust ourselves to God so that he will revenge us of our enemies" (De Wit and López 2013, 172). In the end, the form justice assumed is the result of insistence: "It is certain that there is justice, although it seemed not to be, but when she prayed, there was justice" (172 n. 63). The inefficiency of judges occasions the need to take justice into one's one hands:

> It is necessary that people search in all directions, and if nobody hears them, then they seek how to do justice themselves. It is a lesson so that we do not let ourselves be pushed around by those bribed judges.... We would already be dead if we had continued asking. One needs to defend oneself, I say.... I believe you need to ask, but also to hide oneself and defend oneself: we will not remain only asking. (172 n. 64)

In the interpretation, there is a strong movement back and forth between the text and the life of the group members. In their interpretations, the groups allow a glimpse of this struggle for justice in their references to the following issues:

- the widow's insistence:
  The troubles are the things which at times the people need to do in order that they listen, because those above never listen unless you trouble them, they never want to listen to the people. (De Wit and López 2013, 172 n. 65)

- the rejection of the indolence of the authorities:
  Many ladies continue suffering because they are afraid of being killed, and they continually seek help or ask that the police would do something, but they only say: "Go quietly, señora, for we are keeping watch." (De Wit and López 2013, 172 n. 66)

- the certainty of corruption:
  The system is rotten because it is dependent on a single individual. Another time one sees that we have had those corrupt presidents here who do whatever they feel like. . . . S/he had to talk to the secretary and "ease the hand" (bribe him) to see whether he would let her in or would give him a small signed card for the mayor, or for a

government agency, or for someone who would be able to. (De Wit
and López 2013, 172 n. 67)

- the scarcity of resources of the people to sustain the struggle for
  justice:
  It is pretty expensive to be in court, we know that here very well, if
  we walk in the courts with the ladies and with the condemned nothing is *choto* (free), because you even have to buy the coffee. (De Wit
  and López 2013, 172 n. 68)

When we approach the contexts surrounding these interpretations, the
extraordinary case of the Salvadorian gangs (Maras) comes to the fore, in
which the biblical story is related to the stories of many women—widows—
in El Salvador: "it is the mothers who have lost their husbands in the war
and now have lost their children in gangs" (De Wit and López 2013, 175).
In this manner, they import from their real-life situation elements that are
not present in the text. In the passage from Luke, it does not appear that the
widow is making demands because of her husband's life, but the Salvadorian group assumes that the complaints are due to the death of her husband,
because when a woman requests justice, she does this for a reason that is
truly important, that is, because of her husband or her child.

Though the group of catechists rejected this use of imagination by its
Salvadorian peer group, it followed the same recourse to imagination in
its critical attitude toward the text and its narrative gaps: "It is not known
what really happened because they do not tell what happened when she
returned to the business which she had before she arrived. It is not known
if it was resolved or not, because for the judge it could be that that was the
case, but not for her." The gaps perceived by the group are not deductible
from the argument of the narrative; they also miss the other actors who
could have changed the direction of the events: "No one else appears, it's
not known if there were more people or more judges." Whereupon it is
concluded that "Neither lawyers or prosecutors are present, so the judge
does what he wants, because there is no one to watch out that things keep
functioning" (De Wit and López 2013, 176).

The distance between the interpretations of the two groups—one
adhering to traditional and devout interpretation (as with the catechists),
the other being more imaginative and creative (Salvadorians)—allowed
the groups to recognize their own boundaries and limitations and formed
an extended invitation to the members of the peer group. Thus a member
of the catechists said:

I want to say that I had never seen this Gospel in this way with these words, I feel confused because I feel that there is not much respect for the word of God. I do not say there are no suffering mothers, but then what do we do? That taking law into your own hands scares me. But neither did I see that the woman could take justice into her own hands, because she was poor and was continually asking for help. If she had had money or a gang to back her up, then she herself could have put the judge under pressure instead of continually begging. (De Wit and López 2013, 177)

The following comment accompanied other new questions from the Salvadorian group:

With so many widows how can this reality be understood from the text? Whom should they turn to when their children are killed? Where should the widows go when their husbands are killed? Or their parents? Where does their outcry remain? (De Wit and López 2013, 178)

These and other examples we encountered during this research confront us not only with the polysemy of the term *justice* and its broad meaning, but first and foremost with the diversity of lived experiences, pains, and outcries. It confronts us as well with the diversity of interpretations that allows for criteria for understanding the text to be clarified in accordance with life, faith, and the experience of the community. In this manner, the interpretation of the text is accompanied by a deep concern to read and interpret the text and life adequately according to divine light.

On the other hand, we find the approach to the text by the Mexican martyrs of El Salvador and the group 1 from Tierralta in which justice was linked to human rights protests. They point out:

Look, the judge said at last, "It's true." But you cannot be waiting until the judge says, "Yes," because his conscience reproaches him or her, but because it's up to him to do so. Justice has to do with human rights. We have been in human rights courses and we say that it is not a question of will but an obligation that should be met whether they like it or not, it's not because he wanted to but because it is justice. (De Wit and López 2013, 199)

Among the poor and illiterate, the interpretation of the widow who claims justice from the judge is not only aimed at human rights in general, but also focuses on not forgetting the suffering of the woman. They assure us:

> If you see how from the time of the story of the widow no attention is
> paid to the situation of the poor, who do not know how to read and
> write, have no influence, have nothing, then, why? what good does it do
> to know about the misfortune of a woman like this lady? It is in order to
> continue fighting! (De Wit and López 2013, 202)

Finally, in this sense the group of Caminantes, paired with Tierralta group
2, emphasizes that reading the text helps to analyze what kind of women
undertake the struggle for justice:

> In our country the women are the ones who fight more for justice and
> who denounce impunity. It is women who most frequently endure the
> murder, the persecution, and the silencing for speaking out in front of
> the courts of justice. Beatrice Helen Mack, Nobel Peace Prize winner, is
> a living example of the fight against impunity in Guatemala.... it is, per-
> haps, that women have been affected most ... but there are women who
> have fought and gone ahead; perhaps they have not attained justice that
> they should have received, but at least they have set a precedent so that
> other people could come, and these have been able to create women's
> organizations that unite to work on cases of disappearances, the direct
> attack that women have suffered. (De Wit and López 2013, 219–20)

In this way, as demonstrated, from and through the different interpretations of the text a dialogue between the text and life is established, between
longings for justice and the memory of personal experiences, between
faith and hope, in which the achieving of justice is born from the commitment to persevere despite everything.

### A Transformation toward an Attitude of Solidarity

An additional important element that appears in intercultural Bible reading is an interactive process that initially may hinder mutual enrichment,
but over time provides a sense of solidarity. Due to the experiences that
make up the identity of each group, the defense of one's own points of
view and the preliminary prejudices in relation to being read by others
sometimes generate distance and dissonances in the exchange of reading reports. Nonetheless, these same factors open up something worthy
of being highlighted, that is, the transformation out of solidarity when
recognizing oneself in the pain experienced in the situation of the other.
Examples abound in the reports:

We express our sense of shame that our contributions to their reports were highly critical without having considered a supportive and empathetic attitude that the group Lima had shown in relation to the violence and conflict that we experience in our country.... We saw that it is important first of all to emphasize the positive aspects and then to share our differences, not to criticize but to enrich each other. (De Wit and López 2013, 170—*Semillas del Reino* group, third reading report)

In reviewing these interpretations, one can observe that the groups are suspicious of the readings by the partner group, because among the first reactions they encountered the use of imagination, creativity, or speculation that does not appear in the text. This creates distance between the positions of the peer groups about the reading, but the interaction of the dialogue opens a channel of communication and interest upon learning about the real-life experiences, providing the initial inklings of an approach to what each group understands and supplies with its own meanings. In this regard the catechists group admits to its peer group from El Salvador: "We had difficulty in understanding the meaning of various expressions that were commonplace for you but completely unknown to us. We need to know more about your group" (De Wit and López 2013, 194—catechists, first letter to the partner group). On the other hand, the *Colaboradoras* group believed that the beneficial dialogue had created bonds of friendship and solidarity, and they assured with respect:

S: We wish the same for the whole group of North Arcatao; we are really very pleased with this project of intercultural Bible reading. Go forward with much faith, with much hope, much strength and patience, and that God may bless you. With the same strength and the same unity may you continue the same desire to go forward, in the silence, may God bless you all.
E: We have integrated; I feel that in a deep-down way.
S: Concerning AD: if it would be possible to come to Colombia, we'd be most happy to receive her. Hopefully you can come.... We would feel immensely honored if several *compañeros* from North Arcatao could come as far as Tierralta and we could welcome you here, to get to know you and share. Well, we say goodbye to the friends from Arcatao North. May God bless you!!

In response, North Arcatao considered it no easy task to take leave without making clear the bonds created and affection established:

N: It is hard to say, we have arrived at this point. But I have confidence in that as they have put themselves into our lives and into our affairs, so we've put ourselves into theirs, even knowing, though but a little, about that which they are living through and suffering there. What I mean is why don't we unite into a single continental network to resist together? Over there the initiative of the Americas is moving, and we, the poor—nothing, just watching the parrots fly past. Ladies: continue forward, do not decline, when you have a will; here we'll keep on fighting, we are now brothers and sisters. (De Wit and López 2013, 298—*Arcatao Norte y Colaboradoras* groups)

AD: Dear fellow companions from Tierralta, Colombia, I wish you beautiful things, that you may know how to find the meaning that moves many things across the borders of these countries. We have come to know you and we feel you near. We will look for a way to make our love and our regards reach you, in some trip with someone who connects with your dreams and your countries. We love you dearly. This was the group North Arcatao, from the committee of surviving memory, which comes from the territory of Arcatao. We have called ourselves "North Arcatao" in order to distinguish ourselves from another group participating in this process. We met with other groups here in San Salvador and it has been very nice. Greetings to all.

Despite the different interpretations and approaches to the text of Luke, these and other demonstrations of affection let one see not only a profound interaction around the real-life experiences, but also how the mutual enrichment through reading the text of the widow and the judge brought about a shift toward solidarity with those who have also suffered the pain of injustice and impunity.

To conclude, it is worth noting how intercultural Bible reading opens the path between the narrative of the past (biblical text) and the stories of the present (personal stories) to connect to a memory that once again becomes reality. In these stories, it remains valid not to lose sight of the deep concern of God, which appears in the claim and clamor that everyone should make for justice. Like the widow, the struggle for justice remains valid, much more now on a continent in which things must be made concrete before being archived or deleted, which would open the possibility that they be repeated.

## References

Amnistía Internacional. 2002. *El legado mortal de Guatemala: el pasado impune y las nuevas violaciones de derechos humanos*. Madrid: Amnesty International Publications.

Asamblea Legislativa de El Salvador. 2010. Decreto 458 de 2010. San Salvador: Asamblea legislativa.

Asociación Paz y Esperanza. 2008. *Cinco Años del Informe de la Comisión de la Verdad y la Reconciliación*. Lima: CNDH.

Wit, Hans de, and Edgar López, eds. 2013. *Lectura intercultural de la Biblia en contextos de impunidad en América Latina*. Serie Religión, Cultura y Sociedad 38. Nappanee, India: Facultad de Teología Universidad Javeriana, Prensa.

# Concluding Reflections

*Hans de Wit and Janet Dyk*

The title of this volume—*Bible and Transformation: The Promise of Intercultural Bible Reading*—points to our search for an answer to the question: Can cross-border Bible reading become a catalyst for transformation of the readers themselves, of their understanding of the text, and of their perception of and openness towards the other reader? If so, under what conditions? In these final considerations we harvest the findings from the essays in this volume. What have been the results of reading biblical stories in places of global encounter and dialogue?

## Theory Formation

The first part of this book contributes to theory formation. The place of intercultural hermeneutics within modern and postmodern hermeneutical designs is defined, and there is critical reflection on the concept of transformation. How key concepts of classical emancipation and liberation hermeneutics are redesigned is clarified, and it is made clear how intercultural hermeneutics takes a new place on the hermeneutical playing field. Willingness to interact is seen as a condition for liberation and transformation. Liberation is sought, not by struggle and fostering images of enmity, but through the meeting with the other (Segovia). Difference is engaged as a hermeneutical factor in the interpretation process.

Several essays show the complexity of the concept transformation, warning us not to use the concept too thoughtlessly, too lightly, and too quickly (De Wit, Van Zyl, Schipani, Prior, Autero). 

Within hermeneutics, little empirical research on transformation has been done. Causal relationships between the interpretation of texts and, for example, social transformation are difficult to measure. Transformation appears to be a container concept and is used for often very different effects of reading. The authors share the insight that confrontation with "alterity," with a different reader, is a fundamental condition for transformation. Transformation occurs especially where known "Christian" reading patterns and classic doctrinal teachings are critically questioned. When one is confronted with gaps or inconsistencies within one's frame of understanding and is willing to face up to these, the road to change is opened up (Van Zyl).

The authors agree that the method discussed in this book can make a special contribution to transformation, because the essence of the method is that the Bible reader is invited to practice a productive and critical reevaluation of his or her own dominant reading tradition by means of a careful listening to the interpretation of the same text by the other reader. Schipani shows that the road to shared ownership can be a thorough spiritual exercise, as well as an unusual and risky path. One has to learn to negotiate the meaning of the text, to be able to surrender, live with loss, and abandon acquired frames of understanding. Van Zyl shows what practical factors play a role: language, endurance, smooth communication, and a good facilitator. Deeper aspects interwoven with the identity of readers also play a role: prejudices, fear, assumed positions, and images of the enemy. Prior describes why the hermeneutical adventure of reading with the other may be worthwhile: "We are transformed when we acknowledge that we need each other ... when we experience how intercultural conversations shock and liberate, disturb and challenge, prod and sensitize, refute and confirm, question and transform, interfere and create anew."

### The Case Studies

A fascinating part of this book is formed by the case studies. They take us to the most unusual places, let us get acquainted with the most extraordinary reading groups. They take us far from home and make us sensitive to the miracle of the universal character of the Bible, revealing its potential to transcend culture. They highlight the hermeneutical challenges and opportunities of globalization as a reconfiguration of narrative space.

Transformation is a concept hard to cope with and difficult to measure. It is particularly enriching to notice that a number of case studies show in detail how qualitative research can take place here, how reading reports that contain the deposits of interpretation processes can be encrypted, and how empirical data can be processed to achieve a result (Autero, Jonker, Van der Walt and Barker).

A case study cannot prove more than the results of the case study itself. Jonker notes in his essay that "a small-scale qualitative study does not necessarily deliver representative data, but it does facilitate a deep understanding of community dynamics." Modesty is appropriate in the formulation of the final conclusions of this book. The meetings between groups were mostly transient, the motivation for participation was often not known, and much remained hidden, because reading reports do not reveal everything (Snoek). There has been no follow-up to the question of how sustainable the effect of the meeting with the other has been, and not all meetings were successful (Van Berkum, Ejiogu, Tanja).

Nonetheless, when we review the outcome of the case studies, patterns and opportunities become apparent that go beyond the contextually bound processes of exchange between the members of a single group. The whole is more than the sum of the parts. Triumphalism is not fitting, but neither is excessive modesty.

With only a few exceptions, the reading exchanges resulted in a change of perspective and transformation. Wolverton speaks even of "revelatory moments that appeared in the experience of the majority of the groups." Where there was failure, the limits of the method are pointed out.

## When the Before Has an After

The method of intercultural Bible reading seeks transformation through a meeting of three parties: the biblical text, the reader, and the other reader. We look for what the results are of this meeting, being focused on whether the meeting has been a catalyst for transformation and change. If so, the conditions under which this occurred are of particular interest. What differences can be measured between the beginning and the end of the interpretation process? In presenting the results of the meetings, we follow the order: text, reader, other reader.

When we speak about the *transformation of the text*, we refer to the fact that in the exchange process the text itself underwent a transformation and became a different text. The text acquired a fundamentally different content and status—a new meaning was generated.

By *transformation of the reader*, we mean the understanding the reader has of him- or herself *facing and in confrontation with the text*. The reader starts to reflect critically on his or her own reading strategies. The encounter with the partner group results in a new hermeneutical awareness, a new hermeneutical competence. There is self-disclosure toward the text and the other reader (Autero).

With *transformation of the other reader*, we mean that the view of the other reader, his or her role and presence in the interpretation process, changes fundamentally. The other reader is transformed from being seen as a competitor or being incompetent, from being an inferior partner in dialogue (Autero) to being an ally (Adames Nuñez). The prejudices of the other and "their world" are adjusted. The interpretation process of the other reader becomes a beacon for one's own understanding of the text.

Transformation of the Text

That readers could not see the text in the same manner as before meeting with the partner group was consistently the result of the confrontation with the limits of one's own "acquired frame of understanding" and of the fact that within a text there is always room for another reader, that always in the text something is left behind for another reader.

In and through the encounter, previously hidden cultural conventions and codes were brought to light for the reader (Holter, Sihombing, Ale Díaz and Obeso Perez, Kessler), and new light was thrown on the narrative structure of the story (West, Kessler).

A major source for change of perspective was the characterization of actors in the text by the partner group. The fact that Jonadab in the Tamar story was seen by the partner group as "wise" precipitated an in-depth rereading of the story (Moore). That Mary Magdalene is seen as a grief-stricken woman who in the early morning went to the graveyard—a place of ghosts—(Sihombing), looking for the body of a missing beloved (Ale Díaz and Obeso Perez), changed the perspective of the partner group on the text. The alternative reading strategy of the partner group brings "the world under the text," the power game in the text, the "guilty secret" of the text to the light (Van der Walt and Barker, Moore, Kessler).

Some groups had never before read the stories that played a role in the process (Holter, Marip, Vergara Hoyos). In the encounter with the partner group, the discovery of an unfamiliar text as Luke 18 (the story of the widow and the unjust judge) led to an in-depth discussion about one's own visceral memories and experience with impunity (Vergara Hoyos).

The ethical message of the text is highlighted in the meeting. In the exchanges on the Tamar story, groups helped each other to rid themselves of their admiration for King David. In no case were the acts of Amnon or Jonadab mitigated.

The main transformation is that of the status of the text for the reader. From an historical object, the text became an fellow traveler. The Amsterdam drug addicts expressed that as follows: "Where it used to be a book at a great distance to real life, it became a book relevant to the everyday life of the readers" (Ejiogu). By this proximity the text becomes heterotopic, an "other" place. The text becomes a site where one's own trauma is discussed (Vergara Hoyos), where dissidence is practiced, and where deconstruction of the dominant reading tradition takes place (West). "Thus it seems that the text elicited a potentially emancipating discussion," observes Esa Autero, commenting on the process in the Bolivian group. In this manner, for the women in Grahamstown in the Eastern Cape province of South Africa, the story of Tamar transforms from an unknown text into "a safe and supportive environment for women to speak about issues relating to violence, rape, and abuse" (Van der Walt and Barker).

Transformation of the Reader

The confrontation with alternative reading strategies of the partner group also resulted in more hermeneutical competence and sensitivity. The most profound changes became visible in the reader's understanding of him- or herself "in front of the text."

The following trajectory of the transformation of the reader was repeatedly observed. Through the exchange of reading reports, the one group was confronted with the hermeneutical creativity and sensitivity of the partner group. The ensuing reconsideration of the text led to a broadening of horizons and a new hermeneutical competence. The transformation of the reader is characterized not only by a process of exegetical enablement (De Wit), but also by a new and deeper exploration of the potential of the text to affect behavior. The identification of the partner group with characters in the story, their creativity, the group dynamics, the directives the partner group discovered in the text—all of this led to introspection.

In the process, a broad range of productive ways of reading has been offered. The spectrum of interpretive possibilities was widened by the encounter with the partner group.

The identification patterns and the intimate relationship of the partner group with the text appeared to be an important factor in transformation: "the story of the biblical characters and their own personal stories 'read each other'" (Sihombing). The identification with the powerlessness of Tamar or even with the aggressor Amnon (Ejiogu), with the perseverance of the widow from Luke 18 (Vergara Hoyos), with Mary Magdalene as a woman standing alone and crying at the empty tomb in the dark of the early morning (Sihombing), or with Ruth, the foreigner (Adames Nuñez), led to reflection on one's own process of appropriation. The Indonesian group Rogate is strongly challenged by what the reading of John 20 brought about in one of the participants of the partner group, namely, "sharing Christ with his neighbor": "The Rogate group was willing to adopt a new and potentially dangerous practice of telling their neighbors about Jesus' resurrection" (Autero).

Where the cultural conventions and codes of the text are elucidated from a different cultural context, a critical conversation about the own culture emerges (Holter, Sihombing, Kessler, and Ale Díaz and Obeso Perez): "Eventually, the reading of the partner group provoked new discussions about their own situation in the light of the partner's reading, for example, the impact of traditional (family) structures" (Kessler).

The dialogue with the partner group led the Peruvian group, who read the story of Mary at the empty tomb, to reflect on their own Andean culture in their dealings with the dead. The Colombian group was led to reflect again on their own culture of conflict and violence and the cultural determination of their own method of reading (Madera).

Being hermeneutically frank in breaking the dependence on existing patterns of reading contributed to a change of perspective in the partner group. "By speaking about Tamar's situation and the power dynamics that operate within the story, participants develop an interpretive key to their own, often unnameable, experiences" (Van der Walt and Barker). Hermeneutical courage becomes manifest when participants talk about Tamar or the widow from Luke in the present, as if they were characters from the newspaper (Ejiogu, Vergara Hoyos). One woman wanted "to be Tamar's sister. This woman saw that Tamar needed someone to help her, someone to whom she could talk and with whom she could cry. Having a sister, Tamar would be less lonely" (Van Berkum). Updating of the text, linking the text with a new domain of reference, that of the current reader, led to an analogue process among partner groups. A participant of the Indonesian group "confessed that the experiences and the understanding or verse 16 [of John 20—Eds.] shared by friends from Buenas Nuevas strengthened her to face her own personal struggles" (Autero). The identification in the Ghanaian group of Mary Magdalene as a freedom fighter against the British colonial rule brought the Dutch partner group to wonder with which women in Dutch society they would want to identify Mary. "Though they found the Ghanaian suggestions unexpected, the Dutch group began looking at how they could find such models in the Dutch context and share them with their Ghanaian partners" (Anum).

Group dynamics are decisive in the question of whether distance to the text and to the other reader remains or whether an existential reading process can develop where grief is shared and the space where the text is read is felt to be safe. Where there is no safe space, experiences of readers remain unshared. All essays refer to the fact that a safe space is a precondition for fruitful interaction in the group. "Additionally, the Shalom House group exhibited growth in their own willingness to listen carefully and caringly to one another's stories, and to see themselves as a true group," observed Jeff Moore. In the essay by Van der Walt and Barker, the relationship between disclosure and safety is described: "The ethical concern that was at stake was whether the participant's disclosure of her experience of sexual violence in this context would prove to be beneficial or harmful for her." Autero noted on the Bolivian group: "The Buenas Nuevas group also utilized a loose identification with the grief-stricken Mary and the resurrected Jesus as a platform for sharing difficult personal experiences."

The Transformation of the Other Reader

The willingness to listen and to accept shared ownership are the most important conditions for transformation of the other reader: "It does not hurt to acknowledge that we are not only among the doctors but also among the patients with the disabilities of each one's individual cultural particularities" (Prior). The process of negotiating with the partner group, as interpretive community, on discrepancies and interpretive differences changes one's perception of the partner group.

Knowledge of the context, the struggle, and the wounds of the partner group diminishes prejudices and results in a recognition of one's own vulnerability and the acceptance of the other reader as a full partner in the interpretation process. The other reader becomes a source of knowledge of revelation. When the Bolivian group learned that the Indonesian partner group is "not physically persecuted, but undergoes mental and psychological persecution ... the intercultural reading provided the opportunity to experience transformation in the appreciation of the partner group" (Sihombing; see also Anum, Madera, Adames Nuñez). No longer seeing the other as competitor, as a primitive believer, is the result of a process set in motion by the confrontation with the attitude towards faith of the partner group. "Rogate's stance as (mature) Christians was no longer queried" (Autero).

The transformation of the view of the other reader is perhaps most strongly reflected where sympathy and solidarity with the previously unknown partner group arises: "This study connected us, but the story of violence against the powerless also connects us" (Moore). "Reading 'together' through the exchange of reading reports and responses provided the women of Shalom House with a strong sense of solidarity with the group in the Netherlands" (Moore). "Both the similarities and the particularities of the contexts in which the readings were produced led in most cases to a closer identification with the partner group. To see oneself reflected in the struggles and dreams of another group led to greater solidarity and empathy, which in turn allowed the groups to grow and expand their interpretative spectrum," observed Ricardo González Kindelan concerning the process the Cuban group went through.

Vergara Hoyos describes how twenty groups in Latin and Central America read the story of the widow from Luke 18. All groups have a long and traumatic experience with impunity. When it is discovered that the partner group has the same experience and that its context is one of conflict, solidarity and shared agency begin to form. One participant explained why they should read the story of the widow together with other groups: "To continue fighting." Shared suffering and shared pain "open up something worthy of being highlighted, that is, the transformation out of solidarity when recognizing oneself in the pain experienced in the situation of the other. Examples abound in the reports" (Vergara Hoyos). In the exchange between a Myanmar and a Dutch group, solidarity and social justice play a central role. "Although their approaches and applications were different ... both groups exchanged their perspectives on social justice" (Marip).

### When the Before Does Not Have an After

Interaction with the partner group was not possible in all cases. The examples bring out the limitations of the method and are important witnesses to what occurs in intercultural and interreligious dialogue and what can prevent its success. This method of cross-border reading of Scripture is applicable as well to the multireligious situation in Europe, where in most cities a large variety of Christian communities of faiths live next to one another, but rarely share with one another (Kahl).

Amazingly enough, stagnation and freezing appear to happen precisely between groups that read, live, and believe in the same context (Van Berkum, Ejiogu, Tanja, Jonker). Factors that hinder encounter resemble the opposite of factors that enhance interaction.

The following represents a hierarchy of obstacles. Sometimes these involve practical matters like reading the wrong text, having the reading reports accidentally switched, changes within the memberships of the groups, or incongruence of the time paths for exchange between the groups. More often cases involved instances where one appeared to be unable to step over one's own shadow in order to establish contact with the other group.

The empirical data shows that where readers were unable to appropriate the text, little or only superficial interaction with the partner group was established. The inability of readers to get close to the ancient text has many causes. An important factor is the absence of empathetic imagination that is related to the lack of the experience of tragedy. "Stroom was just no match for Tamar," Tanja concludes in the analysis of the reading of the story of Tamar by an Amsterdam youth group Stroom. In the one group disbelief predominated about whether what is told in the Tamar story "might really have happened" (Ejiogu), and this stood in stark contrast to another group's immediate identification with the story: they read the story "as though this were a newspaper article" (Tanja). No encounter takes place when in the one group the distance to the story was too large ("Why has this story a message for now?" asks one of the participants of Stroom), while a partner group felt itself as direct addressee of the story ("participants spoke in the present tense," Tanja). The decisive factor is the experience of trauma and loss, the (in)ability of empathetic imagination.

An underlying difference in the view of the status of the Bible can form a major obstacle in encounters, equally so when participants do not arrive at self-disclosure and a discussion of their ultimate beliefs (Snoek). At the same time, an endless discussion about the authority and historical significance of the Bible can get in the way of identifying with the story, while the story itself invites readers to identification and self-reflection and not to a discussion of its historical character.

Empathetic imagination is powered by one's own experiences of suffering, by one's own trauma. Vergara Hoyos shows how in the impressive "impunity" project the joint reading of a biblical story contributed to trauma processing. On the other hand, trauma can prevent interaction, both with the story and with the partner group. Where one considers that there is no greater suffering than one's own, identification with the suffering of characters from the story is blocked. "The story is too far away," notes an Amsterdam homeless participant on the story of Tamar. "It makes me fall asleep.... *I have my own problems*" (emphasis added). The coordinator of this group recognizes this as a survival strategy: "By keeping his horizons close by and making his world small, Karel was able to cope" (Tanja).

The reading reports of the socially marginalized groups are full of concepts such as powerlessness, inequality, injustice, loneliness, wounds, and vulnerability. Especially the reading of a story that is fundamental to their own life can be intense and profoundly existential—really a form of trauma processing. In this process no "strangers," no outsiders, are admitted. What then occurs we can call "closed" identification. The encounter with the biblical story is so intense that there is no place for others, especially if these others read the story in a more objectifying manner, with suspicion and from a great distance. That is what occurred in the meeting between the Amsterdam homeless group and the youth group Stroom. "The report from the other group [Stroom] had nothing that this type of reader [the homeless participants] could relate to and thus the report remained closed to them" (Tanja).

Intercultural hermeneutics is a space where we need to exercise negotiation. Where the will and the ability to negotiate is lacking, there will be neither exchange nor growth. The inability to negotiate the interpretation of the text can be related to the inability to liberate oneself from the shackles of the dominant reading tradition. A participant of the Bolivian group makes clear how the story of John 20 should be read: the participant "insisted strongly that the resurrection is the main point of the text and that there is no negotiation on this point" (Autero). Where it is believed that the limits of the hermeneutic tolerance are reached because fundamental insights of the belief system or doctrinal teachings are threatened, the other will be rejected as a competent reader and interlocutor. Often it is fear that maintains this inability or unwillingness to negotiate: "a dialogue might make some 'doubt their faith' or 'lead a weak brother astray,'" observed some Bolivian participants (Autero). Here *hermeneutic discrepancy* is maintained: the avoidance of that which could harm, diminish, devaluate one's own convictions, experiences, and knowledge. Self-disclosure becomes impossible, and people are unwilling to view their own identity as readers as a fragile hermeneutic identity.

Fear feeds prejudices, and prejudices feed fear. We have already seen that also in this project prejudices were often present among the readers. "You tend to look at us as a primitive people," complained the Indonesian group to its Bolivian partner group. "The societal structure as well as the hermeneutical practice of the partner group [the Indonesian group] were seen [by the Bolivian partner group] as inferior and unintelligible in many respects" (Autero). "Many devices have managed to create a social imaginary of fear and rejection toward Haitians in the Dominican Republic," observed Adames Nuñez. Seeing the other as an enemy is indeed a great obstacle for encounter. In his analysis of meetings between groups of black, colored, and white participants in the Western Cape province in South Africa, Jonker shows "how prominent the role of fear was in the responses or participants.... Fear manifested itself in all cultural groups who participated.... The data ... have shown that the experiences of participants before the intercultural exposure were dominated by fear and a lack of knowledge of 'the other.'" However, Jonker also showed that fear may be overcome: "The intercultural meeting on the basis of a shared Bible study created significant changes."

## Final Remarks

Did transformation take place? If so, under what conditions?

Yes, there have been changes and the conditions conducive to that were analyzed and brought to the fore. "The project confirmed that the tool of intercultural Bible reading has transformative power" (Jonker). Whether the changes are sustainable, we do not know. New research is needed. If intercultural encounter is not constantly maintained, the isolated encounter can easily become exotic. However modest transformation has been—some will prefer to speak of change of perspective—it took place on an existential level of the understanding of one's self facing the text and facing the other.

The importance of the reported changes for social transformation could not be measured. The encounter between participants led in many cases to reflection on social problems (violence, rape, hegemony, role of women, murder, injustice, and loss), but about causal relationships between Bible reading and sociopolitical changes no conclusions can be offered. We would like to see social change and liberation as a direct result of cross-border reading of the Bible, but that desire also has a downside. If social transformation is the main objective of the interpretation process, it can easily lead to forms of utilitarian use of biblical texts and taking the interpretation process as hostage. Then there is no longer an encounter with the other, transformation stagnates, and the spiritual dimension of exploring revelation disappears. The result is activism: the meaning of the text that serves "my" vision on necessary social transformation is the right one. We must remember that also fundamentalist reading of Scripture, where the other is excluded, aims at social transformation. Perhaps this is the main function of cross-border and communitarian Bible reading: exploring the infinity of texts and the liberation of the self. This form of Bible reading cannot be defined as apolitical. On the contrary, the method invites not only to read against the grain, but also to read against terror and hermeneutic terrorism. It is reading for the sake of the victims *in* and *of* Scripture.

Was the role of the Bible in the process only instrumental? Would the groups also have met each other without the Bible being involved? That is a question addressed in the analysis of the meeting between the Bolivian and Indonesian group (Autero). The answer is negative, and we believe that this also applies to the other groups. That the joint, cross-border reading of a biblical story is a catalyst for encounter and then also for transformation has been established, we believe. Of the ninety participating groups, there were only four where the interaction could be called a "failure." It is precisely the encounter with the other that prevents the text becoming instrumentalized.

That biblical texts fulfill a unique and not merely instrumental role in the process is related to many factors. Biblical texts, in contrast to secular texts, have a special status: they are part of *Scripture*. They go beyond cultural frontiers, are inexhaustible, and their fundamental narrative character invites people to participate. Above all they touch upon fundamental human experiences. All the texts that play a role in this book witnesses of trauma, loss, absence, empty graves, injustice, murder, rape, and abuse of power, "the other," migration, forgiveness, and hospitality. The cross-border reading of these texts makes the hermeneutic function of the "texts of terror" in the Bible visible. Readers discover that *Scripture* is not a bundle of stories full of angelic dreaminess, but first and foremost a collection of stories about wounds, about trauma.

Amazingly enough, the reading of these texts of terror appears particularly productive and contributes to the processing of trauma and solidarity with places of struggle not seen before. It is not necessary to protect the Bible against itself or against the other reader, as the essays in this book show. Where that occurs, readers are deprived of the opportunity to learn to listen from the "cave of the heart" and hear the voices of other readers:

> At the heart of the intercultural approach is the willingness and ability to listen carefully to each and every voice—to listen deeply from the cave of the heart where buried intuitions are laid bare, intuitions that have been running deeply and quietly, unnoticed, beneath everything else—and the willingness and ability to be open to the Spirit in others who start from a quite different location. (Prior)

The processes described in this book leave behind a fragrance of the joy of shared ownership and the promise of shared agency: "I will not let you go, unless you bless me"—with your interpretation.

# CONTRIBUTORS

**Digna María Adames Nuñez** works as a national expert in Basic Education in the Ministry of Education of the Dominican Republic. For five years she directed the office of the Jesuit Service for refugees and migrants in Santo Domingo, which entailed direct association with the Haitian migrant population in the Dominican Republic. Her research topics and publications include Bible studies from a sociological, political, anthropological, and philosophical perspective. She is also a researcher in the field of social issues of migration and human rights.

**Marisol Ale Díaz** is a biblical scholar and teaches at the Seminario Evangélico Peruano and the Instituto Bíblico in Lima, Peru. She is guest lecturer at the Faculty of Theology and Religion (AETE) and at the Peruvian Bible Society.

**Eric Nii Bortey Anum** is Professor of Biblical Hermeneutics at the University of Cape Coast, Ghana. His areas of expertise are New Testament studies, African biblical hermeneutics, and intercultural hermeneutics. He is a member of the editorial board of International Voices for Biblical Studies of the Society for Biblical Literature.

**Esa Autero** is the Dean of Faculty and Chair of Biblical Studies at the South Florida Bible College and Theological Seminary, Deerfield Beach, Florida. He has written several articles on contextual and empirical hermeneutics that are soon to appear. In his dissertation at the University of Helsinki, Finland, he investigated the influence of socioeconomic status on biblical hermeneutics. He is also the president and founder of *Missio Dei* International, a nonprofit organization that develops curricula for colleges in the developing nations and contextual Bible study materials for communities around the world.

**Kim Barker** is a PhD candidate at the Psychology Department at Rhodes University, South Africa, and will shortly submit her thesis. Her research focuses on the impacts of participating in antirape protests for women who have experienced sexual violence. She is particularly interested in collective practices that facilitate healing and recovery following sexual violence. This year she organized and led Rhodes University's eighth annual silent protest, which is a unique, two-day event, the largest sustained protest against sexual violence in southern Africa. Kim is a pastoral therapist, workshop facilitator, and author.

**Willemien van Berkum** received her Bachelor of Theology from the Theological University of the Reformed Churches in Kampen, the Netherlands. She completed her theological education with a Master of Theology at Vrije Universiteit Amsterdam in 2011. Until September 2014, she worked as the research assistant of Professor Hans de Wit on the field of intercultural hermeneutics and contextual Bible reading. In 2012 she started as an assistant pastor in an old neighborhood in Amsterdam, where she encounters many people with social and psychiatric problems and reads the Bible with them. Together they contextualize the gospel to their own life.

**Janet Dyk** has been affiliated with the Vrije Universiteit intercultural Bible reading project ever since translating the original project application into English in 1999. She has participated both in reading groups and in all of the conferences. As a linguist specializing in Semitic languages, she works as senior researcher at the Eep Talstra Centre for Bible and Computer of the Vrije Universiteit, most recently in the project awarded her by the Netherlands Organization for Scientific Research (NWO), entitled "Does Syntactic Variation Reflect Language Change? Tracing Syntactic Diversity in Biblical Hebrew Texts." Her recent publications include "Deportation or Forgiveness in Hosea 1:6? Verb Valence Patterns and Translation Proposals," *The Bible Translator* 65:235–79 (2014), and (with Percy van Keulen), *Language System, Translation Technique and Textual Tradition in Peshitta Kings* (Brill, 2013).

**Godian Ejiogu** was pastor at the Drugs Pastorate, a project of the Diaconate of the Protestant Church Amsterdam. He is dedicated to working for vulnerable people, for more than twenty years bridging the gap between the poor and the rich in society. He set up projects to contain the social and economic problems of the less privileged in Rotterdam and Amsterdam. Currently he researches the role of peace in the spirituality of Igbo people in Nigeria. He has authored *Christian Cooperation Netherland Nigeria* (1999) and different articles on religious and social issues. His expertise lies in the area of theological social teachings of justice and peace.

**Knut Holter** is Professor of Old Testament Studies at the MHS School of Mission and Theology, Stavanger, Norway, and Extraordinary Professor, Stellenbosch University, South Africa. His research focuses on African interpretive strategies vis-à-vis the Old Testament, and he is currently directing a project on popular enculturation hermeneutics in Maasai biblical interpretation. His books include *Old Testament Research for Africa: A Critical Analysis and Annotated Bibliography of African Old Testament Dissertations, 1967–2000* (2002), and *Contextualized Old Testament Scholarship in Africa* (2008, French and Malagasy versions 2012).

**Louis Jonker** is Professor of Old Testament in the Faculty of Theology, Stellenbosch University, South Africa. His two main areas of research are intercultural Bible reading (he has served, inter alia, as coeditor of the volume *Through the Eyes of Another* [2004]) and biblical literature of the late Persian period, particularly the books of Chronicles, about which he published a commentary in the Understanding the Bible Commentary Series (2013). He is author or coauthor of seven books and more than sixty articles and essays and editor or coeditor of six anthologies. He serves on the editorial boards of two international journals (*Vetus Testamentum* and *Hebrew Bible and Ancient Israel*). He is a fellow of the Alexander von Humboldt Stiftung, Bonn, Germany, and presently serves as chair of the International Cooperation Initiative of the Society of Biblical Literature.

**Werner Kahl** is Professor of New Testament at Frankfurt University and head of studies at the Academy of Mission, University of Hamburg. Areas of expertise include miracle traditions, the Synoptic problem, West African biblical interpretation, and intercultural hermeneutics. He is author of numerous articles and of the following books: *New Testament Miracle Stories in Their Religious-Historical Setting: A Religionsgeschichtliche Comparison from a Structural Perspective* (1994); *Jesus als Lebensretter: Afrikanische Bibelinterpretationen und ihre Relevanz für die neutestamentliche Wissenschaft* (2007).

**Rainer Kessler** is Professor Emeritus of Old Testament, University of Marburg, Germany, and Research Fellow in the Department of Old Testament, University of the Free State. Bloemfontain, South Africa. He is the author of commentaries on Micah (1999) and Malachi (2011), two volumes of collected essays (2006, 2009), and the monograph *The Social History of Ancient Israel* (English translation 2008). Presently, he is preparing a monograph on the ethics of the Old Testament.

**Ricardo González Kindelan** is Coordinator of the Bartolomé G. Lavastida Center, Santiago de Cuba, Cuba. As a sociologist, González Kindelan provides leadership in processes of social transformation. He is studying theology at the Seminario Evangélico de Theología in Matanza, Cuba.

**Ignacio Antonio Madera Vargas** is Professor and Director of Graduate Programs at the Faculty of Theology of the Pontificia Universidad Javeriana, Bogota, Colombia. He has authored the book *Dios Presencia Inquietante* and several articles in collective works on Latin American theology and the theology of religious life. Madera Vargas is involved in research on the significance of theological language and trends in Latin American Christology in contrast to the trends of Christology in the last ten years. He has been involved in research on intercultural reading of the Bible, being part of one of the lower-class communities in the south of the city of Bogotá, where he is active as a priest and theologian.

**La Rip Marip** is Lecturer of Old Testament Studies at Myanmar Institute of Theology, where he has been teaching since 2001. His theological articles appear in Myanmar-based English journals such as *RAYS*, Theology under the Bo Tree (Contextual Theology Series), *Our Theological Journey* (Festschrift), *Thamar Alin* (*Baptist Theological Journal*), and other Myanmar magazines. Currently, he is doing research on Jeremianic female imagery and its challenges to biblical scholars and Myanmar ordinary readers. He is a doctoral candidate in the Faculty of Theology at Vrije Universiteit Amsterdam, the Netherlands.

**Jeff Moore** is Pastor of Webster Groves Christian Church (Disciples of Christ) in St. Louis, Missouri. He serves as an Adjunct Professor at Eden Theological Seminary, where he teaches courses in biblical and ministry studies. He lived and worked in Lesotho from 2003 to 2007, where he taught at Morija Theological Seminary and the National University of

Lesotho and served as the HIV and AIDS Coordinator for the Lesotho Evangelical Church. He works with and serves on boards of directors for agencies that provide housing and services for people facing homelessness and living with HIV. He has facilitated contextual Bible reading groups in many countries and communities, and continues to value the liberative interpretive possibilities of reading the Bible together.

**Manuel Obeso Perez** is a Lutheran theologian and teaches at the Seminario Evangélico Peruano and the Faculty of Theology and Religion (AETE), Lima, Peru. He has participated in the Bridging Gaps program at the Vrije Universiteit Amsterdam.

**John Mansford Prior** lectures in Asian, social, and intercontextual theologies in the postgraduate program at Ledalero Institute of Philosophy, Maumere, Indonesia. A prolific writer, he has been active in grassroots biblical hermeneutics for over forty years.

**Daniel S. Schipani** is Professor of Pastoral Care and Counseling at Anabaptist Mennonite Biblical Seminary, Elkart, Indiana, and Visiting Professor of Practical Theology in numerous programs in Latin and North America and Europe. He is the author of twenty-six books on education and pastoral and practical theology and coedited *Through the Eyes of Another: Intercultural Reading of the Bible* (2004), and *New Perspectives on Contextual and Intercultural Bible Reading* (2015).

**Fernando F. Segovia** is Oberlin Graduate Professor of New Testament and Early Christianity at Vanderbilt University, where he is affiliated with the Divinity School, the Graduate Department of Religion, and the Center for Latin American Studies. He is also Professor Extraordinary in the Old and New Testament Division of the Faculty of Theology, Stellenbosch University. He is a past president of the Society of Biblical Literature. His numerous publications include two recent coedited volumes for Semeia Studies, *Latino/a Biblical Hermeneutics: Problematics, Objectives, Strategies* (2014), and *The Future of the Biblical Past* (2012).

**Batara Sihombing** has been Professor of Biblical Studies and Mission Studies at Abdi Sabda Theological Seminary in Medan, Indonesia, since 1995. He was a visiting professor for three years (2009–2012) at Divinity School of Silliman University, Dumaguete City, Philippines. He is the author of several articles, including "Paul's Fund-Raising Project and the Practice of Auction in the Batak in Indonesia," *Asia Journal of Theology* 17:91–114 (2003); "Hospitality and Indonesian Migrant Workers," *Mission Studies* 30:162–80 (2013); and "The Sermon on the Mount in Light of Wealthy Batak Christians in Indonesia," in *Global Perpspective on the Bible* (2014).

**Hans Snoek** is University Lecturer, Faculty of Theology, at Vrije Universiteit Amsterdam. He worked as a teacher of biblical studies at the Baptist Seminary in Nicaragua for eight years. Presently he is a Lecturer in Biblical Studies at the Windesheim University of Applied Sciences. He is also a researcher affiliated with the intercultural Bible reading project at the Vrije Universiteit Amsterdam.

**Luc Tanja** has been a street pastor since 2011 in a project of the Diaconate of the Protestant Church Amsterdam. He has a master's degree in political science and theology. For many years he was the coordinator of a spiritual community functioning within the Red Light District of Amsterdam.

**José Vicente Vergara Hoyos** has a bachelor's degree in philosophy at the University Minuto de Dios and a master's degree and doctorate in theology from the Pontificia Universidad Javeriana, Bogotá, Colombia. He is Professor at the Centro de Formación Teológica and Assistant Professor of the Postgraduate Program of the Faculty of Theology of the Pontificia Universidad Javeriana. He has been a research fellow in the international project *Through the Eyes of Another: Intercultural Reading of the Bible* and is currently a researcher involved in the project *Teología y Lenguaje*. Vergara Hoyos is a member of the seminar Hermenéutica, Teología y Praxis and director of the Interdisciplinary Seminar Ciencia y Teología. He is the coauthor of the book *Lectura Intercultural de Biblia en Contextos de Impunidad en América Latina* (2013), among other publications.

**Charlene van der Walt** is currently serving as the Gender, Health, and Theology Master's Program Coordinator at the Department of Old and New Testament, Faculty of Theology, Stellenbosch University, South Africa. She also works as a researcher for Inclusive and Affirming Ministries (IAM) on a part-time basis and is an ordained Minister of Religion, serving as pastor in Maitland, South Africa. Her book *Toward a Communal Reading of 2 Samuel 13: Power and Ideology within the Intercultural Bible Reading Process* has recently been published (AMBS, 2014).

**Gerald West** teaches Old Testament and Hebrew Bible and African Biblical Heremeneutics in the School of Religion, Philosophy, and Classics, University of KwaZulu-Natal, South Africa. He also works extensively with the Ujamaa Centre for Community Development and Research, a project in which socially engaged biblical scholars and ordinary African readers of the Bible from poor, working-class, and marginalized communities collaborate for social transformation. He is general editor of the Semeia Studies series and the *Journal of Theology for Southern Africa*.

**Hans de Wit** is Professor at the Faculty of Theology, Vrije Universiteit Amsterdam. De Wit worked from 1980 to 1989 in Chile at the Comunidad Teológica Evangélica de Chile as Professor of Old Testament and Biblical Hermeneutics. In his doctoral dissertation (*Leerlingen van de Armen; Apprentices of the Poor*, 1991), De Wit analyzes the so-called Latin American Biblical Movement and the interface between professional and ordinary readers of the Bible, between exegesis and *lectura popular*. Since 1991 De Wit has been professor at Vrije Universiteit, lecturing in contextual and intercultural biblical hermeneutics and third world theologies. De Wit has been visiting professor in almost all Latin American countries and in many countries in Asia, Africa, and Central and Eastern Europe. De Wit is one of the initiators of the international project *Through the Eyes of Another: Intercultural Reading of the Bible*. Since October 2007, De Wit has held of the prestigious interuniversity Dom Hélder Câmara Chair for Peace and Liberation at Vrije Universiteit Amsterdam. De Wit has written commentaries on Genesis, the prophets, Daniel, and Job and has extensively published on contextual and intercultural hermeneutics and Bible reading with ordinary readers. His work had been translated into more than ten languages.

**Taggert E. Wolverton** is a minister who also currently teaches at the University of South Carolina, Aiken. His primary research area focuses on the spirituality of youth with a specific interest in the way young people appropriate meaning from the Bible. He is presently working on a book-length project linked to his chapter in this volume.

**Danie van Zyl** is the founder and head of the Soklhanya Bible School, an interdenominational Bible training program for lay church leaders teaching in the Xhosa vernacular. Specializing in cross-cultural contextual Bible interpretation, he has published a variety of articles on hermeneutical issues and on African grassroots churches. He is a research associate of the Faculty of Theology at the University of Stellenbosch, South Africa.

# Index of Ancient Sources

# Index of Modern Authors

# Index of Key Terms

CPSIA information can be obtained at www.ICGtesting.com
Printed in the USA
BVOW08s2334181115

427390BV00002B/2/P